THE
CAMBRIDGE EDITION OF
THE LETTERS AND WORKS OF
D. H. LAWRENCE

# LOVE AMONG THE HAYSTACKS

## AND OTHER STORIES

**D. H. LAWRENCE**

EDITED BY
JOHN WORTHEN

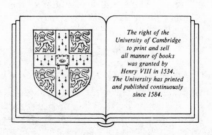

*The right of the University of Cambridge to print and sell all manner of books was granted by Henry VIII in 1534. The University has printed and published continuously since 1584.*

CAMBRIDGE UNIVERSITY PRESS

CAMBRIDGE
LONDON NEW YORK NEW ROCHELLE
MELBOURNE SYDNEY

Published by the Press Syndicate of the University of Cambridge
The Pitt Building, Trumpington Street, Cambridge CB2 1RP
32 East 57th Street, New York, NY 10022, USA
10 Stamford Road, Oakleigh, Melbourne 3166, Australia



Printed in Great Britain at the University Press, Cambridge

*British Library cataloguing in publication data*

Lawrence, D. H.
Love among the haystacks: and other stories. – (The Cambridge edition of the letters and works of D. H. Lawrence)
I. Title. II. Worthen, John. III. Series.
823′.912[F] PR6023.A93

*Library of Congress cataloguing in publication data*

Lawrence, D. H. (David Herbert), 1885–1930.
Love among the haystacks and other stories.
(The Cambridge edition of the letters and works of D. H. Lawrence)
Bibliography.
1. Worthen, John. II. Title. III. Series:
Lawrence, D. H. (David Herbert), 1885–1930. Works. 1979.
PR6023.A93L67 1987 823′.912 86-17606

ISBN 0 521 26836 2

CE

# CONTENTS

# GENERAL EDITORS' PREFACE

D. H. Lawrence is one of the great writers of the twentieth century – yet the texts of his writings, whether published during his lifetime or since, are, for the most part, textually corrupt. The extent of the corruption is remarkable; it can derive from every stage of composition and publication. We know from study of his MSS that Lawrence was a careful writer, though not rigidly consistent in matters of minor convention. We know also that he revised at every possible stage. Yet he rarely if ever compared one stage with the previous one, and overlooked the errors of typists or copyists. He was forced to accept, as most authors are, the often stringent house-styling of his printers, which overrode his punctuation and even his sentence-structure and paragraphing. He sometimes overlooked plausible printing errors. More important, as a professional author living by his pen, he had to accept, with more or less good will, stringent editing by a publisher's reader in his early days, and at all times the results of his publishers' timidity. So the fear of Grundyish disapproval, or actual legal action, led to bowdlerisation or censorship from the very beginning of his career. Threats of libel suits produced other changes. Sometimes a publisher made more changes than he admitted to Lawrence. On a number of occasions in dealing with American and British publishers Lawrence produced texts for both which were not identical. Then there were extraordinary lapses like the occasion when a compositor turned over two pages of MS at once, and the result happened to make sense. This whole story can be reconstructed from the introductions to the volumes in this edition; cumulatively they will form a history of Lawrence's writing career.

The Cambridge edition aims to provide texts which are as close as can now be determined to those he would have wished to see printed. They have been established by a rigorous collation of extant manuscripts and typescripts, proofs and early printed versions; they restore the words, sentences, even whole pages omitted or falsified by editors or compositors; they are freed from printing-house conventions which were imposed on Lawrence's style; and interference on the part of frightened publishers has been eliminated. Far from doing violence to the texts Lawrence would have wished to see published, editorial intervention is essential to recover them. Though we have to accept that some cannot now be recovered in their entirety because early states have not survived, we must be glad that so much evidence remains. Paradoxical as it may seem, the outcome of this recension will be texts which differ, often radically and certainly frequently, from those seen by the author himself.

Editors have adopted the principle that the most authoritative form of the text is to be followed, even if this leads sometimes to a 'spoken' or a 'manuscript' rather than a 'printed' style. We have not wanted to strip off one house-styling in order to impose another. Editorial discretion has been allowed in order to regularise Lawrence's sometimes wayward spelling and punctuation in accordance with his most frequent practice in a particular text. A detailed record of these and other decisions on textual matters, together with the evidence on which they are based, will be found in the textual apparatus or an occasional explanatory note. These give significant deleted readings in manuscripts, typescripts and proofs; and printed variants in forms of the text published in Lawrence's lifetime. We do not record posthumous corruptions, except where first publication was posthumous.

In each volume, the editor's introduction relates the contents to Lawrence's life and to his other writings; it gives the history of composition of the text in some detail, for its intrinsic interest, and because this history is essential to the statement of editorial principles followed. It provides an account of publication and reception which will be found to contain a good deal of hitherto unknown information. Where appropriate, appendixes make available extended draft manuscript readings of significance, or important material, sometimes unpublished, associated with a particular work.

Though Lawrence is a twentieth-century writer and in many respects remains our contemporary, the idiom of his day is not invariably intelligible now, especially to the many readers who are not native speakers of British English. His use of dialect is another difficulty, and further barriers to full understanding are created by now obscure literary, historical, political or other references and allusions. On these occasions explanatory notes are supplied by the editor; it is assumed that the reader has access to a good general dictionary and that the editor need not gloss words or expressions that may be found in it. Where Lawrence's letters are quoted in editorial matter, the reader should assume that his manuscript is alone the source of eccentricities of phrase or spelling. An edition of the letters is still in course of publication: for this reason only the date and recipient of a letter will be given if it has not so far been printed in the Cambridge edition.

# ACKNOWLEDGEMENTS

My thanks go to all the staff of Cambridge University Press who have helped with this volume. I am deeply indebted for the helpful advice, encouragement and scholarship of my fellow Board members: Michael Black, James T. Boulton, F. Warren Roberts and Lindeth Vasey. I owe George Lazarus thanks for many years of generous access to his manuscripts and books, which continued in his contribution to the present volume. W. H. Clarke was most helpful. Gerald Pollinger was his usual generous and informative self. Cornelia Rumpf-Worthen helped me more than I can say.

I am grateful to the following for access to manuscript materials: the two manuscripts and the typescript of 'The Witch à la Mode', the Ellen Clarke Bertrand Library, Bucknell University; the manuscript of 'The Fly in the Ointment', W. H. Clarke; the manuscripts of 'A Lesson on a Tortoise', 'Lessford's Rabbits', 'The Old Adam' and 'Strike-Pay', George Lazarus; the manuscript of 'A Modern Lover', the Berg Collection, New York Public Library; the typescripts of 'The Witch à la Mode', 'Love Among the Haystacks', 'Once—!' and 'New Eve and Old Adam', the Bancroft Library, University of California at Berkeley, which also kindly made available the unpublished manuscript fragments of 'Two Schools' and 'Delilah and Mr Bircumshaw' which appear as Appendixes I and II; the manuscripts of 'Once—!' and the 'Burns Novel' (which appears as Appendix III), and the typescripts of 'A Prelude', 'The Fly in the Ointment' and 'Delilah and Mr. Bircumshaw', the Harry Ransom Humanities Research Center, University of Texas at Austin; the manuscript of 'New Eve and Old Adam', the McFarlin Library, University of Tulsa; the typescripts of 'The Witch à la Mode', 'The Old Adam', 'Her Turn', 'Strike-Pay' and 'New Eve and Old Adam', Viking Press; the manuscript of 'Love Among the Haystacks', its owner.

I must also thank the following for their particular contributions: Helen Baron, Moina and Tom Brown, R. W. Burchfield and the staff of the *Oxford English Dictionary*, Brian Cainen, Bridget P. Carr and the Houghton Library, Harvard University, Christopher Collard, Marianne von Eckhardt, George Evans, David Farmer, W. Forster, Susan Gagg, David

Gerard, Martin Hayes and Croydon Public Library, Michael Herbert, Terry Holmes, Maureen Leach, Alan Newton, Ann Parr, Melissa Partridge, Hans Popper, Peter Preston, Bridget Pugh, Estelle Rebec, Helmut Rumpf, Keith Sagar, Hans Schwarze, Roger Smith, M. J. Stoneburg, Caroline Swinson and the McFarlin Library, University of Tulsa, Lola L. Szladits, Jane Turnbull, John Turner, the Manuscript Department of the University of Virginia Library, Anne Watts and Saint Louis Public Library, Keith Worsop.

*August 1985* J.W.

# CHRONOLOGY

| | |
|---|---|
| 11 September 1885 | Born in Eastwood, Nottinghamshire |
| September 1898–July 1901 | Pupil at Nottingham High School |
| 1902–1908 | Pupil teacher; student at University College, Nottingham |
| between 20 October and 9 November 1907 | Writes 'A Prelude' for the *Nottinghamshire Guardian* Christmas competition |
| 7 December 1907 | First publication: 'A Prelude' in *Nottinghamshire Guardian* |
| October 1908 | Appointed as teacher at Davidson Road School, Croydon |
| Winter 1909 | Writes 'A Lesson on a Tortoise' and 'Lessford's Rabbits' |
| November 1909 | Publishes five poems in *English Review* |
| Late December 1909–Spring 1910 | Writes 'The Virtuous' (revised as 'A Modern Lover') |
| ?1909–1910 | Writes 'Two Schools' and 'Delilah and Mr Bircumshaw' (first version) |
| Early 1910 | Writes 'A Blot' ('The Fly in the Ointment') |
| 3 December 1910 | Engagement to Louie Burrows; broken off on 4 February 1912 |
| 9 December 1910 | Death of his mother, Lydia Lawrence |
| 19 January 1911 | *The White Peacock* published in New York (20 January in London) |
| Late March 1911 | Austin Harrison requests stories for *English Review* |
| ?April 1911 | Writes 'Intimacy' ('The Witch à la Mode') |
| 2 June 1911 | Martin Secker requests short story volume |
| 13–14 June 1911 | Writes first version of 'The Old Adam' |
| August 1911 | Edward Garnett requests stories for *Century* |
| 10 September 1911 | Sends Garnett 'Intimacy' |
| by 25 September 1911 | Garnett returns 'Intimacy' with criticisms |
| by 7 November 1911 | Writes first version of 'Love Among the Haystacks' |
| 11 November 1911 | Sends Garnett 'Love Among the Haystacks'; forwarded to Harrison |

| | |
|---|---|
| 19 November 1911 | Ill with pneumonia; resigns his teaching post on 28 February 1912 |
| January 1912 | Plans short story volume for Secker |
| by 14 February 1912 | Writes 'The Miner at Home'; sent to Garnett |
| 14 March 1912 | Corrects proofs of 'The Miner at Home' |
| 14–17 March 1912 | Writes 'The Collier's Wife Scores' ('Her Turn') and 'Strike-Pay' |
| 16 March 1912 | 'The Miner at Home' in *Nation* |
| *c.* 17 March 1912 | Meets Frieda Weekley; they go to Germany on 3 May |
| 23 May 1912 | *The Trespasser* |
| June 1912 | Writes 'Once—!', revises 'A Blot', rewrites 'Delilah and Mr. Bircumshaw' |
| September 1912–March 1913 | At Gargnano, Lago di Garda, Italy |
| December 1912 | Begins and abandons the 'Burns Novel' |
| February 1913 | *Love Poems and Others* |
| 29 May 1913 | *Sons and Lovers* |
| by 10 June 1913 | Writes 'Eve and the Old Adam' ('New Eve and Old Adam') |
| June–August 1913 | In England |
| 21 June–July 1913 | Plans revision of stories for magazine publication; revises (for typing by Douglas Clayton), first at the Cearne, then at Margate, 'A Blot' as 'The Fly in the Ointment', perhaps 'The Old Adam', 'Strike-Pay', 'The Collier's Wife Scores' as 'Her Turn', perhaps 'Once—!', 'Eve and the Old Adam' as 'New Eve and Old Adam' |
| 8 July 1913 | Sends Clayton stories for typing |
| 11 July 1913 | Revises 'Intimacy' as 'The White Woman' (later as 'The Witch à la Mode') |
| 13 July 1913 | Sends 'The White Woman' for typing |
| 14 July 1913 | Begins to revise the Clayton typescripts; agrees not to have 'New Eve and Old Adam' typed |
| mid-July 1913 | Revises 'Love Among the Haystacks' and sends it to Clayton |
| 20 July 1913 | Sends 'Once—!' to *Smart Set* (rejected; also rejected by *English Review* in October and *Egoist* in December) |
| 28 July 1913 | Sends 'The Fly in the Ointment' to *New Statesman* (accepted) |
| August 1913–June 1914 | In Germany, Switzerland and Italy |

| | |
|---|---|
| 16 August 1913 | 'The Fly in the Ointment' in *New Statesman* |
| 6 September 1913 | 'Her Turn' in *Westminster Gazette* |
| 13 September 1913 | 'Strike-Pay' in *Westminster Gazette* |
| 26 June 1914 | Begins to gather stories for volume publication; considers including 'Love Among the Haystacks', 'Once—!' and 'New Eve and Old Adam' (none included) |
| Late June–mid-July 1914 | Revises stories |
| July 1914–December 1915 | In London, Buckinghamshire and Sussex |
| 13 July 1914 | Marries Frieda Weekley in London |
| 25 July 1914 | Sends Clayton 'Once—!' to be re-typed; sent to J. B. Pinker |
| 29 July 1914 | Tells Clayton not to type 'Love Among the Haystacks' |
| 26 November 1914 | *The Prussian Officer and Other Stories* |
| 30 September 1915 | *The Rainbow*; suppressed by court order on 13 November |
| June 1916 | *Twilight in Italy* |
| July 1916 | *Amores* |
| June 1917 | Ezra Pound tries unsuccessfully to get 'Once—!' published |
| 15 October 1917 | After twenty-one months' residence in Cornwall, ordered to leave by military authorities |
| October 1917–November 1919 | In London, Berkshire and Derbyshire |
| December 1917 | *Look! We Have Come Through!* |
| October 1918 | *New Poems* |
| November 1919–February 1922 | To Italy, then Capri and Sicily |
| 20 November 1919 | *Bay* |
| 10 February 1920 | Asks Pinker for 'The Witch à la Mode', 'Love Among the Haystacks', 'Once—!'; not found |
| November 1920 | Private publication of *Women in Love* (New York), *The Lost Girl* |
| 10 May 1921 | *Psychoanalysis and the Unconscious* (New York) |
| 12 December 1921 | *Sea and Sardinia* (New York) |
| March–August 1922 | In Ceylon and Australia |
| 14 April 1922 | *Aaron's Rod* (New York) |
| September 1922–March 1923 | In New Mexico |
| 23 October 1922 | *Fantasia of the Unconscious* (New York) |
| 24 October 1922 | *England, My England* (New York) |
| March 1923 | *The Ladybird, The Fox, The Captain's Doll* |
| March–November 1923 | In Mexico and USA |

| | |
|---|---|
| 27 August 1923 | *Studies in Classic American Literature* (New York) |
| September 1923 | *Kangaroo* |
| 9 October 1923 | *Birds, Beasts and Flowers* (New York) |
| December 1923–March 1924 | In England, France and Germany |
| March 1924–September 1925 | In New Mexico and Mexico |
| August 1924 | *The Boy in the Bush* (with Mollie Skinner) |
| 10 September 1924 | Death of his father, John Arthur Lawrence |
| 14 May 1925 | *St. Mawr together with The Princess* |
| September 1925–June 1928 | In England and, mainly, in Italy |
| 7 December 1925 | *Reflections on the Death of a Porcupine* (Philadelphia) |
| January 1926 | *The Plumed Serpent* |
| June 1927 | *Mornings in Mexico* |
| 24 May 1928 | *The Woman Who Rode Away and Other Stories* |
| June 1928–March 1930 | In Switzerland and, principally, in France |
| July 1928 | *Lady Chatterley's Lover* privately published (Florence) |
| September 1928 | *Collected Poems* |
| July 1929 | Exhibition of paintings in London raided by police. *Pansies* (manuscript earlier seized in the mail) |
| September 1929 | *The Escaped Cock* (Paris) |
| 6 January 1930 | Hears from Clayton about early manuscripts |
| 30 January 1930 | Asks Clayton for 'Love Among the Haystacks' and 'Once—!' |
| 2 March 1930 | Dies at Vence, Alpes Maritimes, France |
| Summer 1930 | David Garnett plans publication of 'Love Among the Haystacks' and 'Once—!' |
| 25 November 1930 | *Love Among the Haystacks & Other Pieces* (including 'Once—!') published in London by The Nonesuch Press (1933 by Secker and Viking Press) |
| 15 January 1932 | 'The Fly in the Ointment' (manuscript version) in *Young Lorenzo* |
| April–May 1933 | Bumpus Bookshop Exhibition of manuscripts: 'A Modern Lover' rediscovered |
| June 1933 | 'A Modern Lover' typed: sold to *Life and Letters* |
| September 1933 | 'A Modern Lover' in *Life and Letters* |
| by September 1933 | 'The Old Adam', 'Her Turn' and 'Strike-Pay' typed |
| October 1933 | Plans for volume of unpublished stories |

| | |
|---|---|
| by November 1933 | 'New Eve and Old Adam' and 'The Witch à la Mode' typed |
| December 1933 | 'The Old Adam' bought by *Cosmopolitan* (not published); 'The Witch à la Mode' sold to *Lovat Dickson's Magazine* and *Esquire* |
| Spring 1934 | 'Strike-Pay' and 'Her Turn' sold to *Everyman*, *Esquire* and *Lovat Dickson's Magazine* |
| 29 March 1934 | 'Her Turn' in *Everyman* |
| Late May 1934 | Secker proposes *A Modern Lover* volume |
| June 1934 | Contents of *A Modern Lover* agreed for Secker and Viking Press; 'The Witch à la Mode' in *Lovat Dickson's Magazine*, 'Strike-Pay' in *Esquire* |
| Late July 1934 | Secker sends proofs of *A Modern Lover* to Viking Press |
| August 1934 | 'Her Turn' in *Esquire*, 'Strike-Pay' in *Lovat Dickson's Magazine* |
| September 1934 | 'The Witch à la Mode' in *Esquire* |
| 11 October 1934 | *A Modern Lover* published in New York by Viking Press (18 October in London by Secker) |
| 19 October 1936 | 'The Miner at Home' in *Phoenix* |
| February 1938 | 'Delilah and Mr. Bircumshaw' rediscovered |
| Spring 1940 | 'Delilah and Mr. Bircumshaw' in *Virginia Quarterly Review* |
| 1949 | 'A Prelude' republished in *A Prelude* |
| March 1954 | 'Burns Novel' rediscovered |
| 12 August 1957 | 'Burns Novel' in *A Composite Biography* |
| 15 January 1968 | 'Lessford's Rabbits' and 'A Lesson on a Tortoise' in *Phoenix II* |
| July 1971 | 'The Fly in the Ointment' (typescript version) in *The Mortal Coil* |

# CUE-TITLES

## A. Manuscript Locations

| | |
|---|---|
| BucU | Bucknell University |
| Clarke | Mr W. H. Clarke |
| Lazarus | Mr George Lazarus |
| NYPL | New York Public Library |
| UCB | University of California at Berkeley |
| UT | University of Texas |
| UTul | University of Tulsa |
| ViU | University of Virginia |
| YU | Yale University |

## B. Printed Works

(The place of publication is London unless otherwise stated.)

| | |
|---|---|
| Delavenay | Emile Delavenay. *D. H. Lawrence: L'Homme et la Genèse de son Œuvre*. 2 volumes. Paris: Librairie C. Klincksieck, 1969. |
| E.T. | E.T. [Jessie Wood]. *D. H. Lawrence: A Personal Record*. Jonathan Cape, 1935; reprinted Cambridge: Cambridge University Press, 1980. |
| *Letters*, i. | James T. Boulton, ed. *The Letters of D. H. Lawrence*. Volume I. Cambridge: Cambridge University Press, 1979. |
| *Letters*, ii. | George J. Zytaruk and James T. Boulton, eds. *The Letters of D. H. Lawrence*. Volume II. Cambridge: Cambridge University Press, 1981. |
| *Letters*, iii. | James T. Boulton and Andrew Robertson, eds. *The Letters of D. H. Lawrence*. Volume III. Cambridge: Cambridge University Press, 1984. |

| | |
|---|---|
| *A Modern Lover* | D. H. Lawrence. *A Modern Lover*. Secker, 1934. |
| Nehls | Edward Nehls, ed. *D. H. Lawrence: A Composite Biography*. 3 volumes. Madison: University of Wisconsin Press, 1957–9. |
| *OED* | Sir James A. H. Murray and others, eds. *A New English Dictionary on Historical Principles*. 10 volumes. Oxford: Oxford University Press, 1884–1928. |
| *Phoenix* | Edward D. McDonald, ed. *Phoenix: The Posthumous Papers of D. H. Lawrence*. New York: Viking Press, 1936. |
| *Phoenix II* | Warren Roberts and Harry T. Moore, eds. *Phoenix II: Uncollected, Unpublished and Other Prose Works by D. H. Lawrence*. Heinemann, 1968. |
| Roberts | Warren Roberts. *A Bibliography of D. H. Lawrence*. 2nd edn. Cambridge: Cambridge University Press, 1982. |
| Tedlock, *Lawrence MSS* | E. W. Tedlock. *The Frieda Lawrence Collection of D. H. Lawrence Manuscripts: A Descriptive Bibliography*. Albuquerque: University of New Mexico, 1948. |

# INTRODUCTION

# INTRODUCTION

## 1907–13 Early Short Stories

For a number of reasons, some of Lawrence's early short stories were not published in his lifetime; while others, appearing in newspapers and magazines, were never reprinted or collected in book form. This volume presents the entire body of Lawrence's posthumously published, uncollected or unpublished early short fiction, and offers a cross-section of all the latter's most important periods, styles and concerns. It contains unrevised work dating from 1907, at the very start of his writing career (including his very first published work); it also presents two sketches dating from 1909, a year from which very little of his work survives.[1] Five stories written during his period as a teacher in Croydon are included, throwing considerable light on his writing during and after the period of *The White Peacock*, together with three sketches from early in 1912, written during the composition of the penultimate version of *Sons and Lovers*, two stories written abroad later that year, and one story written at the height of his early maturity in the summer of 1913. This volume thus stands as a companion to the collection *The Prussian Officer and Other Stories* (1914); while deprived of the intensive revision received by most of the contents of that volume in 1914, the stories in this edition include a number of characteristic and extremely important works which missed revision or republication only by chance.

The Introduction to *The Prussian Officer*[2] recounts the history of the stories collected there, and describes Lawrence's early plans for a book of short stories. A good deal of his writing and revision of stories in 1911 and early 1912, as well as in 1914, was with such a book in mind. But many of the stories which he wrote between 1907 and 1914 failed to get into *The Prussian Officer* simply because, by 1914, they had not been published. When he began to assemble stories for the collection in the summer of

[1] Two half-page fragments of the third version of *The White Peacock* survive (Roberts E430b and c), but otherwise these two sketches are all we possess of DHL's fiction between the summer of 1908 and the winter of 1909.

[2] Ed. John Worthen (Cambridge, 1983), pp. xix–xxx.

1914, he seems to have planned to include 'Love Among the Haystacks', 'Once—!' and 'New Eve and Old Adam'; he asked his typist Douglas Clayton to send him copies for revision.[3] But, fairly late in the revision of stories for the volume, he decided to make it primarily a collection of published work; only one unpublished story (still not in print after many attempts, and of an awkward length for magazine publication) was included.[4] As a consequence, a number of stories which we know he considered including could find no place in the volume; as well as the three just mentioned, at least two others ('The Witch à la Mode' and 'The Old Adam'), included in plans for a short story volume early in 1912,[5] had to be omitted in 1914. Lawrence's major work of revision of his early stories had come in the summer of 1913, when he decided to publish in magazines everything he could: seven of the twelve stories included in *The Prussian Officer* were substantially revised during July 1913.[6] But seven other stories, equally heavily revised in 1913 but not included in *The Prussian Officer*, are printed here: 'The Fly in the Ointment', 'The Witch à la Mode', 'Love Among the Haystacks', 'Her Turn', 'Strike-Pay', 'Once—!' and 'New Eve and Old Adam'. All except the last of these Lawrence attempted to publish in the summer of 1913: the first, fourth and fifth got into print but not into *The Prussian Officer*.

Another accident also contributed to the fact that a number of stories remained unpublished. After his work on *The Prussian Officer* was finished, in October 1914, Lawrence's writing for the next three years concentrated upon his novels *The Rainbow* and *Women in Love*, his poems and his 'philosophical' work. He only wrote three stories during the whole of that period, and published only two by March 1917.[7] This meant that stories not in print by 1914 tended to get forgotten; and as some were in the possession of his typist Clayton, his sister Ada Clarke and his friend Edward Garnett, rather than with J. B. Pinker (his agent from 1914), they remained unpublished and in some cases actually lost. A letter Lawrence wrote to Pinker in February 1920, when he was planning his second short story volume (iii. 473), produced none of the old stories he was looking

[3] *Letters*, ii. 190; future references in the Introduction to *Letters*, i., ii. and iii. appear in the text in the form (ii. 190).

[4] 'Daughters of the Vicar'.

[5] See Introduction to *The Prussian Officer*, ed. Worthen, p. xxiii, and *Letters*, i. 345.

[6] 'The Prussian Officer' ['Honour and Arms'], 'The Thorn in the Flesh', 'Daughters of the Vicar', 'The Shadow in the Rose Garden', 'The White Stocking', 'A Sick Collier' and 'The Christening'.

[7] 'England, My England' (1915; published in the *English Review*, xxi, October 1915, 238–52), 'The Thimble' (1915) and probably 'The Horse-Dealer's Daughter' (1916). 'The Thimble' was published in *Seven Arts*, i (March 1917), 435–8.

for;[8] he recovered one of them from Edward Garnett in time to include it in *England, My England* (1922),[9] but the others remained unpublished. Two missing stories (and some sketches) surfaced in January 1930, when Clayton wrote to Lawrence reminding him of the manuscripts left in his possession. Lawrence immediately planned to revise and to publish 'Love Among the Haystacks' and 'Once—!', but Clayton was slow in answering, and it was (anyway) too late in Lawrence's life; he died less than two months later. A full history of all the stories' posthumous publication appears below.

Four appendixes are included, containing an unpublished story fragment ('Two Schools') dating from between 1908 and 1911, the unpublished second half of an early version of 'Delilah and Mr. Bircumshaw', the so-called 'Burns Novel' of December 1912, and a guide to the real-life locations of a number of the stories.

## 1907 'A Prelude'

The earliest story printed here was never revised, and in that respect is unique among Lawrence's surviving short fiction. 'A Prelude' was written between 20 October and 9 November 1907.[10] As a Nottingham college student, Lawrence entered the *Nottinghamshire Guardian* 1907 Christmas short story competition; 'Alan and J[essie] asked me why I didn't, and so put me upon doing it to show I could.'[11] He wanted to enter all three competition categories, but as the rules stated 'No Competitor will be awarded more than one prize',[12] and as he himself wished to enter the early version of 'A Fragment of Stained Glass', he asked two friends to enter stories on his behalf. Louie Burrows entered 'The White Stocking', and Jessie Chambers 'A Prelude' in the section 'the MOST ENJOYABLE

[8] 'The Witch à la Mode', 'Love Among the Haystacks', 'Once—!' and 'The Primrose Path'.

[9] Letter to Edward Garnett, 10 November 1921; Tedlock, *Lawrence MSS* 94; the story was 'The Primrose Path'.

[10] On 20 October 'The White Stocking' was finished and 'A Legend' ('A Fragment of Stained Glass') drafted: 'I may write a third' (*Letters*, i. 38). The closing date for competition entries was Saturday 9 November.

[11] *Letters*, i. 38. Alan and Jessie Chambers belonged to the Haggs Farm family at Underwood; Jessie (1887–1944) was responsible for sending some of DHL's poetry manuscripts to Ford Madox Hueffer in 1909, and thus for his first significant publications. See Explanatory note on 5:1.

[12] *Nottinghamshire Guardian*, 10 August 1907, p. 1; see Introduction to *The Prussian Officer*, ed. Worthen, pp. xix–xx.

CHRISTMAS the writer remembers or has ever heard of';[13] it won, and was published under her name.[14] Lawrence made some attempt to deny his authorship; Jessie's sister May asked him for the truth, and received the following letter:

> The tale is Jessie's; do not accept any such reports. Whoever can have promulgated it? The miserable cacklers in Eastwood are always so ready to jump to conclusions and bandy names.
>
> Do not say anything to those at the Haggs [i.e. Jessie's parents and other brothers and sister], it would make them feel so uncomfortable, perhaps vexed – (i. 41)

But Jessie Chambers later confirmed that the story was indeed Lawrence's, and her family too seems to have been allowed into the secret; when the prize money of £3 arrived, 'my father cashed Lawrence's first cheque. As he gave the money to him, father remarked: "Well Bert, it's the first, but I hope it won't be the last."'[15] Given the nature of the competition, Lawrence must have written 'A Prelude' specifically for it; he made no subsequent attempts to revise it or even to recover it, though the terms of the competition allowed him to reprint it 'with acknowledgement as from the "Nottinghamshire Guardian" three months after its publication in the Christmas number';[16] he did revise, and later published, both his other entries.[17] In 1924 he admitted to his bibliographer E. D. McDonald the existence of 'a youthful story in the bad grey print of a provincial newspaper—under a nom de plume. But thank God that has gone to glory in the absolute sense.'[18] P. Beaumont Wadsworth rediscovered it, and published it in a limited edition in 1949;[19] however, a typescript survives at the University of Texas (Roberts E322.2) of the 1907 newspaper text with a note on the first page in Frieda Lawrence's hand: 'I had this by me for several years before it became an ugly little book'. This suggests that the story became known to McDonald (the typescript resembling a number he had made) at some date between 1936 and 1949; if he had known of it before 1936, he would probably have included it in *Phoenix*. Emile Delavenay, too, saw a copy of the 1907 newspaper text 'dans l'exemplaire de Jessie Chambers',[20] probably when he visited her in July 1934.

13 *Nottinghamshire Guardian*, 10 August 1907, p. 1. For Louie Burrows, see *Letters*, i. 29 n. 3.
14 *Nottinghamshire Guardian*, 7 December 1907, p. 17.
15 E.T. 113.
16 *Nottinghamshire Guardian*, 10 August 1907, p. 1.
17 See Introduction to *The Prussian Officer*, ed. Worthen, pp. xli–ii, xlvii.
18 Letter to E. D. McDonald, 31 July 1924.
19 *A Prelude, by D. H. Lawrence* (Merle Press, Thames Ditton, 1949); reprinted in the *Nottinghamshire Guardian*, 10 December 1949, pp. 9, 12.
20 Delavenay, i. 122.

It is possible that Jessie Chambers altered Lawrence's story before she submitted it; he asked Louie Burrows to write out the story she entered for him 'in your style, because mine would be recognised' (i. 38). But the only original text of 'A Prelude' is that of the 1907 *Nottinghamshire Guardian*, which has been adopted as base-text here. The original cross-headings have, however, been removed from the text; they are printed in the Textual apparatus.[21]

## 1909 'A Lesson on a Tortoise', 'Lessford's Rabbits'

In October 1908, Lawrence left the Midlands to teach at the Davidson Road School in Croydon, and sometime during his first two years there he wrote two short stories of school life. They suggest his developing talent for a realistic reporting of daily events, as well as for the ironical presentation of himself as a teacher. There are numerous parallels between the description of free school breakfasts in 'Lessford's Rabbits', and an account in a letter to May Holbrook (née Chambers) of 2 December 1908 (i. 97); there are also parallels between the descriptions of the boys in the letter and in both stories. A letter to Louie Burrows of 28 March 1909 (i. 124), however, reproduces some of the same details of the free breakfasts, and includes a detail of youngsters 'crippled with broken boots' which appears in 'A Lesson on a Tortoise' but not in the May Holbrook letter. Another detail in the story—children going to school on 'snowy days'—would have been most unlikely in November or December 1908 ('November' is the setting of 'A Lesson on a Tortoise'), but not in March or November 1909.[22] The class described, however (Standard VI) corresponds to the class Lawrence was teaching in the winter term of 1909: and paper in both manuscripts (pp. 1–6 in Roberts E196.4a and pp. 1–8 in Roberts E196.5a) is identical with paper Lawrence was using in December 1909.[23] It seems probable, then, that Lawrence wrote or (just possibly) revised the stories in the winter of 1909, probably after finishing

21 The 1949 *Nottinghamshire Guardian* reprint reproduced the 1907 text's illustrations (reduced in size), but provided new and different cross-headings. No short story manuscript or typescript from the whole of DHL's career bears any indication of cross-headings which he inserted.

22 According to the records of the Croydon Natural History and Scientific Society (*Rainfall of the Croydon District* 1905–22), there was no snowfall in Croydon until 27 December 1908 (after school term ended). There was, however, a good deal of snow in late February and early March 1909: and again in November 1909 (see *Letters*, i. 143).

23 For DHL's class teaching, see Nehls, i. 150. DHL used the paper (watermarked MINNESOTA MILL/FINE) on 15 December 1909, when he copied out Ford Madox Hueffer's letter praising *The White Peacock* (MS Lazarus).

*The White Peacock* at the end of October; they may both have been written for Ford Madox Hueffer and the *English Review*. The manuscripts of both stories have Lawrence's 1911–12 address added at the top of the first page in his later hand; the fact that they survived until 1986 in the possession of his publisher William Heinemann suggests that Lawrence may have shown them to someone in the firm, perhaps to their reader the poet Walter de la Mare, with whom he became friendly early in 1912 and who helped him place several of his short stories in magazines. Lawrence asked him on 11 April 1912: 'is there any news of any of my articles?' (i. 383), and he may have been thinking of these school stories as well as of his recent pieces on the miners' strike (see below). The surviving 1909 manuscripts (now in the Lazarus collection) have been adopted as base-texts for this edition.

## 1909–10 'A Modern Lover', 'The Fly in the Ointment', 'Two Schools'

The real-life events upon which 'A Modern Lover' drew can be accurately dated to the period between December 1909 and the spring of 1910 (see the first Explanatory note to the story). Jessie Chambers said that she saw 'the first and quite different version' of the story—'Le personnage de Tom Vickers, inventé, ne figurait pas dans la première version'[24]—before Christmas 1909. If she is right, Lawrence must have written the version surviving in manuscript (Roberts E240.7, originally entitled 'The Virtuous') shortly afterwards. At some stage he revised it extensively, and supplied five new manuscript pages, all in the section about Tom Vickers;[25] it is possible that this was the addition which Jessie Chambers misremembered. The revision cannot, at any rate, have been long after the original composition; by December 1911 Lawrence had apparently forgotten the story's existence, as he then wrote 'The Right Thing to Do', the first version of 'The Shades of Spring' (published 1913 and included in *The Prussian Officer*), on almost exactly the same theme. He only realised the coincidence when he came across the earlier story in Eastwood in March 1912, while revising the later one. He sent 'A Modern Lover' to Garnett as 'a story I wrote three years back, and had forgotten ... before it was ever submitted to a publisher, I would like thoroughly to revise it'

[24] 'The character of Tom Vickers, invented, did not appear in the first version' (Delavenay, ii. 694, 708): Delavenay's summary of a manuscript written by Jessie Chambers, later destroyed by her.

[25] Pp. [37], [38] (the end of section 4), [42], [43], [44].

(i. 372–3). But he probably never worked at it again, and the manuscript remained in Garnett's possession for the next twenty-one years. It was first published in 1933 in *Life and Letters*, from a typescript (no longer extant) made for the literary agency Curtis Brown from the original manuscript. The magazine stated that the story 'came to light during the recent exhibition of D. H. Lawrence's manuscripts at Messrs. J. & G. Bumpus's bookshop'; on 6 April 1933, Curtis Brown had asked Garnett for permission 'to have typewritten copies made of all the unpublished material that you have so kindly loaned to the Exhibition at Bumpus.'[26] The base-text adopted for this edition is the manuscript.

'The Fly in the Ointment' was also first written early in 1910, as 'A Blot': the original title is deleted on the surviving autograph manuscript (Roberts E135.5a) which, however, probably dates from 1912. Helen Corke remembered seeing the story in the summer of 1910 as 'just written';[27] the setting suggests a date some months earlier. Lawrence later revised the story and created the existing manuscript, which closely resembles that of a *Prussian Officer* story, 'The Christening' (Roberts E68.2), written in June 1912; he probably added further revisions to the manuscript in the summer of 1913, before sending it to be typed by Clayton.[28] He then revised Clayton's typescript[29] to create the corrected typescript (Roberts E135.5b) which he sent to the *New Statesman* on 28 July 1913: 'I offer you the enclosed sketch ... Since *Sons and Lovers*, my last novel [published 29 May], has quite a considerable success, and the *New Statesman* was kindly disposed to it, I am in hopes that your generosity may wax to printing an occasional sketch of mine' (ii. 52).[30] The story must have been accepted immediately; the first page of the typescript bears a note of the date and the *New Statesman*'s address: 'Printing Department / 1 Aug 1913 / Fetter Lane E.C.', and the story appeared in the *New Statesman* on 16 August 1913. The differences between the typescript and the *New Statesman* text must have been introduced at the proof stage,

[26] P. 286; letter from Laurence Pollinger (of Curtis Brown) to Edward Garnett: UT.

[27] Helen Corke, *D. H. Lawrence: The Croydon Years* (Austin, 1965), p. 10. A. W. McLeod (see *Letters*, i. 136 n. 3) also saw it in Croydon (ii. 65).

[28] For the 1932 publication of Roberts E135.5a, see 'Other posthumous publication' below.

[29] All the pencil corrections in Roberts E135.5b appear to be in DHL's hand, as well as most of the ink corrections; three ink corrections of typing errors (on pp. 6, 7 and 8) were almost certainly made by Clayton. For further information about Clayton's typing habits, see Introduction to *The Prussian Officer*, ed. Worthen, pp. xxxvi–vii; the only texts in this volume he may have influenced in ways not now discoverable are those of 'Her Turn' and 'Strike-Pay'.

[30] The review of the novel in the *New Statesman*, i (5 July 1913), 408, was by Hubert Bland. The magazine prepared the typescript of the story as setting-copy: DHL's name was moved to the end, and one misspelling (p. 6) and one mistyped word (p. 3) were corrected.

though probably not by Lawrence. We have no record of his correcting proofs; he was at the address he gave the magazine only until 2 August, and left for Germany on 7 August. 'The Fly in the Ointment' was not included in *The Prussian Officer*;[31] since it had been published, and since several forms—autograph manuscript, corrected typescript and magazine text—were all theoretically available, Lawrence may have made a deliberate decision to exclude it. The base-text for this edition is the manuscript E135.5a, emended from the revisions he made to the typescript E135.5b.

'Two Schools', the unpublished story fragment in Appendix I, also almost certainly belongs to the period 1909–10; the surviving manuscript (Roberts E396) is on the 'sermon paper' from Boots Cash Chemists and Stationers characteristic of those years,[32] and used (for example) throughout the first draft of *The Trespasser* (Roberts E407a and b), written between May and August 1910. The pencil manuscript of 'Two Schools' also bears a strong resemblance to the pencil draft (Roberts E284a) of the last part of the first version of 'Odour of Chrysanthemums', which dates from 1909. It is not known why Lawrence abandoned it.

## 1911 'The Witch à la Mode', 'The Old Adam', 'Love Among the Haystacks'

Early in 1911, Lawrence's first novel *The White Peacock* was published; and although he was not yet ready to embark on a full-time career as a writer (particularly as his December 1910 engagement to Louie Burrows meant that he felt obliged to maintain his schoolteacher's regular salary), nevertheless during 1911 a number of things happened which made his eventual career possible. It was probably *The White Peacock* which provoked the editor of the *English Review*, Austin Harrison, to solicit stories from him at the end of March (i. 240 and n. 3, 245); and in August he made contact with Edward Garnett, whose literary advice and support for him with the publisher Duckworth were crucial for the next two years. 'The Witch à la Mode' was written at the latest by 10 September, when Lawrence sent it (almost certainly in the form of the earliest surviving autograph manuscript, entitled 'Intimacy', Roberts E438a) to Garnett, for possible publication in the American magazine *Century* (i. 301, 307). But it had been drafted earlier in the year, probably as early as March or April (i. 258 n. 3)

[31] The other three published stories not included were 'A Prelude', 'Her Turn' and 'Strike-Pay'.

[32] A. W. McLeod described how 'Lawrence . . . asked me, if I was going into Croydon, to get him a lot of sermon paper at Boots'. Sermon paper was a new term to me and I asked whether he was writing theology' (Nehls, i. 90).

and then sent to Harrison at the *English Review* (see below); it draws upon experiences shared by Lawrence and Helen Corke in March 1911 (and perhaps repeated in July).[33] Garnett returned it by 25 September, with advice about revising it for which Lawrence thanked him: 'I myself had felt the drag of the tale, and its slowness in accumulating' (i. 307). In January 1912, it was included in the contents of his projected short story volume (i. 354). Sometime between September 1911 and July 1913 Lawrence rewrote it to create the second autograph manuscript (Roberts E438b); he may have worked on it while staying at Garnett's house between 21 June and 9 July 1913. He wrote to Garnett's son David on 11 July from Broadstairs, asking if he had left behind 'a little story of mine, in MS, called Intimacy . . . send it to me here' (ii. 33). But by 13 July he had found it himself, 'mingled up with Frieda's underclothing. I at once changed its title, "Intimacy", in order to get it out' (ii. 36). E438b shows the title 'Intimacy' altered to 'The White Woman'; the manuscript was extensively revised at the same time. It was sent to Clayton's mother Katharine for typing on 13 July (ii. 37); Lawrence lightly revised the resulting typescript to create the corrected typescript (Roberts E438c). He also changed the title again, to 'The Witch à la Mode'. He almost certainly submitted the story to periodicals in the summer of 1913, but it was not accepted. The last we hear of it in his lifetime is in February 1920, when he asked his (now) ex-agent J. B. Pinker if he had it.[34]

In 1932, Frieda came into possession of a typescript; the following year, Curtis Brown had a new typescript made from E438c, to create the surviving carbon-copies (Roberts E438d and e); the story was first printed, probably from a copy of these typescripts, in June 1934, in *Lovat Dickson's Magazine* (which paid 16 guineas for it),[35] and reprinted in *A Modern Lover* (1934). The base-text for the current edition is the second autograph manuscript (E438b), emended from Lawrence's autograph corrections to the 1913 typescript (E438c).

The publication of Lawrence's short story 'Odour of Chrysanthemums'[36] in Harrison's *English Review* in June 1911 proved to be another turning point. It provoked the young publisher Martin Secker to write to him: 'I was extremely interested in your novel, and the excellent story in

[33] See *Letters*, i. 238–40, 285–6, and Helen Corke, *In Our Infancy* (Cambridge, 1975), pp. 209–10. Helen Corke (1882–1978) was a teacher in Croydon: see *Letters*, i. 129.

[34] *Letters*, iii. 473. Any stories DHL was able to recover in 1920–1 would probably have been published in *England, My England* (1922); compare 'The Primrose Path' (see footnote 9).

[35] Curtis Brown Accounts, 2 July 1934: UT. It was also printed in *Esquire* (Chicago), September 1934, pp. 42–3, 131–2.

[36] Included in *The Prussian Officer*.

this month's *English Review* which I have just read prompts me to ask if you would care to offer me a volume of short stories, when you have sufficient material' (i. 275 n. 2). Secker wrote on 2 June, and Lawrence must have received the letter when he returned to Croydon on 11 June after the Whitsuntide holidays; he replied the next day.

I am very much flattered by your offer to publish a volume of my short stories: to tell the truth, I sit in doubt and wonder because of it.

There have appeared in print, in the *English Review*, two and two only of my tales. Because nobody wanted the things, I have not troubled to write any. So that, at present, I have two good stories published ['Goose Fair' and 'Odour of Chrysanthemums'], three very decent ones lying in the hands of the Editor of the *English Review* ['A Fragment of Stained Glass', 'The White Stocking' and 'Intimacy'], another good one at home [perhaps 'A Modern Lover'], and several slight things sketched out and neglected [e.g. 'The Fly in the Ointment', 'A Lesson on a Tortoise', 'Lessford's Rabbits']. If these would be any good towards an autumn volume, I should be at the top of happiness. If they are not enough—I am in the midst of a novel, and bejungled in work, alas. (i. 275)

But in spite of his work on the novel 'Paul Morel' (published as *Sons and Lovers*), he found time to produce short stories. Only two nights after writing that letter, he told Louie Burrows that 'I've worked quite hard ... written a short story, 32 pages long, in two nights' (i. 276). A remark a fortnight later identifies that story; responding to her 'belated advice' not to spend time on anything except 'Paul Morel', he remarked 'Why mustn't I write Old Adams?' (i. 279). The surviving manuscript of 'The Old Adam' (Roberts E286a) is 26 pages long; however, its paper and appearance are almost identical with those of the first draft of 'Daughters of the Vicar',[37] written 15–16 July 1911, and it may well represent Lawrence's July revision of the story. It was obviously designed for the proposed 'Secker volume' which he was still hoping to put together in January 1912 (i. 345), but it is not clear what then happened to it. There is no record of Lawrence revising it with his other stories in the summer of 1913; nor is there evidence that Clayton typed it, unless we assume that it was one of the typed stories ('short ones') Lawrence was reserving for the *New Statesman* on 20 July, together with 'The Fly in the Ointment' (ii. 44). A surviving carbon-copy typescript (E286b) dates from September 1933: the story was first published, from a text related to E286b, in *A Modern Lover*. The base-text for this edition is the manuscript (E286a).

'Love Among the Haystacks' was written by 7 November 1911; four days later, Lawrence sent it to Edward Garnett for his advice: 'Dare I ask

[37] Roberts E86a, p. 23; E86b, pp. 10–11, [18–24], [27–33], [36–60], [62–7].

Harrison, of the *English Review*, to publish this thing as a little serial?' (i. 327). It drew upon events dating from 1908 (see the first Explanatory note to the story), and may have been first written earlier than 1911; but Lawrence's enthusiastic remark to Garnett of 7 November—'I've got another rather ripping long short story – shall I show it you?' (i. 323)—suggests a recent date of composition or revision.[38] Garnett probably forwarded it to Harrison; it was in the latter's possession on 10 January 1912. Lawrence planned to include it in his projected volume of stories, but he realised that its length reduced its chances of magazine publication: 'I suppose [Harrison] wont have the "Haystacks" one – too long – he doesn't say' (i. 348). Harrison kept it until March, when he must have written complaining about its length; Lawrence replied on 28 March to say 'I am sorry it is so long. I suppose it would not split' (i. 378). Harrison then offered to publish either the early version of 'The Shades of Spring' or 'Love Among the Haystacks', and Lawrence again turned to Garnett for advice: 'Which shall I say? He wants a definite answer directly' (i. 380). Garnett advised 'Love Among the Haystacks', and Lawrence informed Harrison accordingly (i. 381); but when Harrison saw Lawrence in London on 24 or 25 April 'to jaw me' (i. 384), he probably told Lawrence that he would not after all be publishing the story; it never appeared in the *English Review*.

The 1911 version of the story most likely survives in the form of six revised pages in the autograph manuscript (Roberts E211a); when Lawrence sent the manuscript to Clayton for typing in July 1913, he implied to Garnett that he had rewritten a good deal of it, and the new pages probably date from then.[39] However, in July 1914 Lawrence asked Clayton (who retained the manuscript) to send the story back, which 'I want to go over before it is typed. I hope you have it by you' (ii. 190). He was obviously planning to include it in the *The Prussian Officer*, but when his conception of the volume changed, it was not included. He apparently returned the manuscript to Clayton at the end of July 1914, perhaps after engaging in a second stage of revision, and asked him to let it 'lie by for a while. I must work at it later' (ii. 204). He must have been considering giving it the same kind of extensive revision as he had recently given to a number of the *Prussian Officer* stories, but he probably never worked on it again. In 1920, he asked his ex-agent J. B. Pinker for it (iii. 473), but Clayton must have

38 David Garnett claimed to have seen the story's manuscript 'when it was first written' (*Love Among the Haystacks*, 1930, p. v); he might have seen it when DHL sent it to his father in the winter of 1911, but probably saw it in June 1913 before it was revised.

39 *Letters*, ii. 44. In revision, all except the original pp. 10–14 ([12–16]) and the original last page (p. [59]) were replaced.

retained the manuscript: in 1930 he wrote to Lawrence to tell him that a number of manuscripts were in his possession, including 'one or two unpublished things'[40] which Lawrence thought he might revise—'it might turn out quite nice'. He wrote a letter (now lost) to Clayton, asking for the unpublished manuscripts, and wondering if he might sell the published ones; he had started to think of his manuscripts as 'a sort of nest-egg' in 1929.[41] Clayton did not immediately reply, but at the end of January we find Lawrence writing to him again:

> I ... am thinking the best would be if you sent me *all* the MSS. here for me to look at—except those you have advertised ... It may be I shall not even want the typescript of 'Love Among the Haystacks' and 'Once', so if you haven't begun typing, don't, but just send me all the MSS.[42]

It seems that Clayton had taken Lawrence at his word on the matter of selling old manuscripts, and had advertised some for sale (the advertisement has not been traced); but he must also have volunteered to make typescripts of the unpublished ones which Lawrence wanted. Clayton typed 'Love Among the Haystacks' in 1930,[43] a copy of which provided setting-copy for David Garnett's collection *Love Among the Haystacks & Other Pieces* (1930): a carbon-copy (Roberts E211b) of the typescript survives. If Clayton made a typescript in 1913, which Lawrence might have corrected, it is no longer extant. He probably returned the 1911–13 manuscript (E211a) to Lawrence in 1930; it survives in private hands, and has been adopted as base-text for this edition.

## England, Spring 1912 'The Miner at Home', 'Her Turn', 'Strike-Pay'

Following his serious illness in the winter of 1911, Lawrence was obliged to give up school-teaching; he broke off his engagement to Louie Burrows, and began working for the first time as a professional writer. He rewrote *The Trespasser* during January 1912, and 'Paul Morel' between February and April. But he also wrote a number of pieces 'as journalistic as I can make 'em' (i. 376) during the same period. The national miners' strike began in February 1912, and Lawrence used his knowledge of conditions

40 DHL to Nancy Pearn (Curtis Brown's periodical agent), 6 January 1930.
41 DHL to Hon. Dorothy Brett, 23 June 1929.
42 DHL to Douglas Clayton, 30 January 1930.
43 Clayton's 1913 typescripts are on paper watermarked 'EXCELSIOR / SUPERFINE / BRITISH MAKE'; his 1930 on paper watermarked 'PLANTAGENET / BRITISH MAKE'. In 1930 he also added a telephone number to his address on the typescripts.

in his home village of Eastwood (where he lived between February and early May 1912) to produce at least four pieces about it. The first, 'The Miner at Home', was written by 14 February and despatched to Edward Garnett that day, along with another (unidentified) sketch for 'the *Saturday* [*Westminster Gazette*] or the *Nation* . . . The colliery one à propos the Strike, might go down' (i. 366). The *Nation* accepted it, sent proofs on 14 March (i. 375), and published it (under 'Short Studies') two days later. It was reprinted in *Phoenix*. No manuscripts survive; the base-text for this edition is the printing in the *Nation*.

Lawrence's three other pieces about the strike were written between 14 and 17 March; the coincidence of dates suggests that Lawrence was stimulated to write them because of his success with 'The Miner at Home'. He told Garnett, when he had finished, that he was 'sick of 'em', and wondered 'why in the name of all that's fortunate do I kill my own pig before I've driven it to market. There's stuff in all the damned articles that nobody will want to print.'[44] He was right: they found no publisher in 1912. He sent 'Her Turn' under its then title of 'The Collier's Wife Scores' to the *Daily News*, but it was returned by 1 April (i. 379); he then sent it to Hilaire Belloc's radical journal the *Eyewitness* (i. 381), but it did not appear there either. Lawrence revised all three articles in July 1913, and had them typed by Clayton; he almost certainly then revised them again, on the clean typescripts (as he did in the case of 'The Fly in the Ointment'). All three were then sold, which suggests the increase in his reputation after the publication of *Sons and Lovers* in May 1913; two of these sketches of mining-life were bought in 1913 by one of the newspapers which may well have turned them down in 1912. 'Her Turn' (as 'Strike-Pay I, Her Turn') and 'Strike-Pay' (as 'Strike-Pay II, Ephraim's Half-Sovereign', heavily cut) were published in the *Westminster Gazette*, 6 and 13 September 1913.[45] Lawrence may have revised them again in proof. Both sketches were reprinted (from typescripts made from the manuscripts by September 1933) in magazines in England and America in the summer of 1934,[46] and were then collected in *A Modern Lover*. The

[44] *Letters*, i. 376; see also p. 375 n. 3.

[45] They were both also printed, in identical texts, in the *Saturday Westminster Gazette* for the same dates, p. 9. The third piece, 'A Sick Collier', was published in the *New Statesman* on 16 August, and included in *The Prussian Officer*. Some self-censorship in revision may have helped sell the pieces; see Explanatory notes on 136:2, 136:14 and 141:38.

[46] 'Her Turn' was reprinted from a typescript related to Roberts E159.5b in *Everyman* (London), 29 March 1934, pp. 159–60, and (as 'Turnabout is Fair') in *Esquire* (Chicago), August 1934, pp. 50, 156: the former paid 5 guineas for it (Curtis Brown Accounts, 30 April 1934: UT). 'Strike-Pay' was reprinted from a typescript related to Roberts E318b in

original autograph manuscripts of both stories survived in Frieda Lawrence's possession as late as 1937.[47] The manuscript of 'Her Turn' (Roberts E159.5a) is now missing, though its text is recorded in the 1933 typescript (Roberts E159.5b); given the nature of the typist's work as it can be gauged from the text of 'Strike-Pay' (where both manuscript and typescript survive[48]), the words and punctuation of the missing manuscript can no longer be accurately recovered. Base-text for 'Her Turn' adopted for this edition is therefore the *Westminster Gazette* text, which preserves Lawrence's revisions made either in the missing 1913 typescript, or in proof. The base-text for 'Strike-Pay' is the surviving manuscript (Roberts E381a), emended from the *Westminster Gazette* printing so far as the latter's heavily cut version allows (six substantives have been adopted).

## Germany and Italy, 1912 'Delilah and Mr. Bircumshaw', 'Once—!', 'Burns Novel'

After going to Germany on 3 May 1912 with Frieda Weekley (later Lawrence), and finishing 'Paul Morel' for what he believed was the last time early in June, Lawrence worked on at least three and probably four short stories: 'Once—!' (see below), a revision of 'The Fly in the Ointment' (see above), the first version of his *Prussian Officer* story 'The Christening', and probably a revision of 'Delilah and Mr. Bircumshaw'; 'under the influence of Frieda, I am afraid their moral tone would not agree with my countrymen' (i. 420). It was Frieda who dated 'Delilah and Mr. Bircumshaw' to 'her early years with Lawrence, circa 1912–1913'.[49] The earliest surviving version exists only as a manuscript fragment (Roberts E90.5a); a reference in it to Ernest Shackleton suggests an original composition date nearer 1909–10.[50] It is printed as Appendix II.

The 1912–13 version exists in two forms: an unrevised typescript of uncertain date (Roberts E90.5b), and the text published in the *Virginia Quarterly Review* in 1940[51] (reprinted in *Phoenix II*). The typescript and magazine texts differ in many details, and in some short passages; they may well represent versions of a revised and an unrevised text (for example, the

*Esquire*, June 1934, pp. 54–5, 100, and in *Lovat Dickson's Magazine*, iii (August 1934), 129–40; the latter paid 7 guineas for it (Curtis Brown Accounts, 31 August 1934: UT).

47 Lawrence Clark Powell, *The Manuscripts of D. H. Lawrence* (Los Angeles, 1937), pp. 25–6.

48 See, e.g., Textual apparatus at 134:5, 16; 135:2, 9, 11, 28, 29, 35 etc.

49 Tedlock, *Lawrence MSS* 41.

50 See Explanatory note on 194:34. It is possible that the missing pp. 1–8 of E90.5a became the first part of a revised 1912–13 version.

51 Vol. xvi (Spring 1940), 257–66.

1912–13 manuscript and a slightly revised typescript made from it). Although at one point the magazine text is slightly closer than the typescript to the early manuscript fragment (E90.5a),[52] it is impossible to say with certainty which of the two represents the revised text. The typescript (E90.5b), however, corresponds rather more closely to Lawrence's known habits of punctuation,[53] while the magazine text appears to have been heavily normalised. For this reason, the base-text adopted is the typescript (E90.5b), emended only where it is clearly corrupted by typing errors. The Textual apparatus lists these emendations, and also all the variants in the magazine text, since their status cannot be exactly determined; passages of particular interest are also discussed in the Explanatory notes. (For details of the story's rediscovery in the late 1930s, see '1930–71 Other posthumous publication' below.)

'Once—!' was written, with a Bavarian setting (see the first Explanatory note on the story), between June and September 1912; its surviving autograph manuscript (Roberts E296a) dates from then.[54] Clayton typed the story in July 1913, and by 20 July Lawrence had sent the typescript (probably revised, but now unlocated) to the *Smart Set* (ii. 44 and n. 2). By 4 September it had been rejected as 'too hot' (ii. 67), and returned to the magazine's English representative Ezra Pound. Lawrence then asked Pound to forward it to the *English Review*, because—'if Harrison dare print it'—it would 'go excellently well with the two soldier stories' (ii. 82) already accepted ('The Prussian Officer' and 'The Thorn in the Flesh'). Harrison had told Lawrence that he would like to see two more, similar, stories (ii. 81 n. 1 and 82 n. 2), and by 26 October must have received 'Once—!': 'he has got three Soldier Stories, which he is going to publish in a sort of series – perhaps four – so he says – which will make a book afterwards. I hope they'll go all right' (ii. 90). However, Harrison did not accept 'Once—!'. It is unclear whether Lawrence revised it further at this stage; Pound apparently forwarded the typescript rejected by the *Smart Set* directly to Harrison, in which case Lawrence could not have worked on it. However, on 23 October Frieda wrote to Lady Cynthia Asquith that 'L. has just put your black *crêpe de Chine* blouse with the big opal in a story! It's jolly, to watch the stories

[52] See Explanatory note on 148:9. [53] See Explanatory note on 144:37.

[54] Its transparent paper (28.45 × 22.5 cm.) is identical with that used for Letters nos. 463, 464, 467 and 471 (29 June, 3, 8 and 18 July 1912) in *Letters*, i. 419–27, and with pages introduced into 'Paul Morel' during revision in Germany, May–June 1912. It is also possible, however, that DHL took some of the paper with him on his journey to Italy, starting 5 August 1912, and that he finished or rewrote the story either in Mayrhofen in the Tyrol, or in Italy.

coming!'[55] Anita in the surviving manuscript of 'Once—!' wears crêpe de chine, but as a pale blue nightgown, not as a black blouse; and there is no mention of an opal. Yet the coincidence is strong, and suggests that Lawrence may after all have been working on 'Once—!' at the end of October; in which case the typescript made by Clayton may have been revised then, and returned to Harrison.[56] After the latter rejected it, Pound suggested that it be submitted to the newly renamed magazine the *Egoist*, but Lawrence (probably because of Harrison's attitude) was

> a little bit afraid that the poor critics or whoever they are might seize on 'Once' as a flagrant example of my indecency, once it were published and so proceed to chase me out of the herd – or try to. *But* if *The Egoist* is not likely to get me into trouble by publishing 'Once', and I am not likely to get the *Egoist* into trouble by offering them the story, then I don't see why they shouldn't have it, for as much as they can afford. (ii. 131–2)

But the *Egoist* did not accept it.

When collecting stories for *The Prussian Officer* in the summer of 1914, Lawrence came very close to including 'Once—!'. On 2 July he asked Clayton for '*typed* copies of "Once" and "A Sick Collier"' (ii. 190), and included the latter. At the end of July he sent 'Once—!', apparently in its manuscript form, back to Clayton, and asked for a typed copy to be sent to his agent J. B. Pinker 'to show to the editor' (ii. 201, 202); Lawrence also asked Clayton to keep a carbon copy. Clayton noticed pencil brackets round several sentences in the manuscript, and asked Lawrence whether the sentences should be typed, but Lawrence reassured him on 27 July that 'It was right not to omit the sentences in "Once". An editor inserted the brackets.'[57] We do not know with whom Pinker was hoping to place the story; in any case he was unsuccessful.

In June 1917 Lawrence told Pinker that 'Ezra Pound wants to publish that short story "Once", which I believe we have lost between us. It seems he has a copy of the MS. How and where he will bring it out I don't know, his letter is so foolish – as usual. Shall I let him do it?' (iii. 135). Pound presumably retained the 1913 revised typescript he had sent to the *Egoist*, but either Pinker advised against its publication, or Pound was again unable to place it. In 1920 Lawrence asked Pinker whether he knew where the story now was,[58] but nothing came of the request: the manuscript itself

[55] *Frieda Lawrence: The Memoirs and Correspondence*, ed. E. W. Tedlock (1961), p. 200.

[56] The manuscript E296a, too, went to a magazine editor at some stage: see below.

[57] *Letters*, ii. 202; the suggestion (n. 4) that the editor was 'Probably Wright of the *Smart Set*' ignores the fact that Wright was sent Clayton's 1913 typescript.

[58] *Letters*, iii. 473; see similar requests for 'The Witch à la Mode' and 'Love Among the Haystacks' above, pp. xxix, xxxi.

remained with Clayton. In 1930 the latter at last wrote to Lawrence about it (see the description of the events of January 1930, pp. xxxi–xxxii above), and made a typescript of which the carbon-copy survives (Roberts E296b); the typescript must have been the setting-copy for the text printed in *Love Among the Haystacks & Other Pieces*.[59] The 1913 typescript of 'Once—!' is lost, and along with it Lawrence's revisions; the base-text for this edition is the manuscript (E296a).

After their journey to Italy in August–September 1912, Lawrence and Frieda spent the winter at Gargnano, on Lake Garda. In November, he finished *Sons and Lovers* there, but within a month ('since I am feeling hard pushed again') told McLeod that he was planning a new novel:

> It is to be a life of Robert Burns – but I shall make him live near home, as a Derbyshire man – and shall fictionise the circumstances. But I have always loved him, in a way. He seems a good deal like myself – nicer in most ways. I think I can do him almost like an autobiography. Tell Miss Mason the *Life* came all right . . . If it would amuse you, just peep round and see if you can spot anything interesting about Burns, in the library, during the holiday. I've only got Lockhart's *Life*. I should like to know more about the Highland Mary episode. Do you think it's interesting? (i. 487)

The fact that Lockhart's biography of Burns[60] had already arrived suggests that he had been planning the novel for at least a fortnight; it might even have been the 'novel – purely of the common people – fearfully interesting' (i. 431) he had told Edward Garnett he was thinking about in August, and which—as 'Scargill Street' (i. 466)—he had planned to start after *Sons and Lovers*.[61] However, it was a 'new novel' that he described to Garnett in December: 'a sort of life of Robert Burns. But I'm not Scotch. So I shall just transplant him to home – or on the hills of Derbyshire – and do as I like with him as far as circumstances go, but I shall stick to the man. I have

59 Two corrections in ink to E296b do not appear in the printed text, and may not have been included in the ribbon copy; see Textual apparatus 152:1 and Explanatory note on 159:38.

60 In what may be DHL's hand, 'Beginning of a *Burn's n*ovel' appears on the surviving MS (Roberts E59.3), p. 10 verso. DHL also originally named one character 'Mary Burns' (see Textual apparatus for 203:19–22). He had read J. G. Lockhart's 1828 *Life of Burns*, probably in the Everyman's Library edition of 1907; see *Letters*, i. 504 n. 5 for other Burns materials he knew, including an essay by W. E. Henley (see Explanatory note on 200:19). In 1927 he re-read Lockhart's biography, and on 5 December wrote to Donald Carswell (whose wife Catherine was planning a new Burns biography) that it 'Made me spit! Those damned middle-class Lockharts grew lilies of the valley up their arses, to hear them talk . . . My word, you can't know Burns unless you can hate the Lockharts and all the estimable bourgeois and upper classes as he really did—the narrow-gutted pigeons. Don't, for God's sake, be mealy mouthed like them. *I'd* like to write a Burns life.'

61 See also Explanatory note on 202:28.

always been fond of him, as of a sort of brother. Now, I'll write a novel of him. Tell me if you approve' (i. 489). Lawrence was ill around 21 December, but—in bed on the 24th—was 'writing a bit at a new novel, which seems to me to be so far more clever than good' (i. 491). This was almost certainly the 'Burns Novel', but by 29 December he had apparently abandoned it in favour of another novel (surviving as the twenty-page manuscript of 'Elsa Culverwell') which he thought would be less 'unwieldy, because it'll be further off from me and won't come down on my head so often' (i. 497).[62] This sounds very different from the 'Burns Novel', which was to have been written 'almost like an autobiography' and would have presented yet another male hero; the writer who declared on 23 December that he would do his 'work for women, better than the suffrage' (i. 490) would take women as his central characters in 'Elsa Culverwell', in its apparent development 'The Insurrection of Miss Houghton' (rewritten as *The Lost Girl*), and in 'The Sisters' (the early version of *The Rainbow* and *Women in Love*).

By 17 January 1913, he was wondering about the 'Burns Novel' 'if I shall ever get it done'; 'The Insurrection of Miss Houghton' was by then 80 pages long, and would grow to 200 (i. 505, 536). He probably never went back to the 'Burns Novel'; all that survive are two fragments (Roberts E59.3) which remained in Germany, in the possession of Frieda's elder sister Else Jaffe, until 1954: Lawrence probably left them with her when he and Frieda stayed in Bavaria April–June 1913. They were first printed by Edward Nehls in 1957;[63] here they appear as Appendix III.

## Germany, 1913 'New Eve and Old Adam'

After abandoning 'The Insurrection of Miss Houghton' in March 1913, Lawrence wrote the first draft of 'The Sisters' (ii. 20); he finished this in Bavaria in May 1913. Then, just as he had done the previous year, he wrote a number of short stories: 'I have written the best short story I have ever done – about a German officer in the army and his orderly ['The Prussian Officer' ('Honour and Arms')]. Then there is another good autobiographical story – I think it is good ['Eve and the Old Adam']: then there is another story in course of completion which interests me ['Vin Ordinaire' ('The Thorn in the Flesh')]' (ii. 21). The last two stories were completed by 10 June; see Explanatory notes for further details confirming

[62] See D. H. Lawrence, *The Lost Girl*, ed. John Worthen (Cambridge, 1981), pp. xix–xxiv; the surviving 'Elsa Culverwell' fragment is included, pp. 343–58.

[63] Nehls, i. 184–95; see also pp. 561–2 n. 38. Else Jaffe, née von Richthofen (1874–1973).

this dating.[64] As soon as he was back in England, Lawrence began to revise his unpublished short stories with a view to magazine publication (ii. 26); he probably revised 'Eve and the Old Adam', giving it first the title 'Renegade Eve and the Old Adam', and then 'New Eve and Old Adam', early in July 1913. He sent it to Clayton for typing around 8 July (ii. 30, 38), but told Garnett on 14 July that Katharine Clayton

said she thought the story I called 'The New Eve' – previously I think 'Renegade Eve' – that is the one where the telegram comes 'Meet me Marble Arch 7.30 Richard' – was unworthy of me, and so Douglas didn't type it. Perhaps she's right – it amuses me. (ii. 38)

He wrote to Katharine Clayton the same day: 'Yes, we'll leave the "New Eve" for the present' (ii. 38). The story was therefore not typed in the summer of 1913. Early in July 1914, Lawrence seriously considered it for *The Prussian Officer*, and on 2 July asked Clayton 'I wonder if you have got, and if you could let me have at once, the MS. of "Love Among the Haystacks", and "The Old Adam and the New Eve", or a story with a title something like that' (ii. 190); but within a week, his conception of the volume had changed.

The surviving autograph manuscript (Roberts E268a) shows the title changes noted above, and contains a great deal of interlinear revision, some of which may date from 1914. There are no subsequent references to it in Lawrence's correspondence, and the whereabouts of the manuscript for the next sixteen years is likewise unknown: it may have remained with Clayton. In 1930, Frieda Lawrence deposited a text of the story, almost certainly the manuscript, with Curtis Brown (see p. xli below). In 1933, Curtis Brown had a typed copy made, with a view to periodical publication; the surviving carbon-copy typescript (Roberts E268b) bears the characteristic Curtis Brown stamp 'MUST AWAIT AMERICAN RELEASE' on its first page.[65] The typist, working from Lawrence's heavily corrected (and often minute) handwriting, made a number of important errors; on two occasions whole lines of text were omitted, a number of words were misread (including the last one in the story), and Lawrence's characteristic punctuation was not reproduced at all accurately. This typescript was the source of the English first edition, and consequently of the American first

[64] The paper of the surviving autograph manuscript (Roberts E268a) of 'New Eve and Old Adam' is identical with that of pp. 11–16 of the manuscript of 'The Prussian Officer' ['Honour and Arms'], Roberts E326.5, and both are very similar to the paper of DHL's letter to Ernest Collings, 13 May 1913: UT.

[65] A pencil note on p. 1—'7/1935'—is misleading; the story was in print by October 1934, in a text similar to that of Roberts E268b.

edition, in *A Modern Lover*. The base-text for this edition is the autograph manuscript (E268a), emended on a small number of occasions from the carbon-copy typescripts (E268b and c) where the latter made a sensible choice between conflicting manuscript readings.

## Publication 1930–33 *Love Among the Haystacks*

In his introductory 'Reminiscence' to the volume *Love Among the Haystacks & Other Pieces* (1930), David Garnett described how its contents had been sent to his father Edward, 'who tried without success to place them. After Lawrence's death they were brought to me to publish' (p. v). It has already been shown how it was, in fact, Douglas Clayton who had retained possession of the manuscripts of 'Love Among the Haystacks' and 'Once—!' (and of the other two pieces which David Garnett printed); Clayton may have given typescripts of the four pieces to Edward Garnett (his uncle by marriage), with the latter passing them on to David for The Nonesuch Press.[66] Publication proceeded quickly, with a contract for the book being sent to Frieda Lawrence and to Lawrence's brother George (joint administrators of the Lawrence estate, 1930–2) at the end of August 1930.[67] David Garnett made no attempt either to add to, or to edit, the contents he had thus acquired; with only some very slight modification to the texts of Clayton's typescripts, probably made by the printer, the book was published on 25 November 1930, in what Lawrence's and (now) Frieda's agent at the firm of Curtis Brown, Laurence Pollinger, noted as a 'limited edition ... over subscribed several weeks ahead of publication'.[68]

In 1933, Martin Secker issued a reprint in England, and the Viking Press brought it out in America in mid-October; both included Garnett's 'Reminiscence', but—following a suggestion from Frieda Lawrence[69]—the American edition also included the 1912 version of the essay 'Christs in the Tirol'. The remainder of the American edition was set from a copy

[66] The other two were 'A Chapel Among the Mountains' and 'A Hay-Hut Among the Mountains'; see *Letters*, ii. 204. David Garnett had been a third partner (with Vera Mendel and Francis Meynell) in The Nonesuch Press from its foundation in 1923; see his *The Familiar Faces* (1962), pp. 16–20.

[67] Laurence Pollinger to Frieda, 28 August 1930: UT.

[68] Pollinger to Richard Everitt (Curtis Brown New York), 30 May 1933: UT. Of the 1600 copies, 550 were sent to America for publication by Random House.

[69] Pollinger to Frieda, 27 February 1933; Pollinger to Richard Everitt, 29 April and 30 May 1933; Richard Everitt to Pollinger, 20 May 1933: UT.

of Secker's edition,[70] which in turn was a reprint of the 1930 edition with only slight editorial and printing-house modifications.

## Publication 1933–34 *A Modern Lover*

After Lawrence's death in March 1930, Frieda deposited with the Curtis Brown agency in London a number of Lawrence manuscripts to be kept in the bank. The batch included manuscript or typescript versions of the unpublished 'The Witch à la Mode', 'The Old Adam' and 'New Eve and Old Adam', as well as of 'Her Turn' and 'Strike-Pay'.[71] Thus versions of five of the seven items to be included in the 1934 collection *A Modern Lover* had been brought together.[72] But in 1930 no move was made to publish them; instead, there were prolonged negotiations between Curtis Brown, Secker, William Heinemann and the Viking Press to produce what was first thought of as a 'Definitive Collected Works' (to include all Lawrence's unpublished writing), later modified into a series of collections, or single volumes, of the unpublished materials. And, of course, further unpublished manuscripts came to light. In March 1932 Frieda took away from the Curtis Brown office in London a typescript of 'The Witch à la Mode' (perhaps Roberts E438c), which they must have reacquired by the following year; by the summer of 1932, the manuscript of 'Intimacy' (Roberts E438a) had joined those Frieda had already deposited with Curtis Brown, and yet another typescript of 'The Witch à la Mode' was being held in New York.[73]

But still no efforts were made to publish this material. A request from the American magazine *Cosmopolitan* in January 1933 for unpublished stories received the response from Pollinger: 'Don't believe there are ... any *new* things in so far as I know and apart from possible hoards in Barclay's Bank'.[74] This attitude was confirmed by the Curtis Brown office

70 Richard Everitt to Pollinger, 27 July 1933: UT. Secker published a pocket edition in 1934, and the book was issued as No. 14 of the Phoenix Books at Berne in 1943 by Scherz.

71 Curtis Brown internal memo, 3 April 1930: UT.

72 The final contents were the surviving first part of the 1920–1 novel *Mr Noon*, 'A Modern Lover', 'The Old Adam', 'Her Turn', 'Strike-Pay', 'The Witch à la Mode' and 'New Eve and Old Adam'. A note on p. 5 of the English edition erroneously stated that the six stories 'belong to Lawrence's earliest phase of authorship, and were written in 1910–11'. In fact they dated from 1910–13: see above. The American edition (Viking Press, 1934) contained no such note; its dust-jacket simply noted that 'Most of them are from his earlier productive period ...'

73 Note signed W.A., 7 March 1932; List of D. H. Lawrence's Manuscripts in Barclay's Bank, *c.* March 1932; Additional List of D. H. Lawrence Manuscripts held in New York Office, 1 July 1932: UT.

74 Note by Pollinger on a letter to him from Helen Everitt, 16 January 1933: UT.

a fortnight later: 'I am afraid everything of a short story nature has been used in one form or another in this country by now ... We'll let you know of course if any cache *is* discovered, as is very apt to happen in this case:- D.H.L. having left material in one place or another apparently all over the world'.[75] The Barclay's Bank 'cache' was either forgotten or deliberately ignored. However, in the spring of 1933, the London bookshop Bumpus staged an exhibition of Lawrence manuscripts; and Frieda—through Curtis Brown—loaned a number of the Bank's holdings, including the fragments of 'Two Schools' and the early 'Delilah and Mr Bircumshaw'.[76] The exhibition also provoked the rediscovery of other unpublished manuscripts; some, presumably, in the Bank, while Edward Garnett found 'A Modern Lover' among his papers and sent it to Bumpus. Pollinger arranged for all the new discoveries to be typed after the exhibition was over, and a typescript of 'A Modern Lover' was made in June 1933, while 'The Old Adam', 'Her Turn' and 'Strike-Pay' (both the latter believed to be unpublished) were typed by September.[77] But neither Pollinger nor Lawrence's main English publisher Martin Secker were, at this stage, considering volume publication for the stories; an outline of Secker's future plans, drafted in July 1933, included an 'Omnibus Stories' for April–June 1934,[78] and a cheap edition of the 1932 collection *The Lovely Lady*, but no plans for the unpublished stories.[79] Periodical publication, however, went ahead; in September 1933 'A Modern Lover' was sold to *Life and Letters*,[80] and in November Pollinger sent typescripts of a number of stories he had 'now unearthed' to the New York office, including 'The Witch à la Mode', 'The Old Adam', 'Her Turn', 'Strike-Pay' and 'New Eve and Old Adam'. In December, the New York office confirmed that they were offering all of them for periodical publication.[81]

By November 1933, therefore, all the items eventually to appear in *A Modern Lover* had been recovered and typed, in texts that would provide setting-copy for their eventual volume publication; no further reference to the original manuscripts appears to have been made. The first mention of a volume came in a letter from Pollinger to Frieda in October 1933, suggesting that Secker's plans for 1935 might include 'a collection of

75 Nancy Pearn to Helen Everitt, 2 February 1933: UT.
76 Note signed L.P., 6 March 1933: UT.
77 Curtis Brown Accounts, 1 July and 1 October 1933: UT.
78 *The Tales of D. H. Lawrence* (1934).
79 Pollinger to Richard Everitt, 14 July 1933: UT.
80 Curtis Brown Accounts, 1 October 1933: UT.
81 Pollinger to Richard Everitt, 15 November 1933; Helen Everitt to Pollinger, 6 December 1933: UT.

stories (I think there are about ten unpublished in book form)'.[82] By December, either Pollinger or Secker had made a list of the contents of a volume to be called *A Modern Lover and Other Stories*: it would consist of 'A Modern Lover', 'The Old Adam (alternative title, Intimacy)', 'The Vicar's Garden', 'Strike Pay', 'Her Turn', 'The Witch à la Mode', 'New Eve and Old Adam', 'Two Marriages', 'Legend' and 'Mr Noon'.[83] At this stage, the early version of 'The Witch à la Mode' was being confused with 'The Old Adam', while 'The Vicar's Garden', 'Two Marriages' and 'Legend' had not yet been recognised as early versions of three stories published in *The Prussian Officer*.[84] The volume was not assembled with any great care; Pollinger and Secker simply put together all their unpublished typescripts, in no particular order. As a result, stories such as 'The Mortal Coil' and 'The Thimble' (published in America during the war but never published in England) were not even considered; when Secker saw the latter, during discussion of the volume which eventually became *Phoenix*, he remarked that 'we ought to have had it for "A Modern Lover"'.[85]

The publication date of 1935 had been suggested so as to allow time for full periodical publication of the contents first. In December 1933, *Cosmopolitan* bought 'The Old Adam', but, although they appear to have paid for it, they never published it; however, by the spring of 1934 'Two Marriages', 'The Witch à la Mode', 'Her Turn' and 'Strike-Pay' had all been sold.[86] In April 1934, after its periodical publication, 'Two Marriages' was recognised for what it was, and Pollinger noted that it should 'come off Fiction Volume'; but as late as May 1934 Curtis Brown London and New York were still offering 'The Vicar's Garden' and 'Legend' as unpublished stories.[87] Only on 11 June was the proposed volume's list of contents finally agreed to;[88] Secker, who had recognised 'Two Marriages', may have helped discard the other two items.[89]

Matters were now urgent, as it had become clear during the first half of 1934 that, with negotiations over the material which eventually became

[82] Pollinger to Frieda, 4 October 1933: UT.

[83] Curtis Brown Records, 5 page list, *c.* December 1933: UT.

[84] 'The Shadow in the Rose Garden', 'Daughters of the Vicar' and 'A Fragment of Stained Glass'.

[85] Martin Secker to Pollinger, 11 March 1935: UT.

[86] Curtis Brown New York to Curtis Brown London, 21 December 1933; Curtis Brown London to Curtis Brown New York, 21 December 1933; Nancy Pearn to Frieda, 13 March 1934: UT.

[87] Pollinger to Richard Everitt, 8 May 1934; note by Pollinger on a letter to him from Richard Everitt, 11 May 1934: UT.

[88] See footnote 72 above.

[89] Pollinger to P. P. Howe (Secker's associate), 16 April 1934; Secker to Pollinger, 17 April 1934: UT.

*Phoenix* still going on, neither Secker nor the Viking Press were going to have a Lawrence book in their autumn lists. Late in May, Secker apparently proposed *A Modern Lover* for prior publication.[90] This meant that Frieda Lawrence would have to be consulted, and at first she failed to respond to Pollinger's requests for a decision.[91] She had always been unhappy about the volume publication of Lawrence's unpublished work, sending (for example) Curtis Brown a telegram in February 1934: 'SELL UNPUBLISHED MATERIAL TO MAGAZINES FIRST AUTHORISE SECKER PUBLISHING PORCUPINE ONLY NO HURRY LAWRENCE'.[92] But the Viking Press, in particular, wanted a quick decision on *A Modern Lover*, and in mid-June cabled her for permission to go ahead.[93] In fact, both Secker and the Viking Press (with the approval of their respective Curtis Brown agencies) went ahead with their plans for the book long before Frieda actually agreed to it. A letter from Secker's office to Pollinger of 11 June confirmed title and contents, and noted: 'There are all early stories and would be stated to be such, with the exception of "Mr Noon", which would also be dated, with an explanation of its non-continuance... We should propose to publish in September or October'.[94]

Frieda, however, protested at the very idea of the book when she finally replied. She thought it would appear too soon after Secker's omnibus *Tales*; and, above all, 'before giving Secker *unpublished* fiction let it be sold in *magazines first*'.[95] Pollinger tried to reassure her on 9 July that every possible story had already been sold: 'The remainder is unsaleable serially, and there is no point in not letting Secker bring it out ... simultaneously with the Viking Press this Autumn'.[96] He wrote to Secker the same day in terms which suggested that the book was now a certain prospect; and, before he could have heard again from Frieda, queried whether the first story, 'A Modern Lover', was yet set up in type: the New York Curtis Brown office wanted a copy of the story (which they insisted they had never seen) for the Viking Press.[97] Secker could not yet provide galley proofs,

90 Pollinger to Secker, 24 May 1934: UT.
91 Pollinger to Frieda, 24 May and 6 June 1934: UT.
92 Frieda to Curtis Brown London, 1 February 1934: UT. The reference is to Secker's February 1934 Adelphi Library reprint of Lawrence's *Reflections on the Death of a Porcupine* (Philadelphia, 1925).
93 Richard Everitt to Pollinger, 14 June 1934: UT.
94 Howe to Pollinger, 11 June 1934: UT. See footnote 72. Secker also rejected the idea of including the animal sketches 'Adolf' and 'Rex'; they 'do not seem to be "stories" or to go well with the other contents.' They were published in *Phoenix*.
95 Frieda to Pollinger, 2 July 1934: UT. 96 UT.
97 Pollinger to Secker, 9 and 16 July 1934; Pollinger to Howe, 18 July 1934: UT. Typed

though they were 'due at any moment', but he promised to send a copy of the *Life and Letters* text. In fact, he managed to send a copy of the proofs of his edition which became the setting-copy for the whole of the Viking Press edition; the magazine text of 'A Modern Lover' either failed to arrive on time, or was ignored.

It would be wrong to criticise Pollinger for ignoring Frieda's wishes; he knew the market much better than she did (especially from the distance of New Mexico, where she was now living), and the demands she made on Pollinger had a great deal to do with her desire to prove herself as astute a business-person as her late husband.[98] She also regarded the unpublished manuscripts as a crucial, but diminishing, part of her future financial security. At the end of July—now several stages behind the fast-moving processes of publication—she asked Pollinger: 'What is Secker wanting to put into a "modern Lover"? Send me a list as the list I have seems different'. She probably had a copy of the December 1933 list, with its three rejected items. She also added a postscript: 'Let Nancy Pearn sell all she can—';[99] but it was now too late for further periodical publication of the stories. In mid-August Pollinger sent her a set of Secker's proofs, and announced the Viking Press publication date as 8 October;[100] although Secker had planned to publish simultaneously, he brought out his edition on 18 October. A day later, Pollinger sent Frieda two copies of the English edition.[101]

Early in November, a copy of Secker's contract for the book was at last sent to Frieda; after still further delays (and reminders from Pollinger), she finally signed it and returned it early in May 1935.[102] The delay was a final proof of her reluctance to acknowledge the book; but it also marked a most significant change in the publication of Lawrence's work that, by May 1935, her publisher was no longer Martin Secker, but William Heinemann. The firm which had brought out Lawrence's first book in 1911 would be responsible for his work in England for the next forty-five years.

carbon-copies of the other six items in the book survive in the possession of Viking Press.

98 Cf. DHL to Pollinger, 11 October 1929: 'Hope my wife doesn't bother you – I ask her to leave my affairs alone, but she feels the usual "call"'.

99 Frieda to Pollinger, 27 July 1934: UT.

100 Pollinger to Frieda, 17 August 1934: UT. The book was copyrighted in the USA on 11 October, which suggests that was the day of publication.

101 Copies were also sent to DHL's brother George and sisters Emily King and Ada Clarke; letters from Pollinger to Frieda, 19 and 21 October 1934: UT.

102 Pollinger to Frieda, 7 November 1934 and 4 January 1935; Pollinger to A. S. Frere-Reeves, 7 May 1935: UT.

## 1930–71 Other posthumous publication

Ada Clarke had, in the meanwhile, printed 'The Fly in the Ointment' (as 'A Fly in the Ointment') from the manuscript Roberts E135.5a in her possession. It appeared in *Young Lorenzo* as 'one of the earliest examples of his work which has not been published previously':[103] she was unaware of its 1913 publication. In 1936, E. D. McDonald included 'The Miner at Home' in *Phoenix*; he had known of its existence since at least 1925, when he had recorded its 1912 publication in his *Bibliography*.[104] A text of 'Delilah and Mr. Bircumshaw' suddenly turned up in 1938, discovered in a desk drawer of Gerald Duckworth (presumably after being sent to Edward Garnett); Curtis Brown attempted to place it, but eventually told Frieda that they had 'exhausted all the available markets', and returned it to her.[105] However, in 1939—perhaps after yet another text of it had been discovered—she told the *Virginia Quarterly Review* of its existence, and they agreed to print it if they could establish that it had not previously been published. Letters to a number of Lawrence collectors and scholars (including McDonald) failed to elicit any record of previous publication, and it was printed in the Spring 1940 number.[106] In 1968 Warren Roberts and Harry T. Moore reprinted the magazine text (wrongly as 'unfinished') in *Phoenix II*, together with the 1949 text of 'A Prelude', Ada Clarke's text of 'The Fly in the Ointment' and David Garnett's text of 'Once—!'; they also printed, for the first time, 'A Lesson on a Tortoise' and 'Lessford's Rabbits'.[107] In 1957, Edward Nehls published the 'Burns Novel' fragments in his *Composite Biography*;[108] in 1971 Keith Sagar printed the typescript version of 'The Fly in the Ointment' in *The Mortal Coil and Other Stories*.[109] Few of the posthumous publications, from 1930

[103] Ada Lawrence and G. Stuart Gelder, *Young Lorenzo* (Florence, 1932), pp. 213, 215–30.

[104] *Phoenix* 775–9; *A Bibliography of the Writings of D. H. Lawrence* (Philadelphia, 1925), p. 119.

[105] Pollinger to Frieda, 24 February 1938: ViU; Edith Haggard (Curtis Brown Ltd) to Frieda, 4 January 1939: UT.

[106] Laurence Lee to Frieda, 20 October 1939, 10, 23, 25 January and 17 February 1940; Frieda to Lee, 11 December 1939, 26 January and 6 March 1940; letters between William Jay Gould and Ben Abramson, Edward Burchard, Norman Hickox, Carmin Jones and E. D. McDonald, January 1940: ViU.

[107] 'A Prelude', 'The Fly in the Ointment' (as 'A Fly …', error from *Young Lorenzo*), 'Once—!' (as 'Once'), 'Delilah and Mr. Bircumshaw', *Phoenix II* 3–12, 13–17, 44–52, 84–91; 'Lessford's Rabbits', 'A Lesson on a Tortoise', *Phoenix II* 18–23, 24–8.

[108] Nehls, i. 184–95.

[109] Penguin Books, Harmondsworth, 1971, pp. 60–6. Sagar used the *New Statesman* printing of 1913 as base-text, occasionally emending from Roberts E135.5a and E135.5b; since he also referred to the text in *Young Lorenzo*, a number of errors from the latter were incorporated.

to 1971, fully considered the textual history of the stories, or attempted to publish them in their best versions. Some printings depended upon unreliable typescripts; others upon unreliable printed texts; others again were of early versions, while Lawrence's revised versions were either unknown, or ignored. This edition prints, for the first time, accurate texts of the final versions of the stories.

## Reception

The first critical response ever addressed to Lawrence's work appeared in the same issue of the *Nottinghamshire Guardian* in which 'A Prelude' had been published; the competition report on 7 December 1907 noted that

> In "A Prelude" however, a simple theme was handled with a freshness and simplicity altogether charming, and there was no hesitation in awarding the prize of £3 in this section to its writer, ROSALIND ... (p. 6)[110]

There is, however, no extant critical reaction to the collier sketches or other stories which Lawrence published in 1912 and 1913; not until 1930 do we get any further commentary on the stories included in this volume.

*Love Among the Haystacks & Other Pieces*, containing the title story and 'Once—!', appeared in England only nine months after Lawrence's death, and—like *Assorted Articles* in April and *The Virgin and the Gypsy* in May and October—was often taken as an opportunity by its reviewers to make some general statement about his importance as a writer. But as with the reception of *A Modern Lover* in 1934, the relatively early date of the work it contained provoked a number of reviewers to contrast the 'time when his art was practically untinged with philosophy' (*Times Literary Supplement*, 18 December 1930, p. 1083) with his later writing. Henry Tracy in the *Saturday Review of Literature* remarked on 30 December 1933 that 'one perceives what Lawrence might have been if he had been content to remain merely a good author; if he had not elected to fight the English ethos single-handed' (x, 379)—though the *New York Times Book Review* of 11 January 1931 had found 'the Lawrence philosophy beginning to ferment already' (p. 15). 'Once—!' reminded several reviewers of Lawrence's last novel, *Lady Chatterley's Lover* (1928), though the *TLS*

[110] 'On the first page of each Story much be written ... the competitor's nom de plume' (*Nottinghamshire Guardian*, 10 August 1907, p. 1). DHL's nom de plume for himself (on the early version of 'A Fragment of Stained Glass') was 'Herbert Richards' (his second and unused third names); 'Rosalind', suggestive of a heroine in the woods whose sex is not what it at first appears, may have been Jessie Chambers's choice for herself.

reckoned that the story 'was saved by a sense of humour' (p. 1083); the *London Mercury* of March 1931, however, thought it 'coarse ... one of Lawrence's first attempts at disclosing the slightly pornographic streak which he was afterwards to develop so strongly' (xxiii, 503); the *Saturday Review of Literature* found it 'innocence turned voluptuous' (x, 379). (The same magazine thought that '"Love Among the Haystacks" ... could be read aloud in a Baptist deacon's family'.) Lorine Pruette, however, in the *New York Herald Tribune Books* on 8 February 1931, saw 'Once—!' as the start of an 'exploration in the feminine reactions to sex which resulted finally in the sureness and realism of "Lady Chatterley's Lover"' (p. 7), a rare piece of praise for the novel. In general there was agreement that 'Love Among the Haystacks' was the important piece in the volume, with 'its exquisite descriptions, its amazing verve, its fierce and difficult values ... it is the germ of *The Rainbow*' (*New Statesman*, 24 January 1931, xxxvi, 472). In it, reviewers saw Lawrence 'upon his own ground' (*New York Herald Tribune Books*, p. 7) and praised his 'vivid objectivity' (*TLS*, p. 1083), even if they did so largely in order to contrast the 'charmingly innocent tale of Nottinghamshire' with the 'tortured man, the mouthpiece of moral revolt' (*Saturday Review of Literature*, x, 379) which he later became; *Lady Chatterley's Lover* loomed large behind many reviews.

In 1934, the six stories belonging to *A Modern Lover* were published, together with the first part of *Mr Noon*. By 1934 there was often a more jaundiced attitude towards Lawrence and his unpublished work; whereas the 1930 volume had elicited comments such as 'It is rather astonishing that none of these pieces should have found a publisher when they were written' (*TLS*, p. 1083), in December 1934 L. A. G. Strong noted of the stories that 'Lawrence evidently had not chosen to put them into a volume. Some readers may wonder why they have been reprinted now' (*19th Century*, p. vi). Dilys Powell in the *London Mercury* for February 1935 remarked that 'For Lawrence this book is only second-rate' (xxxi, 397), Currie Cabot wrote that 'There is no story in this collection that touches Lawrence at his absolute best' (*Saturday Review of Literature*, 10 November 1934, xi, 273), and Ferner Nuhn opined that the book 'will not change Lawrence's status greatly' (*The Nation*, 24 October 1934, cxxxix, 384). But even more clearly than in 1930, the links with Lawrence's other early work were seen; his career was starting to be understood chronologically and historically. It was obvious to Joseph Sell in the *Manchester Evening News* on 25 October 1934 how several stories came 'from the same social and geographical landscape' as *Sons and Lovers* (p. 8), while several reviewers, like Peter Monro Jack, noticed how the story 'A Modern Lover' itself appeared to be 'an overflow from "Sons and Lovers"'; the characters 'Really ... are Morel and Miriam' (*New York Times Book Review*, 4 November 1934, xxix, 7); it was 'yet another story on the Miriam theme' (*Everyman*, 2 November 1934, p. 82); H. J. Davis in the *Canadian Forum* for January 1935 linked it with 'that other Muriel story', 'The Fly in the Ointment' (xv, 159). Dilys Powell in the *London Mercury* saw its heroine as a version of Emily in *The White Peacock*, and also noticed how Winifred in 'The Witch à la Mode' 'is the Helen of the poems, the destructive spiritual woman of "The Trespasser"' (xxxi, 397), while Currie Cabot in the *Saturday Review of Literature* actually treated 'The Witch à la Mode' as an early version of the novel (xi, 273). But Dilys Powell also recognised that, within the six stories, there were distinctions to be made: '"New Eve and Old Adam" suggests a later date', and 'introduces a woman character whom we do not find in the novels before "The Rainbow" (1915)' (xxxi, 397).

In particular, reviewers singled out 'The Old Adam' and 'The Witch à la Mode' as examples of 'Lawrence's view of modern love' (*New York Times Book Review*, xxix, 7), 'the repulsion and attraction between a man and a woman' (*New York Herald Tribune Books*, 21 October 1934, p. 15), of 'sexual relationships depicted in suspense' (*TLS*, 25 October 1934, p. 731). On the other hand, 'A Modern Lover' divided reviewers into those who thought it 'admirably done ... the volume's best justification' (*TLS*, p. 731)—Lorine Pruette saw in it 'the grace and certainty of the master craftsman' (*New York Herald Tribune Books*, p. 16)—and those who regarded it as 'superficially realistic, only hinting at emotional depths' (*New York Times Book Review*, xxix, 7). In one of the more perceptive reviews, David Garnett suggested how the story's self-consciousness and 'ridiculous fine-writing' could in *A Modern Lover* be seen giving way to the maturity of Lawrence's 1912–13 work; Garnett also correctly dated the individual stories, putting 'New Eve and Old Adam' 'provisionally' in 'the summer of 1913', after Lawrence's return to England with Frieda (*New Statesman*, 27 October 1934, p. 587); perhaps he saw it at the Cearne when Lawrence was revising it. But that suggests the volume's interest for the more intelligent reviewers, though its contents might be 'slight and sketchy' (*TLS*, p. 731) by the highest standards of Lawrence's work, the stories were 'invaluable ... in a study of his literary and psychological development' (*London Mercury*, xxix, 397). It was in such terms that Lawrence criticism would increasingly speak.

# *LOVE AMONG THE HAYSTACKS AND OTHER STORIES*

## Note on the texts

'A Prelude': base-text is the first printing in the *Nottinghamshire Guardian*, 7 December 1907, p. 17 (Per), emended by reference to the text in *A Prelude* (Merle Press, Thames Ditton, 1949), pp. 29–47 (E1).

Throughout, E1 replaced Per's 'mother' by 'Mother', and replaced the unspaced 'em' dash at the end of Per's cut-off sentences with three dots; these readings are not recorded in the Textual apparatus.

'A Lesson on a Tortoise': base-text is the autograph manuscript Roberts E196.5a (MS), emended by reference to the first printing in *Phoenix II* 24–8 (E1).

'Lessford's Rabbits': base-text is the autograph manuscript Roberts E196.4a (MS), emended by reference to the first printing in *Phoenix II* 18–23 (E1).

'A Modern Lover': base-text is the autograph manuscript Roberts E240.7 (MS), emended by reference to the first printing in *Life and Letters*, ix (September–November 1933), 257–86 (Per) and to the text in *A Modern Lover* 11–44 (E1).

Throughout, Per used single inverted commas for quotations; the preferred reading of MS in respect of ages is without a hyphen (e.g. 'twenty one'); these readings are not recorded in the Textual apparatus.

The particularly light punctuation of the dialogue is a feature of MS.

'The Fly in the Ointment': base-text is the autograph manuscript Roberts E135.5a (MS), emended by reference to the corrected typescript Roberts E135.5b (TS and TSR), to the first printing in the *New Statesman*, i (16 August 1913), 595–7 (Per), and to the first printing of MS in *Young Lorenzo* (Florence, 1932), pp. 211–30 (O1).

Throughout, O1 used spaced 'em' dashes; these readings are not recorded in the Textual apparatus.

The particularly light punctuation of the dialogue is a feature of MS.

'The Witch à la Mode': base-text is the autograph manuscript Roberts E438b (MS), emended by reference to the corrected typescript Roberts E438c (TS), to the carbon-copy typescripts Roberts E438d and e (TCC), to the first printing in *Lovat Dickson's Magazine*, ii (June 1934), 697–718 (Per), and to the text in *A Modern Lover* 103–28 (E1).

'The Old Adam': base-text is the autograph manuscript Roberts E286a (MS), emended by reference to the carbon-copy typescript Roberts E286b (TCC) and to the first printing in *A Modern Lover* 47–71 (E1).

'Love Among the Haystacks': base-text is the autograph manuscript Roberts E211a (MS), emended by reference to the carbon-copy typescript Roberts E211b (TCC) and to the first printing in *Love Among the Haystacks & Other Pieces* (The Nonesuch Press, 1930), pp. 1–56 (E1).

Throughout, E1 printed 'labourer', 'labour', 'Vicar', 'Vicarage', 'on to' and 'Aye'; DHL usually wrote these as 'laborer', 'labor', 'vicar', 'vicarage', 'onto' and 'Ay'; his practice has been preserved, and E1's variants are not recorded in the Textual apparatus.

'The Miner at Home': base-text is the first printing in the *Nation*, x (16 March 1912), 981–2 (Per), emended by reference to the text in *Phoenix* 775–9 (E1).

'Her Turn': base-text is the first printing in the *Westminster Gazette*, 6 September 1913, p. 2 (Per), emended by reference to the carbon copy typescript Roberts E159.5b (TCC) and the text in *A Modern Lover* 75–83 (E1).

E1 printed 'Mr.' and 'Mrs.' without a full stop: these variants are not recorded in the Textual apparatus.

'Strike-Pay': base-text is the autograph manuscript Roberts E381a (MS), emended by reference to the first printing (heavily cut) in the *Westminster Gazette*, 13 September 1913, p. 2 (Per), to the carbon-copy typescript Roberts E381b (TCC) and to the text in *A Modern Lover* 87–100 (E1).

Throughout, TCC and E1 reproduced 'half-a-crown', 'four-and-sixpence', 'five-and-sixpence'; it was DHL's habit to write these without hyphens; his practice has been preserved, and the variants of TCC and E1 in this regard are not recorded in the Textual apparatus.

'Delilah and Mr. Bircumshaw': base-text is the ribbon copy typescript Roberts E90.5b (TS). The Textual apparatus records all the variants in the first printing in the *Virginia Quarterly Review*, xvi (Spring 1940), 257–66 (Per) and the text in *Phoenix II* 84–91 (E1), with the exception of the American forms 'Ill-humor', 'jeweled', 'Pretense' and 'willful'. It also records emendations of base-text from Per and from the early manuscript fragment Roberts E90.5a (MS).

'Once—!': base-text is the autograph manuscript Roberts E296a (MS), emended by reference to the carbon-copy typescript E296b (TCC) and the first printing in *Love Among the Haystacks & Other Pieces* (The Nonesuch Press, 1930), pp. 83–96 (E1).

TCC and E1 frequently employed '2 em' dashes where MS practice is equivalent to the 'em' dash; these readings are not recorded in the Textual apparatus.

'New Eve and Old Adam': base-text is the autograph manuscript Roberts E268a (MS), emended by reference to the carbon-copy typescripts Roberts E268b and c (TCC) and the first printing in *A Modern Lover* 131–66 (E1).

DHL was inconsistent in inserting full stops after the story's internal division numbering; this edition has silently deleted them. TCC and E1 inserted double inverted commas at the start of new paragraphs of the letter quoted at the end of the story; these readings are not recorded in the Textual apparatus, and neither is the name 'Cyriack' in MS; see Explanatory note on 165:7.

The apparatus records all textual variants between the base-texts and the texts here printed, except for the following silent emendations:

1 Incomplete quotation marks and missing full stops at the end of sentences have been supplied.
2 DHL's typists and typesetters consistently adopted the forms 'to-day', 'to-night', 'to-morrow', 'good-night' and 'good-bye' (DHL wrote these as one unhyphenated word); 'apologize', 'realize', 'recognize' and 'scrutinize' (DHL spelled these and their derivative forms with an 's'); 'Mr.' and 'Mrs.' (DHL usually wrote these without a full stop). In all these cases, DHL's manuscript practice has been adopted where appropriate manuscripts survive; in 'Delilah and Mr. Bircumshaw' the practice of TS and in 'A Prelude' and 'Her Turn' the practice of Per has been preserved.
3 DHL sometimes presented colloquial contractions without joining them up. e.g. 'did n't', 'would n't'; typists and typesetters consistently presented these as 'didn't', 'wouldn't'. In all cases, this normalisation has been accepted or adopted.
4 Omitted and misplaced apostrophes have been corrected.
5 Italicised punctuation variants have only been recorded when they form part of another variant.
6 DHL's typesetters normally presented the titles of his stories in bold capitals, and DHL and his typists sometimes put a full stop after his titles in manuscript and typescript; emendation to lower case type and deletion of those full stops have not been recorded.
7 Clearly inadvertent errors made by DHL (e.g. 'you' for 'your') and by typists and typesetters (e.g. 'wide-opem', 'Feoffrey', 'o'clack') have not been recorded.

Inconsistencies in DHL's hyphenation have been regularised according to majority usage. Inconsistencies in paragraphing have also been regularised where DHL's manuscripts are unclear.

# A Prelude*

*"Sweet is pleasure after pain ...... "**

In the kitchen of a small farm a little woman* sat cutting bread and butter. The glow of the clear, ruddy fire was on her shining cheek and white apron; but grey hair will not take the warm caress of firelight.

She skilfully spread the softened butter, and cut off great slices from the floury loaf in her lap. Already two plates were piled, but she continued to cut.

Outside the naked ropes of the creeper tapped and lashed at the window.

The grey-haired mother looked up, and setting the butter on the hearth, rose and went to look out. The sky was heavy and grey as she saw it in the narrow band over the near black wood. So she turned and went to look through the tiny window which opened from the deep recess on the opposite side of the room. The northern sky was blacker than ever.

She turned away with a little sigh, and took a duster from the red, shining warming-pan to take the bread from the oven. Afterwards she laid the table for five.

There was a rumbling and a whirring in the corner, and the clock struck five. Like clocks in many farmers' kitchens, it was more than half an hour fast. The little woman hurried about, bringing milk and other things from the dairy; lifting the potatoes from the fire, peeping through the window anxiously. Very often her neck ached with watching the gate for a sign of approach.

There was a click of the yard gate. She ran to the window, but turned away again, and, catching up the blue enamelled teapot, dropped into it a handful of tea from the caddy, and poured on the water. A clinking scrape of iron shod boots sounded outside, then the door opened with a burst as a burly, bearded man entered. He drooped at the shoulders, and leaned forward as a man who has worked heavily all his life.

"Hello, mother," he said loudly and cheerfully. "Am I first? Aren't any of the lads down yet? Fred will be here in a minute."

"I wish they would come," said his wife, "or else it'll rain before they're here."

"Ay," he assented, "it's beginning, and it's cold rain an' all. Bit of sleet, I think," and he sat down heavily in his armchair, looking at his wife as she knelt and turned the bread, and took a large jar of stewed apples from the oven.*

"Well mother," he said with a pleasant comfortable little smile, "here's another Christmas for you and me. They keep passing us by."

"Ay," she answered, the effects of her afternoon's brooding now appearing. "They come and go, but they never find us any better off."

"It seems so," he said, a shade of regret appearing momentarily over his cheerfulness. "This year we've certainly had some very bad luck. But we keep straight—and we never regret that Christmas, see, it's twenty-seven years since—twenty-seven years."

"No, perhaps not, but there's Fred as hasn't had above three pounds for the whole year's work, and the other two at the pit."

"Well, what can I do? If I hadn't lost the biggest part of the hay, and them two beast—"*

"If—! Besides what prospects has he? Here he is working year in year out for you and getting nothing at the end of it. When you were his age, when you were 25, you were married and had two children. How can he ask anybody to marry him?"

"I don't know that he wants to. He's fairly contented. Don't be worrying about him and upsetting him. He'd only go and leave us if he got married. Besides, we may have a good year next year, and we can make this up."

"Ay, so you say."

"Don't fret yourself to-night, lass. It's true things haven't gone as we hoped they would. I never thought to see you doing all the work you have to do, but we've been very comfortable, all things considered, haven't we?"

"I never thought to see my first lad a farm labourer at 25, and the other two in the pit. Two of my sons in the pit!"

"I'm sure I've done what I could, and"——but they heard a scraping outside, and he said no more.

The eldest son tramped in, his great boots and his leggings all covered with mud. He took off his wet overcoat, and stood on the hearthrug, his hands spread out behind him in the warmth of the fire.

Looking smilingly at his mother, as she moved about the kitchen, he said:

"You do look warm and cosy, mother. When I was coming up with the last load I thought of you trotting about in that big, white apron, getting tea ready, watching the weather. There are the lads. Aren't you quite contented now—perfectly happy?"

She laughed an odd little laugh, and poured out the tea. The boys came in from the pit, wet and dirty, with clean streaks down their faces where the rain had trickled. They changed their clothes and sat at the table. The elder was a big, heavy, loosely-made fellow, with a long nose and chin, and comical wrinkling round his eyes. The younger, Arthur, was a handsome lad, dark-haired, with ruddy colour glowing through his dirt, and dark eyes. When he talked and laughed the red of his lips and whiteness of his teeth and eyeballs stood out in startling contrast to the surrounding black.

"Mother, I'm glad to see thee," he said, looking at her with frank, boyish affection.

"There mother, what more can you want?" asked her husband.

She took a bite of bread and butter, and looked up with a quaint, comical glance, as if she were given only her just dues, but for all that it pleased and amused her, only she was half shy, and a grain doubtful.

"Lad," said Henry, "it's Christmas Eve. The fire ought to burn its brightest."

"Yes, I will have just another potato, seeing as Christmas is the time for feeding. What are we going to do? Are we going to have a party, mother?"

"Yes, if you want one."

"Party," laughed the father, "who'd come?"

"We might ask somebody. We could have Nellie Wycherley,* who used to come, an' David Garton."

"We shall not do for Nellie nowadays," said the father. "I saw her on Sunday morning on the top road. She was drivin' home with another young woman, an' she stopped an' asked me if we'd got any holly with berries on, an' I said we hadn't."

Fred looked up from the book he was reading over tea. He had dark brown eyes, something like his mother's, and they always drew attention when he turned them on anyone.

"There is a tree covered in the wood," he said.

"Well," answered the irrepressible Henry, "that's not ours, is it? An' if she's got that proud she won't come near to see us, am I goin' choppin' trees down for her? If she'd come here an' say she wanted a bit, I'd fetch her half the wood in. But when she sits in the trap and looks down on you an' asks, 'Do you happen to hev a bush of berried holly in your hedges? Preston can't find a sprig to decorate the house, and I hev some people coming down from town,' then I tell her we're all crying because we've none to decorate ourselves, and we want it the more 'cause nobody's coming, neither from th' town nor th' country, an' we're likely to forget it's Christmas if we've neither folks nor things to remind us."

"What did she say?" asked the mother.

"She said she was sorry, an' I told her not to bother, it's better lookin' at folks than at bits o' holly. The other lass was laughing, an' she wanted to know what folks. I told her any as hadn't got more pricks than a holly bush to keep you off."

"Ha! ha!" laughed the father; "did she take it?"

"The other girl nudged her, and they both began a laughing. Then Nellie told me to send down the guysers* to-night. I said I would, but they're not going now."

"Why not?" asked Fred.

"Billy Simpson's got a gathered face,* an' Wardy's gone to Nottingham."

"The company down at Ramsley Mill will have nobody to laugh at to-night," said Arthur.

"Tell ye what!" exclaimed Henry, "we'll go."

"How can we, three of us?" asked Arthur.

"Well," persisted Henry, "we could dress up so as they'd niver know us, an' hae a bit o' fun. Hey!" he suddenly shouted to Fred, who was reading, and taking no notice. "Hey, we're going to the Mill guysering."

"Who is?" asked the elder brother, somewhat surprised.

"You, an' me, an' our Arthur. I'll be Beelzebub."

Here he distorted his face to look diabolic, so that everybody roared.

"Go," said his father, "you'll make our fortunes."

"What!" he exclaimed, "by making a fool of myself? They say

fools for luck. What fools wise folk must be. Well, I'll be the devil—are you shocked, mother? What will you be, Arthur?"

"I don't care," was the answer. "We can put some of that red paint on our faces, and some soot, they'd never know us. Shall we go, Fred?"

"I don't know."

"Why, I should like to see her with her company, to see if she has very fine airs. We could leave some holly for her in the scullery."

"All right, then."

After tea all helped with the milking and feeding. Then Fred took a hedge knife and a hurricane lamp and went into the wood to cut some of the richly berried holly. When he got back he found his brothers roaring with laughter before the mirror. They were smeared with red and black, and had fastened on grotesque horsehair moustaches, so that they were entirely unrecognisable.

"Oh, you are hideous," cried their mother. "Oh, it is shameful to disfigure the work of the Almighty like that!"

Fred washed and proceeded to dress. They could not persuade him to use paint or soot. He rolled his sleeves up to the shoulder, and wrapped himself in a great striped horse rug. Then he tied a white cloth round his head, as the Bedouins do,* and pulled out his moustache to fierce points. He looked at himself with approval, took an old sword from the wall, and held it in one naked, muscular arm.

"Decidedly," he thought, "it is very picturesque, and I look very fine."

"Oh, that is grand," exclaimed his mother, as he entered the kitchen. His dark eyes glowed with pleasure to hear her say it. He seemed somewhat excited, this bucolic young man. His tanned skin shone rich and warm under the white cloth, its coarseness hidden by the yellow lamplight. His eyes glittered like a true Arab's, and it was to be noticed that the muscles of his sunbrowned arm were tense with the grip of the broad hand.

It was remarkable how the dark folds of the rug and the flowing burnouse* glorified this young farmer, who, in his best clothes looked awkward and ungainly, and whose face a linen collar showed coarse, owing to exposure to the weather, and long application to heavy labour.

They set out to cross the two of their own fields, and two of their neighbour's which separated their home from the mill. A few uncertain flakes of snow were eddying down, melting as they settled.

The ground was wet, and the night very dark. But they knew the way well, and were soon at the gate leading to the mill yard. The dog began to bark furiously, but they called to him, "Trip, Trip," and knowing their voices, he was quieted.

Henry gave a thundering knock, and bawled in stentorian tones, "Dun yer want guysers?"

A man came to the door, very tall, very ungainly, very swarthy.

"We non want yer," he said, talking down his nose.

"Here comes Beelzebub," banged away Henry, thumping a pan which he carried. "Here comes Beelzebub, an' he's come to th' right place."

A big, bonny farm girl came to the door.

"Who is it?" she asked.

"Beelzebub, you know him well," was the answer.

"I'll ask Miss Ellen if she wants you."

Henry winked a red and black wink at the maid, saying, "Never keep Satan on the doorstep," and he stepped into the scullery.

The girl ran away, and soon was heard a laughing, and bright talking of women's voices drawing nearer to the kitchen.

"Tell them to come in," said a voice.

The three trooped in, and glanced round the big kitchen. They could only see Betty, seated as near to them as possible on the squab, her father, black and surly, in his armchair, and two women's figures in the deep shadows of one of the great ingle-nook seats.

"Ah," said Beelzebub, "this is a bit more like it, a bit hotter. The Devil feels at home here."

They began the ludicrous old Christmas play that everyone knows so well. Beelzebub acted with much force, much noise, and some humour. St. George, that is Fred, played his part with zeal and earnestness most amusing, but at one of the most crucial moments he entirely forgot his speech, which, however, was speedily rectified by Beelzebub. Arthur was nervous and awkward, so that Beelzebub supplied him with most of his speeches.

After much horseplay, stabbing, falling on the floor, bangings of dripping-pans and ludicrous striving to fill in the blanks, they came to an end.

They waited in silence.

"Well, what next," asked a voice from the shadows.

"It's your turn," said Beelzebub.

"What do you want?"

"As little as you have the heart to give."

"But," said another voice, one they knew well, "We have no heart to give at all."

"You did not know your parts well," said Blanche, the stranger. "The big fellow in the blanket deserves nothing."

"What about me?" asked Arthur.

"You," answered the same voice, "oh, you're a nice boy, and a lady's; thanks* are enough reward for you."

He blushed, and muttered something unintelligible.

"There'll be the Devil to pay," suggested Beelzebub.

"Give the Devil his dues, Nell," said Blanche, choking again with laughter. Nellie threw a large silver coin on to the flagstone floor, but she was nervous, and it rolled to the feet of Preston in his armchair.

"'Alf-a-crern!" he exclaimed, "gie 'em thripence, an' they're non worth that much."

This was too much for the chivalrous St. George. He could bear no longer to stand in this ridiculous garb before his scornful lady-love and her laughing friend.

He snatched off his burnouse and his robe, flung them over one arm, and with the other caught back Beelzebub, who would have gone to pick up the money. There he stood, St. George metamorphosed into a simple young farmer, with ruffled curly black hair, a heavy frown and bare arms.

"Won't you let him have it?" asked Blanche. "Well, what do you want?" she continued.

"Nothing, thanks. I'm sorry we troubled you."

"Come on," he said, drawing the reluctant Beelzebub, and the three made their exit. Blanche laughed and laughed again to see the discomfited knight tramp out, rolling down his shirt sleeves.

Nellie did not laugh. Seeing him turn, she saw him again as a child, before her father had made money by his cattle-dealing, when she was a poor, wild little creature. But her father had grown rich, and the mill was a big farm, and when the old cattle dealer had died, she became sole mistress. Then Preston, their chief man, came with Betty and Sarah, to live in, and take charge of the farm.

Nellie had seen little of her old friends since then. She had stayed a long time in town, and when she called on them after her return found them cool and estranged. So she had not been again, and now it was almost a year since she had spoken many words to Fred.

Her brief meditations were disturbed by a scream from Betty in the scullery, followed by the wild rush of that damsel into the kitchen.

"What's up?" asked her father.

"There's somebody there got hold of my legs."

Nellie felt suddenly her own loneliness. Preston struck a match and investigated. He returned with a bunch of glittering holly, thick with scarlet berries.

"Here's yer somebody," said he, flinging the bunch down on the table.

"Oh, that is pretty!" exclaimed Blanche. Nellie rose, looked, then hurried down the passage to the sitting-room, followed by her friend. There, to the consternation of Blanche, she sat down and began to cry.

"Whatever is the matter?" asked Blanche.

It was some time before she had a reply, then, "It's so miserable," faltered Nellie, "and so lonely. I do think Will and Harry and Louie and all the others were mean not to come, then this wouldn't have happened. It was such a shame—such a shame."

"What was a shame?" asked Blanche.

"Why, when he had got me that holly, and come down to see——" she ended, blushing.

"Who do you mean—the Bedouin?"

"And I had not seen him for months, and he will think I am just a mean, proud thing."

"You don't mean to say you care for him!"

Nellie's tears began to flow again. "I do, and I wish this miserable farm and bit of money had never come between us. He'll never come again, never, I know."

"Then," said Blanche, "you must go to him."

"Yes, and I will."

"Come along, then."

In the meantime the disappointed brothers had reached home. Fred had thrown down his Bedouin wardrobe, and put on his coat muttering something about having a walk up to the village. Then he had gone out, his mother's eyes watching his exit with helpless grief, his father looking over his spectacles in a half-surprised paternal sympathy. However, they heard him tramp down the yard and enter the barn, and they knew he would soon recover. Then the lads went out, and nothing was heard in the kitchen save the beat of the clock and the rustle of the newspaper, or the rattle of the board, as the mother rolled out paste for the mince-pies.

In the pitch-dark barn, the rueful Bedouin told himself that he expected no other than this, and that it was high time he ceased fooling himself with fancies, that he was well-cured, that even had she invited him to stay, how could he; how could he have asked her; she must think he wanted badly to become master of Ramsley Mill. What a fool he had been to go—what a fool!

"But," he argued, "let her think what she likes. I don't care. She may remember if she can that I used to sole her boots with my father's leather, and she went home in mine. She can remember that my mother taught her how to write and sew decently. I should think she must sometimes."

Then he admitted to himself that he was sure she did not forget. He could feel quite well that she was wishing that this long estrangement might cease.

"But," came the question, "why doesn't she end it? Pah, it's only my conceit; she thinks more of those glib, grinning fellows from the clerks' stools. Let her, what do I care!"

Suddenly he heard voices from the field at the back, and sat up listening.

"Oh, it's a regular slough," said someone. "We can never get through the gate. See, let us climb the stackyard fence. They've put some new rails in. Can you manage, Blanche? Here, just between the lilac bush and the stack. What a blessing they keep Chris at the front! Mind, bend under this plum tree. Dare we go, Blanche?"

"Go on, go on," whispered Blanche, and they crept up to the tiny window, through which the lamplight streamed uninterrupted. Fred stole out of the barn, and hid behind the great water-butt. He saw them stoop and creep to the window and peep through.

In the kitchen sat the father, smoking and appearing to read, but really staring into the fire. The mother was putting the top crusts on the little pies, but she was interrupted by the need to wipe her eyes.

"Oh, Blanche," whispered Nellie, "he's gone out."

"It looks like it," assented the other.

"Perhaps he's not, though," resumed the former bravely. "He's very likely only in the parlour."

"That's all right, then," said Blanche. "I thought we should have seen him looking so miserable. But, of course, he wouldn't let his mother see it."

"Certainly not," said Nellie.

Fred chuckled.

"But," she continued doubtfully, "if he has gone out, whatever shall we do? What can we tell his mother?"

"Tell her we came up for fun."

"But if he's out?"

"Stay till he comes home."

"If it's late?"

"It's Christmas Eve."

"Perhaps he doesn't care after all."

"You think he does, so do I; and you're quite sure you want him."

"You know I do, Blanche, and I always have done."

"Let us begin, then."

"What? 'Good King Wenceslaus?'"

The mother and father started as the two voices suddenly began to carol outside. She would have run to the door, but her husband waved her excitedly back. "Let them finish," he said, his eyes shining. "Let them finish."

The girls had retired from the window lest they should be seen, and stood near the water-butt. When the old carol was finished, Nellie began the beautiful song of Giordani's:—

> Turn once again, heal thou my pain,
> Parted from thee, my heart is sore.*

As she sang she stood holding a bough of the old plum tree, so close to Fred that by leaning forward he could have touched her coat. Carried away by the sweet pathos of her song, he could hardly refrain from rising and flinging his arms round her.

She finished, the door opened, showing a little woman holding out her hands.

Both girls made a motion towards her, but—"Nell, Nell," he whispered, and caught her in his arms. She gave a little cry of alarm and delight. Blanche stepped into the kitchen, and shut the door, laughing.

She sat in the low rocking-chair swinging to and fro in a delighted excitement, chattering brightly about a hundred things. And with a keen woman's eye she noticed the mother put her hands on her husband's as she sat on the sofa by his chair, and saw him hold the shining stiffened hand in one of his, and stroke it with old, undiminished affection.

Soon the two came in, Nellie all blushing. Without a word she ran and kissed the little mother, lingering a moment over her before she turned to the quiet embrace of the father. Then she took off her hat, and brushed back the brown tendrils all curled so prettily by the damp.

Already she was at home.

# A Lesson on a Tortoise

It was the last lesson on Friday afternoon, and this, with Standard VI, was Nature Study from half past three till half past four. The last lesson of the week is a weariness to teachers and scholars. It is the end; there is no need to keep up the tension of discipline and effort any longer, and, yielding to weariness, a teacher is spent.

But Nature Study is a pleasant lesson. I had got a big old tortoise, who had not yet gone to sleep, though November* was darkening the early afternoon, and I knew the boys would enjoy sketching him. I put him under the radiator to warm while I went for a large empty shell that I had sawn in two to show the ribs of some ancient tortoise absorbed in his bony coat. When I came back I found Joe, the old reptile, stretching slowly his skinny neck, and looking with indifferent eyes at the two intruding boys who were kneeling beside him. I was too good-tempered to send them out again into the playground, too slack with the great relief of Friday afternoon. So I bade them put out the Nature books ready. I crouched to look at Joey, and stroked his horny, blunt head with my finger. He was quite lively. He spread out his legs and gripped the floor with his flat, hand-like paws, then he slackened again as if from a yawn, drooping his head meditatively.

I felt pleased with myself, knowing that the boys would be delighted with the lesson. "He will not want to walk" I said to myself. "And if he takes a sleepy stride, they'll be just in ecstasy, and I can easily calm him down to his old position." So I anticipated their entry. At the end of playtime I went to bring them in. They were a small class of about thirty—my own boys. A difficult, mixed class, they were, consisting of six Gordon Home boys,* five boys from a fairly well-to-do Home for the children of actors,* and a set of commoners varying from poor lads who hobbled to school, crippled by broken enormous boots,* to boys who brought soft, light shoes to wear in school on snowy days. The Gordons were a difficult set; you could pick them out: crop haired, coarsely dressed lads, distrustful, always ready to assume the defensive. They would lie till it made my heart sick, if they were charged with offence, but they were willing, and would respond beautifully to an appeal. The actors were of different fibre: some gentle, a pleasure even to look at; others polite and obedient, but indifferent, covertly insolent and vulgar; all of them more or less gentlemanly.

The boys crowded round the table noisily as soon as they discovered Joe. "Is he alive?—Look, his head's coming out! He'll bite you?—He *won't*!"—with much scorn—"Please Sir, do tortoises bite?" I hurried them off to their seats in a little group in front, and pulled the table up to the desks. Joe kept fairly still. The boys nudged each other excitedly, making half audible remarks concerning the poor reptile, looking quickly from me to Joe and then to their neighbours. I set them sketching, but in their pleasure at the novelty they could not be still:

"Please Sir—shall we draw the marks on the shell? Please Sir, has he only got four toes?"—"Toes!" echoes somebody, covertly delighted at the absurdity of calling the grains* of claws 'toes'. "Please Sir, he's moving—Please Sir!"

I stroked his neck and calmed him down:

"Now don't make me wish I hadn't brought him. That's enough Miles—you shall go to the back and draw twigs if I hear you again! Enough now—be still, get on with the drawing, it's hard!"

I wanted peace for myself. They began to sketch diligently. I stood and looked across at the sunset, which I could see facing me through my window, a great gold sunset, very large and magnificent, rising up in immense gold beauty beyond the town, that was become a low dark strip of nothingness under the wonderful up-building of the western sky. The light, the thick, heavy golden sunlight which is only seen in its full dripping splendour in town, spread on the desks and the floor like gold lacquer. I lifted my hands, to take the sunlight on them, smiling faintly to myself, trying to shut my fingers over its tangible richness.

"Please Sir!"—I was interrupted. "Please Sir, can we have rubbers?"

The question was rather plaintive. I had said they should have rubbers no more. I could not keep my stock, I could not detect the thief among them, and I was weary of the continual degradation of bullying them to try to recover what was lost among them. But it was Friday afternoon, very peaceful and happy. Like a bad teacher, I went back on my word:

"Well—!" I said, indulgently.

My monitor, a pale, bright, erratic boy, went to the cupboard and took out a red box.

"Please Sir!" he cried, then he stopped and counted again in the box. "Eleven! There's only eleven, Sir, and there were fifteen when I put them away on Wednesday—!"

The class stopped, every face upturned. Joe sunk, and lay flat on his shell, his legs limp. Another of the hateful moments had come. The sunset was smeared out, the charm of the afternoon was smashed like a fair glass that falls to the floor. My nerves seemed to tighten, and to vibrate with sudden tension.

"Again!" I cried, turning to the class in passion, to the upturned faces, and the sixty watchful eyes.

"Again! I am sick of it, sick of it I am! A thieving, wretched set!—a skulking, mean lot!" I was quivering with anger and distress.

"Who is it? You must know! You are all as bad as one another, you hide it—a miserable—!" I looked round the class in great agitation. The Gordons, with their distrustful faces, were noticeable.

"Marples!" I cried to one of them, "where are those rubbers?"

"I don't know where they are:—I've never 'ad no rubbers"—he almost shouted back, with the usual insolence of his set. I was more angry:

"You must know! They're gone—they don't melt into air, they don't fly—who took them then? Rawson, do you know anything of them?"

"No Sir!" he cried, with impudent indignation.

"No, you intend to know nothing! Wood, have you any knowledge of these four rubbers?"

"No!" he shouted, with absolute insolence.

"Come here!" I cried, "come here! Fetch the cane, Burton. We'll make an end, insolence and thieving and all."

The boy dragged himself to the front of the class, and stood slackly, almost crouching, glaring at me. The rest of the Gordons sat upright in their desks, like animals of a pack ready to spring. There was tense silence for a moment. Burton handed me the cane, and I turned from the class to Wood. I liked him best among the Gordons.

"Now my lad!" I said "I'll cane you for impudence first."

He turned swiftly to me; tears sprang to his eyes.

"Well" he shouted at me "you always pick on the Gordons—you're always on to us—!"

This was so manifestly untrue that my anger fell like a bird shot in a mid-flight.

"Why!" I exclaimed, "what a disgraceful untruth! I am always excusing you, letting you off—!"

"But you pick on us—you start on us—you pick on Marples, an' Rawson, an' on me. You always begin with the Gordons."

"Well" I answered, justifying myself. "Isn't it natural? Haven't your boys stolen—haven't these boys stolen—several times—and been caught?"

"That doesn't say as we do now," he replied.

"How am I to know? You don't help me. How do I know? Isn't it natural to suspect you—?"

"Well, it's not us. We know who it is. Everybody knows who it is—only they won't tell."

"Who know?" I asked.

"Why Rawson, and Maddock, and Newling, and all of 'em."

I asked these boys if they could tell me. Each one shook his head, and said "No Sir." I went round the class. It was the same. They lied to me every one.

"You see" I said to Wood.

"Well—they won't own up" he said. "I shouldn't 'a done if you hadn't 'a been goin' to cane me."

This frankness was painful, but I preferred it. I made them all sit down. I asked Wood to write his knowledge on a piece of paper, and I promised not to divulge. He would not. I asked the boys he had named, all of them. They refused. I asked them again—I appealed to them.

"Let them all do it then!" said Wood. I tore up scraps of paper, and gave each boy one.

"Write on it the name of the boy you suspect. He is a thief and a sneak. He gives endless pain and trouble to us all. It is your duty."

They wrote furtively, and quickly doubled up the papers. I collected them in the lid of the rubber box, and sat at the table to examine them. There was dead silence, they all watched me. Joe had withdrawn into his shell, forgotten.

A few papers were blank; several had 'I suspect nobody';—these I threw in the paper basket; two had the name of an old thief, and these I tore up; eleven bore the name of my assistant-monitor, a splendid, handsome boy, one of the oldest of the actors. I remembered how deferential and polite he had been when I had asked him, how ready to make barren suggestions; I remembered his shifty, anxious look during the questioning; I remembered how eager he had been to do things for me before the monitor came in the room. I knew it was he—without remembering.

"Well!" I said, feeling very wretched when I was convicted that the papers were right. "Go on with the drawing."

They were very uneasy and restless, but quiet. From time to time they watched me. Very shortly, the bell rang. I told the two monitors to collect up the things, and I sent the class home. We did not go into prayers. I, and they, were in no mood for hymns and the evening prayer of gratitude.

When the monitors had finished, and I had turned out all the lights but one, I sent home Curwen, and kept my assistant-monitor a moment.

"Ségar, do you know anything of my rubbers?"

"No Sir"—he had a deep, manly voice, and he spoke wth earnest protestation—flushing.

"No? Nor my pencils?—nor my two books?"

"No Sir! I know nothing about the books."

"No? The pencils then—?"

"No Sir! Nothing! I don't know anything about them."

"Nothing, Ségar?"

"No Sir."

He hung his head, and looked so humiliated, a fine, handsome lad, that I gave it up. Yet I knew he would be dishonest again, when the opportunity arrived.

"Very well! You will not help as monitor any more. You will not come into the class room, until the class comes in—any more. You understand?"

"Yes Sir"—he was very quiet.

"Go along then."

He went out, and silently closed the door. I turned out the last light, tried the cupboards, and went home.

I felt very tired, and very sick. The night had come up, the clouds were moving darkly, and the sordid streets near the school felt like disease in the lamplight.

# Lessford's Rabbits

On Tuesday mornings I have to be at school at half past eight to administer the free breakfasts. Dinners are given in the canteen in one of the mean steets, where the children feed in a Church Mission room* appropriately adorned by Sunday School cartoons showing the blessing of the little ones, and the feeding of the five thousand.* We serve breakfasts, however, in school, in the wood-work room high up under the roof.

Tuesday morning sees me rushing up the six short flights of stone stairs, at twenty-five minutes to nine. It is my disposition to be late.* I generally find a little crowd of children waiting in the 'art' room—so called because it is surrounded with a strip of black-board too high for the tallest boy to reach—which is a sort of ante-room to the workshop where breakfast is being prepared. I hasten through the little throng to see if things are ready. There are two big girls putting out the basins, and another one looking in the pan to see if the milk is boiling. The room is warm, and seems more comfortable because the windows are high up under the beams of the slanting roof, and the walls are all panelled with ruddy gold, varnished wood. The work bench is in the form of three sides of a square—or of an oblong—as the dining tables of the ancients used to be, I believe. At one of the extremities are the three vises, and at the other the great tin pan, like a fish kettle,* standing on a gas ring. When the boys' basins are placed along the outer edge of the bench, the girls' on the inner, and the infants' on the lockers against the wall, we are ready. I look at the two rows of assorted basins, and think of the three bears. Then I admit the thirty, who bundle to their places and stand in position, girls on the inside facing boys on the outside, and quaint little infants with their toes kicking the lockers along the walls.

Last week the Infant mistress* did not come up, so I was alone. She is an impressive woman, who always commands the field. I stand in considerable awe of her. I feel like a reckless pleasure boat with one extravagant sail misbehaving myself in the track of a heavy earnest coaster when she bears down on me. I was considerably excited to find myself in sole charge. As I ushered in the children, the caretaker, a little fierce-eyed man with hollow cheeks and a walrus moustache, entered with the large basket full of chunks of bread. He glared around without bidding me good-morning.

"Miss Culloch not come?" he asked.

"As you see," I replied.

He grunted, and put down the basket. Then he drew himself up like a fiery prophet, and stretching forth his hairy arm towards the opposite door, shouted loudly to the children:

"None of you's got to touch that other door there! You hear—you're to leave it alone!"

The children stared at him without answering.

"A brake as I'm making for these doors," he said confidentially to me, thrusting* forward his extraordinarily hairy lean arms, and putting two fingers of one hand into the palm of the other, as if to explain his invention. I bowed.

"Nasty things them swing doors"—he looked up at me with his fierce eyes, and suddenly swished aside his right arm:

"They come to like *that*!" he exclaimed, "and a child's fingers is cut off—clean!"—he looked at me for ratification. I bowed.

"It'll be a good thing, I think," he concluded, considerably damped. I bowed again. Then he left me. The chief, almost the only duty of a caretaker, is to review the works of the head and of the staff, as a reviewer does books: at length and according to his superior light.

I told one of the girls to give three chunks of bread to each child, and, having fished a mysterious earwig out of the scalding milk, I filled the large enamelled jug— such as figures and has figured in the drawing lessons of every school in England, I suppose—and doled out the portions—about three quarters of a pint per senior, and half a pint per infant. Everything was ready. I had to say grace. I dared not launch into the Infant mistress' formula, thanking the Lord for his goodness—, "and may we eat and drink to thine everlasting glory—Amen." I looked at the boys, dressed in mouldering garments of remote men, at the girls with their rat-tailed hair,* and at the infants, quaint little mites on whom I wished, but could not bring myself, to expend my handkerchief, and I wondered what I should say. The only other grace I knew was "For these and for all good things may the Lord make us truly thankful." But I wondered whom we should thank for the bad things. I was becoming desperate. I plunged:

"Ready now—hands together, close eyes. 'Let us eat, drink and be merry, for tomorrow we die'."* I felt myself flushing with confusion—what did I mean? But there was a universal clink of iron spoons on the basins, and a snuffling, slobbering sound of children feeding. They had not noticed, so it was all right. The infants were kneeling and squatting by the lockers, the boys were stretching wide their eyes and their mouths at the same time, to admit the spoon. They spilled the milk on their jackets and wiped it off with their sleeves, continuing to eat all the time.

"Don't slobber, lads, be decent," I said, rebuking them from my superior sphere. They ate more carefully, glancing up at me when the spoon was at their mouths.

I began to count the number—nine boys, seven girls, and eleven infants. Not many. We could never get many boys to give in their names for free meals. I used to ask the Kelletts, who were pinched and pared thin with poverty:

"Are you sure you don't want either dinners or breakfasts, Kellett?"

He would look at me curiously, and say, with a peculiar small movement of his thin lips,

"No Sir."

"But have you plenty—quite plenty?"

"Yes Sir,"—he was very quiet, flushing at my questions. None—or very few—of the boys could endure to accept the meals. Not many parents would submit to the indignity of the officer's inquiries, and the boys, the most foolishly sensitive animals in the world, would, many of them, prefer to go short rather than to partake of charity meals of which all their school-mates were aware.

"Halket*—where is Halket?" I asked.

"Please Sir, his mother's got work" replied Lessford, one of my own boys, a ruddy, bonny lad—many of those at breakfast were pictures of health. Lessford was brown-skinned and had fine dark eyes. He was a reticent, irresponsible creature, with a radical incapacity to spell and to read and to draw, but who sometimes scored at arithmetic. I should think he came of a long line of unrelievedly poor people.* He was skilled in street lore, and cute at arithmetic, but blunt and blind to everything that needed a little delicacy of perception. He had an irritating habit of looking at me furtively with his handsome dark eyes, glancing covertly again and again. Yet he was not a sneak; he gave himself the appearance of one.

He was a well-built lad, and he looked well in the blue jersey he wore—there were great holes at the elbows, showing the whitish shirt and a brown bit of Lessford. At breakfasts he was a great eater. He would have five solid pieces of bread, and then ask for more.

We gave them bread and milk one morning, cocoa and currant bread the next. I happened to go one cocoa morning to take charge. Lessford, I noticed, did not eat by any means so much as on bread mornings. I was surprised. I asked him if he did not care for currant loaf, but he said he did. Feeling curious, I asked the other teachers what they thought of him. Mr Hayward, who took a currant bread morning, said he was sure the boy had a breakfast before he came to school;—Mr Jephson, who took a milk morning, said the lad was voracious, that it amused him to try to feed him up. I watched—turning suddenly to ask if anyone wanted a little more milk, and glancing over the top of the milk pan as I was emptying it.

I caught him: I saw him push a piece of bread under his jersey, glancing furtively with a little quiver of apprehension up at me. I did not appear to notice, but when he was going downstairs I followed him and asked him to go into the class-room with me. I closed the door and sat down at my table: he stood hanging his head and marking with his foot on the floor. He came to me, very slowly, when I bade him. I put my hand on his jersey, and felt something underneath. He did not resist me, and I drew it out. It was his cap. He smiled, he could not help it, at my discomfiture. Then he pulled his lips straight and looked sulky. I tried again—and this time I found three pieces of bread in a kind of rough pocket inside the waist of his trousers. He looked at them blackly as I arranged them on the table before him, flushing under his brown skin.

"What does this mean?" I asked. He hung his head, and would not answer.

"You may as well tell me—what do you want this for?"

"Eat," he muttered, keeping his face bent. I put my hand under his chin and lifted up his face. He shut his eyes, and tried to move his face aside, as if from a very strong light which hurt him.

"That is not true" I said "I know perfectly well it is not true. You have a breakfast before you come. You do not come to eat. You come to take the food away."

"I never!" he exclaimed sulkily.

"No" I said. "You did not take any yesterday. But the day before you did."

"I never, I never!!" he declared, more emphatically, in the tone of one who scores again. I considered.

"Oh no—the day before was Sunday. Let me see. You took some on Thursday—yes, that was the last time—. You took four or five pieces of bread—" I hung fire; he did not contradict; "five, I believe" I added. He scraped his toe on the ground. I had guessed aright. He could not deny the definite knowledge of a number.

But I could not get another word from him. He stood and heard all I had to say, but he would not look up, or answer anything. I felt angry.

"Well" I said "if you come to breakfasts any more, you will be reported."

Next day, when asked why he was absent from breakfast, he said his father had got a job.

He was a great nuisance for coming with dirty boots. Evidently he went roaming over fields and everywhere. I concluded he must have a strain of gipsy in him, a mongrel form common in the south of London. Halket was his great friend. They never played together at school, and they had no apparent common interests. Halket was a debonair, clever lad who gave great promise of turning out a neer-do-well. He was very lively, soon moved from tears to laughter; Lessford was an inveterate sulker. Yet they always hung together.

One day my bread-stealer arrived at half past two, when the register was closed.* He was sweating, dishevelled, and his breast was heaving; he gave no word of explanation, but stood near the great blackboard, his head dropped, one leg loosely apart, panting.

"Well!" I exclaimed "this is a nice thing! What have you to say?" I rose from my chair.

Evidently he had nothing to say.

"Come on" I said finally. "No foolery! Let me hear it." He knew he would have to speak. He looked up at me, his dark eyes blazing:

"My rabbits has all gone!" he cried, as a man would announce his wife and children slain. I heard Halket exclaim. I looked at him. He was half out of the desk, his mercurial face blank with dismay.

"Who's 'ad 'em?" he said, breathing the words almost in a whisper.

"Did you leave th' door open?"

Lessford bent forward like a serpent about to strike as he asked this. Halket shook his head solemnly:

"No! I've not been near 'em today."

There was a pause. It was time for me to reassume my position of authority. I told them both to sit down, and we continued the lesson. Halket crept near his comrade and began to whisper to him, but he received no response. Lessford sulked fixedly, not moving his head for more than an hour.

At playtime I began to question Halket:

"Please Sir—we had some rabbits in a place on the allotments. We used to gather manure for a man, and he let us have half of his tool-house in the garden—."

"How many had you—rabbits?"

"Please Sir—they varied. When we had young ones we used to have sixteen sometimes. We had two brown does and a black buck."

I was somewhat taken back by this.

"How long have you had them?"

"A long time now Sir. We've had six lots of young ones."

"And what did you do with them?"

"Fatten them, Sir"—he spoke with a little triumph, but he was reluctant to say much more.

"And what did you fatten them on?"

The boy glanced swiftly at me. He reddened, and for the first time became confused.

"Green stuff, what we had given us out of the gardens, and what we got out of the fields."

"And bread." I answered quietly.

He looked at me. He saw I was not angry, only ironical. For a few moments he hesitated, whether to lie or not. Then he admitted, very subdued:

"Yes Sir."

"And what did you do with the rabbits?"—he did not answer—"Come, tell me. I can find out whether or not."

"Sold them."—He hung his head guiltily.

"Who did the selling?"

"I, Sir—to a green-grocer."

"For how much?"

"Eight-pence each."

"And did your mothers know?"

"No Sir." He was very subdued and guilty.

"And what did you do with the money?"

"Go to the Empire—generally."

I asked him a day or two later if they had found the rabbits. They had not. I asked Halket what he supposed had become of them.

"Please Sir—I suppose somebody must 'a stole them. The door was not broken. You could open our padlock with a hair-pin. I suppose somebody must have come after us last night when we'd fed them. I think I know who it is, too, Sir." He shook his head wisely—"There's a place where you can get into the allotments off the field——."

# A Modern Lover*

## 1.

The road was heavy with mud. It was labour to move along it. The old, wide way, forsaken and grown over with grass, used not to be so bad. The farm traffic from Coney Grey must have cut it up. The young man crossed carefully again to the strip of grass on the other side.

It was a dreary, out-of-doors track, saved only by low fragments of fence and occasional bushes from the desolation of the large spaces of arable and of grass lands on either side, where only the unopposed wind and the great clouds mattered, where even the little grasses bent to one another indifferent of any traveller. The abandoned road used to seem clean and firm. Cyril Mersham stopped to look round and to bring back old winters to the scene, over the ribbed red land, and the purple wood. The surface of the field seemed suddenly to lift and break. Something had startled the peewits, and the fallow flickered over with pink gleams of birds white-breasting the sunset. Then the plovers turned, and were gone in the dusk behind.

Darkness was issuing out of the earth, and clinging to the trunks of the elms which rose like weird statues lessening down the wayside. Mersham laboured forwards, the earth sucking and smacking at his feet. In front the Coney Grey farm was piled in shadow on the road. He came near to it, and saw the turnips heaped in a fabulous heap up the side of the barn, a buttress that rose almost to the eaves, and stretched out towards the cart-ruts in the road. Also, the pale breasts of the turnips got the sunset, and they were innumerable orange glimmers piled in the dusk. The two labourers who were pulping at the foot of the mound stood shadow-like to watch as he passed, breathing the sharp scent of turnips.

It was all very wonderful and glamourous,* here, in the old places that had seemed so ordinary. Three-quarters of the scarlet sun was settling among the branches of the elm in front, right ahead where he would come soon. But when he arrived at the brow where the hill swooped downwards, where the broad road ended suddenly, the sun had vanished from the space before him, and the evening star was white where the night urged up against the retreating, rose-coloured billow of day. Mersham passed through the stile and sat upon the remnant of the thorn-tree on the brink* of the valley. All the wide space before him was full of a mist of rose, nearly to his feet. The large ponds were hidden, the farms, the fields, the far-off coal-mine, under the rosy outpouring of twilight. Between him and the spaces of Leicestershire and the hills of Derbyshire, between him and all the South-Country which he had fled, was the splendid rose-red strand of sunset, and the white star keeping guard.

Here, on the lee-shore of day, was only the purple showing of the woods and the great hedge below him: and the roof of the farm below him, with a film of smoke rising up. Unreal, like a dream which wastes a sleep with unrest, was the South and its hurrying to and fro. Here, on the further shore of the sunset, with the flushed tide at his feet, and the large star flashing with strange laughter, did he himself naked walk with lifted arms into the quiet flood of life.

What was it he wanted, sought in the slowly lapsing tide of days. Two years he had been in the large city in the south. There always his soul had moved among the faces that swayed on the thousand currents in that node of tides, hovering and wheeling and flying low over the faces of the multitude like a sea-gull over the waters, stooping now and again, and taking a fragment of life—a look, a contour, a movement—to feed upon. Of many people, his friends, he had asked that they would kindle again the smouldering embers of their experience; he had blown the low fires gently with his breath, and had leaned his face towards their glow, and had breathed in the words that rose like fumes from the revived embers, till he was sick with the strong drug of sufferings and ecstasies and sensations, and the dreams that ensued. But most folk had choked out the fires of their fiercer experience with rubble of sentimentality and stupid fear, and rarely could he feel the hot destruction of Life fighting out its way.

Surely, surely somebody could give him enough of the philtre of life to stop the craving which tortured him hither and thither, enough to satisfy for a while, to intoxicate him till he could laugh the crystalline laughter of the star, and bathe in the retreating flood of twilight like a naked boy in the surf, clasping the waves and beating them and answering their wild clawings with laughter sometimes, and sometimes gasps of pain.

He rose, and stretched himself. The mist was lying in the valley like a flock of folded* sheep: Orion had strode into the sky, and the Twins* were playing towards the west. He shivered, stumbled down the path, and crossed the orchard, passing among the dark trees as if among people he knew.

## 2.

He came into the yard. It was exceedingly, painfully muddy. He felt a disgust of his own feet, which were cold, and numbed, and heavy.

The window of the house was uncurtained, and shone like a yellow moon, with only a large leaf or two of ivy, and a cord of honeysuckle hanging across it. There seemed a throng of figures moving about the fire. Another light gleamed mysteriously among the out-buildings. He heard a voice in the cow-shed, and the impatient movement of a cow, and the rhythm of milk in the bucket.

He hesitated in the darkness of the porch, then he entered without knocking. A girl was opposite him, coming out of the dairy doorway with a loaf of bread. She started; and they stood a moment looking at each other across the room. They advanced to each other; he took her hand, plunged overhead, as it were, for a moment in her great brown eyes. Then he let her go, and looked aside, saying some words of greeting. He had not kissed her; he realised that when he heard her voice:

"When did you come?"

She was bent over the table cutting bread and butter. What was it in her bowed, submissive pose, in the dark small head with its black hair twining and hiding her face, that made him wince and shrink and close over his soul that had been open like a foolhardy flower to the nights? Perhaps it was her very submission, which trammelled him, throwing the responsibility of her wholly on him, making him shrink from the burden of her.

Her brothers were home from the pit. They were two well-built lads of twenty and twenty one. The coal-dust over their faces was like a mask, making them inscrutable, hiding any glow of greeting, making them strangers. He could only see their eyes wake with a sudden smile, which sank almost immediately, and they turned aside. The mother was kneeling at a big brown stew-jar in front of the open oven. She did not rise, but gave him her hand, saying:

"Cyril!* How are you?" Her large dark eyes wavered and left him. She continued with the spoon in the jar.

His disappointment rose as water suddenly heaves up the side of a ship. A sense of dreariness revived, a feeling, too, of the cold wet mud that he had struggled through.

These were the people who, a few months before, would look up in one fine broad glow of welcome whenever he entered the door, even if he came daily. Three years before, their lives would draw together into one flame, and whole evenings long would flare with magnificent mirth, and with play. They had known each other's lightest and deepest feelings. Now, when he came back to them after a long absence, they withdrew, turned aside. He sat down on the sofa under the window deeply chagrined. His heart closed tight like a fir-cone, which had been open and full of naked seeds when he came to them.

They asked him questions of the South. They were starved for news, they said, in that God-forsaken hole.

"It is such a treat to hear a bit of news from outside," said the mother.

News! He smiled, and talked, plucking for them the leaves from off his tree, leaves of easy speech,. He smiled, rather bitterly as he slowly reeled off his news, almost mechanically. Yet he knew—and that was the irony of it—that they did not want his "records": they wanted the timorous buds of his hopes, and the unknown fruits of his experiences, full of the taste of tears and what sunshine of gladness had gone to their ripening. But they asked for his "news", and, because of some subtle perversity, he gave them what they begged, not what they wanted, not what he desired most sincerely to give them.

Gradually he exhausted his store of talk, that he had thought was limitless. Muriel moved about all the time laying the table and listening, only looking now and again across the barren garden of his talk into his windows. But he hardened his heart and turned his head from her. The boys had stripped to their waists, and had knelt on the hearth-rug and washed themselves in a large tin bowl, the mother sponging and drying their backs. Now they stood wiping themselves, the firelight bright and rosy on their fine torses,* their heavy arms swelling and sinking with a life. They seemed to cherish the firelight on their bodies. Benjamin, the younger, leaned his breast to the warmth, and threw back his head, showing his teeth in a voluptuous little smile. Mersham watched them, as he had watched the peewits and the sunset.

Then they sat down to their dinners, and the room was dim with the steam of food. Presently the father and the eldest brother were in from the cow-sheds, and all assembled at table. The conversation went haltingly: a little badinage on Mersham's part, a few questions on politics from the father. Then there grew an acute, fine feeling of discord. Mersham, particularly sensitive, reacted. He became extremely attentive to the others at table, and to his own manner of eating. He used English that was exquisitely accurate, pronounced with the Southern accent, very different from the heavily sounded speech of the home folk. His nicety contrasted the more with their rough, country habit. They became shy and awkward, fumbling for something to say. The boys ate their dinners hastily, shovelling up the mass as a man shovels gravel. The eldest son clambered* roughly with a great hand at the plate of bread and butter. Mersham tried to shut his eyes. He kept up all the time a brilliant tea-talk that they failed to appreciate in that atmosphere. It was evident to him. Without forming the idea, he felt how irrevocably he was removing them from him, though he had loved them. The irony of the situation appealed to him, and added brightness and subtlety to his wit. Muriel, who had studied him so thoroughly, confusedly understood. She hung her head over her plate, and ate little. Now and again she would look up at him, toying all the time with her knife—though it was a family for ugly hands—and would address him some barren question. He always answered the question, but he invariably disregarded her look of earnestness, lapped in his unbreakable armour of light irony. He acknowledged, however, her power, in the flicker of irritation that accompanied his reply. She quickly hid her face again.

They did not linger at tea, as in the old days. The men rose, with an "Ah well!", and went about their farm work. One of the lads lay sprawling for sleep on the sofa; the other lighted a cigarette and sat with his arms on his knees, blinking into the fire. Neither of them ever wore a coat in the house, and their shirt-sleeves, and their thick bare necks irritated the stranger still further by accentuating his strangeness. The men came tramping in and out to the boiler. The kitchen was full of bustle, of the carrying of steaming water, and of draughts. It seemed like a place out of doors. Mersham shrank up in his corner, and pretended to read the "Daily News."* He was ignored, like an owl sitting in the stalls of cattle.

"Go in the parlour Cyril! Why don't you! It's comfortable there."

Muriel turned to him with this reproach, this remonstrance, almost chiding him. She was keenly aware of his discomfort, and of his painful discord with his surroundings. He rose without a word and obeyed her.

## 3.

The parlour was a long, low room with red colourings. A bunch of mistletoe hung from the beam, and thickly-berried holly was over the pictures—over the little, gilt-blazed water-colours that he hated so much because he had done them in his teens, and nothing is so hateful as the self one has left. He dropped in the tapestried chair—called the Countess'*—and thought of the changes which this room had seen in him. There, by that hearth, they had threshed the harvest of their youth's experience, gradually burning the chaff of sentimentality and false romance that covered the real grain of life. How infinitely far away, now, seemed "Jane Eyre" and George Eliot. These had marked the beginning. He smiled as he traced the graph onwards, plotting the points with Carlyle and Ruskin, Schopenhauer and Darwin and Huxley, Omar Khayyam, the Russians, Ibsen and Balzac, then Guy de Maupassant and Madame Bovary. They had parted in the midst of "Madame Bovary". Since then had come only Nietzsche and William James.* They had not done so badly, he thought, during those years which now he was apt to despise a little, because of their dreadful strenuousness, and because of their later deadly, unrelieved seriousness. He wanted her to come in and talk about the old times. He crossed to the other side the fire and lay in the big horse-hair chair, which pricked the back of his head. He looked about, and stuffed behind him the limp green cushions that were always sweating down.*

It was a week after Christmas. He guessed they had kept up the holly and mistletoe for him. The two photographs of himself* still occupied the post of honor on the mantel-piece, but between them was a stranger. He wondered who the fellow could be; good-looking, he seemed to be; but a bit of a clown beside the radiant, subtle photos of himself. He smiled broadly at his own arrogance. Then he remembered that Muriel and her people were leaving the farm come Lady-day.* Immediately, in valediction, he began to call up the old days, when they had romped and played so boisteriously, dances, and wild charades, and all mad games. He was just telling himself that those were the days, the days of unconscious ecstatic fun, and he was smiling at himself over his information, when she entered.

She came in, hesitating. Seeing him sprawling in his old abandonment, she closed the door softly. For a moment or two she sat, her elbows on her knees, her chin in her hands, sucking her little finger, and withdrawing it from her lips with a little pop, looking all the while in the fire. She was waiting for him, knowing all the time he would not begin. She was trying to feel him, as it were. She wanted to assure herself of him after so many months. She dared not look at him directly. Like all brooding, constitutionally earnest souls, she gave herself away unwisely, and was defenceless when she found herself pushed back, rejected so often with contempt.

"Why didn't you tell me you were coming?" she asked at last.

"I wanted to have exactly one of the old tea-times, and evenings."

"Ay!"—she answered with hopeless bitterness. She was a dreadful pessimist. People had handled her so brutally, and had cheaply thrown away her most sacred intimacies.

He laughed, and looked at her kindly.

"Ah well, if I'd thought about it I should have known this was what to expect. It's my own fault."

"Nay" she answered, still bitterly, "it's not your fault. It's ours. You bring us to a certain point, and when you go away, we lose it all again, and receive you like creatures* who have never known you."

"Never mind" he said easily "—if it is so, it is!—How are you?"

She turned and looked full at him. She was very handsome; heavily moulded, coloured richly. He looked back smiling into her big, brown, serious eyes:

"Oh I'm very well" she answered, with puzzled irony. "How are you?"

"Me? You tell me. What do you think of me?"

"What do I think—?" she laughed a little nervous laugh and shook her head.—"I don't know. Why—you look well—and very much of a gentleman."

"Ah—and you are sorry?"

"No—No I am not! No! Only you're different, you see."

"Ah, the pity!* I shall never be as nice as I was at twenty one, shall I?" He glanced at his photo on the mantel-piece, and smiled, gently chaffing her.

"Well—you're different—it isn't that you're not so nice—but different. I always think you're like that, really!"

She too glanced at the photo, which had been called the portrait of an intellectual prig, but which was really that of a sensitive, alert, exquisite boy. The subject of the portrait lay smiling at her. Then he turned voluptuously like a cat spread out in the chair:

"And this is the last of it all—!"

She looked up at him startled and pitiful.

"Of this phase, I mean" he continued, indicating with his eyes the room, the surroundings. "Of Crossleigh Bank, I mean, and this part of our lives."

"Ay!" she said, bowing her head, and putting into the exclamation all her depth of sadness and regret. He laughed:

"Aren't you glad?" he asked.

She looked up, startled, a little shocked.

"Goodbye's a fine word" he explained. "It means you're going to have a change, and a change is what you, of all people, want."

Her expression altered as she listened:

"It's true" she said "I do."

"So you ought to say to yourself 'What a treat—I'm going to say goodbye directly to the most painful phase of my life!'—you make up your mind it shall be the most painful, by refusing to be hurt so much in the future. There you are! 'Men at most times are masters of their fates etcetera.'"[*]

She pondered his method of reasoning, and turned to him with a little laughter that was full of pleading and yearning.

"Well—!" he said, lying amiably smiling,—

"Isn't it so?—and aren't you glad?"

"Yes!" she nodded. "I am,—very glad."

He twinkled playfully at her, and asked, in a soft voice:

"Then what do you want?"

"Yes" she replied, a little breathlessly. "What do I?"—she looked at him with a rash challenge that pricked him.

"Nay" he said evading her, "do you even ask me that?"

She veiled her eyes, and said, meekly, in excuse:

"It's a long time since I asked you anything, isn't it?"

"Ay! I never thought of it. Whom have you asked in the interim?"

"Whom have I asked—?"—she arched her brows and laughed a monosyllable of scorn.

"No one, of course—!" he said smiling, "The world asks questions of you, you ask questions of me, and I go to some oracle in the dark, don't I?"

She laughed with him.

"No!" he said, suddenly serious, "supposing you must answer me a big question—something I can never find out by myself."

He lay out indolently in the chair and began smiling again. She turned to look with intensity at him, her hair's fine foliage all loose round her face, her dark eyes haunted with doubt, her finger at her lips. A slight perplexity flickered over his eyes.

"At any rate" he said "you have something to give me."

She continued to look at him with dark, absorbing eyes. He probed her with his regard. Then he seemed to withdraw, and his pupil dilated with thought.

"You see" he said "life's no good but to live—and you can't live your life by yourself. You must have a flint and steel, both, to make the sparks fly. Supposing you be my flint, my white flint, to spurt out red fire for me."

"But how do you mean?" she asked breathlessly.

"You see" he continued, thinking aloud as usual "—thought—that's not life. It's like washing and combing and carding and weaving the fleece that the year of life has produced. Now I think—we've carded* and woven to the end of our bundle—nearly. We've got to begin again—you and me—living together—see?—Not speculating and poetising together—see?"

She did not cease to gaze absorbedly at him.

"Yes—?" she whispered, urging him on.

"You see—I've come back to you—to you—."

He waited for her.

"But" she said huskily "I don't understand."

He looked at her with aggressive frankness, putting aside all her confusions.

"Fibber!"—he said gently.

"But—" she turned in her chair from him "but not clearly!"

He frowned slightly:

"Nay, you should be able by now to use the algebra of speech. Must I count up on your fingers for you what I mean, unit by unit, in bald arithmetic?"

"No—no!" she cried justifying herself, "but how can I understand—the change in you? You used to say—you couldn't.—Quite opposite."

He lifted his head as if taking in her meaning.

"Ah yes, I have changed. I forget. I suppose I must have changed in myself. I'm older—I'm twenty six. I used to shrink from the thought of having to kiss you, didn't I?" he smiled very brightly, and added, in a soft voice "Well—I don't now."

She flushed darkly and hid her face from him.

"Not" he continued, with slow, brutal candour—"Not that I know any more than I did then—what love is—as you know it—but—I think you're beautiful—and we know each other so well—as we know nobody else—don't we? And so we . . . "

His voice died away, and they sat in a tense silence, listening to the noise outside, for the dog was barking loudly. They heard a voice speaking and quieting him. Cyril Mersham listened. He heard the clatter of the barn door latch, and a slurring ring of a bicycle bell brushing the wall.

"Who is it?" he asked, unsuspecting.

She looked at him, and confessed with her eyes, guiltily, beseeching. He understood immediately.

"Good Lord!—Him?"—he looked at the photo on the mantelpiece. She nodded with her usual despair, her finger between her lips again. Mersham took some moments to adjust himself to the new situation.

"Well!—so *he's* in my place! Why didn't you tell me?"

"How could I?—he's not!—besides—you never would have a place—." She hid her face.

"No—" he drawled, thinking deeply, "I wouldn't. It's my fault, altogether—"—then he smiled, and said whimsically "but I thought you kept an old pair of my gloves in the chair beside you."

"So I did, so I did!" she justified herself again with extreme bitterness "till you asked me for them. You told me to—to take another man—and I did as you told me—as usual."

"Did I tell you?—did I tell you? I suppose I must. I suppose I am a fool. And do you like him?"

She laughed aloud, with scorn and bitterness:

"He's very good—and he's very fond of me!"

"Naturally!" said Mersham, smiling and becoming ironical—"and how firmly is he fixed?"

## 4.

She was mortified, and would not answer him. The question for him now, was how much did this intruder count. He looked and saw she wore no ring—but perhaps she had taken it off for his coming. He began diligently to calculate what attitude he might take. He had looked for many women to wake his love, but he had been always disappointed. So he had kept himself virtuous, and waited. Now he would wait no longer. No woman and he could ever understand each other so well as he and Muriel whom he had fiercely educated into womanhood along with his own struggling towards a manhood of independent outlook. They had breathed the same air of thought, they had been beaten with the same storms of doubt and disillusionment, they had expanded together in days of pure poetry. They had grown so; spiritually, or rather psychically, as he preferred to say, they were married; and now he found himself thinking of the way she moved about the house—.

The outer door had opened and a man had entered the kitchen, greeting the family cordially, and without any formality. He had the throaty, penetrating voice of a tenor singer, and it came distinctly over the vibrating rumble of the men's talking. He spoke good, easy English. The boys asked him about the "iron-men" and the electric haulage, and he answered them with rough technicalities; so Mersham concluded he was a working electrician* in the mine. They continued to talk casually for some time, though there was a false note of secondary interest in it all. Then Benjamin came forward and broke the check, saying, with a dash of braggart taunting,

"Muriel's in th' parlour, Tom, if you want her."

"Oh is she! I saw a light in, I thought she might be"—he affected indifference, as if he were kept thus at every visit. Then he added, with a touch of impatience, and of the proprietor's interest: "What is she doing?"

"She's talking. Cyril Mersham's come from London."

"What!—is *he* here?"

Mersham sat listening, smiling. Muriel saw his eyelids lift. She had run up her flag of challenge taut, but continually she slackened towards him with tenderness. Now her flag flew out bravely. She rose, and went to the door.

"Hello!" she said, greeting the stranger with a little song of welcome in one word, such as girls use when they become aware of the presence of their sweethearts.

"You've got a visitor I hear," he answered.

"Yes! Come along, come in!"

She spoke softly, with much gentle caressing.

He was a handsome man, well set up, rather shorter than Mersham. The latter rose indolently, and held out his hand, smiling curiously into the beautiful, generous blue eyes of the other.

"Cyril—Mr Vickers."

Tom Vickers crushed Mersham's hand, and answered his steady smiling regard with a warm expansion of feeling, then bent his head slightly confused.

"Sit here, will you?" said Mersham, languidly indicating the arm-chair.

"No, no, thanks, I won't. I shall do here, thanks." Tom Vickers took a chair and placed it in front of the fire. He was confusedly charmed with Mersham's natural frankness and courtesy.

"If I'm not intruding" he added, as he sat down.

"No, of course not" said Muriel, in her wonderfully soft, fond tones—the indulgent tone of a woman who will sacrifice anything to love.

"Couldn't!" added Mersham lazily. "We're always a public meeting, Muriel and I. Aren't we Miel?* We're discussing affinities, that ancient topic. You'll do for an audience. We agree so beastly well, we two. We always did. It's her fault. Does she treat you so badly?"

The other was rather bewildered. Out of it all he dimly gathered that he was suggested as the present lover of Muriel, while Mersham referred to himself as the one discarded. So he smiled, reassured.

"How—'badly'?" he asked.

"Agreeing with you on every point?"

"No, I can't say she does that" said Vickers, smiling, and looking with little warm glances at her.

"Why, we never disagree, you know!" she remonstrated, in the same deep indulgent tone.

"I see" Mersham said languidly, yet keeping his wits keenly to the point. "*You* agree with everything *she* says. Lord, how interesting!"

Muriel arched eyelids with a fine flare of intelligence across at him, and laughed.

"Something like that" answered the other man, also indulgently, as became a healthy male towards one who lay limply in a chair and said clever nothings in a lazy drawl. Mersham noted the fine limbs, the solid, large thighs, and the thick wrists. He was classifying his rival among the men of handsome, healthy animalism, and good intelligence, who are children in simplicity, who can add two and two, but never xy and yx.* His contours, his movements, his repose were, strictly, lovable. "But," said Mersham to himself, "if I were blind, or sorrowful, or very tired, I should not want him. He is one of the men, as George Moore says, whom his wife would hate after a few years for the very way he walked across the floor.* I can imagine him with a family of children, a fine father. But unless he had a domestic wife—"

Muriel had begun to make talk to him.

"Did you cycle?" she asked, in that irritating private tone so common to lovers, a tone that makes a third person an impertinence.

"Yes—I was rather late" he replied, in the same caressing manner. The sense did not matter, the caress was everything.

"Didn't you find it very muddy?"

"Well, I did—but not any worse than yesterday."

Mersham sprawled his length in the chair, his eyelids almost shut, his fine white hands hanging over the arms of the chair like dead white stoats from a bough. He was wondering how long Muriel would endure to indulge her sweetheart thus. Soon she began to talk second hand to Mersham. They were speaking of Tom's landlady.

"You don't care for her, do you?" she asked, laughing insinuatingly, since the shadow of his dislike for other women heightened the radiance of his affection for her.

"Well—I can't say that I love her."

"How is it you always fall out with your landladies after six months? You must be a wretch to live with."

"Nay, I don't know that I am. But they're all alike, they're jam and cakes at first, but after a bit they're dry bread."

He spoke with solemnity, as if he uttered a universal truth. Mersham's eyelids flickered now and again. Muriel turned to him:

"Mr Vickers doesn't like lodgings," she said.

Mersham understood that Vickers therefore wanted to marry her; he also understood that as the pretendant tired of his landladies, so his wife and he would probably weary one another. He looked this intelligence at Muriel, and drawled:

"Doesn't he?—Lodgings are ideal. A good lodger can always boss the show, and have his own way. It's the time of his life."

"I don't think—!" laughed Vickers.

"It's true" drawled Mersham torpidly, giving his words the effect of droll irony. "You're evidently not a good lodger. You only need to sympathise with a landlady—against her husband generally—and she'll move heaven and earth for you."*

"Ah!" laughed Muriel, glancing at Mersham—"Tom doesn't believe in sympathising with women—especially married women."

"I don't!" said Tom emphatically—"it's dangerous."

"You leave it to the husband" said Mersham.

"I do that! I don't want 'em coming to me with their troubles. I should never know the end—."

"Wise of you!—poor women!—So you'll broach your barrel of sympathy for your wife, eh, and for nobody else?"

"That's it—isn't that right?"

"Oh quite! Your wife will be a privileged person. Sort of home brewed beer to drink 'ad infinitum'. Quite all right, that!"

"There's nothing better" said Tom, laughing.

"Except a change" said Mersham—"Now I'm like a cup of tea to a woman."

Muriel laughed aloud at this preposterous cynicism, and knitted her brows to bid him cease playing ball with bombs.

"A fresh cup each time. Women never weary of tea. Muriel, I can see you having a rich time. Sort of long after-supper drowse with a good husband."

"Very delightful!" said Muriel sarcastically.

"If she's got a good husband what more can she want?" asked Tom, keeping the tone of banter, but really serious and somewhat resentful.

"A lodger—to make things interesting."

"Why" said Muriel, intervening "do women like you so?"

Mersham looked up at her, quietly smiling into her eyes. She was really perplexed. She wanted to know what he put in the pan to make the balance go down so heavily on his side. He tried, as usual, to answer her seriously and truthfully, so he said "Because I can make them believe that black is green or purple:—which it is in reality." Then, smiling broadly as she wakened again with admiration for him, he added "But you're trying to make me conceited, Miel—to stain my virgin modesty."

Muriel glanced up at him with softness and understanding, and laughed low. Tom gave a guffaw at the notion of Mersham's virgin modesty. Muriel's brow twitched* with irritation, and she turned from her sweetheart to look in the fire.

5.

Mersham, all unconsciously, had now developed the situation to the climax he desired. He was sure that Vickers would not count seriously in Muriel's movement towards himself. So he turned away uninterested.

The talk drifted for some time, after which he suddenly bethought himself:

"I say, Mr Vickers, will you sing for us? You do sing, don't you?"

"Well—nothing to speak of," replied the other modestly, wondering at Mersham's sudden change of interest. He looked at Muriel.

"Very well" she answered him, indulging him now like a child. "But" she turned to Mersham "—but do you really—?"

"Yes of course—play some of the old songs. Do you play any better?"

She began "Honour and Arms."*

"No, not that!" cried Mersham. "Something quiet—'sois triste et sois belle'"*—he smiled gently at her, suggestively "—try 'Du bist wie eine Blume' or 'Pur dicesti.'"*

Vickers sang well, though without much imagination. But the songs they sang were the old songs that Mersham had taught Muriel years before, and she played with one of his memories in her heart. At the end of the first song, she turned and found him looking at her, and they met again in the poetry of the past.

"Daffodils!" he said softly, his eyes full of memories.

She dilated, quivered with emotion, in response. They had sat on the rim of the hill, where the wild daffodils stood up to the sky, and there he had taught her, singing line by line "Du bist wie eine Blume". He had no voice, but a very accurate ear.

The evening wore on to ten o'clock. The lads came through the room on their way to bed. The whole house was asleep save the father, who sat alone in the kitchen, reading "The Octopus."* They went in to supper.

Mersham had roused himself and was talking well. Muriel stimulated him, always, and turned him to talk of art and philosophy,—abstract things that she loved, of which only he had ever spoken to her, of which only he could speak, she believed, with such beauty. He used quaint turns of speech, contradicted himself waywardly, then said something sad and whimsical, all in a wistful, irresponsible manner so that even the men leaned indulgent and deferential to him.

"Life" he said, and he was always urging this on Muriel in one form or another, "Life is beautiful, so long as it is consuming you. When it is rushing through you, destroying you, life is glorious. It is best to roar away, like a fire with a great draught, white hot to the last bit. It's when you burn a slow fire and save fuel that life's not worth having."

"You believe in a short life and a merry" said the father.

"Needn't be either short or merry. Grief is part of the fire of life—and suffering—they're the root of the flame of joy, as they say. No! With life, we're like the man who was so anxious to provide for his old age, that he died at thirty from inanition."

"That's what we're not likely to do" laughed Tom.

"Oh I don't know. You live most intensely in human contact—and that's what we shrink from, poor timid creatures, from giving our souls to somebody to touch; for they, bungling fools, will generally paw it with dirty hands."

Muriel looked at him with dark eyes of grateful understanding. She herself had been much pawed, brutally, by her brothers. But then she had been foolish in offering herself.

"And" concluded Mersham "you are washed with the whitest fire of life—when you take a woman you love—and understand—."

Perhaps Mersham did not know what he was doing. Yet his whole talk lifted Muriel as in a net, like a sea-maiden out of the waters, and placed her in his arms, to breathe his thin, rare atmosphere. She looked at him, and was certain of his pure earnestness, and believed implicitly he could not do wrong.

Vickers believed otherwise. He would have expressed his opinion, whatever it might be, in an: "Oh ay, he's got plenty to say, and he'll keep on saying it—but hang it all—!" For Vickers was an old-fashioned, inarticulate lover, such as has been found the brief joy and the unending disappointment of a woman's life. At last he found he must go, as Mersham would not precede him. Muriel did not kiss him goodbye, nor did she offer to go out with him to his bicycle. He was angry at this, but more angry with the girl than with the man. He felt that she was fooling about, 'showing-off' before the stranger. Mersham was a stranger to him, and so, in his idea, to Muriel. Both young men went out of the house together, and down the rough brick track to the barn. Mersham made whimsical little jokes: "I wish my feet weren't so fastidious. They dither when they go in a soft spot like a girl who's touched a toad. Hark at that poor old wretch—she sounds as if she'd got whooping cough."

"A cow is not coughing when she makes that row" said Vickers.

"Pretending, is she, to get some Owbridge's?* Don't blame her—. I guess she's got chilblains, at any rate—do cows have chilblains, poor devils—?"

Vickers laughed, and felt he must take this man into his protection. "Mind" he said, as they entered the barn, which was very dark. "Mind your forehead against this beam." He put one hand on the beam, and stretched out the other to feel for Mersham. "Thanks!' said the latter gratefully. He knew the position of the beam to an inch, however dark the barn, but he allowed Vickers to guide him past it. He rather enjoyed being taken into Tom's protection.

Vickers carefully struck a match, bowing over the ruddy core of light and illuminating himself like some beautiful lantern in the midst of the high darkness of the barn. For some moments he bent over his bicycle lamp, trimming and adjusting the wick, and his face, gathering all the light on its ruddy beauty, seemed luminous, and wonderful.* Mersham could see the down on his cheeks above the razor line, and the full lips in shadow beneath the moustache, and the brush of the eyebrows between the light.

"After all" said Mersham "he's very beautiful, she's a fool to give him up."

Tom shut the lamp with a snap, and carefully crushed the match under his foot. Then he took the pump from the bicycle, and crouched on his heels in the dimness inflating the tyre. The swift, unerring, untiring stroke of the pump, the light balance and the fine elastic adjustment of the man's body to his movements, pleased Mersham.

"She could have" he was saying to himself "some glorious hours with this man—yet she'd rather have me, because I can make her sad and set her wondering."

But to the man, he was saying:

"You know love isn't the twin soul business. With you, for instance, women are like apples on a tree. You can have one that you can reach. Those that look best are overhead, but it's no good bothering with them. So you stretch up, perhaps you pull down a bough and just get your fingers round a good one. Then it swings back and you feel wild and you say your heart's broken. But there are plenty of apples as good for you no higher than your chest."

Vickers smiled, and thought there was something in it—generally; but for himself, it was nothing. They went out of the barn to the yard gate. He watched the young man swing over his saddle and vanish, calling "goodnight."

"Sic transit," he murmured—meaning Tom Vickers, and beautiful lustihood that is unconscious like a blossom.*

Mersham went slowly in the house. Muriel was clearing away the supper things, and laying the table again for the men's breakfasts. But she was waiting for him as clearly as if she had stood watching in the doorway. She looked up at him, and instinctively he lifted his face towards her as if to kiss her. They smiled, and she went on with her work.

The father rose, stretching his burly form, and yawning. Mersham put on his overcoat.

"You will come a little way with me?" he said. She answered him with her eyes. The father stood, large and silent, on the hearth-rug. His sleepy, mazed disapproval had no more effect than a little breeze which might blow against them. She smiled brightly at her lover, like a child, as she pinned on her hat.

It was very dark outside in the starlight. He groaned heavily, and swore with extravagance as he went ankle deep in mud.

"See, you should follow me. Come here," she commanded, delighted to have him in charge.

"Give me your hand" he said, and they went hand in hand over the rough places. The fields were open, and the night went up to the magnificent stars. The wood was very dark, and wet; they leaned forward and stepped stealthily, and gripped each other's hands fast with a delightful sense of adventure. When they stood and looked up a moment, they did not know how the stars were scattered among the tree-tops till he found the three jewels of Orion right in front. There was a strangeness everywhere, as if all things had ventured out alive to play in the night, as they do in fairy tales; the trees, the many stars, the dark spaces, and the mysterious waters below uniting in some unknown magnificent game.

They emerged from the wood onto the bare hillside. She came down from the wood-fence into his arms, and he kissed her, and they laughed low together. Then they went on across the wild meadow where there was no path.

"Why don't you like him?" he asked playfully.

"Need you ask?" she said, simply.

"Yes! Because he's heaps nicer than I am."

She laughed a full laugh of amusement.

"He is! Look! He's like summer, brown and full of warmth. Think how splendid and fierce he'd be—"

"Why do you talk about him?" she said.

"Because I want you to know what you're losing—and you won't till you see him in my terms. He is very desirable—I should choose *him* in preference to me—for myself."

"Should you?" she laughed. "But" she added with soft certainty "you don't understand."

"No—I don't! I suppose it's love;—your sort, which is beyond me. I shall never be blindly in love, shall I?"

"I begin to think you never will" she answered, not very sadly: "you won't be blindly anything."

"The voice of love!" he laughed; and then "No, if you pull your flowers to pieces, and find how they pollinate, and where are the ovaries, you don't go in blind ecstasies over them.*—But they mean more to you: they are intimate, like friends of your heart, not like wonderful dazing fairies."*

"Ay!" she assented, musing over it with the gladness of understanding him. "—And then?"

Softly, almost without words she urged him to the point.

"Well" he said "you think I'm a wonderful magical person, don't you?—and I'm not—I'm not as good, in the long run, as your Tom, who thinks *you* are a wonderful magical person." She laughed and clung to him as they walked. He continued, very carefully and gently. "Now, I don't imagine for a moment that you are princessy or angelic or wonderful. You often make me thundering mad because you're an ass— —"

She laughed low with shame and humiliation.

"Nevertheless—I come from the south to you—because—well, with you I can be just as I feel, conceited or idiotic, without being afraid to be myself—" he broke off suddenly: "I don't think I've tried to make myself out to you—any bigger or better than I am—?"—he asked her, wistfully.

"No!" she answered, in beautiful deep assurance. "No! That's where it is! You have always been so honest. You are more honest than anybody ever—"—she did not finish, being deeply moved. He was silent for some time, then he continued, as if he must see the question to the end with her:

"But you know—I do like you not to wear corsets. I like to see you move inside your dress."

She laughed, half shame, half pleasure.

"I wondered if you'd notice," she said.

"I did—directly"—there was a space of silence, after which he resumed "You see—we would marry tomorrow—but I can't keep myself. I am in debt—."

She came close to him, and took his arm.

"—And what's the good of letting the years go, and the beauty of one's youth—?"

"No—," she admitted, very slowly and softly, shaking her head.

"So—well!—you understand, don't you?—and—if you're willing—you'll come to me, won't you?—just naturally; as you used to come and go to church with me?—and it won't be—it won't be me coaxing you—reluctant?—will it?"

They had halted in front of a stile which they would have to climb. She turned to him in silence, and put up her face to him. He took her in his arms, and kissed her, and felt the night-mist with which his moustache was drenched, and he bent his head and rubbed his face on her shoulder, and then pressed his lips on her neck. For a while they stood in silence clasped together. Then he heard her voice, muffled in his shoulder, saying:

"But—but you know—it's much harder for the woman—it means something so different for a woman."

"One can be wise" he answered, slowly and gently, "one need not blunder into calamities."*

She was silent for a time. Then she spoke again.

"Yes but—if it should be—you see—I couldn't bear it."

He let her go, and they drew apart, and the embrace no longer choked them from speaking. He recognised the woman defensive, playing the coward against her own inclinations, and even against her knowledge.

"If—if!" he exclaimed sharply, so that she shrank with a little fear, "there need be no ifs—need there?"

"I don't know" she replied, reproachfully, very quietly.

"If I say so—" he said, angry with her mistrust. Then he climbed the stile, and she followed.

"But you *do* know," he exclaimed. "I have given you books—."

"Yes—but—."

"But what?" he was getting really angry.

"It's so different for a woman—you don't know."

He did not answer this. They stumbled together over the mole-hills, under the oak trees.

"And look—how we should have to be—creeping together in the dark—"*

This stung him;—at once, it was as if the glamour went out of life. It was as if she had tipped over the frail vessel that held the wine of his desire, and had emptied him of all his vitality. He had played a difficult, deeply-moving part all night, and now the lights suddenly switched out, and there was left only weariness. He was silent, tired, very tired, bodily and spiritually. They walked across the wide, dark meadow with sunken heads. Suddenly she caught his arm.

"Don't be cold with me!" she cried.

He bent and kissed in acknowledgment the lips she offered him for love.

"No" he said drearily "no, it is not coldness—only—I have lost hold—for tonight." He spoke with difficulty. It was hard to find a word to say. They stood together, apart, under the old thorn tree for some minutes, neither speaking. Then he climbed the fence, and stood on the highway above the meadow.

At parting also he had not kissed her. He stood a moment and looked at her. The water in a little brook under the hedge was running, chuckling with extraordinary loudness: away on Nethermere they heard the sad, haunting cry of the wild fowl from the North. The stars still twinkled intensely. He was too spent to think of anything to say; she was too overcome with grief and fear and a little resentment. He looked down at the pale blotch of her face upturned from the low meadow beyond the fence. The thorn boughs tangled above her, drooping behind her like the roof of a hut. Beyond was the great width of the darkness. He felt unable to gather his energy to say anything vital.

"Goodbye!" he said. "I'm going back—on Saturday. But—you'll write to me—goodbye."

He turned to go. He saw her white uplifted face vanish, and her dark form bend under the boughs of the tree, and go out into the great darkness. She did not say goodbye.*

# The Fly in the Ointment

Muriel had sent me some mauve primroses,* slightly weather beaten, and some honeysuckle-twine threaded with grey-green rosettes,* and some timid hazel catkins. They had arrived in a forlorn little cardboard box, just as I was rushing off to school.

"Stick 'em in water!" I said to Mrs Williams,* and I left the house. But those mauve primroses had set my tone for the day: I was dreamy and reluctant; school and the sounds of the boys were unreal, unsubstantial; beyond these, were the realities of my poor winter-trodden primroses, and the pale hazel catkins that Muriel had sent me. Altogether, the boys must have thought me a vacant fool; I regarded them as a punishment upon me.

I rejoiced exceedingly when night came, with the evening star, and the sky flushed dark blue, purple, over the golden pomegranates of the lamps. I was as glad as if I had been hurrying home to Muriel, as if she would open the door to me, would keep me a little while in the fireglow, with the splendid purple of the evening against the window, before she laughed and drew up her head proudly and flashed on the light over the tea-cups. But Eleanor, the girl, opened the door to me, and I poured out my tea in solitary state.

Mrs Williams had set out my winter posy for me on the table, and I thought of all the beautiful things we had done, Muriel and I, at home in the midlands, of all the beautiful ways she had looked at me, of all the beautiful things I had said to her—or had meant to say. I went on imagining beautiful things to say to her looking* at me with her wonderful eyes from among the fir boughs in the wood. Meanwhile I talked to my landlady about the neighbours.

Although I had much work to do, and although I laboured away at it, in the end there was nothing done. Then I felt very miserable, and sat still and sulked. At a quarter to eleven I said to myself:

"This will never do—" and I took up my pen and wrote a letter to Muriel:

"It was not fair to send me those robins"—we called the purple primroses 'robins', for no reason, unless that they bloomed in winter—"they have bewitched me. Their wicked, bleared little pinkish eyes follow me about and I have to think of you and home, instead of doing what I've got to do. All the time while I was teaching I had a grass-hopper chirruping away in my head, as if it were midsummer there, and the arithmetic rattled like the carts on the street. Poor lads! I read their miserable pieces of composition on 'Pancakes' over and over, and never saw them, thinking—'the primrose flowers now because it is so sheltered under the plum-trees—those old trees with gummy bark—' You like biting through a piece of hard bright gum—if your lips did not get so sticky— —"

I will not say at what time I finished my letter. I can recall a sensation of being dim, oblivious of everything, smiling to myself as I sealed the envelope; of putting my books and papers in their places without the least knowledge of so doing, keeping the atmosphere of Strelley Mill close round me in my London lodging. I cannot remember turning off the electric light. The next thing of which I am conscious is pushing at the kitchen door.

The kitchen is at the back of the house. Outside in the dark was a little yard and a hand's-breadth of garden backed up by the railway embankment. I had come down the passage from my room in the front of the house, and stood pushing at the kitchen door to get a glass for some water. Evidently the oilcloth* had turned up a little, and the edge of the door was under it. I woke up irritably, swore a little, pushed harder and heard the oilcloth rip. Then I bent and put my hand through the small space to flatten the oilcloth.

The kitchen was in darkness save for the red embers lying low in the stove. I started, but rather from sleepy wonder than anything else. The shock was not quite enough to bring me to. Pressing himself flat into the corner between the stove and the wall was a fellow. I wondered, and was disturbed: the greater part of me was away in the midlands still. So I stood looking and blinking.

"Why?" I said, helplessly. I think this very mildness must have terrified him. Immediately he shrunk together, and began to dodge about between the table and the stove, whining, snarling, with an incredibly mongrel sound:

"Don't yer touch me—don't yer come grabbin' at me—I'll hit you between the eyes with this poker—I ain't done nothin' to you—don't yer touch me, yer bloody coward."

All the time he was writhing about in the space in which I had him trapped, between the table and stove. I was much too dazed to do anything but stare. Then my blood seemed to change its quality. I came awake, sick and sharp with pain. It was such a display as I had seen before, in school, and I felt again the old misery of helplessness and disgust. He dared not, I knew, strike, unless by trying to get hold of him I terrified him to the momentary madness of such a slum-rat.

"Stop your row!" I said, standing still and leaving him his room. "Shut your miserable row. Do you want to waken the children."

"Ah but don't you touch 'im,* don't you come no nearer!"

He had stopped writhing about, and was crouching at the defensive. The little frenzy, too, had gone out of his voice.

"Put the poker down, you fool,—" I pointed to the corner of the stove, where the poker used to stand. I supplied him with the definite idea of placing the poker in the corner, and, in his crazy witless state, he could not reject it. He did as I told him, but indefinitely, as if the action were second hand. The poker, loosely dropped into the corner, slid to the ground with a clatter. I looked from it to him, feeling him like a burden upon me, and in some way I was afraid of him, for my heart began to beat heavily. His own indefinite clumsiness, and the jangle of the poker on the hearth, and then my sudden spiritual collapse, unnerved him still more. He crouched there abjectly.

I took a box of matches from the mantel piece and lit the gas at the pendant that hung in the middle of the bare little room. Then I saw that he was a youth of nineteen or so, narrow at the temples, with thin, pinched-looking brows. He was not ugly, nor did he look ill-fed. But he evidently came of a low breed.* His hair had been cut close to his skull, leaving a tussocky fringe over his forehead to provide him with a "topping", and to show that it was no prison crop which had bared him.

"I wasn't doin' no harm" he whined, resentfully, with still an attempt at a threat in his tones. "I 'aven't done nuffin' to you, you leave me alone. What harm have I done?"

"Be quiet" I said. "You'll wake the children and the people."

I went to the door and listened. No one was disturbed. Then I closed the door, and pulled down the wide-opened window, which was letting in the cold night air. As I did so I shivered, noting how ugly and shapeless the mangle looked in the yard, with the moonlight on its frosty cover.

The fellow was standing abjectly in the same place. He had evidently been ricketty as a child. I sat down in the rocking chair.

"What did you come in here for?" I asked, almost pleading.

"Well" he retorted insolently "an' wouldn't you go somewhere, if you 'edn't a place to go to of a night like this."

"Look here" I said coldly, a flash of hate in my blood, "none of your chelp."*

"Well I only come in for a warm" he said, afraid not to appear defiant.

"No you didn't," I replied. "You came to take something. What did you want from here?" I looked round the kitchen unhappily. He looked back at me uneasily, then at his dirty hands, then at me again. He had brown eyes, in which low cunning floated like oil on the top of much misery.

"I might 'a took some boots," he said, with a little vaunt.

My heart sank. I hoped he would say 'food'. And I was responsible for him. I hated him.

"You want your neck breaking," I said. "We can hardly afford boots as it is."

"I ain't never done it before! This is the first time— —"

"You miserable swine!" I said. He looked at me with a flash of rat-fury.

"Where do you live?" I asked.

"Exeter Road."

"And you don't do any work?"

"I couldn't never get a job—except—I used to deliver laundry—"

"And they turned you off for thieving?"

He shifted and stirred uneasily in his chair.* As he was so manifestly uncomfortable, I did not press him.

"Who do you live with?"

"I live at 'ome."

"What does your father do?"

But he sat stubborn, and would not answer. I thought of the gangs of youths who stood at the corners of the mean streets near the school, there all day long, month after month, fooling with the laundry girls, and insulting passers-by.

"But" I said "what are you going to do?"

He hung his head again and fidgetted in his chair. Evidently what little thought he gave to the subject made him uncomfortable. He could not answer.

"Get a laundry girl to marry you and live on her?" I asked, sarcastically.

He smiled sicklily, evidently even a little bit flattered. What was the good of talking to him.

"And loaf at the street corners till you go rotten?" I said.

He looked up at me sullenly:

"Well I can't get a job" he replied, with insolence. He was not hopeless, but like a man born without expectations, apathetic, looking to be provided for, sullenly allowing everything.

"No" I said "if a man is worthy of his hire,* the hire is worthy of a man—and I'm damned if you *are* a man."

He grinned at me with sly insolence.

"And would any women have you?" I asked.

Then he grinned slyly to himself, ducking his head to hide the joke. And I thought of the coloured primroses, and of Muriel's beautiful, pensive face. Then of him with his dirty clothes and his nasty skin! Then, that given a woman, he would be a father.

"Well," I said, "it's a knock-out."

He gave me a narrow, sleering* look.

"You don't know everyfing," he said in contempt.

I sat and wondered.

And I knew I could not understand him, that I had no fellow feeling with him. He was something beyond me.

"Well," I said, helplessly, "you'd better go."

I rose, feeling he had beaten me. He could affect and alter me, I could not affect nor alter him. He shambled off down the path. I watched him skulk under the lamp posts, afraid of the police. Then I shut the door.

In the silence of the sleeping house I stood quite still for some minutes, up against the unpassable* fact of this man, beyond which I could not get. I could not accept him; I simply hated him. Then I climbed the stairs. It was like a nightmare. I thought he was a blot,* like a blot fallen on my mind, something black and heavy out of which I could not extricate myself.

As I hung up my coat I felt Muriel's fat letter in my pocket. It made me a trifle sick.

"No," I said, with a flush of rage against her perfect serene purity, "I don't want to think of her."

And I wound my watch up sullenly, feeling alone and wretched.

# The Witch à la Mode*

When Bernard Coutts* alighted at East Croydon he knew he was tempting Providence.

"I may just as well," he said to himself, "stay the night here, where I am used to the place, as go to London. I can't get to Connie's forlorn spot* tonight, and I'm tired to death, so why shouldn't I do what is easiest!" He gave his luggage to a porter.

Again, as he faced the approaching tram-car:

"I don't see why I shouldn't go down to Purley, I shall just be in time for tea."

Each of these concessions to his desires, he made against his conscience. But beneath his sense of shame his spirit exulted.

It was an evening of March.* In the dark hollow below Crown Hill the buildings accumulated, bearing the black bulk of the Church tower up into the rolling and smoking sunset.

"I know it so well," he thought—"And love it," he confessed, secretly, in his heart.

The car ran on familiarly. The young man listened for the swish, watched for the striking of the blue splash overhead, at the bracket. The sudden fervour of the sparks, splashed out of the mere wire, pleased him.

"Where does it come from?" he asked himself, and a spark struck bright again. He smiled a little, roused.*

The day was dying out. One by one the arc lamps fluttered or leaped alight, the strand of copper overhead glistened against the dark sky that now was deepening to the colour of monkshood. The tram-car dipped as it ran, seeming to exult. As it came clear of the houses, the young man, looking west, saw the evening star advance, a bright thing approaching from a long way off, as if it had been bathing in the surf of the daylight, and now was walking shorewards to the night. He greeted the naked star, with a bow of the head, his heart surging as the car leaped.

"It seems to be greeting me across the sky—the star," he said, amused by his own vanity.

Above the colouring of the afterglow the blade of the new moon hung sharp and keen. Something recoiled in him.

"It is like a knife to be used at a sacrifice," he said,* to himself. Then secretly: "I wonder for whom?"

He refused to answer this question, but he had the sense of Constance, his betrothed, waiting for him in the Vicarage in the north. He closed his eyes.

Soon the car was running full tilt from the shadow to the fume of yellow light at the terminus, where shop on shop and lamp beyond lamp heaped golden fire on the floor of the blue night. The car, like an eager dog, ran in home, sniffing with pleasure the fume of lights.

Coutts flung away up-hill. He had forgotten he was tired. From a distance he could distinguish the house, by the broad white cloths of alyssome* flowers that hung down the garden walls. He ran up the steep path to the door, smelling the hyacinths in the dark, watching for the pale fluttering of daffodils, and the steadier show of white crocuses on the grassy banks.

Mrs Braithwaite* herself opened the door to him.

"There!" she cried. "I expected you. I had your card saying you would cross from Dieppe today. You wouldn't make up your mind to come here, not till the last minute, would you? No—that's what I expected. You know where to put your things: I don't think we've altered anything in the last year."

Mrs Braithwaite chattered on, laughing all the time. She was a young widow, whose husband had been dead two years. Of medium height, sanguine in complexion and temper, there was a rich, oily glisten in her skin and black hair,* suggesting the flesh of a nut. She was dressed for the evening in a long gown of soft, mole-coloured satin.

"Of course I'm delighted you've come," she said at last, lapsing into conventional politeness, and then, meeting his eyes, she began to laugh at her attempt at formality.

She led Coutts into a small, very warm room, that had a dark foreign sheen, owing to the black of the curtains and hangings, covered thick with glistening Indian embroidery, and to the sleekness of some Indian ware. A rosy old gentleman,* with exquisite white hair and side-whiskers, got up shakily and stretched out his hand. His cordial expression of welcome was rendered strange by a puzzled wondering look of old age, and by a certain stiffness of his countenance, which now would only render a few expressions. He wrung the new-comer's hand heartily, his manner contrasting pathetically with his bowed and trembling form.

"Oh, why—why yes, it's Mr Coutts!—hm?—Ay. Well, and how are you—hm? Sit down, sit down." The old man rose again, bowing, waving the young man into a chair. "Ay!—well, and how are you?—What? Have some tea—Come on, come along, here's the tray. Laura, ring for fresh tea for Mr Coutts. But I'll do it." He suddenly remembered his old gallantry, forgot his age and uncertainty. Fumbling, he rose to go to the bell-push.

"It's done Pater—the tea will be in in a minute," said his daughter, in high distinct tones. Mr Cleveland sank with relief into his chair.

"You know, I'm beginning to be troubled with rheumatism," he explained in confidential tones. Mrs Braithwaite glanced at the young man, and smiled. The old gentleman babbled and chattered. He had no knowledge of his guest beyond the fact of his presence: Coutts might have been any other young man, for all his host was aware.

"You didn't tell us you were going away—why didn't you?" asked Laura, in her distinct tones, between laughing and reproach. Coutts looked at her ironically, so that she fidgetted with some crumbs on the cloth.

"I don't know," he said. "Why do we do things?"

"I'm sure I don't know. Why do we? Because we want to, I suppose;" and she ended again with a little run of laughter. Things were so amusing, and she was so healthy.

"Why *do* we do things, Pater," she suddenly asked in a loud voice, glancing with a little chuckle of laughter at Coutts.

"Eh?—Why do we do things? What things?" said the old man, beginning to laugh with his daughter.

"Why, any of the things that we do."

"Eh?—Oh." The old man was illuminated, and delighted. "Well now, that's a difficult question. I remember, when I was a little younger, we used to discuss Free Will*—got very hot about it—" he laughed—and Laura laughed, then said, in a high voice:

"Oh, Free Will! We shall really think you're 'passé' if you revive that, Pater."

Mr Cleveland looked puzzled for a moment. Then, as if answering a conundrum, he repeated:

"Why do we do things?—now why *do* we do things."

"I suppose," he said, in all good faith, "it's because we can't help it.—Eh?—what?"

Laura laughed, Coutts showed his teeth in a smile.

"That's what I think, Pater," she said loudly.

"And are you still engaged to your Constance?" she asked of Coutts, with a touch of mockery this time. Coutts nodded.

"And how is she?" asked the widow.

"I believe she is very well—unless my delay has upset her," said Coutts, his tongue between his teeth. It hurt him to give pain to his fiancée, and yet he did it wilfully.

"Do you know she always reminds me of a Bunbury— I call her your Miss Bunbury,"* Laura laughed.

Coutts did not answer.

"We missed you *so* much when you first went away," Laura began, re-establishing the proprieties.

"Thank you," he said. She began to laugh wickedly.

"On Friday evenings," she said, adding quickly: "Oh, and this is Friday evening, and Winifred* is coming just as she used—how long ago?—ten months?"

"Ten months," Coutts corroborated.

"Did you quarrel with Winifred?" she asked suddenly.

"Winifred never quarrels," he answered.

"I don't believe she does. Then why *did* you go away? You are such a puzzle to me, you know—and I shall never rest till I have it out of you. Do you mind?"

"I like it," he said, quietly, flashing a laugh at her.

She laughed, then settled herself in a dignified, serious way.

"No, I can't make you out at all—nor can I Winifred. You *are* a pair! But it's you who are the real wonder. When are you going to be married?"

"I don't know—when I am sufficiently well off."*

"I *asked* Winifred to come tonight," Laura confessed. The eyes of the man and woman met.

"Why is she so ironic to me?—does she really like me?" Coutts asked of himself. But Laura looked too bonny and jolly to be fretted by love.

"And Winifred won't tell me a word," she said.

"There is nothing to tell," he replied.

Laura looked at him closely for a few moments. Then she rose and left the room.

Presently there arrived a German lady* with whom Coutts was slightly acquainted. At about half past seven came Winifred Varley. Coutts heard the courtly old gentleman welcoming her in the hall, heard her low voice in answer. When she entered, and saw him, he knew it was a shock to her, though she hid it as well as she could. He suffered too. After hesitating for a second in the doorway, she came forward, shook hands without speaking, only looking at him with rather frightened blue eyes. She was of medium height, sturdy in build. Her face was white, and impassive, without the least trace of a smile. She was a blonde of twenty eight, dressed in a white gown just short enough not to touch the ground. Her throat was solid and strong, her arms heavy and white and beautiful, her blue eyes heavy with unacknowledged passion. When she had turned away from Coutts, she flushed vividly. He could see the pink in her arms and throat, and he flushed in answer.

"That blush would hurt her," he said to himself, wincing.

"I did not expect to see you," she said, with a reedy timbre of voice, as if her throat were half closed. It made his nerves tingle.

"No—nor I you—at least—." He ended indefinitely—

"You have come down from Yorkshire?" she asked. Apparently she was cold and self-possessed. Yorkshire meant the rectory where his fiancée lived: he felt the sting of sarcasm.

"No," he answered. "I am on my way there."

There was a moment's pause. Unable to resolve the situation, she turned abruptly to her hostess.

"Shall we play then?"

They adjourned to the drawing room. It was a large room upholstered in dull yellow. The chimney-piece took Coutts' attention. He knew it perfectly well, but this evening it had a new lustrous fascination. Over the mellow marble of the mantel rose an immense mirror, very translucent and deep, like deep grey water.* Before this mirror, shining white as moons on a soft grey sky, was a pair of statues in alabaster, two feet high. Both were nude figures. They glistened under the side lamps, rose clean and distinct from their pedestals. The Venus leaned slightly forward, as if anticipating someone's coming. Her attitude of suspense made the young man stiffen. He could see the clean suavity of her shoulders and waist reflected white on the deep mirror. She shone, catching, as she leaned forward, the glow of the lamp on her lustrous marble loins.

Laura played Brahms; the delicate, winsome German lady played Chopin; Winifred played on her violin a Grieg sonata,* to Laura's accompaniment. After having sung twice, Coutts listened to the music. Unable to criticise, he listened till he was intoxicated. Winifred, as she played, swayed slightly. He watched the strong forward thrust of her neck, the powerful and angry striking of her arm. He could see the outline of her figure: she wore no corsets: and he found her of resolute, independent build. Again he glanced at the Venus bending in suspense. Winifred was blonde with a solid whiteness, an isolated woman.

All evening, little was said, save by Laura. Miss Syfurt exclaimed continually "Oh, that is fine! You play gra-and, Miss Varley, don't you know. If I could play the violin—ah the violin!"

It was not later than ten o'clock when Winifred and Miss Syfurt rose to go, the former to Croydon, the latter to Ewell.

"We can go by car together to West Croydon," said the German lady, gleefully, as if she were a child. She was a frail, excitable little woman of forty, naïve and innocent. She gazed with bright brown eyes of admiration on Coutts.

"Yes, I am glad," he answered.

He took up Winifred's violin, and the three proceeded downhill to the tram terminus. There a car was on the point of departure. They hurried forward. Miss Syfurt mounted the step. Coutts waited for Winifred. The conductor called:

"Come along please, if you're going."

"No," said Winifred. "I prefer to walk this stage."

"We can walk from West Croydon," said Coutts.

The conductor rang the bell.

"Aren't you coming?" cried the frail excitable little lady from the footboard. "Aren't you coming?—Oh!"

"I walk from West Croydon every day: I prefer to walk here, in the quiet," said Winifred.

"Aw! Aren't you coming with me?" cried the little lady, quite frightened. She stepped back in supplication towards the footboard. The conductor impatiently buzzed the bell. The car started forward, Miss Syfurt staggered, was caught by the conductor.

"Aw!" she cried, holding her hand out to the two who stood on the road, and breaking almost into tears of disappointment. As the tram darted forward she clutched at her hat. In a moment she was out of sight.

Coutts stood wounded to the quick by this pain given to the frail, child-like lady.

"We may as well," said Winifred, "walk over the hill to the 'Swan'." Her note had that intense, reedy quality which always set the man on edge. It* was the note of her anger, or more often of her tortured sense of discord. The two turned away, to climb the hill again. He carried the violin: for a long time neither spoke.

"Ah, how I hate her, how I hate her!" he repeated in his heart. He winced repeatedly at the thought of Miss Syfurt's little cry of supplication. He was in a position where he was not himself, and he hated her for putting him there, forgetting that it was he who had come, like a moth to the candle. For half a mile he walked on, his head carried stiffly, his face set, his heart twisted with painful emotion. And all the time, as she plodded, head down, beside him, his blood beat with hate of her, drawn to her, repelled by her.

At last, on the high-up, naked down, they came upon those meaningless pavements that run through the grass, waiting for the houses to line them. The two were thrust up into the night, above the little flowering of the lamps in the valley. In front was the daze of light from London, rising midway to the zenith, just fainter than the stars. Across the valley, on the blackness of the opposite hill, little groups of lights like gnats seemed to be floating in the darkness. Orion was heeled over the west. Below, in a cleft in the night, the long low garland of arc-lamps strung down the Brighton Road, where now and then the golden tram-cars flew low along the track, passing each other with a faint angry sound.

"It is a year last Monday since we came over here," said Winifred, as they stopped to look about them.

"I remember—but I didn't know it was then," he said. There was a touch of hardness in his voice. "I don't remember our dates."

After a wait, she said in very low passionate tones:

"It *is* a beautiful night."

"The moon has set, and the evening star," he answered. "Both were out as I came down."

She glanced swiftly at him to see if this speech was a bit of symbolism. He was looking across the valley with a set face. Very slightly, by an inch or two, she nestled towards him.

"Yes," she said, half stubborn, half pleading. "But the night is a very fine one for all that."

"Yes," he replied, unwillingly.

Thus, after months of separation, they dovetailed into the same love and hate.

"You are staying down here?" she asked at length, in a forced voice. She never intruded a hair's breadth on the most trifling privacy: in which she was Laura's antithesis; so that this question was almost an impertinence for her. He felt her shrink.

"Till the morning—then Yorkshire," he said cruelly.

He hated it that she could not bear outspokenness.

At that moment a train across the valley threaded the opposite darkness with its gold thread. The valley re-echoed with vague throat. The two watched the express, like a gold and black snake, curve and dive seawards into the night. He turned, saw her full fine face tilted up to him. It showed pale, distinct and firm, very near to him. He shut his eyes and shivered.

"I hate trains," he said, impulsively.

"Why?" she asked, with a curious, tender little smile that caressed, as it were, his emotion towards her.

"I don't know: they pitch one about here and there..."

"I thought," she said, with faint irony, "that you preferred change."

"I do like *life*. But now I should like to be nailed to something, if it was only a cross."

She laughed sharply, and said, with keen sarcasm:

"Is it so difficult, then, to let yourself be nailed to a cross? I thought the difficulty lay in getting free."

He ignored her sarcasm on his engagement.

"There is nothing now that matters," he said, adding quickly, to forestall her: "Of course I'm wild when dinner is late, and so on——but—apart from those things—nothing seems to matter."

She was silent.

"One goes on—remains in office, so to speak: and life's all right—only, it doesn't seem to matter."

"This does sound like complaining of trouble because you've got none," she laughed.

"Trouble.—" he repeated. "No, I don't suppose I've got any. Vexations, which most folk call trouble—: but something I really grieve about in my soul, no, nothing. I wish I had—."

She laughed again, sharply: but he perceived in her laughter a little keen despair.

"I find a lucky pebble. I think, now I'll throw it over my left shoulder, and wish. So I spit over my little finger, and throw the white pebble behind me, and then, when I want to wish, I'm done. I say to myself 'Wish', and myself says back 'I don't want anything.' I say again 'Wish, you fool', but I'm as dumb of wishes as a newt. And then, because it rather frightens me, I say in a hurry 'A million of money.' Do *you* know what to wish for when you see the new moon?"

She laughed quickly.

"I think so," she said. "But my wish varies."

"I wish mine did," he said, whimsically lugubrious.

She took his hand in a little impulse of love.

They walked hand in hand on the ridge of the down, bunches of lights shining below, the big radiance of London advancing like a wonder in front.

"You know— —," he began, then stopped.

"I don't—," she ironically urged.

"Do you want to?" he laughed.

"Yes, one is never at peace with oneself till one understands."

"Understands what?" he asked brutally. He knew she meant that she wanted to understand the situation he and she were in.

"How to resolve the discord," she said, balking the issue. He would have liked her to say, "What you want of me."

"Your foggy weather of symbolism as usual," he said.

"The fog is not of symbols," she replied, in her metallic voice of displeasure. "It may be symbols are candles in a fog— —."

"I prefer my fog without candles. I'm the fog, eh? Then I'll blow out your candles, and you'll see me better. Your candles of speech, symbols and so forth only lead you wronger. I'm going to wander blind, and go by instinct, like a moth that flies and settles on the wooden box his mate is shut up in."

"Isn't it an ignis fatuus you are flying after, at that rate," she said.

"May be, for if I breathe outwards, in a positive movement towards you, you move off. If I draw in a vacant sigh of soulfulness, you flow nearly to my lips."

"This is a very interesting symbol," she said, with sharp sarcasm.

He hated her, truly. She hated him. Yet they held hands fast as they walked.

"We are just the same as we were a year ago," he laughed. But he hated her, for all his laughter.

When, at the 'Swan and Sugar Loaf' they mounted the car, she climbed to the top, in spite of the sharp night. They nestled side by side, shoulders caressing, and all the time that they ran under the round lamps, neither spoke.

At the gate of a small house in a dark, tree-lined street, both waited a moment. From her garden leaned an almond tree whose buds, early this year, glittered in the light of the street-lamp, with theatrical effect.* He broke off a twig.

"I always remember this tree," he said, "how I used to feel sorry for it when it was full out, and so lively, at midnight in the lamplight. I thought it must be tired."

"Will you come in?" she asked tenderly.

"I did get a room in town," he answered, following her.

She opened the door with her latch-key, showing him as usual into her drawing room. Everything was just the same, cold in colouring, warm in appointment: ivory-coloured walls, blond, polished floor, with thick ivory-coloured rugs: three deep armchairs in pale amber, with large cushions: a big black piano, a violin-stand beside it: and the room very warm with a clear red fire, the brass shining hot. Coutts, according to his habit, lit the piano candles and lowered the blinds.

"I say," he said. "This is a variation from your line!"

He pointed to a bowl of magnificent scarlet anemones, that stood on the piano.

"Why?" she asked, pausing in arranging her hair at the small mirror.

"On the *piano*!" he admonished.

"Only while the table was in use," she smiled, glancing at the litter of papers that covered her table.

"And then—*red* flowers!" he said.

"Oh, I thought they were such a fine piece of colour," she replied.

"I would have wagered you would buy freesias," he said.

"Why?" she smiled. He pleased her thus.

"Well—for their cream and gold and restrained, bruised purple: and their scent. I cannot believe you bought scentless flowers!"

"What!" She went forward, bent over the flowers.

"I had not noticed," she said, smiling curiously, "that they were voiceless."*

She touched the velvet black centres.

"Would you have bought them had you noticed?" he asked.

She thought for a moment, curiously.

"I don't know—probably I should not."

"You would never buy scentless flowers," he averred. "Any more than you'd love a man because he was handsome."

"I did not know," she smiled. She was pleased.

The housekeeper entered with a lamp, which she set on a stand.

"You will illuminate me?" he said to Winifred. It was her habit to talk to him by candle-light.

"I have thought about you—now I will look at you," she said, quietly smiling.

"I see—to confirm your conclusions," he asked.

Her eyes lifted quickly in acknowledgement of his guess.

"That is so," she replied.

"Then," he said, "I will wash my hands."

He ran upstairs. This sense of freedom, of intimacy, was very fascinating. As he washed, the little everyday action of twining his hands in the lather set him suddenly considering his other love. At her house, he was always polite and formal: gentlemanly, in short. With Connie he felt the old, manly superiority, he was the knight, strong and tender, she the beautiful maiden with a touch of God on her brow. He kissed her, he softened and selected his speech for her, he forbore from being the greater part of himself. She was his betrothed, his wife, his queen, whom he loved to idealise, and for whom he carefully modified himself. She should rule him later on—that part of him which was hers. But he loved her too, with a pitying, tender love. He thought of her tears upon her pillow in the northern rectory, and he bit his lip, held his breath under the strain of the situation. Vaguely, he knew she would bore him. And Winifred fascinated him. He and she really played with fire. In her house, he was roused and keen. But she was not and never could be frank. So he was not frank even to himself. Saying nothing, betraying nothing, immediately they were together they began the same game. Each shuddered, each, defenceless and exposed, hated the other by turns. Yet they came together again. Coutts felt a vague fear of Winifred—she was intense and unnatural, and he became unnatural and intense, beside her.

When he came downstairs she was fingering the piano from the score of 'Walküre.'*

"First wash in England," he announced, looking at his hands. She laughed swiftly. Impatient herself of the slightest soil, his indifference to temporary grubbiness amused her.

He was a tall, bony man, with small hands and feet. His features were rough and rather ugly, but his smile was taking. She was always fascinated by the changes in him. His eyes, particularly, seemed quite different at times: sometimes hard, insolent, blue, sometimes dark, full of warmth and tenderness, sometimes flaring like an animal's. He sank wearily into a chair.

'My chair," he said, as if to himself.

She bowed her head. Of compact physique, uncorseted, her figure bowed richly to the piano. He watched the shallow concave between her shoulders, marvelling at its rich solidity. She let one arm fall loose: he looked at the shadows in the dimples of her elbows. Slowly, smiling a look of brooding affection, of acknowledgment, upon him for a forgetful moment, she said:

"And what you have done lately?"

"Simply nothing," he replied quietly. "For all that these months have been so full of variety, I think they will sink out of my life: they will evaporate and leave no result: I shall forget them."

Her blue eyes were dark and heavy upon him, watching. She did not answer. He smiled faintly at her.

"And you?" he said at length.

"With me it is different," she said quietly.

"You sit with your crystal," he laughed.

"While you tilt—"* she hung on her ending.—

He laughed, sighed, and they were quiet awhile.

"I've got such a skinful of heavy visions, they come sweating through my dreams," he said.

"Whom have you read?" she smiled.

"Meredith—very healthy,"* he laughed.

She laughed quickly, being caught.

"Now have you found out all you want?" he asked.

"Oh no," she cried with full throat.

"Well, finish at any rate. I'm not diseased. How are you?"

"But—but—" she stumbled on doggedly. "What *do* you intend to do?"

He hardened the line of his mouth and eyes, only to retort with immediate lightness:

"Just go on—"

This was their battle-field: she could not understand how he could marry: it seemed almost monstrous to her: she fought against his marriage. She looked up at him, witch-like from under bent brows. Her eyes were dark blue and heavy. He shivered, shrank with pain. She was so cruel to that other, common, every-day part of him.

"I wonder you dare go on like it," she said.

"Why dare?" he replied. "What's the odds?"

"I don't know," she answered, in deep, bitter displeasure.

"And I don't care," he said.

"But—" she continued, slowly, gravely pressing the point: "You know what you intend to do."

"Marry—settle—be a good husband, good father, partner in the business, get fat, be an amiable gentleman—Q.E.F."*

"Very good," she said, deep and final.

"Thank you."

"I did not congratulate you," she said.

"Ah!" his voice tailed off into sadness and self mistrust. Meanwhile she watched him heavily. He did not mind being scrutinised: it flattered him.

"Yes, it is, or may be, very good," she began, "but *why all* this?—*why*?"

"And why not?—And why?—because I want to."

He could not leave it thus flippantly.

"You know, Winifred, we should only drive each other into insanity, you and I: become abnormal."*

"Well," she said, "and even so, why the other?"

"My marriage?—I don't know. Instinct."

"One has so many instincts," she laughed bitterly.

That was a new idea to him.

She raised her arms, stretched them above her head in a weary gesture. They were fine, strong arms. They reminded Coutts of Euripides' 'Bacchae':* white, round arms, long arms. The lifting of her arms lifted her breasts. She dropped suddenly as if inert, lolling her arms against the cushions.

"I really don't see why you should be," she said drearily, though always with the touch of a sneer, "why we should always be—fighting."

"Ah yes you do," he replied. It was a deadlock, which he could not sustain.

"Besides," he laughed, "it's your fault."

"Am I *so* bad," she sneered.

"Worse," he said.

"But,"—she moved irritably. "Is this to the point?"

"What point?" he answered—then smiling "you know you only like a wild-goose chase."

"I do," she answered plaintively. "I miss you very much. You snatch things from the Kobolds* for me."

"Exactly," he said in a biting tone. "Exactly! That's what you want me for. I am to be your crystal, your 'genius'. My length of blood and bone you don't care a rap for. Ah yes, you like me for a crystal-glass, to see things in: to hold up to the light. I'm a blessed Lady-of-Shalott-looking-glass* for you."

"You talk to *me*," she said, dashing his fervour, "of my fog of symbols."

"Ah well, if so, 'tis your own asking."

"I did not know it." She looked at him coldly. He was angry.

"No," he said.

Again, they hated each other.

"The old ancients," he laughed, "gave the Gods the suet and intestines:* at least I believe so. They ate the rest. You shouldn't be a Goddess."

"I wonder, among your rectory acquaintances, you haven't learned better manners," she answered, in cold contempt. He closed his eyes, lying back in his chair, his legs sprawled towards her.

"I suppose we're civilised savages," he said sadly. All was silent.

At last, opening his eyes again, he said, "I shall have to be going directly, Winifred: it is past eleven"—then the appeal in his voice changed to laughter—"though I know I shall be winding through all the Addios in 'Traviata'* before you can set me travelling." He smiled at her, then closed his eyes once more, conscious of deep, but vague suffering. She lay in her chair, her face averted, rosily, towards the fire. Without glancing at her, he was aware of the white approach of her throat, towards her breast. He seemed to perceive her with another, unknown sense, that acted all over his body. She lay perfectly still and warm in the fire glow. He was dimly aware that he suffered.

"Yes," she said at length, "if we were linked together we should only destroy each other."

He started, hearing her admit, for the first time, this point of which he was so sure.

"You should never *marry* anyone," he said.

"And you," she asked in irony, "must offer your head to harness, and be bridled, and driven?"

"There's the makings of quite a good, respectable trotter in me," he laughed. "Don't you see it's what I *want* to be."

"I am not sure," she laughed in return.

"I think so."

"Ah well, if you think so."

They were silent for a time. The white lamp burned steady as moonlight, the red fire like sunset: there was no stir or flicker.

"And what of you?" he asked, at last.

She crooned a faint, tired laugh.

"If you are jetsam, as you say you are," she answered, "I am flotsam. I shall lie stranded."

"Nay," he pleaded. "When were you wrecked?"

She laughed quickly, with a sound like the tinkle of tears.

"Oh dear, Winifred!" he cried despairingly.

She lifted her arms towards him, hiding her face between them, looking up through the white closure with dark, uncanny eyes, like an invocation. His breast lifted towards her up-tilted arms. He shuddered, shut his eyes, held his throat rigid. He heard her drop her arms heavily.

"I must go," he said in a dull voice.

The rapidly chasing quivers that ran in tremors down the front of his body and limbs made him stretch himself, stretch hard.

"Yes," she assented gravely, "you must go."

He turned to her. Again looking up darkly, from under her lowered brows, she lifted her hands like small white orchids towards him. Without knowing, he gripped her wrists with a grasp that circled his blood-red nails with white rims.

"Goodbye," he said, looking down at her. She made a small moaning sound in her throat, lifting her face, so that it came open and near to him like a suddenly-risen flower, borne on a strong white stalk. She seemed to extend, to fill the world, to become atmosphere and all. He did not know what he was doing. He was bending forward, his mouth on hers, her arms round his neck, and his own hands, still fastened onto her wrists, almost bursting the blood under his nails with the intensity of their grip. They remained for a few moments thus, rigid. Then, weary of the strain, she relaxed. She turned her face, offered him her throat, white, hard, and rich, below the ear. Stooping still lower, so that he quivered in every fibre at the strain, he laid his mouth to the kiss. In the intense silence, he heard the deep, dull pulsing of her blood, and the minute click of a spark within the lamp.

Then he drew her from the chair up to him. She came, arms always round his neck, till at last she lay along his breast as he stood, feet planted wide, clasping her tight, his mouth on her neck. She turned suddenly to meet his full red mouth in a kiss. He felt his moustache prick back into his lips. It was the first kiss she had genuinely given. Dazed, he was conscious of the throb of one great pulse, as if his whole body were a heart that contracted in throbs. He felt, with an intolerable ache, as if he, the heart, were setting the pulse in her, in the very night, so that everything beat from the throb of his overstrained, bursting body.

The hurt became so great it brought him out of the reeling stage to distinct consciousness. She clipped her lips, drew them away, leaving him her throat. Already she had had enough. He opened his eyes as he bent with his mouth on her neck, and was startled: there stood the objects of the room, stark; there, close below his eyes, were the half sunk lashes of the woman, swooning on her unnatural ebb of passion. He saw her thus, knew she wanted no more of him than that kiss. And the heavy form of this woman hung upon him, his mouth was grown to her throat in a kiss: and even so, as she lay in his arms, she was gradually dismissing him. His whole body ached like a swollen vein, with heavy intensity, while his heart grew dead with misery and despair. This woman gave him anguish and a cutting-short like death: to the other woman he was false. As he shivered with suffering, he opened his eyes again, and caught sight of the pure ivory of the lamp. His heart flashed with rage.

A sudden involuntary blow of his foot, and he sent the lamp-stand spinning. The lamp leaped off, fell with a smash on the fair, polished floor. Instantly a bluish hedge of flame quavered, leaped up before them. She tightened her hold round his neck, and buried her face against his throat. The flame veered at her, blue, with a yellow tongue that licked her dress and her arm. Convulsive, she clutched him, almost strangled him, though she made no sound.

He gathered her up and bore her heavily out of the room. Slipping from her clasp, he brought his arms down her form, crushing the starting blaze of her dress. His face was singed. Staring at her, he could scarcely see her.

"I am not hurt," she cried. "But you?"

The housekeeper was coming, the flames were sinking and waving-up in the drawing room. He broke away from Winifred, threw one of the great woollen rugs onto the flame, then stood a moment looking at the darkness.

Winifred caught at him as he passed her.

"No, no," he answered, as he fumbled for the latch. "I'm not hurt. Clumsy fool I am—clumsy fool!"

In another instant he was gone, running with burning red hands held out blindly down the street.

# The Old Adam*

The maid who opened the door was just developing into a handsome womanhood. Therefore she seemed to have the insolent pride of one newly come to an inheritance. She would be a splendid woman to look at, having just enough of Jewish blood to enrich her comeliness into beauty. At nineteen her fine grey eyes looked challenge, and her warm complexion, her black hair looped up slack, enforced the sensuous folding of her mouth.

She wore no cap nor apron, but a well-looking sleeved overall such as even very ladies don.

The man she opened to was tall and thin, but graceful in his energy. He wore white flannels, carried a tennis-racket. With a light bow to the maid he stepped beside her on the threshold. He was one of those who attract by their movement, whose movement is watched unconsciously, as we watch the flight of a sea bird waving its wings leisurely. Instead of entering the house, the young man stood beside the maid-servant and looked back into the blackish evening. When in repose, he had the diffident, ironic bearing so remarkable in the educated youth of today, the very reverse of that traditional aggressiveness of youth.

"It is going to thunder, Kate," he said.

"Yes, I think it is," she replied, on an even footing.

The young man stood a moment looking at the trees across the road, and on the oppressive twilight.

"Look," he said, "there's not a trace of colour in the atmosphere, though it's sunset; all a dark, lustrous grey; and those oaks kindle green like a low fire*—see!"

"Yes," said Kate, rather awkwardly.

"A troublesome sort of evening: must be because it's your last with us."

"Yes," said the girl, flushing and hardening.

There was another pause, then:

"Sorry you're going?" he asked, with a faint tang of irony.

"In some ways," she replied, rather haughtily.

He laughed as if he understood what was not said, then, with an "Ah well!" he passed along the hall.

The maid stood for a few moments clenching her young fists, clenching her very breast in revolt. Then she closed the door.

Edward Severn went into the dining room. It was eight o'clock, very dark for a June evening: on the dusk blue walls only the gilt frames of the pictures glinted pale. The clock occupied the room with its delicate ticking.

The door opened into a tiny conservatory that was lined with a grape vine. Severn could hear, from the garden beyond, the high prattling of a child. He went to the glass door.

Running down the grass by the flower-border was a little girl of three,* dressed in white. She was very bonny, very quick and intent in her movements; she reminded him of a field-mouse which plays alone in the corn, for sheer joy. Severn lounged in the doorway, watching her. Suddenly she perceived him. She started, flashed into greeting, gave a little gay jump, and stood quite still again, as if pleading.

"Mr Severn," she cried, in wonderfully coaxing tones: "Com' and see this."

"What?" he asked.

"Com' and see it," she pleaded.

He laughed, knowing she only wanted to coax him into the garden; and he went.

"Look," she said, spreading out her plump little arm.

"What?" he asked.

The baby was not going to admit that she had tricked him thither for her amusement.

"All gone up to buds," she said, pointing to the closed marigolds. Then "See!" she shrieked, flinging herself at his legs, grasping the flannel of his trousers, and tugging at him wildly. She was a wild little Menad.* She flew shrieking like a revelling bird down the garden, glancing back to see if he were coming. He had not the heart to desist, but went swiftly after her. In the obscure garden, the two white figures darted through the flowering plants, the baby, with her full silk skirts, scudding like a ruffled bird, the man, lithe and fleet, snatching her up and smothering his face in her. And all the time her piercing voice re-echoed from his low calls of warning and of triumph as he hunted her. Often she was really frightened of him, then she clung fast round his neck, and he laughed and mocked her in a low, stirring voice, whilst she protested.

The garden was large for a London suburb. It was shut in by a high, dark embankment, that rose above a row of black poplar trees. And over the spires of the trees, high up, slid by the golden-lighted trains, with the soft movement of caterpillars, and a hoarse, subtle noise.

Mrs Thomas* stood in the dark doorway watching the night, the trains, the flash and run of the two white figures.

"And now we must go in," she heard Severn say.

"No," cried the baby, wild and defiant as a bacchanal.* She clung to him like a wild cat.

"Yes," he said—"Where's your mother?"

"Give me a *swing*," demanded the child.

He caught her up. She strangled him hard with her young arms.

"I said where's your mother?" he persisted, half smothered.

"She's op'tairs," shouted the child. "Give me a swing."

"I don't think she is," said Severn.

"She is. Give me a swing, a swi-i-ing!"

He bent forward, so that she hung from his neck like a great pendant. Then he swung her, laughing low to himself while she shrieked with fear. As she slipped he caught her to his breast.

"Mary!" called Mrs Thomas, in that low, songful tone of a woman when her heart is roused and happy.

"Mary!" she called, long and sweet.

"Oh no," cried the child quickly.

But Severn bore her off. Laughing, he bowed his head and offered to the mother the baby who clung round his neck.

"Come along here," said Mrs Thomas roguishly, clasping the baby's waist with her hands.

"Oh no," cried the child, tucking her head into the young man's neck.

"But it's bed-time," said the mother. She laughed as she drew at the child to pull her loose from Severn. The baby clung tighter, and laughed, feeling no determination in her mother's grip. Severn bent his head to loosen the child's hold, bowed, and swung the heavy baby on his neck. The child clung to him, bubbling with laughter, the mother drew at her baby, laughing low, while the man swung gracefully, giving little jerks of laughter.

"Let Mr Severn undress me," said the child, hugging close to the young man, who had come to lodge with her parents when she was scarce a month old.*

"You're in high favour tonight," said the mother to Severn. He laughed, and all three stood a moment watching the trains pass and re-pass in the sky beyond the garden-end. Then they went indoors, and Severn undressed the child.

She was a beautiful girl, a bacchanal with her wild, dull-gold hair tossing about like a loose chaplet, her hazel eyes shining daringly, her small, spaced teeth glistening in little passions of laughter within her red, small mouth. The young man loved her. She was such a little bright wave of wilfulness, so abandoned to her impulses, so white and smooth as she lay at rest, so startling as she flashed her naked limbs about. But she was growing too old for a young man to undress.

She sat on his knee in her high waisted night-gown, eating her piece of bread and butter with savage little bites of resentment: she did not want to go to bed. But Severn made her repeat a Pater Noster. She lisped over the Latin, and Mrs Thomas, listening, flushed with pleasure: although she was a Protestant, and although she deplored the unbelief of Severn, who had been a Catholic.

The mother took the baby to carry her to bed. Mrs Thomas was thirty-four years old,* full-bosomed and ripe. She had dark hair that twined lightly round her low, white brow. She had a clear complexion, and beautiful brows, and dark blue eyes. The lower part of her face was heavy.

"Kiss me," said Severn to the child.

He raised his face as he sat in the rocking chair. The mother stood close beside, looking down at him, and holding the laughing rogue of a baby against her breast. The man's face was uptilted, his heavy brows set back from the laughing tenderness of his eyes, which looked dark, because the pupil was dilated. He pursed up his handsome mouth, his thick close cut moustache roused.

He was a man who gave tenderness, but who did not ask for it. All his own troubles he kept, laughingly, to himself. But his eyes were very sad when quiet, and he was too quick to understand sorrow, not to know it.

Mrs Thomas watched his fine mouth lifted for kissing. She leaned forward, lowering the baby, and suddenly, by a quick change in his eyes, she knew he was aware of her heavy woman's breasts approaching down to him. The wild rogue of a baby bent her face to his, and then, instead of kissing him, suddenly licked his cheek with her wet, soft tongue. He started back in aversion, and his eyes and his teeth flashed with a dangerous laugh.

"No no," he laughed, in low, strangled tones. "No dog-licks my dear, oh no!"

The baby chuckled with glee, gave one wicked jerk of laughter, that came out like a bubble escaping.

He put up his mouth again, and again his face was horizontal below the face of the young mother. She looked down on him as if by a kind of fascination.

"Kiss me then," he said with thick throat.

The mother lowered the baby. She felt scarcely sure of her balance. Again the child, when near to his face, darted out her tongue to lick him. He swiftly averted his face, laughing in his throat.

Mrs Thomas turned her face aside: she would see no more.

"Come then," she said to the child. "If you won't kiss Mr Severn nicely——."

The child laughed over the mother's shoulder like a squirrel crouched there. She was carried to bed.

It was still not quite dark: the clouds had opened slightly. The young man flung himself into an arm chair, with a volume of French verse.* He read one lyric, then he lay still.

"What, all in the dark!" exclaimed Mrs Thomas, coming in. "And reading by *this* light." She rebuked him with timid affectionateness. Then, glancing at his white flannelled limbs sprawled out in the gloom, she went to the door. There she turned her back to him, looking out.

"Don't these flags smell strongly in the evening," she said at length.

He replied with a few lines of the French he had been reading. She did not understand. There was a peculiar silence.

"A peculiar brutal, carnal scent, iris," he drawled at length. "Isn't it?"

She laughed shortly, saying: "Eh, I don't know about that."

"It is," he asserted calmly.

He rose from his chair, went to stand beside her at the door.

There was a great sheaf of yellow iris near the window. Further off, in the last twilight, a gang of enormous poppies balanced and flapped their gold-scarlet, which even the darkness could not quite put out.

"We ought to be feeling very sad," she said after a while.

"Why?" he asked.

"Well—isn't it Kate's last night?" she said, slightly mocking.

"She's a tartar, Kate," he said.

"Oh, she's too rude, she is really! The way she criticises the things you do, and her insolence—"

"The things *I* do?" he asked.

"Oh no, you can't do anything wrong. It's the things *I* do." Mrs Thomas sounded very much incensed.

"Poor Kate, she'll have to lower her key," said Severn.

"Indeed she will, and a good thing too."

There was silence again.

"It's lightning," he said at last.

"Where?" she asked, with a suddenness that surprised him. She turned, met his eyes for a second. He sunk his head abashed.

"Over there in the north east," he said, keeping his face from her. She watched his hand rather than the sky.

"Oh," she said uninterestedly.

"The storm will wheel round, you'll see," he said.

"I hope it wheels the other way then."

"Well it won't. You don't like lightning, do you? You'd even have to take refuge with Kate if I weren't here."

She laughed quietly at his irony.

"No," she said, quite bitterly. "Mr Thomas* is never in when he's wanted."

"Well, as he won't be urgently required, we'll acquit him, eh?"

At that moment a white flash fell across the blackness.

They looked at each other laughing. The thunder came broken and hesitatingly.

"I think we'll shut the door," said Mrs Thomas, in normal, sufficiently distant tones. A strong woman, she locked and bolted the stiff fastenings easily. Severn pressed on the light. Mrs Thomas noticed the untidiness of the room. She rang, and presently Kate appeared.

"Will you clear baby's things away," she said, in the contemptuous tone of a hostile woman. Without answering, and in her superb unhastening way, Kate began to gather up the small garments. Both women were aware of the observant, white figure of the man standing on the hearth. Severn balanced with a fine, easy poise, and smiled to himself, exulting a little, to see the two women in this state of hostility. Kate moved about with bowed, defiant head. Severn watched her curiously: he could not understand her: and she was leaving tomorrow. When she had gone out of the room, he remained still standing, thinking. Something in his lithe, vigorous balance, so alert, and white, and independent, caused Mrs Thomas to glance at him from her sewing.

"I will let the blinds down," he said, becoming aware that he was attracting attention.

"Thank you," she replied conventionally.

He let the lattice blinds down, then flung himself into his chair.

Mrs Thomas sat at the table, near him, sewing. She was a good-looking woman, well made. She sat under the one light that was turned on. The lamp shade was of red silk lined with yellow. She sat in the warm-gold light. There was established between the two a peculiar silence, like suspense, almost painful to each of them, yet which neither would break. Severn listened to the snap of her needle, looked from the movement of her hand to the window, where the lightning beat and fluttered through the lattice. The thunder was as yet far off.

"Look," he said, "at the lightning."

Mrs Thomas started at the sound of his voice, and some of the colour went from her face. She turned to the window.

There between the cracks of the venetian blinds, came the white flare of lightning, then the dark. Several storms were in the sky. Scarcely had one sudden glare fluttered and palpitated out, than another covered the window with white. It dropped, and another flew up, beat like a moth for a moment, then vanished. Thunder met and overlapped, two battles were fought together in the sky.

Mrs Thomas went very pale. She tried not to look at the window, yet, when she felt the lightning blench the lamplight, she watched, and each time a flash leaped on the window, she shuddered. Severn, all unconsciously, was smiling with roused eyes.

"You don't like it?" he said at last, gently.

"Not much," she answered, and he laughed.

"Yet all the storms are a fair way off," he said. "Not one near enough to touch us,"

"No but," she replied, at last laying her hands in her lap, and turning to him, "it makes me feel worked up. You don't know how it makes me feel as if I couldn't contain myself."

She made a helpless gesture with her hand. He was watching her closely. She seemed to him pathetically helpless and bewildered: she was eight years older than he. He smiled in a strange, alert fashion, like a man who feels in jeopardy.

She bent over her work, stitching nervously. There was a silence in which neither of them could breathe freely.

Presently a bigger flash than usual whitened through the yellow lamplight. Both glanced at the window, then at each other. For a moment it was a look of greeting: then his eyes dilated to a smile, wide with recklessness. He felt her waver, lose her composure, become incoherent. Seeing the faint helplessness of coming tears, he felt his heart thud to a crisis. She hid her face at her sewing.

Severn sank in his chair, half suffocated by the beating of his heart. Yet, time after time, as the flashes came, they looked at each other, till in the end they both were panting, and afraid, not of the lightning but of themselves and of each other.

He was so much moved that he became conscious of his perturbation. "What the deuce is up?" he asked himself, wondering. At twenty-seven, he was quite chaste. Being highly civilised, he prized women for their intuition, and because of the delicacy with which he could transfer to them his thoughts and feelings, without cumbrous argument. From this to a state of passion he could only proceed by fine gradations, and such a procedure he had never begun. Now he was startled, astonished, perturbed, yet still scarcely conscious of his whereabouts. There was a pain in his chest that made him pant, and an involuntary tension in his arms, as if he must press someone to his breast. But the idea that this someone was Mrs Thomas would have shocked him too much had he formed it. His passion had run on subconsciously, till now it had come to such a pitch it must drag his conscious soul into allegiance. This, however, would probably never happen; he would not yield allegiance, and blind emotion, in this direction, could not carry him alone.

Towards eleven o'clock Mr Thomas came in.

"I wonder you come home at all," Severn heard Mrs Thomas say as her husband stepped indoors.

"I left the office at half past ten," the voice of Thomas replied, disagreeably.

"Oh, don't try to tell me that old tale," the woman answered contemptuously.

"I didn't try anything at all, Gertie," he replied with sarcasm. "Your question was answered."

Severn imagined him bowing with affected, magisterial dignity, and he smiled. Mr Thomas was something in the law.

Mrs Thomas left her husband in the hall, came and sat down

again at table, where she and Severn had just finished supper, both of them reading the while.

Thomas came in, flushed very red. He was of middle stature, a thickly built man of forty, good looking. But he had grown round-shouldered with thrusting forward his chin in order to look the aggressive, strong-jawed man. He *had* a good jaw: but his mouth was small and nervously pinched. His brown eyes were of the emotional, affectionate sort, lacking pride or any austerity.

He did not speak to Severn nor Severn to him. Although as a rule the two men were very friendly, there came these times when, for no reason whatever, they were sullenly hostile. Thomas sat down heavily, and reached his bottle of beer. His hands were thick, and in their movement, rudimentary. Severn watched the thick fingers grasp the drinking-glass as if it were a treacherous enemy.

"Have you *had* supper, Gertie?" he asked, in tones that sounded like an insult. He could not bear that these two should sit reading as if he did not exist.

"Yes," she replied, looking up at him in impatient surprise. "It's late enough." Then she buried herself again in her book. Severn ducked low and grinned. Thomas swallowed a mouthful of beer.

"I wish you could answer my questions, Gertie, without superfluous *de*-tail," he said nastily, thrusting out his chin at her as if cross-examining.

"Oh," she said indifferently, not looking up. "Wasn't my answer right, then."

"Quite—I thank you," he answered, bowing with great sarcasm. It was utterly lost on his wife.

"Hm-hm!" she murmured in abstraction, continuing to read.

Silence resumed. Severn was grinning to himself, chuckling.

"I *had* a compliment paid me tonight Gertie," said Thomas, quite amicably, after a while. He still ignored Severn.

"Hm-hm!" murmured his wife. This was a well-known beginning. Thomas valiantly struggled on with his courtship of his wife, swallowing his spleen.

"Councillor Jarndyce,* in full committee—are you listening, Gertie—?"

"Yes," she replied, looking up for a moment.

"You know Councillor Jarndyce's style," Thomas continued, in the tone of a man determined to be patient and affable: "—the Courteous Old English Gentleman——"

"Hm-hm!" replied Mrs Thomas.

"He was speaking in reply to——" Thomas gave innumerable wearisome details, which no one heeded . . .

"Then he bowed to me, then to the chairman.—'I am compelled to say, Mr Chairman, that we have *one* cause for congratulation: we are inestimably fortunate in *one* member of our staff: there is *one* point of which we can always be sure:—the point of *law*: and it is an important point, Mr Chairman."

"He bowed to the chairman, he bowed to me. And you should have heard the applause all round that Council Chamber—that great, horseshoe table; you don't know how impressive it is. And every face turned to me, and all round the board, 'Hear-Hear!'. You don't know what respect I command in *business*, Mrs Thomas."

"Then let it suffice you," said Mrs Thomas, calmly indifferent. Mr Thomas bit his bread and butter.

"The fat-head's had two drops of Scotch, so he's drawing on his imagination," thought Severn, chuckling deeply.

"I thought you said there was no meeting tonight," Mrs Thomas suddenly and innocently remarked after a while.

"There was a meeting *in camera*," replied her husband, drawing himself up with official dignity. His excessive and wounded dignity convulsed Severn; the lie disgusted Mrs Thomas in spite of herself.

Presently Thomas, always courting his wife and insultingly overlooking Severn, raised a point of politics, passed a lordly opinion very offensive to the young man. Severn had risen, stretched himself, and laid down his book. He was leaning on the mantel-piece in an indifferent manner, as if he scarcely noticed the two talkers. But hearing Thomas pronounce like a boor upon the Woman's Bill,* he roused himself, and coolly contradicted his landlord. Mrs Thomas shot a look of joy at the white-clad young man who lounged so scornfully on the hearth. Thomas cracked his knuckles one after another, and lowered his brown eyes, which were full of hate. After a sufficient pause, for his timidity was stronger than his impulse, he replied with a phrase that sounded final. Severn flipped the sense out of it with a few words. In the argument Severn, more cultured and far more nimble witted than his antagonist, who hauled up his answers with a lawyer's show of invincibility, but who had not any fineness of perception, merely spiked his opponent's pieces and smiled at him. Also the young man enjoyed himself by looking down scornfully, straight into the brown eyes of his senior all the time, so that Thomas writhed.

Mrs Thomas, meanwhile, took her husband's side against the women, without reserve. Severn was angry: he was scornfully angry with her. Mrs Thomas glanced at him from time to time, a little ecstasy lighting her fine blue eyes. The irony of her part was delicious to her. If she had sided with Severn, that young man would have pitied the forlorn man, and been gentle with him.

The battle of words had got quieter and more intense. Mrs Thomas made no move to check it. At last Severn was aware he and Thomas were both getting over heated. Thomas had doubled and dodged painfully, like a half frenzied rabbit that will not realise it is trapped. Finally his efforts had moved even his opponent's pity. Mrs Thomas was not pitiful. She scorned her husband's dexterity of argument, when his intellectual dishonesty was so evident to her. Severn uttered his last phrases, and would say no more. Then Thomas cracked his knuckles one after the other, turned aside consumed with morbid humiliation, and there was silence.

"I will go to bed," said Severn. He would have spoken some conciliatory words to his landlord; he lingered with that purpose: but he could not bring his throat to utter his purpose.

"Oh, before you go, do you mind, Mr Severn, helping Mr Thomas down with Kate's box. You may be gone before he's up in the morning, and the cab comes at ten. Do you mind?"

"Why should I?" replied Severn.

"Are you ready, Joe?" she asked her husband.

Thomas rose with the air of a man who represses himself and is determined to be patient.

"Where is it?" he asked.

"On the top landing. I'll tell Kate, and then we shan't frighten her. She has gone to bed."

Mrs Thomas was quite mistress of the situation: both men were humble before her. She led the way, with a candle, to the third floor. There on the little landing, outside the closed door, stood a large tin trunk. The three were silent because of the baby.

"Poor Kate," Severn thought. "It's a shame to kick her out into the world, and all for nothing." He felt an impulse of hate towards womankind.

"Shall I go first, Mr Severn?" asked Thomas.

It was surprising how friendly the two men were, as soon as they had something to do together, or when Mrs Thomas was absent. Then they were comrades, Thomas, the elder, the thick-set, playing the protector's part, though always deferential to the younger, whimsical man.

"I had better go first," said Thomas kindly. "And if you put this round the handle, it won't cut your fingers."

He offered the young man a little, flexible book from his pocket. Severn had such small, fine hands, that Thomas pitied them.

Severn raised one end of the trunk. Leaning back, and flashing a smile to Mrs Thomas, who stood with the candle, he whispered: "Kate's got a lot more impedimenta than I have."

"I know it's heavy," laughed Mrs Thomas.

Thomas, waiting at the brink of the stairs, saw the young man tilting his bare throat towards the smiling woman, and whispering words which pleased her.

"At your pleasure Sir," he said in his most grating and official tones.

"Sorry," Severn flung out scornfully.

The elder man retreated very cautiously, stiffly lowering himelf down one stair, looking anxiously behind.

"Are you holding the light for *me*, Gertie," he snapped sarcastically, when he had managed one stair. She lifted the candle with a swoop. He was in a bustle and a funk. Severn, always indifferent, smiled slightly, and lowered the box with negligent ease of movement. As a matter of fact, three-quarters of the heavy weight pressed on Thomas. Mrs Thomas watched the two figures from above.

"If I slip now," thought Severn, as he noticed the anxious red face of his landlord, "I should squash him like a shrimp," and he laughed to himself.

"Don't come yet," he called softly to Mrs Thomas, whom he heard following. "If you slip, your husband's bottommost under the smash. 'Beware the fearful avalanche.'"*

He laughed, and Mrs Thomas gave a little chuckle. Thomas, very red and flustered, glanced irritably back at them, but said nothing.

Near the bottom of the staircase there was a twist in the stairs. Severn was feeling particularly reckless. When he came to the turn he chuckled to himself, feeling his house-slippers unsafe on the narrowed, triangular stairs. He loved a risk above all things, and a subconscious instinct made the risk doubly sweet when his rival was under the box. Though Severn would not knowingly have hurt a hair of his landlord's head.

When Thomas was beginning to sweat with relief, being only one step from the landing, Severn did slip, quite accidentally. The great box crashed as if in pain, Severn glissaded down the stairs, Thomas was flung backwards across the landing, and his head went thud against the banister post. Severn, seeing no great harm done, was struggling* to his feet, laughing and saying: "I'm awfully sorry—" when Thomas got up. The elder man was infuriated like a bull. He saw the laughing face of Severn and he went mad. His brown eyes flared.

"You sod,* you did it on purpose!" he shouted, and straightway he fetched the young man two heavy blows, upon the jaw and ear. Thomas, a footballer and boxer in his youth, had been brought up among the roughs of Swansea; Severn in a religious college in France. The young man had never been struck in the face before. He instantly went white and mad with rage. Thomas stood on guard, fists up. But on the small, lumbered landing there was no room for fight. Moreover Severn had no instinct of fisticuffs. With open, stiff fingers, the young man sprang on his adversary. In spite of the blows he received, but did not feel, he flung himself again forward, and then, catching Thomas' collar, brought him down with a crash. Instantly his exquisite hands were dug in the other's thick throat, the linen collar having been torn open. Thomas fought madly, with blind, brute strength. But the other lay wrapped on him like a white steel, his rare intelligence concentrated, not scattered: concentrated on strangling Thomas swiftly. He pressed forward, forcing his landlord's head over the edge of the next flight of stairs. Thomas, stout and full-blooded, lost every trace of self possession: he struggled like an animal at slaughter. The blood came out of his nose over his face, he made horrid choking sounds as he struggled.

Suddenly Severn felt his face turned between two hands. With a shock of real agony, his met* the eyes of Kate. She bent forward, she captured his eyes.

"What do you think you're doing?" she cried in frenzy of indignation. She leaned over him in her nightdress, her two black plaits hanging perpendicular. He hid his face, and took his hands away. As he kneeled to rise, he glanced up the stairs. Mrs Thomas stood against the banisters, motionless in a trance of horror and remorse. He saw the remorse plainly. Severn turned away his face, and was wild with shame.

He saw his landlord kneeling, his hands at his throat, choking, rattling, and gasping. He put his arms round the heavy man, and raised him, saying tenderly:

"Let me help you up."

He had got Thomas up against the wall, when the choked man began to slide down again in collapse, gasping all the time pitifully.

"No, stand up, you're best standing up," commanded Severn sharply, rearing his landlord up again. Thomas managed to obey, stupidly. His nose still bled, he still held his throat and gasped with a crowing sound. But his breathing was getting deeper.

"Water, Kate,—and sponge—cold," said Severn.

Kate was back in an instant. The young man bathed his landlord's face and temples and throat. The bleeding ceased directly, the stout man's breathing became a series of irregular, jerky gasps, like a child that has been sobbing hard. At last he took a long breath, and his breast settled into its regular stroke, with little, fluttering interruptions. Still holding his hand to his throat, he looked up with dazed, piteous brown eyes, mutely wretched and appealing. He moved his tongue as if to try it, put back his head a little and moved the muscles of his throat. Then he replaced his hands on the place that ached.

Severn was grief-stricken: he would willingly, at that moment, have given his right hand for the man he had hurt.

Mrs Thomas, meanwhile, stood on the stairs watching. For a long time, she dared not move, knowing she would sink down. She watched. One of the crises of her life was passing. Full of remorse, she passed over into the bitter land of repentance. She must no longer allow herself to hope for anything for herself. The rest of her life must be spent in self abnegation: she must seek for no sympathy, must ask for no grace in love, no grace and harmony in living. Henceforward, as far as her own desires went, she was dead. She took a fierce joy in the anguish of it.

"Do you feel better?" Severn asked of the sick man. Thomas looked at the questioner with tragic brown eyes, in which was no anger, only mute self-pity. He did not answer, but looked like a wounded animal, very pitiable. Mrs Thomas quickly repressed an impulse of impatient scorn, replacing it with a numb, abstract sense of duty, lofty and cold.

"Come," said Severn, full of pity and gentle as a woman. "Let me help you to bed."

Thomas, leaning heavily on the young man, whose white garments were dabbed with blood and water, stumbled forlornly into his room. There Severn unlaced his boots and got off the remnant of his collar. At this point Mrs Thomas came in. She had taken her part: she was weeping also.

"Thank you, Mr Severn," she said coldly. Severn, dismissed, slunk out of the room. She went up to her husband, took his pathetic head upon her bosom, and pressed it there. As Severn went downstairs, he heard the few sobs of the husband, among the quick sniffing of the wife's tears. And he saw Kate, who had stood on the stairs to see all went well, climb up to her room with cold, calm face.

He locked up the house, put everything in order. Then he heated some water to bathe his face, which was swelling painfully. Having finished his fomentation, he sat thinking bitterly, with a good deal of shame.

As he sat, Mrs Thomas came down for something. Her bearing was cold and hostile. She glanced round to see all was safe. Then:

"You will put out the light when you go to bed, Mr Severn," she said, more formally than a landlady at the sea-side would speak. He was insulted: any ordinary being would turn off the light on retiring. Moreover, almost every night it was he who locked up the house, and came last to bed.

"I will, Mrs Thomas," he answered. He bowed, his eyes flickering with irony, because he knew his face was swollen.

She returned again after having reached the landing.

"Perhaps you wouldn't mind helping *me* down with the box," she said, quietly and coldly. He did not reply, as he would have done an hour before, that he certainly should not help her, because it was a man's job and she must not do it. Now, he rose, bowed, and went upstairs with her. Taking the greater part of the weight, he came quickly downstairs with the load.

"Thank you—it is very good of you. Goodnight," said Mrs Thomas, and she retired.

In the morning Severn rose late. His face was considerably swollen. He went in his dressing gown across to Thomas' room. The other man lay in bed looking much the same as ever, but mournful in aspect, though pleased within himself at being coddled.

"How are you this morning?" Severn asked.

Thomas smiled, looked, almost with tenderness, up at his friend: "Oh, I'm all right, thanks," he replied.

He looked at the other's swollen and bruised cheek, then again, affectionately, into Severn's eyes.

"I'm sorry"—with a glance of indication—"for that," he said simply. Severn smiled with his eyes, in his own, winsome manner.

"I didn't know we were such essential brutes," he said. "I thought I was so civilised …"

Again he smiled, with a wry, stiff mouth. Thomas gave a deprecating little grunt of a laugh.

"Oh I don't know," he said. "It shows a man's got some fight in him."

He looked up in the other's face appealingly. Severn smiled, with a touch of bitterness. The two men grasped hands.

To the end of their acquaintance, Severn and Thomas were close friends, with a gentleness in their bearing one towards the other. On the other hand, Mrs Thomas was only polite and formal with Severn, treating him as if he were a stranger.

Kate, her fate disposed of by her 'betters', passed out of their three lives.

# Love Among the Haystacks*

## 1.

The two large fields lay on a hillside facing south. Being newly cleared of hay, they were golden green, and they shone almost blindingly in the sunlight. Across the hill, half way up, ran a high hedge, that flung its black shadow finely across the molten glow of the sward. The stack was being built just above the hedge. It was of great size, massive, but so silvery and delicately bright in tone that it seemed not to have weight. It rose dishevelled and radiant among the steady, golden-green glare of the field. A little further back was another, finished stack.

The empty wagon was just passing through the gap in the hedge. From the far-off corner of the bottom field, where the sward was still striped grey with winrows,* the loaded wagon launched forward, to climb the hill to the stack. The white dots of the hay-makers showed distinctly among the hay.

The two brothers* were having a moment's rest, waiting for the load to come up. They stood wiping their brows with their arms, sighing from the heat and the labor of placing the last load. The stack they rode was high, lifting them up above the hedge tops, and very broad, a great slightly hollowed vessel into which the sunlight poured, in which the hot sweet scent of hay was suffocating. Small and inefficacious the brothers looked, half submerged in the loose, great trough, lifted high up as if on an altar reared to the sun.

Maurice, the younger brother, was a handsome young fellow of twenty one, careless and debonnair, and full of vigour. His grey eyes, as he taunted his brother, were bright and baffled with a strong emotion. His swarthy face had the same peculiar smile, expectant and glad and nervous, of a young man roused for the first time in passion.

"Tha sees," he said, as he leaned on the pommel of his fork, "tha thowt as tha 'd done me one, didna ter?"* He smiled as he spoke, then fell again into his pleasant torment of musing.

"I thought nowt—tha knows so much," retorted Geoffrey, with the touch of a sneer. His brother had the better of him. Geoffrey was a very heavy, hulking fellow, a year older than Maurice. His blue eyes were unsteady, they glanced away quickly; his mouth was morbidly sensitive. One felt him wince away, through the whole of his great body. His inflamed self-consciousness was a disease in him.

"Ah but though, I know tha did," mocked Maurice. "Tha went slinkin' off—" Geoffrey winced convulsively—"thinking as that wor the last night as any of us 'ud ha'e ter stop* here, an' so tha'd leave me to sleep out, though it wor thy turn——"

He smiled to himself, thinking of the result of Geoffrey's ruse.

"I didna go slinkin' off, neither," retorted Geoffrey, in his heavy, clumsy manner, wincing at the phrase. "Didna my feyther* send me to fetch some coal—"

"Oh yes, oh yes—we know all about it. But tha sees what tha missed, my lad."

Maurice, chuckling, threw himself on his back in the bed of hay. There was absolutely nothing in his world, then, except the shallow ramparts of the stack, and the blazing sky. He clenched his fists tight, threw his arms across his face, and braced his muscles again. He was evidently very much moved, so acutely that it was hardly pleasant, though he still smiled. Geoffrey, standing behind him, could just see his red mouth, with the young moustache like black fur, curling back and showing the teeth in a smile. The elder brother leaned his chin on the pommel of his fork, looking out across the country.

Far away was the faint blue heap of Nottingham. Between, the country lay under a haze of heat, with here and there a flag of colliery smoke waving. But near at hand, at the foot of the hill, across the deep-hedged highroad, was only the silence of the old church and the castle farm, among their trees. The large view only made Geoffrey more sick. He looked away, to the wagons crossing the field below him, the empty cart like a big insect moving down hill, the load coming up, rocking like a ship, the brown head of the horse ducking, the brown knees lifted and planted strenuously. Geoffrey wished it would be quick.

"Tha didna think—"

Geoffrey started, coiled within himself, and looked down at the handsome lips moving in speech below the brown arms of his brother.

"Tha didna think *'er* 'd be theer* wi' me—or tha wouldna ha' left me to it," Maurice said, ending with a little laugh of excited memory. Geoffrey flushed with hate, and had an impulse to set his foot on that moving, taunting mouth, which was there below him. There was silence for a time, then, in a peculiar tone of delight, Maurice's voice came again, spelling out the words, as it were:

"Ich bin klein, mein Herz ist rein
Ist niemand d'rin als Christ allein."*

Maurice chuckled, then, convulsed at a twinge of recollection, keen as pain, he twisted over, pressed himself into the hay.

"Can thee thy prayers in German,"* came his muffled voice.

"I non want," growled Geoffrey.

Maurice chuckled. His face was quite hidden, and in the dark he was going over again his last night's experiences.

"What about kissing 'er under th' ear, Sorry," he said, in a curious, uneasy tone. He writhed, still startled and inflamed by his first contact with love.

Geoffrey's heart swelled within him, and things went dark. He could not see the landscape.

"An' there's just a nice two-handful of her bosom,"* came the low, provocative tones of Maurice, who seemed to be talking to himself.

The two brothers were both fiercely shy of women, and until this hay harvest, the whole feminine sex had been represented by their mother, in* presence of any other women they were dumb louts. Moreover, brought up by a proud mother, a stranger in the country, they held the common girls as beneath them, because beneath their mother, who spoke pure English, and was very quiet. Loud-mouthed and broad tongued, the common girls were. So the two* young men had grown up virgin but tormented.

Now again Maurice had the start of Geoffrey, and the elder brother was deeply mortified. There was a danger of his sinking into a morbid* state, from sheer lack of living, lack of interest. The foreign governess at the vicarage,* whose garden lay beside the top field, had talked to the lads through the hedge, and had fascinated them. There was a great elder bush, with its broad creamy flowers crumbling onto the garden path, and into the field. Geoffrey never smelled elder-flower without starting and wincing, thinking of the strange foreign voice that had so startled him as he mowed out with the scythe in the hedge bottom. A baby had run through the gap, and the Fräulein, calling in German, had come brushing down the flowers in pursuit. She had started so on seeing a man standing there in the shade, that for a moment she could not move: and then she had blundered onto the rake which was lying by his side. Geoffrey, forgetting she was a woman when he saw her pitch forward, had picked her up carefully, asking: "Have you hurt you?"

Then she had broken into a laugh, and answered in German, showing him her arms, and knitting her brows. She was nettled* rather badly.

"You want a dock leaf," he said.

She frowned in a puzzled fashion.

"A do-ock leaf?" she repeated.

He had rubbed her arms with the green leaf.

And now, she had taken to Maurice. She had seemed to prefer himself at first. Now she had sat with Maurice in the moonlight, and had let him kiss her. Geoffrey sullenly suffered, making no fight.

Unconsciously, he was looking at the vicarage garden. There she was, in a golden brown dress. He took off his hat, and held up his right hand in greeting to her. She, a small golden figure, waved her hand negligently from among the potato rows. He remained arrested in the same posture, his hat in his left hand, his right arm upraised, thinking. He could tell by the negligence of her greeting that she was waiting for Maurice. What did she think of himself? Why wouldn't she have him?

Hearing the voice of the wagoner leading the load, Maurice rose. Geoffrey still stood in the same way, but his face was sullen, and his upraised hand was slack with brooding. Maurice faced up-hill. His eyes lit up and he laughed. Geoffrey dropped his own arm, watching.

"Lad!" chuckled Maurice. "I non knowed 'er wor there." He waved his hand clumsily. In these matters Geoffrey did better. The elder brother watched the girl. She ran to the end of the path, behind the bushes, so that she was screened from the house. Then she waved her handkerchief wildly. Maurice did not notice the manœuvre. There was the cry of a child. The girl's figure vanished, re-appeared holding a white childish bundle, and came down the path. There she put down her charge, sped up-hill to a great ash-tree, climbed quickly to a large horizontal bar that formed the fence there, and, standing poised, blew kisses with both her hands, in a foreign fashion that excited the brothers. Maurice laughed aloud, as he waved his red handkerchief.

"Well, what's the danger?" shouted a mocking voice from below. Maurice collapsed, blushing furiously.

"Nowt!" he called.

There was a hearty laugh from below.

The load rode up, sheered with a hiss against the stack, then sank back upon the scotches.* The brothers ploughed across the mass of hay, taking the forks. Presently a big, burly man, red and glistening, climbed to the top of the load. Then he turned round, scrutinised the hillside from under his shaggy brows. He caught sight of the girl under the ash-tree.

"Oh that's who it is," he laughed. "I thought it was some such bird, but I couldn't see her."

The father laughed in a hearty, chaffing way, then began to teem* the load. Geoffrey, on the stack above, received his great forkfuls, and swung them over to Maurice, who took them, placed them, building the stack. In the intense sunlight, the three worked in silence, knit together in a brief passion of work. The father stirred slowly for a moment, getting the hay from under his feet. Geoffrey waited, the blue tines of his fork glittering* in expectation: the mass rose, his fork swung beneath it, there was a light clash of blades, then the hay was swept onto the stack, caught by Maurice, who placed it judiciously. One after another, the shoulders of the three men bowed and braced themselves. All wore light blue, bleached shirts, that stuck close to their backs. The father moved mechanically, his thick, rounded shoulders bending and lifting dully; he worked monotonously. Geoffrey flung away his strength. His massive shoulders swept and flung the hay extravagantly.

"Dost want to knock me ower?" asked Maurice angrily. He had to brace himself against the impact. The three men worked intensely, as if some will urged them. Maurice was light and swift at the work, but he had to use his judgment. Also, when he had to place the hay along the far ends, he had some distance to carry it. So he was too slow for Geoffrey. Ordinarily, the elder would have placed the hay as far as possible where his brother wanted it. Now, however, he pitched his forkfuls into the middle of the stack. Maurice strode swiftly and handsomely across the bed, but the work was too much for him. The other two men, clenched in their receive and deliver, kept up a high pitch of labor. Geoffrey still flung the hay at random. Maurice was perspiring heavily with heat and exertion, and was getting worried. Now and again, Geoffrey wiped his arm across his brow, mechanically, like an animal. Then he glanced with satisfaction at Maurice's moiled condition, and caught the next forkful.

"Wheer dost think thou'rt hollin' it,* fool?" panted Maurice, as his brother flung a forkful out of reach.

"Wheer I'n a mind," answered Geoffrey.

Maurice toiled on, now very angry. He felt the sweat trickling down his body: drops fell into his long black lashes, blinding him, so that he had to stop and angrily dash his eyes clear. The veins stood out in his swarthy neck. He felt he would burst, or drop, if the work did not soon slacken off. He heard his father's fork dully scrape the cart-bottom.

"There, the last," the father panted. Geoffrey tossed the last light lot at random, took off his hat, and, steaming in the sunshine as he wiped himself, stood complacently watching Maurice struggle with clearing the bed.

"Don't you think you've got your bottom corner a bit far out," came the father's voice from below. "You'd better be drawing in* now, hadn't you."

"I thought you said next load," Maurice called, sulkily.

"Ay! All right. But isn't this bottom corner—?"

Maurice, impatient, took no notice.

Geoffrey strode over the stack, and stuck his fork in the offending corner.

"What—here . . . ?" he bawled in his great voice.

"Ay—isn't it a bit loose?" came the irritating voice.

Geoffrey pushed his fork in the jutting corner, and, leaning his weight on the handle, shoved. He thought it shook. He thrust again with all his power. The mass swayed.

"What art up to, tha fool!" cried Maurice, in a high voice.

"Mind who tha 'rt callin' a fool," said Geoffrey, and he prepared to push again. Maurice sprang across, elbowed his brother aside. On the yielding, swaying bed of hay, Geoffrey lost his foot hold, and fell grovelling. Maurice tried the corner.

"It's solid enough," he shouted angrily.

"Ay—all right," came the conciliatory voice of the father—"you do get a bit of rest now there's such a long way to cart it," he added reflectively.

Geoffrey had got to his feet.

"Tha 'll mind who tha 'rt nudging, I can tell thee," he threatened heavily; adding, as Maurice continued to work, "An' tha non ca's* him a fool again, dost hear?"

"Not till next time," sneered Maurice.

As he worked silently round the stack, he neared where his brother stood like a sullen statue, leaning on his fork-handle, looking out over the countryside. Maurice's heart quickened in its beat. He worked forward, until a point of his fork caught in the leather of Geoffrey's boot, and the metal rang sharply.

"Are ter going to* shift thysen?" asked Maurice threateningly. There was no reply from the great block. Maurice lifted his upper lip like a dog. Then he put out his elbow, and tried to push his brother into the stack, clear of his way.

"Who are ter shovin'?" came the deep, dangerous voice.

"Thaïgh,"* replied Maurice, with a sneer.

And straightway the two brothers set themselves against each other, like opposing bulls, Maurice trying his hardest to shift Geoffrey from his footing, Geoffrey leaning all his weight in resistance. Maurice, insecure in his footing, staggered a little, and Geoffrey's weight followed him. He went slithering over the edge of the stack.

Geoffrey turned white to the lips, and remained standing, listening. He heard the fall. Then a flush of darkness came over him, and he remained standing only because he was planted. He had not strength to move. He could hear no sound from below, was only faintly aware of a sharp shriek from a long way off. He listened again. Then he filled with sudden panic.

"Feyther!" he roared, in his tremendous voice:

"Feyther! Feyther!"

The valley re-echoed with the sound. Small cattle on the hill-side looked up. Men's figures came running from the bottom field, and much nearer, a woman's figure was racing across the upper field. Geoffrey waited in terrible suspense.

"Ah-h!" he heard the strange, wild voice of the girl cry out. "Ah-h!"—and then some foreign wailing speech. Then "Ah-h!—Are you dea-ed!"

He stood sullenly erect on the stack, not daring to go down, longing to hide in the hay, but too sullen to stoop out of sight. He heard his oldest brother* come up, panting:

"Whatever's amiss!" and then the laborer, and then his father.

"What *ever* have you been doing?" he heard his father ask, while yet he had not come round the corner of the stack. And then, in a low, bitter tone:

"Ehe, he's done for! I'd no business to ha' put it all on that stack."

There was a moment or two of silence, then the voice of Henry, the eldest brother, said crisply:

"He's not dead—he's coming round."

Geoffrey heard, but was not glad. He had as lief Maurice were dead. At least that would be final: better than meeting his brother's charges, and of seeing his mother pass to the sick-room. If Maurice was killed, he himself would not explain, no, not a word, and they could hang him if they liked. If Maurice were only hurt, then everybody would know, and Geoffrey could never lift his face again. What added torture, to pass along, everybody knowing. He wanted something that he could stand back to, something definite, if it were only the knowledge that he had killed his brother. He *must* have something firm to back up to, or he would go mad. He was so lonely, he who above all needed the support of sympathy.

"No, he's commin' to, I tell you he is," said the laborer.

"He's not dea-ed, he's not dea-ed," came the passionate, strange sing-song of the foreign girl. "He's not dead—no-o."

"He wants some brandy—look at the colour of his lips," said the crisp, cold voice of Henry. "Can you fetch some?"

"Wha-at?—Fetch—?." Fräulein did not understand.

"Brandy," said Henry, very distinct.

"Brrandy!" she re-echoed.

"You go, Bill,"* groaned the father.

"Ay, I'll go," replied Bill, and he ran across the field.

Maurice was not dead, nor going to die. This Geoffrey now realised. He was glad after all that the extreme penalty was revoked. But he hated to think of himself going on—. He would *always* shrink now. He had hoped and hoped for the time when he would be careless, bold as Maurice, when he would not wince and shrink. Now he would always be the same, coiling up in himself like a tortoise with no shell.

"Ah-h! He's getting better!" came the wild voice of the Fräulein, and she began to cry, a strange sound, that startled the men, made the animal bristle within them. Geoffrey shuddered as he heard, between her sobbing, the impatient moaning of his brother, as the breath came back.

The laborer returned at a run, followed by the vicar.* After the brandy, Maurice made more moaning hiccuping noise. Geoffrey listened in torture. He heard the vicar asking for explanations. All the muted, anxious voices replied in brief phrases.

"It was that other," cried the Fräulein. "He knocked him over—Ha!"

She was shrill and vindictive.

"I don't think so," said the father, to the vicar, in a quite audible but private tone, speaking as if the Fräulein did not understand his English.

The vicar addressed his children's governess in bad German. She replied in a torrent which he would not confess was too much for him. Maurice was making little moaning, sighing noises.

"Where's your pain, boy, eh?," the father asked, pathetically.

"Leave him alone a bit," came the cool voice of Henry. "He's winded, if no more."

"You'd better see that no bones are broken," said the anxious vicar.

"It wor a blessing as he should a dropped on that heap of hay just there," said the laborer. "If he'd happened to ha' catched hisself on this nog o' wood 'e wouldna ha' stood much chance."

Geoffrey wondered when he would have courage to venture down. He had wild notions of pitching himself headforemost from the stack: if he could only extinguish himself, he would be safe. Quite frantically, he longed not-to-be. The idea of going through life thus coiled up within himself in morbid self-consciousness, always lonely, surly, and a misery, was enough to make him cry out.—What would they all think when they knew he had knocked Maurice off that high stack.

They were talking to Maurice down below. The lad had recovered in great measure, and was able to answer faintly.

"Whatever was you doin'?" the father asked gently. "Was you playing about with our Geoffrey?—Ay, and where is he?"

Geoffrey's heart stood still.

"I dunno," said Henry, in a curious, ironic tone.

"Go an' have a look," pleaded the father, infinitely relieved over one son, anxious now concerning the other. Geoffrey could not bear that his eldest brother should climb up and question him in his high-pitched drawl of curiosity. The culprit doggedly set his feet on the ladder. His nailed boots slipped a rung.

"Mind yourself," shouted the overwrought father.

Geoffrey stood like a criminal at the foot of the ladder, glancing furtively at the group. Maurice was lying, pale and slightly convulsed, upon a heap of hay. The Fräulein was kneeling beside his head.

The vicar had the lad's shirt full open down the breast, and was feeling for broken ribs. The father kneeled on the other side, the laborer and Henry stood aside.

"I can't find anything broken," said the vicar, and he sounded slightly disappointed.

"There's nowt broken to find," murmured Maurice, smiling.

The father started. "Eh?" he said, "Eh?," and he bent over the invalid.

"I say it's not hurt me," repeated Maurice.

"What were you doing?" asked the cold, ironic voice of Henry. Geoffrey turned his head away: he had not yet raised his face.

"Nowt as I know on,"* he muttered in a surly tone.

"Why!" cried Fräulein in reproachful tone. "I see him—knock him over!" She made a fierce gesture with her elbow. Henry curled his long moustache sardonically.

"Nay lass, niver," smiled the wan Maurice. "He was fur enough away from me when I slipped."

"Oh ah!" cried the Fräulein, not understanding.

"Yi," smiled Maurice indulgently.

"I think you're mistaken," said the father, rather pathetically, smiling at the girl as if she were 'wanting'.*

"Oh no," she cried. "I *see* him."

"Nay lass," smiled Maurice quietly.

She was a Pole, named Paula Jablonowsky:* young, only twenty years old, swift and light as a wild cat, with a strange, wild-cat way of grinning. Her hair was blonde and full of life, all crisped into many tendrils with vitality, shaking round her face. Her fine blue eyes were peculiarly lidded, and she seemed to look piercingly, then languorously like a wild cat. She had somewhat Slavonic cheekbones, and was very much freckled. It was evident that the vicar, a pale, rather cold man, hated her.

Maurice lay pale and smiling in her lap, whilst she cleaved to him like a mate. One felt instinctively that they were mated. She was ready at any minute to fight with ferocity in his defence, now he was hurt. Her looks at Geoffrey were full of fierceness. She bowed over Maurice and caressed him with her foreign-sounding English.

"You say what you lai-ike," she laughed, giving him lordship over her.

"Hadn't you better be going and looking what has become of Marjery?," asked the vicar in tones of reprimand.

"She is with her mother—I heared her. I will go in a whai-ile," smiled the girl, coolly.

"Do you feel as if you could stand?" asked the father, still anxiously.

"Ay, in a bit," smiled Maurice.

"You want to get up?" caressed the girl, bowing over him, till her face was not far from his.

"I'm in no hurry," he replied, smiling brilliantly.

This accident had given him quite a strange new ease, an authority. He felt extraordinarily glad. New power had come to him all at once.

"You in no hurry," she repeated, gathering the meaning. She smiled tenderly: she was in his service.

"She leaves us in another month—Mrs Inwood could stand no more of her," apologised the vicar quietly to the father.

"Why, is she——?"

"Like a wild thing—disobedient and insolent."

"Ha!"

The father sounded abstract.

"No more foreign governesses for me."

Maurice stirred, looked up at the girl.

"You stand up?" she asked brightly. "You well?"

He laughed again, showing his teeth winsomely. She lifted his head, sprung to her feet, her hands still holding his head, then she took him under the arm-pits and had him on his feet before anyone could help. He was much taller than she. He grasped her strong shoulders heavily, leaned against her, and, feeling her round, firm breast doubled up against his side, he smiled, catching his breath.

"You see I'm all right," he gasped. "I was only winded."

"You all raïght?," she cried, in great glee.

"Yes, I am."

He walked a few steps after a moment.

"There's nowt ails me, father," he laughed.

"Quite well, you?" she cried in a pleading tone. He laughed outright, looked down at her, touching her cheek with his fingers.

"That's it—if tha likes."

"If I lai-ike!" she repeated, radiant.

"She's going at the end of three weeks," said the vicar consolingly to the farmer.

2.

While they were talking, they heard the far-off hooting of a pit.

"There goes th' loose 'a,"* said Henry, coldly. "We're *not* going to get that corner up today."

The father looked round anxiously.

"Now Maurice, are you sure you're all right?" he asked.

"Yes, I'm all right. Haven't I told you?"

"Then you sit down there, and in a bit you can be getting dinner out. Henry, you go on the stack. Wheer's Jim?—Oh, he's minding the horses. Bill, and you Geoffrey, you can pick* while Jim loads."

Maurice sat down under the wych elm to recover. The Fräulein had fled back. He made up his mind to ask her to marry him. He had got fifty pounds of his own, and his mother would help him. For a long time he sat musing, thinking what he would do. Then, from the float* he fetched a big basket covered with a cloth, and spread the dinner. There was an immense rabbit pie, a dish of cold potatoes, much bread, a great piece of cheese, and a solid rice pudding.

These two fields were four miles from the home farm. But they had been in the hands of the Wookeys for several generations, therefore the father kept them on, and everyone looked forward to the hay harvest at Greasley: it was a kind of picnic. They brought dinner and tea in the milk-float, which the father drove over in the morning. The lads and the laborers cycled. Off and on, the harvest lasted a fortnight. As the highroad from Alfreton to Nottingham ran at the foot of the fields, some one usually slept in the hay under the shed to guard the tools. The sons took it in turns. They did not care for it much, and were for that reason anxious to finish the harvest on this day. But work went slack and disjointed after Maurice's accident.

When the load was teemed, they gathered round the white cloth, which was spread under a tree between the hedge and the stack, and, sitting on the ground, ate their meal. Mrs Wookey sent always a clean cloth, and knives and forks and plates for everybody. Mr Wookey was always rather proud of this spread, everything was so proper.

"There now," he said, sitting down jovially. "Doesn't this look nice now—Eh?"

They all sat round the white spread, in the shadow of the tree and the stack, and looked out up the fields as they ate. From their shady coolness, the gold sward seemed liquid, molten with heat. The horse with the empty wagon wandered a few yards, then stood feeding. Everything was still as a trance. Now and again, the horse beween the shafts of the load that stood propped beside the stack, jingled his loose bit as he ate. The men ate and drank in silence, the father reading the newspaper, Maurice leaning back on a saddle, Henry reading the *Nation*,* the others eating busily.

Presently "Helloa! Er's 'ere again!" exclaimed Bill. All looked up. Paula was coming across the field carrying a plate.

"She's bringing something to tempt your appetite, Maurice," said the eldest brother ironically. Maurice was mid-way through a large wedge of rabbit pie, and some cold potatoes.

"Ay, bless me if she's not," laughed the father. "Put that away, Maurice, it's a shame to disappoint her."

Maurice looked round very shamefaced, not knowing what to do with his plate.

"Gi'e it over here," said Bill. "I'll polish him off."

"Bringing something for the invalid?" laughed the father to the Fräulein. "He's looking up nicely."

"I bring him some chicken, hm!" She nodded her head at Maurice childishly. He flushed and smiled.

"Tha doesna mean ter bust 'im," said Bill.

Everybody laughed aloud. The girl did not understand, so she laughed also. Maurice ate his portion very sheepishly.

The father pitied his son's shyness.

"Come here and sit by me," he said. "Eh, Fräulein! Is that what they call you?"

"I sit by you, father," she said innocently.

Henry threw his head back and laughed long and noiselessly.

She settled near to the big, handsome man.

"My name," she said, "is Paula Jablonowsky."

"Is what?" said the father, and the other men went into roars of laughter.

"Tell me again," said the father. "Your name—?"

"Paula."

"Paula? Oh—well, it's a rum sort of name, eh? His name—," he nodded at his son—

"Maurice—I know." She pronounced it sweetly, then laughed into the father's eyes. Maurice blushed to the roots of his hair.

They questioned her concerning her history, and made out that she came from Hanover, that her father was a shop-keeper, and that she had run away from home because she did not like her father. She had gone to Paris.

"Oh," said the father, now dubious. "And what did you do there?"

"In school—in a young ladies' school."

"Did you like it?"

"Oh no—no laïfe—no life!"

"What?"

"When we go out—two and two—all together—no more. Ah, no life, no life."

"Well, that's a winder!"* exclaimed the father. "No life in Paris! And have you found much life in England?"

"No—ah no. I don't like it." She made a grimace at the vicarage.

"How long have you been in England?"

"Chreestmas—so."

"And what will you do?"

"I will go to London, or to Paris. Ah, Paris!!—Or get married!" She laughed into the father's eyes.

The father laughed heartily.

"Get married, eh? And who to?"

"I don't know. I am going away."

"The country's too quiet for you?" asked the father.

"Too quiet—hm!" she nodded in assent.

"You wouldn't care for making butter and cheese?"

"Making butter—hm!" She turned to him with a glad, bright gesture. "—I like it."

"Oh," laughed the father, "you would, would you."

She nodded vehemently, with glowing eyes.

"She'd like anything in the shape of a change," said Henry judicially.

"I think she would," agreed the father. It did not occur to them that she fully understood what they said. She looked at them closely, then thought, with bowed head.

"Hullo!" exclaimed Henry, the alert. A tramp was slouching towards them through the gap. He was a very seedy, slinking fellow, with a tang of horsey braggadocio about him. Small, thin, and ferrety, with a week's red beard bristling on his pointed chin, he came slouching forward.

"Han yer got a bit of a job goin'?" he asked.

"A bit of a job," repeated the father. "Why, can't yer see as we've a'most done?"

"Ay—but I noticed you was a hand short, an' I thowt as 'appen you'd gie me half a day."

"What, are *you* any good in a hay close?" asked Henry, with a sneer.

The man stood slouching against the haystack. All the others were seated on the floor. He had an advantage.

"I could work aside any on yer," he bragged.

"Tha looks it," laughed Bill.

"And what's your regular trade?" asked the father.

"I'm a jockey by rights. But I did a bit o' dirty work for a boss o' mine, an' I was landed. '*E* got the benefit, *I* got kicked out. '*E* axed me—an' then 'e looked as if 'e'd never seed me."

"Did he though!" exclaimed the father sympathetically.

"'E did that!" asserted the man.

"But we've got nothing for you," said Henry coldly.

"What does the boss say?" asked the man, impudent.

"No, we've no work you can do," said the father. "You can have a bit o' something to eat, if you like."

"I should be glad of it," said the man.

He was given the chunk of rabbit pie that remained. This he ate greedily. There was something debased, parasitic about him, which disgusted Henry. The others regarded him as a curiosity.

"That was nice and tasty," said the tramp, with gusto.

"Do you want a piece of bread 'n cheese?" asked the father.

"It'll help to fill up," was the reply.

The man ate this more slowly. The company was embarrassed by his presence, and could not talk. All the men lit their pipes, the meal over.

"So you dunna want any help?," said the tramp at last.

"No—we can manage what bit there is to do."

"You don't happen to have a fill of bacca* to spare, do you?"

The father gave him a good pinch.

"You're all right here," he said, looking round. They resented this familiarity. However, he filled his clay pipe and smoked with the rest.

As they were sitting silent, another figure came through the gap in the hedge, and noiselessly approached. It was a woman. She was rather small, and finely made. Her face was small, very ruddy, and comely, save for the look of bitterness and aloofness that it wore. Her hair was drawn tightly back under a sailor hat. She gave an impression of cleanness, of precision and directness.

"Have you got some work?" she asked of her man. She ignored the rest. He tucked his tail between his legs.

"No, they haven't got no work for me. They've just gave me a draw of bacca."

He was a mean crawl* of a man.

"An' am I goin' to wait for you out there on the lane all day?"

"You nedn't if you don't like. You could go on."

"Well, are you coming?" she asked contemptuously.

He rose to his feet in a ricketty fashion.

"You nedn't be in such a mighty hurry," he said. "If you'd wait a bit you might get summat."

She glanced for the first time over the men. She was quite young, and would have been pretty, were she not so hard and callous-looking.

"Have you had your dinner?" asked the father.

She looked at him with a kind of anger, and turned away. Her face was so childish in its contours, contrasting strangely with her expression.

"Are you coming?" she said to the man.

"He's had his tuck-in. Have a bit, if *you* want it," coaxed the father.

"What have you had?" she flashed, to the man.

"He's had all what was left o' th' rabbit pie," said Geoffrey, in an indignant, mocking tone, "and a great hunk o' bread an' cheese."

"Well, it was gave me," said the man.

The young woman looked at Geoffrey, and he at her. There was a sort of kinship between them. Both were at odds with the world. Geoffrey smiled satirically. She was too grave, too deeply incensed even to smile.

"There's a cake here though—you can have a bit o' that," said Maurice blithely.

She eyed him with scorn.

Again she looked at Geoffrey. He seemed to understand her. She turned, and in silence departed. The man remained obstinately sucking at his pipe. Everybody looked at him with hostility.

"We'll be getting to work," said Henry, rising pulling off his coat. Paula got to her feet. She was a little bit confused by the presence of the tramp.

"I go," she said, smiling brilliantly. Maurice rose and followed her sheepishly.

"A good grind,* eh?" said the tramp, nodding after the Fräulein. The men only half understood him, but they hated him.

"Hadn't you better be getting off?," said Henry.

The man rose obediently. He was all slouching, parasitic insolence. Geoffrey loathed him, longed to exterminate him. He was exactly the worst foe of the hypersensitive; insolence without sensibility, preying on sensibility.

"Aren't you goin' to give me summat for her?—it's nowt she's had all day, to my knowin'. She'll 'appen eat it if I take it 'er—though she gets more than I've any knowledge of"—this with a lewd wink of jealous spite. "And then tries to keep a tight hand on me——" he sneered, taking the bread and cheese, and stuffing it in his pocket.

## 3.

Geoffrey worked sullenly all afternoon, and Maurice did the horse-raking.* It was exceedingly hot. So the day wore on, the atmosphere thickened, and the sunlight grew blurred. Geoffrey was picking with Bill—helping to load the wagons from the winrows. He was sulky, though extraordinarily relieved: Maurice would not tell. Since the quarrel neither brother had spoken to the other. But their silence was entirely amicable, almost affectionate. They had both been deeply moved, so much so that their ordinary intercourse was interrupted: but underneath, each felt a strong regard for the other. Maurice was peculiarly happy, his feeling of affection swimming over everything. But Geoffrey was still sullenly hostile to the most part of the world. He felt isolated. The free and easy intercommunication between the other workers left him distinctly alone. And he was a man who could not bear to stand alone, he was too much afraid of the vast confusion of life surrounding him, in which he was helpless. Geoffrey mistrusted himself with everybody.

The work went on slowly. It was unbearably hot, and everyone was disheartened.

"We s'll have getting-on-for another day of it," said the father at tea-time, as they sat under the tree.

"Quite a day," said Henry.

"Somebody 'll have to stop, then," said Geoffrey. "It 'ud better be me."

"Nay lad, I'll stop," said Maurice, and he hid his head in confusion.

"Stop again tonight!" exclaimed the father. "I'd rather you went home."

"Nay, I'm stoppin'," protested Maurice.

"He wants to do his courting," Henry enlightened them.

The father thought seriously about it.

"I don't know——" he mused, rather perturbed.

But Maurice stayed. Towards eight o'clock, after sundown, the men mounted their bicycles, the father put the horse in the float, and all departed. Maurice stood in the gap of the hedge and watched them go, the cart rolling and swinging downhill, over the grass stubble, the cyclists dipping swiftly like shadows, in front. All passed through the gate, there was a quick clatter of hoofs on the roadway under the lime trees, and they were gone. The young man was very much excited, almost afraid, at finding himself alone.

Darkness was rising from the valley. Already, up the steep hill the cart-lamps crept indecisively, and the cottage windows were lit. Everything looked strange to Maurice, as if he had not seen it before. Down the hedge a large lime tree teemed with scent* that seemed almost like a voice speaking. It startled him. He caught a breath of the over-sweet fragrance, then stood still, listening expectantly.

Up hill, a horse whinneyed. It was the young mare. The heavy horses went thundering across to the far hedge.

Maurice wondered what to do. He wandered round the deserted stacks restlessly. Heat came in wafts, in thick strands. The evening was a long time cooling. He thought he would go and wash himself. There was a trough of pure water in the hedge bottom. It was filled by a tiny spring that filtered over the brim of the trough down the lush hedge bottom of the lower field. All round the trough, in the upper field, the land was marshy, and there the meadow-sweet stood like clots of mist, very sickly smelling in the twilight. The night did not darken, for the moon was in the sky, so that as the tawny colour drew off the heavens they remained pallid with a dimmed moon. The purple bell-flowers in the hedge went black, the ragged robin turned its pink to a faded white, the meadow-sweet gathered light as if it were phosphorescent, and it made the air ache with scent.

Maurice kneeled on the slab of stone bathing his hands and arms, then his face. The water was deliciously cool. He had still an hour before Paula would come: she was not due till nine. So he decided to take his bath at night instead of waiting till morning. Was he not sticky, and was not Paula coming to talk to him? He was delighted the thought had occurred to him. As he soused his head in the trough, he wondered what the little creatures that lived in the velvetty silt at the bottom would think of the taste of soap. Laughing to himself, he squeezed his cloth into the water. He washed himself from head to foot, standing in the fresh, forsaken corner of the field, where no one could see him by daylight, so that now, in the veiled grey tinge of moonlight, he was no more noticeable than the crowded flowers. The night had on a new look: he never remembered to have seen the lustrous grey sheen of it before, nor to have noticed how vital the lights looked, like live folk inhabiting the silvery spaces. And the tall trees, wrapped obscurely in their mantles, would not have surprised him had they begun to move in converse. As he dried himself, he discovered little wanderings in the air, felt on his sides soft touches and caresses that were peculiarly delicious: sometimes they startled him, and he laughed as if he were not alone. The flowers, the meadow-sweet particularly haunted him. He reached to put his hand over their fleeciness. They touched his thighs. Laughing, he gathered them and dusted himself all over with their cream dust and fragrance. For a moment he hesitated in wonder at himself: but the subtle glow in the hoary and black night reassured him. Things never had looked so personal and full of beauty, he had never known the wonder in himself before.

At nine o'clock he was waiting under the elder bush, in a state of high trepidation, but feeling that he was worthy, having a sense of his own wonder. She was late. At a quarter past nine she came, flitting swiftly, in her own eager way.

"No she would *not* go to sleep," said Paula, with a world of wrath in her tone. He laughed bashfully. They wandered out into the dim, hillside field.

"I have sat—in that bedroom—for an hour, for hours," she cried indignantly. She took a deep breath: "Ah, breathe!" she smiled.

She was very intense, and full of energy.

"I want—" she was clumsy with the language—"I want—I should laïke—to run—there!" She pointed across the field.

"Let's run then," he said, curiously.

"Yes!"

And in an instant she was gone. He raced after her. For all he was so young and limber, he had difficulty in catching her. At first he could scarcely see her, though he could hear the rustle of her dress. She sped with astonishing fleetness. He overtook her, caught her by the arm, and they stood panting, facing one another with laughter.

"I could win," she asserted blithely.

"Tha couldna," he replied, with a peculiar, excited laugh. They walked on, rather breathless. In front of them suddenly appeared the dark shapes of the three feeding horses.

"We ride a horse?," she said.

"What, bareback?," he asked.

"You say?"—She did not understand.

"With no saddle?"

"No saddle—yes—no saddle."

"Coop lass!"* he said to the mare, and in a minute he had her by the forelock, and was leading her down to the stacks, where he put a halter on her. She was a big, strong mare. Maurice seated the Fräulein, clambered himself in front of the girl, using the wheel of the wagon as a mount, and together they trotted up-hill, she holding lightly round his waist. From the crest of the hill they looked round.

The sky was darkening with an awning of cloud. On the left the hill rose black and wooded, made cosy by a few lights from cottages along the highway. The hill spread to the right, and tufts of trees shut round. But in front was a great vista of night, a sprinkle of cottage candles, a twinkling cluster of lights, like an elfish fair in full swing, at the colliery, an encampment of light at a village, a red flare on the sky far off above an iron foundry, and in the farthest distance the dim breathing of town-lights. As they watched the night stretch far out, her arms tightened round his waist, and he pressed his elbows to his side, pressing her arms closer still. The horse moved restlessly. They clung to each other.

"Tha doesna want to go right away?" he asked the girl behind him.

"I stay with you," she answered softly, and he felt her crouching close against him. He laughed curiously. He was afraid to kiss her, though he was urged to do so. They remained still, on the restless horse, watching the small lights lead deep into the night, an infinite distance.

"I don't want to go," he said, in a tone half pleading.

She did not answer. The horse stirred restlessly.

"Let him run," cried Paula, "fast!"

She broke the spell, startled him into a little fury. He kicked the mare, hit her and away she plunged downhill. The girl clung tightly to the young man. They were riding bareback down a rough, steep hill. Maurice clung hard with hands and knees. Paula held him fast round the waist, leaning her head on his shoulders, and thrilling with excitement.

"We shall be off, we shall be off," he cried, laughing with excitement, but she only crouched behind, and pressed tight to him. The mare tore across the field. Maurice expected every moment to be flung onto the grass. He gripped with all the strength of his knees. Paula tucked herself behind him, and often wrenched him almost from his hold. Man and girl were taut with effort.

At last the mare came to a standstill, blowing. Paula slid off, and in an instant Maurice was beside her. They were both highly excited. Before he knew what he was doing, he had her in his arms, fast, and was kissing her, and laughing. They did not move for some time. Then, in silence, they walked towards the stacks.

It had grown quite dark, the night was thick with cloud. He walked with his arm round Paula's waist, she with her arm round him. They were near the stacks when Maurice felt a spot of rain.

"It's going to rain," he said.

"Rain!" she echoed, as if it were trivial.

"I s'll have to put the stack-cloth on," he said gravely. She did not understand.

When they got to the stacks, he went round to the shed, to return staggering in the darkness under the burden of the immense and heavy cloth. It had not been used once during the hay harvest.

"What are you going to do?" asked Paula, coming close to him in the darkness.

"Cover the top of the stack with it," he replied. "Put it over the stack, to keep the rain out."

"Ah!" she cried. "Up there!" He dropped his burden.

"Yes," he answered.

Fumblingly, he reared the long ladder up the side of the stack. He could not see the top. "I hope it's solid," he said, softly.

A few smart drops of rain sounded drumming on the cloth. They seemed like another presence. It was very dark indeed between the great buildings of hay. She looked up the black wall, and shrank to him.

"You carry it up there?" she asked.

"Yes," he answered.

"I help you?," she said.

And she did. They opened the cloth. He clambered first up the steep ladder, bearing the upper part, she followed closely, carrying her full share. They mounted the shaky ladder in silence, stealthily.

## 4.

As they climbed the stacks a light stopped at the gate on the highroad. It was Geoffrey, come to help his brother with the cloth. Afraid of his own intrusion, he wheeled his bicycle silently towards the shed. This was a corrugated iron erection, on the opposite side of the hedge from the stacks. Geoffrey let his light go in front of him, but there was no sign from the lovers. He thought he saw a shadow slinking away. The light of the bicycle lamp sheered* yellowly across the dark, catching a glint of rain-drops, a mist of darkness, shadow of leaves and strokes of long grass. Geoffrey entered the shed—no one was there. He walked slowly and doggedly round to the stacks. He had passed the wagon, when he heard something sheering down upon him. Starting back under the wall of hay, he saw the long ladder slither across the side of the stack, and fall with a bruising ring.

"What wor that?" he heard Maurice, aloft, ask cautiously.

"Something fall," came the curious, almost pleased voice of the Fräulein.

"It wor niver th' ladder," said Maurice. He peered over the side of the stack. He lay down, looking.

"It is an' a'!" he exclaimed. "We knocked it down with the cloth, dragging it over."

"We fast* up here?," she exclaimed with a thrill.

"We are that—without I shout and make 'em hear at the vicarage."

"Oh no," she said quickly.

"I don't want to," he replied, with a short laugh. There came a swift clatter of rain-drops on the cloth. Geoffrey crouched under the wall of the other stack.

"Mind where you tread—here, let me straighten this end," said Maurice, with a peculiar intimate tone, a command and an embrace. "We s'll have to sit under it. At any rate we shan't get wet."

"Not get wet!" echoed the girl, pleased, but agitated.

Geoffrey heard the slide and rustle of the cloth over the top of the stack, heard Maurice telling her to "Mind!"

"Mind!" she repeated. "Mind! You say 'Mind!'."

"Well, what if I do!" he laughed. "I don't want you to fall over th' side, do I?" His tone was masterful, but he was not quite sure of himself.

There was silence a moment or two.

"Maurice!" she said, plaintive.

"I'm here," he answered, tenderly, his voice shaky with excitement, that was near to distress. "There, I've done. Now should we sit* under this corner."

"Maurice!" she was rather pitiful.

"What? You'll be all right," he remonstrated, tenderly indignant.

"I be all raïght," she repeated, "I be all right, Maurice?"

"Tha knows tha will—I canna ca' thee Powla. Should I ca' thee Minnie?" It was the name of a dead sister.

"Minne!" she exclaimed in surprise.

"Ay, should I?"

She answered in full-throated German. He laughed shakily.

"Come on—come on under. But do yer wish you was safe in th' vicarage? Should I shout for somebody?" he asked.

"I don't wish, no!" She was vehement.

"Art sure?," he insisted, almost indignantly.

"Sure—I quite sure." She laughed.

Geoffrey turned away at the last words. Then the rain beat heavily. The lonely brother slouched miserably to the hut, where the rain played a mad tattoo. He felt very miserable, and jealous of Maurice.

His bicycle lamp, downcast, shone a yellow light on the stark floor of the shed or hut with one wall open. It lit up the trodden earth, the shafts of tools lying piled under the beam, beside the dreary grey metal of the building. He took off the lamp, shone it round the hut. There were piles of harness, tools, a big sugar box, a deep bed of hay—then the beams across the corrugated iron, all very dreary and stark. He shone the lamp into the night: nothing but the furtive glitter of rain-drops through the mist of darkness, and black shapes hovering round.

Geoffrey blew out the light and flung himself onto the hay. He would put the ladder up for them in a while, when they would be wanting it. Meanwhile he sat and gloated over Maurice's felicity. He was imaginative, and now he had something concrete to work upon. Nothing in the whole of life stirred him so profoundly, and so utterly, as the thought of this woman. For Paula was strange, foreign, different from the ordinary girls: the rousing, feminine quality seemed in her concentrated, brighter, more fascinating than in anyone he had known, so that he felt most like a moth near a candle. He would have loved her wildly—but Maurice had got her. His thoughts beat the same course, round and round: what was it like when you kissed her, when she held you tight round the waist; how did she feel towards Maurice, did she love to touch him; was he fine and attractive to her; what did she think of himself—she merely disregarded him, as she would disregard a horse in a field; why should she do so, why couldn't he make her regard himself, instead of Maurice: he would never command a woman's regard like that, he always gave in to her too soon: if only some woman would come and take him for what he was worth, though he was such a stumbler and showed to such disadvantage, ah, what a grand thing it would be; how he would kiss her. Then round he went again in the same course, brooding almost like a madman. Meanwhile the rain drummed deep on the shed, then grew lighter and softer. There came the drip, drip of the drops falling outside.

Geoffrey's heart leaped up his chest, and he clenched himself, as a black shape crept round the post of the shed and, bowing, entered silently. The young man's heart beat so heavily, in plunges, he could not get his breath to speak. It was shock, rather than fear. The form felt towards him. He sprang up, gripped it with his great hands, panting

"Now then!"

There was no resistance, only a little whimper of despair.

"Let me go," said a woman's voice.

"What are you after?" he asked, in deep, gruff tones.

"I thought 'e was 'ere," she wept despairingly, with little, stubborn sobs.

"An' you've found what you didn't expect, have you?"

At the sound of his bullying she tried to get away from him.

"Let me go," she said.

"Who did you expect to find here?" he asked, but more his natural self.

"I expected my husband—him as you saw at dinner. Let me go."

"Why, is it you?" exclaimed Geoffrey. "Has he left you?"

"Let me go," said the woman sullenly, trying to draw away. He realised that her sleeve was very wet, her arm slender under his grasp. Suddenly he grew ashamed of himself: he had no doubt hurt her, gripping her so hard. He relaxed, but did not let her go.

"An' are you searching round after that snipe* as was here at dinner?" he asked. She did not answer.

"Where did he leave you?"

"I left him—here. I've seen nothing of him since."

"I s'd think it's good riddance," he said. She did not answer. He gave a short laugh, saying:

"I should ha' thought you wouldn't ha' wanted to clap eyes on him again."

"He's my husband—an' he's not goin' to run off, if I can stop him."

Geoffrey was silent, not knowing what to say.

"Have you got a jacket on?" he asked at last.

"What do you think?—You've got hold of it."

"You're wet though, aren't you?"

"I shouldn't be dry, comin' through that teemin' rain.—But 'e's not here, so I'll go."

"I mean," he said humbly, "are you wet through?"

She did not answer. He felt her shiver.

"Are you cold?" he asked, in surprise and concern.

She did not answer. He did not know what to say.

"Stop a minute," he said, and he fumbled in his pocket for his matches. He struck a light, holding it in the hollow of his large, hard palm. He was a big man, and he looked anxious. Shedding the light on her, he saw she was rather pale, and very weary looking. Her old sailor hat was sodden and drooping with rain. She wore a fawn-coloured jacket of smooth cloth. This jacket was black-wet where the rain had beaten—her skirt hung sodden, and dripped onto her boots. The match went out.

"Why you're wet through," he said.

She did not answer.

"Shall you stop in here while it gives over?" he asked.* She did not answer.

"'Cause if you will, you'd better take your things off, an' have th' rug. There's a horse rug in the box."

He waited, but she would not answer. So he lit his bicycle lamp, and rummaged in the box, pulling out a large brown blanket, striped with scarlet and yellow. She stood stock still. He shone the light on her. She was very pale, and trembling fitfully.

"Are you that cold?" he asked in concern. "Take your jacket off, and your hat, and put this right over you."

Mechanically, she undid the enormous fawn-coloured buttons, and unpinned her hat. With her black hair drawn back from her low, honest brow, she looked little more than a girl, like a girl driven hard with womanhood by stress of life. She was small, and natty, with neat little features. But she shivered convulsively.

"Is something a-matter with you?" he asked.

"I've walked to Bulwell and back," she quivered, "looking for him—an' I've not touched a thing since this morning." She did not weep—she was too dreary-hardened to cry. He looked at her in dismay, his mouth half open: 'Gormin' '* as Maurice would have said.

"'Aven't you had nothing to eat!" he said.

Then he turned aside to the box. There, the bread remaining was kept, and the great piece of cheese, and such things as sugar and salt, with all table utensils: there was some butter.

She sat down drearily on the bed of hay. He cut her a piece of bread and butter, and a piece of cheese. This she took, but she ate listlessly.

"I want a drink," she said.

"We 'aven't got no beer," he answered. "My father doesn't have it."

"I want water," she said.

He took a can and plunged through the wet darkness, under the great black hedge, down to the trough. As he came back he saw her in the half-lit little cave sitting bunched together. The soaked grass wet his feet—he thought of her. When he gave her a cup of water, her hand touched his, and he felt her fingers hot and glossy.* She trembled so she spilled the water.

"Do you feel badly?" he asked.

"I can't keep myself still—but it's only with being tired and having nothing to eat."

He scratched his head contemplatively, waited while she ate her piece of bread and butter. Then he offered her another piece.

"I don't want it just now," she said.

"You'll have to eat summat," he said.

"I couldn't eat any more just now."

He put the piece down undecidedly on the box. Then there was another long pause. He stood up with bent head. The bicycle, like a restful animal, glittered behind him, turning towards the wall. The woman sat hunched on the hay, shivering.

"Can't you get warm?" he asked.

"I shall by an' by—don't you bother. I'm taking your seat—are you stopping here all night?"

"Yes."

"I'll be goin' in a bit," she said.

"Nay, I non want you to go. I'm thinkin' how you could get warm."

"Don't you bother about me," she remonstrated, almost irritably.

"I just want to see as the stacks is all right. You take your shoes an' stockin's an' *all* your wet things off: you can easy wrap yourself all over in that rug, there's not so much of you."

"It's raining—I s'll be all right—I s'll be going in a minute."

"I've got to see as the stacks is safe. Take your wet things off."

"Are you coming back?" she asked.

"I mightn't, not till morning."

"Well, I s'll be gone in ten minutes, then. I've no rights to be here, an' I s'll not let anybody be turned out for me."

"You won't be turning me out."

"Whether or no, I shan't stop."

"Well, shall you if I come back?" he asked. She did not answer.

He went. In a few moments, she blew the light out. The rain was falling steadily, and the night was a black gulf. All was intensely still. Geoffrey listened everywhere: no sound save the rain. He stood between the stacks, but only heard the trickle of water, and the light swish of rain. Everything was lost in blackness. He imagined death was like that, many things dissolved in silence and darkness, blotted out, but existing. In the dense blackness he felt himself almost extinguished. He was afraid he might not find things the same. Almost frantically, he stumbled, feeling his way, till his hand touched the wet metal. He had been looking for a gleam of light.

"Did you blow the lamp out?" he asked, fearful lest the silence should answer him.

"Yes," she answered humbly. He was glad to hear her voice. Groping into the pitch dark shed, he knocked against the box, part of whose cover served as table. There was a clatter and a fall.

"That's the lamp, an' the knife, an' the cup," he said. He struck a match.

"Th' cup's not broke." He put it into the box.

"But th' oil's spilled out o' th' lamp. It always was a rotten old thing." He hastily blew out his match, which was burning his fingers. Then he struck another light.

"You don't want a lamp, you know you don't. And I s'll be going directly, so you come an' lie down an' get your night's rest. I'm not taking any of your place."

He looked at her by the light of another match. She was a queer little bundle, all brown, with gaudy border folding in and out, and her little face peering at him. As the match went out she saw him beginning to smile.

"I can sit right at this end," she said. "You lie down."

He came and sat on the hay, at some distance from her. After a spell of silence:

"Is he really your husband?" he asked.

"He is!" she answered grimly.

"Hm!" Then there was silence again.

After a while: "Are you warm now?"

"Why do you bother yourself?"

"I don't bother myself—do you follow him because you like him?" He put it very timidly. He wanted to know.

"I don't—I wish he was dead"—this with bitter contempt. Then doggedly "But he's my husband."

He gave a short laugh.

"By Gad!" he said.

Again, after a while:

"Have you been married long?"

"Four years."

"Four years—why, how old are you?"

"Twenty three."

"Are you turned twenty three?"

"Last May."

"Then you're four month older than me." He mused over it. They were only two voices in the pitch-black night. It was eerie. Silence again.*

"And do you just tramp about?" he asked.

"He reckons he's looking for a job. But he doesn't like work in any shape or form. He was a stable man when I married him, at Greenhalgh's, the horse dealers, at Chesterfield, where I was housemaid. He left that job when the baby was only two month, and I've been badgered about from pillar to post ever sin'. They say a rolling stone gathers no moss——"

"An' where's the baby."

"It died when it was ten month old."

Now the silence was clinched* between them. It was quite a long time before Geoffrey ventured to say, sympathetically,

"You haven't much to look forward to."

"I've wished many a score time when I've started shiverin' an' shakin' at nights, as I was taken bad for death. But we're not that handy at dying." He was silent.

"But whatever shall you do?," he faltered.

"I s'll find him, if I drop by th' road."

"Why?" he asked, wondering, looking her way, though he saw nothing but solid darkness.

"Because I shall. He's not going to have it all his own road."*

"But why don't you leave him?"

"Because he's *not goin' to have it all his own road.*"

She sounded very determined, even vindictive. He sat in wonder, feeling uneasy, and vaguely miserable on her behalf. She sat extraordinarily still. She seemed like a voice only, a presence.

"Are you warm now?" he asked, half afraid.

"A bit warmer—but my feet—!" She sounded pitiful.

"Let me warm them with my hands," he asked her. "I'm hot enough."

"No thank you," she said, coldly.

Then, in the darkness, she felt she had wounded him. He was writhing under her rebuff, for his offer had been pure kindness.

"They're 'appen dirty," she said, half mocking.

"Well—mine is—an' I have a bath a'most every day," he answered.

"I don't know when they'll get warm," she moaned to herself.

"Well then, put them in my hands."

She heard him faintly rattling the match box, and then a phosphorescent glare began to fume in his direction. Presently he was holding two smoking, blue-green blotches of light* towards her feet. She was afraid. But her feet ached so, and the impulse drove her on, so she placed her soles lightly on the two blotches of smoke. His large hands clasped over her instep, warm and hard.

"They're like ice!" he said, in deep concern.

He warmed her feet as best he could, putting them close against him. Now and again convulsive tremors ran over her. She felt his warm breath on the balls of her toes, that were bunched up in his hands. Leaning forward, she touched his hair delicately with her fingers. He thrilled. She fell to gently stroking his hair, with timid, pleading finger-tips.

"Do they feel any better?" he asked, in a low voice, suddenly lifting his face to her. This sent her hand sliding softly over his face, and her finger-tips caught on his mouth. She drew quickly away. He put his hand out to find hers, in his other palm holding both her feet. His wandering hand met her face. He touched it curiously. It was wet. He put his big fingers cautiously on her eyes, into two little pools of tears.

"What's a matter?" he asked, in a low, choked voice.

She leaned down to him, and gripped him tightly round the neck, pressing him to her bosom in a little frenzy of pain. Her bitter disillusionment with life, her unalleviated shame and degradation during the last four years, had driven her into loneliness, and hardened her till a large part of her nature was caked and sterile. Now she softened again, and her spring might be beautiful. She had been in a fair way to make an ugly old woman.

She clasped the head of Geoffrey to her breast, which heaved and fell, and heaved again. He was bewildered, full of wonder. He allowed the woman to do as she would with him. Her tears fell on his hair, as she wept noiselessly; and he breathed deep as she did. At last she let go her clasp. He put his arms round her.

"Come and let me warm you," he said, folding her up on his knee, and lapping her with his heavy arms against himself. She was small and 'câline'.* He held her very warm and close. Presently she stole her arms round him.

"You *are* big," she whispered.

He gripped her hard, started, put his mouth down, wanderingly, seeking her out. His lips met her temple. She slowly, deliberately turned her mouth to his, and with opened lips, met him in a kiss, his first love kiss.

## 5.

It was breaking cold dawn when Geoffrey woke. The woman was still sleeping in his arms. Her face in sleep moved all his tenderness: the tight shutting of her mouth, as if in resolution to bear what was very hard to bear, contrasted so pitifully with the small mould of her features. Geoffrey pressed her to his bosom: having her, he felt he could bruise the lips of the scornful, and pass on erect, unabateable.* With her to complete him, to form the core of him, he was firm and whole. Needing her so much, he loved her fervently.

Meanwhile the dawn came like death, one of those slow, livid mornings that seem to come in a cold sweat. Slowly, and painfully, the air began to whiten. Geoffrey saw it was not raining. As he was watching the ghastly transformation outside, he felt aware of something. He glanced down: she was open eyed, watching him: she had golden brown, calm eyes, that immediately smiled into his. He also smiled, bowed softly down and kissed her. They did not speak for some time. Then:

"What's thy name?" he asked curiously.

"Lydia,"* she said.

"Lydia!" he repeated, wonderingly. He felt rather shy.

"Mine's Geoffrey Wookey," he said.

She merely smiled at him.

They were silent for a considerable time. By morning light, things look small. The huge trees of the evening were dwindled to hoary, small, uncertain things, trespassing in the sick pallor of the atmosphere. There was a dense mist, so that the light could scarcely breathe. Everything seemed to quiver with cold and sickliness.

"Have you often slept out?" he asked her.

"Not so very," she answered.

"You won't go after *him*?" he asked.

"I s'll have to," she replied, but she nestled in to Geoffrey. He felt a sudden panic.

"You mustn't," he exclaimed, and she saw he was afraid for himself. She let it be, was silent.

"We couldn't get married?" he asked, thoughtfully.

"No."

He brooded deeply over this. At length:

"Would you go to Canada* with me?"

"We'll see what you think in two months' time," she replied quietly, without bitterness.

"I s'll think the same," he protested, hurt.

She did not answer, only watched him steadily. She was there for him to do as he liked with; but she would not injure his fortunes, no, not to save his soul.

"Haven't you got no relations?" he asked.

"A married sister at Crich?"

"On a farm?"

"No—married a farm-laborer—but she's very comfortable. I'll go there, if you want me to, just till I can get another place in service."

He considered this.

"Could you get on a farm?" he asked wistfully.

"Greenhalgh's was a farm."

He saw the future brighten: she would be a help to him. She agreed to go to her sister, and to get a place of service,—until Spring, he said, when they would sail for Canada. He waited for her assent.

"You will come with me then?" he asked.

"When the time comes," she said.

Her want of faith made him bow his head: she had reason for it.

"Shall you walk to Crich or go from Langley Mill to Ambergate? But it's only ten mile to walk. So we can go together up Hunt's Hill—you'd have to go past our lane-end, then I could easy nip down an' fetch you some money—" he said, humbly.

"I've got half a sovereign by me—it's more than I s'll want."

"Let's see it," he said.

After a while, fumbling under the blanket, she brought out the piece of money. He felt she was independent of him. Brooding rather bitterly, he told himself she'd forsake him. His anger gave him courage to ask:

"Shall you go in service in your maiden name?"

"No."

He was bitterly wrathful with her—full of resentment.

"I bet I s'll niver see you again," he said, with a short, hard laugh. She put her arms round him, pressed him to her bosom, while the tears rose to her eyes. He was reassured, but not satisfied.

"Shall you write to me tonight?"

"Yes, I will."

"And can I write to you—who shall I write to?"

"Mrs Bredon."

"'Bredon'!" he repeated bitterly.

He was exceedingly uneasy.

The dawn had grown quite wan. He saw the hedges drooping wet down the grey mist. Then he told her about Maurice.

"Oh, you *shouldn't*!" she said. "You should ha' put the ladder up for them, you *should*."

"Well—I don't care."

"Go and do it now—and I'll go."

"No, don't you. Stop an' see our Maurice, go on, stop an' see him—then I s'll be able to tell him."

She consented in silence. He had her promise she would not go before he returned. She adjusted her dress, found her way to the trough, where she performed her toilet.

Geoffrey wandered round to the upper field. The stacks loomed wet in the mist, the hedge was drenched. Mist rose like steam from the grass, and the near hills were veiled almost to a shadow. In the valley, some peaks of black poplar showed fairly definite, jutting up. He shivered with chill.

There was no sound from the stacks, and he could see nothing. After all, he wondered were they up there. But he reared the ladder to the place whence it had been swept, then went down the hedge to gather dry sticks. He was breaking off thin dead twigs under a holly tree when he heard, on the perfectly still air: "Well I'm dashed!"

He listened intently. Maurice was awake.

"Sithee here!" the lad's voice exclaimed.

Then, after a while, the foreign sound of the girl:

"What—oh, thair!"

"Ay, th' ladder's there, right enough."

"You said it had fall down."

"Well, I heard it drop—an' I couldna feel it nor see it."

"You said it had fall down—you lie, you liar."

"Nay, as true as I'm here—"

"You tell me lies—make me stay here*—you tell me lies——." She was passionately indignant.

"As true as I'm standing here—," he began.

"Lies!—lies!—lies!" she cried. "I don't believe you, never. You *mean*, you *mean, mean, mean*!!"

"A' raïght, then!" he was now incensed, in his turn.

"You are bad, mean, mean, mean."

"Are yer commin' down?" asked Maurice coldly.

"No—I will not come with you—mean, to tell me lies."

"Are ter commin down?"

"No, I don't want you."

"A' raïght then!"

Geoffrey, peering through the holly tree, saw Maurice negotiating the ladder. The top rung was below the brim of the stack, and rested on the cloth, so it was dangerous to approach. The Fräulein watched him from the end of the stack, where the cloth thrown back showed the light, dry hay. He slipped slightly,—she screamed. When he had got onto the ladder, he pulled the cloth away, throwing it back, making it easy for her to descend.

"Now are ter comin?" he asked.

"No;" she shook her head violently, in a pet.

Geoffrey felt slightly contemptuous of her. But Maurice waited.

"Are ter comin?" he called again.

"No," she flashed, like a wild cat.

"All right, then I'm going."

He descended. At the bottom, he stood holding the ladder.

"Come on, while I hold it steady," he said.

There was no reply. For some minutes he stood patiently with his foot on the bottom rung of the ladder. He was pale, rather washed-out in his appearance, and he drew himself together with cold.

"Are ter commin', or aren't ter?" he asked at length.

Still there was no reply.

"Then stop up till tha'rt ready," he muttered, and he went away. Round the other side of the stacks he met Geoffrey.

"What, are thaïgh here?" he exclaimed.

"Bin here a' naïght," replied Geoffrey. "I come to help thee wi' th' cloth, but I found it on, an' th' ladder down, so I thowt tha'd gone."

"Did ter put th' ladder up?"

"I did a bit sin."*

Maurice brooded over this, Geoffrey struggled with himself to get out his own news. At last he blurted:

"Tha knows that woman as wor here yis'day dinner—'er come back, an' stopped i' th' shed a' night, out o' th' rain."

"Oh—ah!" said Maurice, his eye kindling, and a smile crossing his pallor.

"An' I s'll gi'e her some breakfast."

"Oh ah!" repeated Maurice.

"It's th' man as is good-for-nowt, not her," protested Geoffrey. Maurice did not feel in a position to cast stones.

"Tha pleases thysen," he said, "what ter does." He was very quiet, unlike himself. He seemed bothered and anxious, as Geoffrey had not seen him before.

"What's up wi' thee?" asked the elder brother, who in his own heart was glad, and relieved.

"Nowt," was the reply.

They went together to the hut. The woman was folding the blanket. She was fresh from washing, and looked very pretty. Her hair, instead of being screwed tightly back, was coiled in a knot low down, partly covering her ears. Before, she had deliberately made herself plain-looking: now she was neat and pretty, with a sweet, womanly gravity.

"Hello, I didn't think to find you here," said Maurice, very awkwardly, smiling. She watched him gravely without reply. "But it was better in shelter than outside, last night," he added.

"Yes," she replied.

"Shall you get a few more sticks," Geoffrey asked him. It was a new thing for Geoffrey to be leader. Maurice obeyed. He wandered forth into the damp, raw morning. He did not go to the stack, as he shrank from meeting Paula.

At the mouth of the hut, Geoffrey was making the fire. The woman got out coffee from the box: Geoffrey set the tin to boil. They were arranging breakfast when Paula appeared. She was hat-less. Bits of hay stuck in her hair, and she was white-faced—altogether, she did not show to advantage.*

"Ah—you!" she exclaimed, seeing Geoffrey.

"Hello!" he answered. "You're out early."

"Where's Maurice?"

"I dunno, he should be back directly."

Paula was silent.

"When have you come?" she asked.

"I come last night, but I could see nobody about. I got up half an hour sin', an' put th' ladder up ready to take the stack-cloth up."*

Paula understood, and was silent. When Maurice returned with the faggots, she was crouched warming her hands. She looked up at him, but he kept his eyes averted from her. Geoffrey met the eyes of Lydia, and smiled. Maurice put his hands to the fire.

"You cold?" asked Paula tenderly.

"A bit," he answered, quite friendly, but reserved. And all the while the four sat round the fire, drinking their smoked coffee, eating each a small piece of toasted bacon, Paula watched eagerly for the eyes of Maurice, and he avoided her. He was gentle, but would not give his eyes to her looks. And Geoffrey smiled constantly to Lydia, who watched gravely.

The German girl succeeded in getting safely into the vicarage, her escapade unknown to anyone save the housemaid. Before a week was out, she was openly engaged to Maurice, and when her month's notice expired, she went to live at the farm.

Geoffrey and Lydia kept faith one with the other.

# The Miner at Home

Like most colliers, Bower* had his dinner before he washed himself. It did not surprise his wife that he said little. He seemed quite amiable, but evidently did not feel confidential. Gertie was busy with the three children, the youngest of whom lay kicking on the sofa, preparing to squeal, therefore she did not concern herself overmuch with her husband, once having ascertained, by a few shrewd glances at his heavy brows and his blue eyes, which moved conspicuously in his black face, that he was only pondering.

He smoked a solemn pipe until six o'clock. Although he was really a good husband, he did not notice that Gertie was tired. She was getting irritable at the end of the long day.

"Don't you want to wash yourself?" she asked, grudgingly, at six o'clock. It was sickening to have a man sitting there in his pit-dirt, never saying a word, smoking like a Red Indian.

"I'm ready when you are," he replied.

She laid the baby on the sofa, barricaded it in with pillows, and brought from the scullery a great panchion,* a bowl of heavy red earthenware like brick, glazed inside to a dark mahogany color. Tall and thin and very pale, she stood before the fire holding the great bowl, her grey eyes flashing.

"Get up, our Jack, this minute, or I'll squash thee under this blessed panchion."

The fat boy of six, who was rolling on the rug in the firelight, said broadly:

"Squash me, then."

"Get up," she cried, giving him a push with her foot.

"Gi'e ower,"* he said, rolling jollily.

"I'll smack you," she said grimly, preparing to put down the panchion.

"Get up, theer," shouted the father.

Gertie ladled water from the boiler with a tin ladling can. Drops fell from her ladle hissing into the red fire, splashing on to the white hearth, blazing like drops of flame on the flat-topped steel fender. The father gazed at it all, unmoved.

"I've told you," he said "to put cold water in that panchion first. If one o' th' children goes an' falls in——"

"You can see as 'e doesn't, then," snapped she. She tempered the bowl with cold water, dropped in a flannel and a lump of soap, and spread the towel over the fender to warm.

Then, and only then, Bower rose. He wore no coat, and his arms were freckled black. He stripped to the waist, hitched his trousers into the strap,* and kneeled on the rug to wash himself. There was a great splashing and spluttering. The red firelight shone on his cap of white soap, and on the muscles of his back, on the strange working of his red and white muscular arms, that flashed up and down like individual creatures.

Gertie sat with the baby clawing at her ears and hair and nose. Continually she drew back her face and head from the cruel little baby-clasp. Jack was hanging on to the kitchen door.

"Come away from that door," cried the mother.

Jack did not come away, but neither did he open the door and run the risk of incurring his father's wrath. The room was very hot, but the thought of a draught is abhorrent to a miner.

With the baby on one arm, Gertie washed her husband's back. She sponged it carefully with the flannel, and then, still with one hand, began to dry it on the rough towel.

"Canna ter put th' childt down an' use both hands," said her husband.

"Yes; an' then if th' childt screets, there's a bigger to-do than iver.* There's no suitin' some folk."

"The childt 'ud non screet."

Gertie plumped it down. The baby began to cry. The wife rubbed her husband's back till it grew pink, whilst Bower quivered with pleasure. As soon as she threw the towel down:

"Shut that childt up," he said.

He wrestled his way into his shirt. His head emerged, with black hair standing roughly on end. He was rather an ugly man, just above medium height, and stiffly built. He had a thin black moustache over a full mouth, and a very full chin that was marred by a blue seam, where a horse had kicked him when he was a lad in the pit.

With both hands on the mantelpiece above his head, he stood

looking in the fire, his whitish shirt hanging like a smock over his pit trousers.

Presently, still looking absently in the fire, he said:

"Bill Andrews was standin' at th' pit top, an' give ivery man as 'e come up one o' these."

He handed to his wife a small, whitey-blue paper, on which was printed simply:

"February 14th, 1912.*

"To the Manager—

"I hereby give notice to leave your employment fourteen days from above date.

"Signed——."

Gertie read the paper, blindly dodging her head from the baby's grasp.

"An' what d'you reckon that's for?" she asked.

"I suppose it means as we come out."

"I'm sure!" she cried in indignation. "Well, *tha'rt* not goin' to sign it."

"It'll ma'e no diff'rence whether I do or dunna—t'others will."

"Then let 'em!" She made a small clicking sound in her mouth. "This 'ill ma'e th' third strike as we've had sin' we've been married; an' a fat lot th' better for it you are, arena you?"*

He squirmed uneasily.

"No, but we mean to be," he said.

"I'll tell you what, colliers is a discontented lot, as doesn't know what they *do* want. That's what they are."

"Tha'd better not let some o' th' colliers as there is hear thee say so."

"I don't care who hears me. An' there isn't a man in Eastwood but what'll say as th' last two strikes* has ruined the place. There's that much bad blood now atween th' mesters an' th' men as there isn't a thing but what's askew. An' what *will* it be, I should like to know!"

"It's not on'y here; it's all ower th' country alike," he gloated.

"Yes; it's them blessed Yorkshire an' Welsh colliers as does it. They're that bug* nowadays, what wi' talkin' an' spoutin', they hardly know which side their back-side hangs. Here, take this childt!"

She thrust the baby into his arms, carried out the heavy bowlful of black suds, mended the fire, cleared round, and returned for the child.

"Ben Haseldine said, an *he's* a union man—he told me when he come for th' union money yesterday, as th' men doesn't *want* to come out—not our men. It's th' union."

"Tha knows nowt about it, woman. It's a' woman's jabber, from beginnin' to end."

"You don't intend us to know. Who wants th' Minimum Wage? Butties* doesn't. There th' butties 'll be, havin' to pay seven shillin' a day to men as 'appen isn't worth a penny more than five."

"But the butties is goin' to have eight shillin', accordin' to scale."

"An' then th' men as can't work tip-top, an' is worth, 'appen, five shillin' a day, they get the sack: an' th' old men, an' so on. . ."

"Nowt o' th' sort, woman, nowt o' th' sort. Tha's got it off 'am-pat.* There's goin' to be inspectors for all that, an' th' men 'll get what they're worth, accordin' to age, an' so on."

"An' accordin' to idleness an'—an' what somebody says about 'em. I'll back! There 'll be a lot o' fairness!"

"Tha talks like a woman as knows nowt. What does thee know about it?"

"I know what you did at th' last strike. And I know this much, when Shipley men had *their* strike tickets, not one in three signed 'em—so there. An' *tha'rt* not goin' to!"

"We want a livin' wage," he declared.

"Hanna you got one?" she cried.

"Han we?" he shouted. "Han we? Who does more chunterin' than thee when it's a short wik, an' tha gets' appen a scroddy* twenty-two shillin'? Tha goes at me 'ard enough then."

"Yi; but what better shall you be? What better *are* you for th' last two strikes—tell me that?"

"I'll tell thee this much, th' mesters doesna mean us to ha'e owt. They promise, but they dunna keep to it, not they. Up comes Friday night, an' nowt to draw, an' a woman fit to ha'e yer guts out for it."

"It's nowt but th' day-men as wants the blessed minimum wage—it's not butties."

"It's time as th' butties *did* ha'e ter let their men make a fair day's wage. Four an' sixpence a day is about as much as 'e's allowed to addle,* whoiver he may be."

"I wonder what you'll say next. You say owt as is put in your mouth, that's a fac'. What are thee, dost reckon?—are ter a butty, or day man, or ostler, or are ter a mester?*—for tha might be, ter hear thee talk."

"I nedna neither. It ought to be fair a' round."

"It ought, hang my rags,* it ought! Tha'rt very fair to me, for instance."

"An' arena I?"

"Tha thinks 'cause tha gi'es me a lousy thirty shillin' reg'lar tha'rt th' best man i' th' Almighty world. Tha mun be waited on han' an' foot, an' sided wi'* whativer tha' says. But I'm *not!* No, an' I'm not, not when it comes to strikes. I've seen enough on 'em."

"Then niver open thy mouth again if it's a short wik, an' we're pinched."

"We're niver pinched that much. An' a short wik isn't no shorter than a strike wik; put that i' thy pipe an' smoke it. It's th' idle men as wants the strikes."

"Shut thy mouth, woman. If every man worked as hard as I do——"

"He wouldn't ha'e as much to do as me; an' 'e wouldna. But *I've* nowt to do, as tha'rt flig*ter tell me. No, it's th' idle men as wants th' strike. It's a union strike this is, not a men's strike. You're sharpenin' th' knife for your own throats."

"Am I not sick of a woman as listens to every tale as is poured into her ears. No, I'm not takin' th' kid. I'm goin' out."

He put on his boots determinedly.

She rocked herself with vexation and weariness.

# Her Turn

She was his second wife, and so there was between them that truce which is never held between a man and his first wife.

He was one for the women, and as such an exception among the colliers. In spite of their prudery, the neighbour women liked him; he was big, naïve, and very courteous with them, as he was even with his second wife.

Being a large man of considerable strength and perfect health, he earned good money in the pit. His natural courtesy saved him from enemies while his good humour made him always welcome. So he went his own way, had plenty of friends, a good job down pit.

He gave his wife thirty-five shillings a week. He had two grown-up sons at home, and they paid twelve shillings each. There was only one child by the second marriage, so Radford* considered his wife did well.

Eighteen months ago, Bryan and Wentworth's men were out on strike for eleven weeks. During that time, Mrs. Radford could neither cajole nor entreat nor nag the eleven shillings strike-pay* from her husband. So that when the second strike* came on, she was prepared for action.

Radford was going, quite inconspicuously, to the publican's wife at the "Golden Horn."* She is a large, easy-going lady of forty, and her husband is sixty-three, moreover crippled with rheumatism. She sits in the little bar-parlour of the wayside public-house, knitting for dear life, and sipping a moderate glass of Scotch. When a decent man arrives at the three-foot width of bar, she rises, serves him, scans him over, and, if she likes his looks, says:

"Won't you step inside, sir?"

If he steps inside, he will find not more than one or two men present. The room is warm and quite small. The landlady knits. She gives a few polite words to the stranger, then resumes her conversation with the man most important to her. She is straight, highly-coloured, with indifferent brown eyes.

"What was that you asked me, Mr. Radford?"

"What is the difference between a donkey's tail and a rainbow?" asked Radford, who had a consuming passion for conundrums.

"All the difference in the world," replied the landlady.

"Yes, but what special difference?"

"I s'll have to give it up again. You'll think me a donkey's head, I'm afraid."

"Not likely. But just you consider now, wheer——."

The conundrum was still under weigh,* when a girl entered. She was swarthy, a fine animal. After she had gone out:

"Do you know who that is?" asked the landlady.

"I can't say as I do," replied Radford.

"She's Frederick Pinnock's daughter, from Stony Ford. She's courting our Willy."

"And a fine lass, too."

"Yes, fine enough, as far as that goes. What sort of a wife'll she make him, think you?"

"You just let me consider a bit," said the man. He took out a pocket-book and a pencil. The landlady continued to talk to the other guests.

Radford was a big fellow, black-haired, with a brown moustache, and darkish blue eyes. His voice, naturally deep, was pitched in his throat, and had a peculiar tenor quality, rather husky, and disturbing. He modulated it a good deal as he spoke, as men do who talk much with women. Always there was a certain indolence in his carriage.

"Our mester's lazy," his wife said of him. "There's many a bit of a job wants doin', but get him to do it if you can."

But she knew he was merely indifferent to the little jobs, and not lazy.

He sat writing for about ten minutes, at the end of which time he read:

"I see a fine girl full of life,
I see her just ready for wedlock,
But there's jealousy between her eyebrows
And jealousy on her mouth.
I see trouble ahead....
Willy is delicate.
She would do him no good.
She would have no thought for his ailment.*
She would only see what she wanted——."

So in phrases, he got down his thoughts. He had to fumble for expression, and anything serious he wanted to say he wrote in "poetry," as he called it.

Presently, the landlady rose, saying:

"Well, I s'll have to be looking after our mester. I s'll be in again before we close."

Radford sat quite comfortably on. In a while he too bade the company good-night.

When he got home, at a quarter-past eleven, his sons were in bed, and his wife sat awaiting him. She was a woman of medium height, fat, and sleek, a dumpling. He black hair was parted smooth, her narrow-opened eyes were sly and satirical; she had a peculiar twang in her rather sleering* voice.

"Our missis is a puss-puss," he said easily, of her. Her extraordinarily smooth, sleek face was remarkable. She was very healthy.

He never came in drunk. Having taken off his coat and his cap, he sat down to supper in his shirt-sleeves. Do as he might, she was fascinated by him. He had a strong neck, with the crisp hair growing low. Let her be angry as she would, yet she had a passion for that neck of his, particularly when she saw the great vein rib under the skin.

"I think, missis," he said, "I'd rather ha'e a smite* o' cheese than this meat."

"Well, can't you get it yourself?"

"Yi, surely I can," he said, and went out to the pantry.

"I think if yer comin' in at this time of night you can wait on yourself," she justified herself.

She moved uneasily in her chair. There were several jam tarts alongside the cheese on the dish he brought.

"Yi, Missis, them tan-tafflins* 'll go down very nicely," he said.

"Oh, will they! Then you'd better help to pay for them," she said, suavely.

"Now what art after?"

"What am I after? Why, can't you think?" she said sarcastically.

"I'm not for thinkin', this hour, Missis."

"No, I know you're not. But wheer's my money? You've been paid th' Union* to-day. Wheer do I come in?"

"Th's got money, an' tha mun use it."

"Thank yer. An' 'aven't you none, as well?"

"I hadna, not till we was paid, not a ha'ep'ny."

"Then you ought to be ashamed of yourself to say so."

"'Appen so!"

"We'll go shares wi' th' Union money," she said. "That's nothing but what's right."

"We shonna. Tha's got plenty o' money as tha can use."

"Oh, all right," she cried, "I will do."

She went to bed. It made her feel sharp that she could not get at him.

The next day she was just as usual. But at eleven o'clock she took her purse and went up-town. Trade was very slack. Men stood about in gangs, men were playing marbles everywhere in the streets. It was a sunny morning. Mrs. Radford went into the furnisher-and-upholsterer's shop.

"There's a few things," she said to Mr. Allcock,* "as I'm wantin' for the house, and I might as well get them now, while the men's at home, and can shift me the furniture."

She put her fat purse on to the counter with a click. The man should know she was not wanting "strap."* She bought linoleum for the kitchen, a new wringer, a breakfast service, a spring mattress, and various other things, keeping a mere thirty shillings, which she tied in a corner of her handkerchief. In her purse was some loose silver.

Her husband was gardening in a desultory fashion when she got back home. The daffodils were out. The colts in the field at the end of the garden were tossing their velvety brown necks.

"Sithee here, Missis," called Radford, from the shed which stood half-way down the path. Two doves in a cage were cooing.

"What have you got?" asked the woman as she approached. He held out to her in his big earthy hand a tortoise. The reptile was very, very slowly issuing its head again to the warmth.

"He's wakkened up betimes,"* said Radford.

"He's like th' men, wakened up for a holiday," said the wife. Radford scratched the little beast's scaley head.

"We pleased to see him out," he said.

They had just finished dinner, when a man knocked at the door.

"From Allcock's!" he said.

The plump woman took up the clothes-basket containing the crockery she had bought.

"Whativer hast got theer?" asked her husband.

"We've been wantin' some breakfast cups for ages, so I went up-town an' got 'em this mornin'," she replied.

He watched her taking out the crockery.

"Hm!" he said. "Tha's been on th' spend, seemly!"

Again there was a thud at the door. The man had put down a roll of linoleum. Mr. Radford went to look at it.

"They come rolling in!" he exclaimed.

"Who's grumbled more than you about the raggy oilcloth of this kitchen?" sang the insidious cat-like voice of the wife.

"It's all right; it's all right," said Radford. The carter came up the entry carrying another roll, which he deposited with a grunt at the door.

"An' how much do you reckon this lot is?" asked Radford.

"Oh, they're all paid for, don't yer worry," replied the wife.

"Shall yer gi'e me a hand, Mester?" asked the carter.

Radford followed him down the entry, in his easy, slouching way. His wife went after. His waistcoat was hanging loose over his shirt. She watched his easy movement of well-being, as she followed him, and she laughed to herself. The carter took hold of one end of the wire mattress, dragged it forth.

"Well, this is a corker!"* said Radford, as he received the burden. They walked with it up the entry.

"There's th' mangle!" said the carter.

"What dost reckon tha's been up to, Missis?" asked the husband.

"I said to myself last wash-day, if I had to turn that mangle again, tha'd ha'e ter wash the clothes thyself."

Radford followed the carter down the entry again. In the street women were standing watching, and dozens of men were lounging round the cart. One officiously helped with the wringer.

"Give him thrippence," said Mrs. Radford.

"Gi'e 't him thy-sen," replied her husband.

"I've no change under half-a-crown."

Radford tipped the carter and returned indoors. He surveyed the array of crockery, linoleum, mattress, mangle, and other goods crowding the house and the yard.

"Well, this is a winder!"* he repeated.

"We stood in need of 'em enough."

"I hope tha's got plenty more from wheer they came from," he replied dangerously.

"That's just what I haven't." She opened her purse. "Two half-crowns; that's ivery copper I've got i' th' world."

He stood very still as he looked.

"It's right," she said.

There was a certain smug sense of satisfaction about her. A wave of anger came over him, blinding him. But he waited and waited. Suddenly his arm leapt up, the fist clenched, and his eyes blazed at her. She shrank away, pale and frightened. But he dropped his fist to his side, turned, and went out muttering. He went down to the shed that stood in the middle of the garden. There he picked up the tortoise, and stood with bent head, rubbing its horny head.

She stood hesitating, watching him. Her heart was heavy, and yet there was a curious, cat-like look of satisfaction round her eyes. Then she went indoors and gazed at her new cups, admiringly.

The next week he handed her his half-sovereign without a word.

"You'll want some for yourself," she said, and she gave him a shilling.* He accepted it.

# Strike-Pay

Strike-money is paid in the Primitive Methodist Chapel. The crier was round quite early on Wednesday morning to say that paying would begin at ten o'clock.

The Primitive Methodist Chapel is a big barn of a place, built, designed, and paid for by the colliers themselves. But it threatened to fall down from its first form, so that a professional architect had to be hired at last to pull the place together.

It stands in the Square. Forty years ago, when Bryan and Wentworth opened their pits,* they put up the 'Squares' of miner's dwellings. They are two great quadrangles of houses, enclosing a barren stretch of ground, littered with broken pots and rubbish, which forms a square, unpaved, a great, sloping, lumpy playground for the children, a drying ground for many women's washing.

Wednesday is still wash-day with some women. As the men clustered round the Chapel, they heard the thud-thud-thud! of many ponches,* women pounding away at the wash-tub with a wooden pestle. In the Square the white clothes were waving in the wind from a maze of clothes lines, and here and there women were pegging out, calling to the miners, or to the children who dodged under the flapping sheets.

Ben Townsend, the Union agent, has a bad way of paying. He takes the men in order of his round, and calls them by name. A big, oratorical man with a grey beard, he sat at the table in the Primitive schoolroom, calling name after name. The room was crowded with colliers, and a great group pushed up outside. There was much confusion. Ben dodged from the Scargill Street list to the Queen Street. For this Queen Street men were not prepared. They were not to the fore.

"Joseph Grooby—Joseph Grooby! Now Joe, where are you?"

"Hold on a bit, Sorry!" cried Joe from outside. "I'm shovin' up."*

There was a great noise from the men.

"I'm takin' Queen Street. All you Queen Street men should be ready. Here you are, Joe," said the Union agent loudly.

"Five children!" said Joe, counting the money suspiciously.

"That is right, I think," came the mouthing voice. "Fifteen shillings, is it not?"

"A bob a kid," said the collier.

"Thomas Sedgwick—How are you, Tom? Missis better?"

"Ay, 'er's shapin' nicely. Tha'rt hard at work today, Ben." This was a sarcasm on the idleness of a man who had given up the pit to become a Union agent.

"Yes, I rose at four to fetch the money—"

"Dunna hurt thysen," was the retort, and the men laughed.

"No.—John Merfin!"

But the colliers, tired with waiting, excited by the strike spirit, began to rag. Merfin was young and dandiacal. He was choir-master at the Wesleyan Chapel.

"Does your collar cut, John?" asked a sarcastic voice out of the crowd.

"Hymn Number Nine. 'Diddle-diddle dumpling, my son John Went to bed with his best suit on'"*—came the solemn announcement.

Mr Merfin, his white cuffs down to his knuckles, picked up his half sovereign, and walked away loftily.

"Sam Coutts!"* cried the pay-master.

"Now lad, reckon it up," shouted the voice of the crowd, delighted.

Mr Coutts was a straight-backed neer-do-well. He looked at his twelve shillings sheepishly.

"Another two bob—he had twins a-Monday night—get thy money, Sam, tha's earned it—tha's addled it,* Sam, dunna go be-out it. Let 'im ha'e two bob for 'is twins, mister," came the clamour from the men around.

Sam Coutts stood grinning awkwardly.

"You should ha' given us notice, Sam," said the pay-master suavely. "We can make it all right for you next week——"

"Nay nay nay," shouted a voice, "pay on delivery—the goods is theer right enough."

"Get thy money Sam, tha's addled it," became the universal cry, and the Union agent had to hand over another florin, to prevent a disturbance. Sam Coutts grinned with satisfaction.

"Good shot, Sam," the men acclaimed.

"Ephraim Wharmby," shouted the payman.

A slim lad came forward.

"Gi'e him sixpence for what's on t'road," said a sly voice.

"Nay nay," replied Ben Townsend, "pay on delivery—."*

There was a roar of laughter. The miners were in high spirits. In the town they stood about in gangs, talking and laughing. Many sat on their heels in the market place. In and out of the public-houses they went, and on every bar the half-sovereigns clicked.*

"Comin' ter Nottingham wi' us, Ephraim?" said Sam Coutts to the slender, pale young fellow of about twenty two.

"I'm non walkin' that far of a gleamy day* like this."

"He hasna got the strength," said somebody, and a laugh went up.

"How's that?" asked another pertinent voice.

"He's a married man, mind yer," said Chris Smitheringale, "an' it ta'es a bit o' keepin' up."

The youth was teased in this manner for some time.*

"Come on ter Nottingham wi's, tha'll be safe for a bit," said Coutts.

A gang set off, although it was only eleven o'clock. It was a nine miles walk. The road was crowded with colliers travelling on foot to see the match between Notts and Aston Villa.* In Ephraim's gang were Sam Coutts, with his fine shoulders and his extra florin, Chris Smitheringale, fat and smiling, and John Wharmby, a remarkable man, tall, erect as a soldier, black haired and proud; he could play any musical instrument, he declared.

"I can play owt from a comb up'ards. If there's music to be got outer a thing, I back I'll get it. No matter what shape or form of instrument you set before me, it doesn't signify if I niver clapped eyes on it before, I's warrant I'll have a tune out of it in five minutes."

He beguiled the first two miles so. It was true, he had caused a sensation by introducing the mandoline into the townlet, filling the hearts of his fellow-colliers with pride as he sat on the platform in evening dress, a fine soldierly man, bowing his black head, and scratching the mewing mandoline with hands that had only to grasp the 'instrument' to crush it entirely.

Chris stood a can round at the White Bull at Gilt Brook, John Wharmby took his turn at Kimberley top.

"We wunna drink again," they decided, "till we're at Cinder Hill. We'll non stop i' Nuttall."

They swung along the high-road under the budding trees. In Nuttall churchyard the crocuses blazed with yellow at the brim of the balanced, black yews. White and purple crocuses clipt up* over the graves, as if the churchyard were bursting out in tiny tongues of flame.

"Sithee," said Ephraim, who was an ostler down pit. "Sithee, here comes the Colonel. Luthee* at his 'osses how they pick their toes up, the beauties!"

The Colonel drove past the men, who took no notice of him.

"Hast heered,* Sorry—," said Sam, "as they'n com'n out i' Germany, by the thousand, an' begun riotin'."

"An' commin' out i' France simbilar,"* cried Chris.

The men all gave a chuckle.

"Sorry," shouted John Wharmby, much elated, "we oughtna ter go back under a twenty perzent rise."*

"We should get it," said Chris.

"An' easy! They can do nowt bi-out us, we'n on'y ter stop out long enough."

"I'm willin'!" said Sam, and there was a laugh. The colliers looked at one another. A thrill went through them as if an electric current passed.

"We'n on'y ter stick out, an' we s'll see who's gaffer."*

"Us!" cried Sam. "Why, what can they do again' us, if we come out all ower th' world?"

"Nowt!" said John Wharmby. "Th' mesters is bobbin' about like corks on a rassivoy* a'ready." There was a large natural reservoir, like a lake, near Bestwood, and this supplied the simile.

Again there passed through the men that wave of elation, quickening their pulses. They chuckled in their throats. Beyond all consciousness was this sense of battle and triumph in the hearts of the working men at this juncture.

It was suddenly suggested at Nuttall that they should go over the fields to Bulwell, and into Nottingham that way. They went single file across the fallow, past the wood, and then over the railway, where now no trains were running. Two fields away was a troop of pit ponies.* Of all colours, but chiefly of red or brown, they clustered thick in the field, scarcely moving, and the two lines of trodden earth patches showed where fodder was placed down the field.

"Theer's th' pit 'osses," said Sam. "Let's run 'em."

"It's like a circus turned out. See them skewbawd* uns—seven skewbawd," said Ephraim warmly.

The ponies were inert, unused to freedom. Occasionally one walked round. But there they stood, two thick lines of ruddy brown and pie-bald and white, across the trampled field. It was a beautiful day, mild, pale blue, a 'growing-day,' as the men said, when there was the silence of swelling sap everywhere.

"Let's ha'e a ride," said Ephraim.

The younger men went up to the horses.

"Come on—co-oop Taffy*—co-oop Ginger."

The horses tossed away. But having got over the excitement of being above-ground, the animals were feeling dazed and rather dreary. They missed the warmth and the movement of the pit. They looked as if life were a blank to them.

Ephraim and Sam caught a couple of steeds, on whose backs they went careering round, driving the rest of the sluggish herd from end to end of the field. The horses were good specimens, on the whole, and in fine condition. But they were out of their element.

Performing too clever a feat, Ephraim went rolling from his mount. He was soon up again, chasing his horse. Again he was thrown. Then the men proceeded on their way.

They were drawing near to miserable Bulwell, when Ephraim, remembering his turn was coming to stand drinks, felt in his pocket for his beloved half-sovereign, his strike-pay. It was not there. Through all his pockets he went, his heart sinking like lead.

"Sam," he said, "I believe I'n lost that ha'ef a sovereign."

"Tha's got it somewheer about thee," said Chris.

They made him take off his coat and waistcoat. Chris examined the coat, Sam the waistcoat, whilst Ephraim searched his trousers.

"Well," said Chris, "I'n foraged* this coat, an' it's non theer."

"An' I'll back my life as th' on'y bit a metal on this wa'scoat is the buttons," said Sam.

"An't it's non in my breeches," said Ephraim.

He took off his boots and his stockings. The half-sovereign was not there. He had not another coin in his possession.

"Well," said Chris, "we mun go back an' look for it."

Back they went, four serious-hearted colliers, and searched the field, but in vain.

"Well," said Chris, "wes'll ha'e ter share wi' thee, that's a'."

"I'm willin'," said John Wharmby.

"An' me," said Sam.

"Two bob each," said Chris.

Ephraim, who was in the depths of despair, shamefully accepted their six shillings.

In Bulwell they called in a small public-house, which had one long room with a brick floor, scrubbed benches and scrubbed tables. The central space was open. The place was full of colliers, who were drinking. There was a great deal of drinking during the strike, but not a vast amount drunk. Two men were playing skittles, and the rest were betting. The seconds sat on either side the skittle board, holding caps of money, sixpences and coppers, the wagers of the 'backers.'

Sam, Chris, and John Wharmby immediately put money on the man who had their favour. In the end Sam declared himself willing to play against the victor. He was the Bestwood champion. Chris and John Wharmby backed him heavily, and even Ephraim the Unhappy* ventured sixpence.

In the end, Sam had won half a crown, with which he promptly stood drinks and bread and cheese for his comrades. At half past one they set off again.

It was a good match between Notts and Villa—no goals at half-time, two-none for Notts at the finish. The colliers were hugely delighted, especially as Flint, the forward for Notts, who was an Underwood man well known to the four comrades, did some handsome work, putting the two goals through.*

Ephraim determined to go home as soon as the match was over. He knew John Wharmby would be playing the piano at the 'Punch Bowl,' and Sam, who had a good tenor voice, singing, while Chris cut in with witticisms, until evening. So he bade them farewell, as he must get home. They, finding him somewhat of a damper on their spirits, let him go.

He was the sadder for having witnessed an accident near the football ground.* A navvy working at some drainage, carting an iron tip-tub of mud and emptying it, had got with his horse onto the deep deposit of ooze, which was crusted over. The crust had broken, the man had gone under the horse, and it was some time before the people had realised he had vanished. When they found his feet sticking out, and hauled him forth, he was dead, stifled dead in the mud. The horse was at length hauled out, after having its neck nearly pulled from the socket.

Ephraim went home vaguely impressed with a sense of death, and loss, and strife. Death was loss greater than his own, the strike was a battle greater than that he would presently have to fight.

He arrived home at seven o'clock, just when it had fallen dark. He lived in Queen Street with his young wife, to whom he had been married two months, and with his mother-in-law, a widow of sixty four. Maud was the last child remaining unmarried, the last of eleven.

Ephraim went up the entry. The light was burning in the kitchen. His mother-in-law was a big, erect woman, with wrinkled, loose face, and cold blue eyes. His wife was also large, with very vigorous fair hair, frizzy like unravelled rope. She had a quiet way of stepping, a certain cat-like stealth, in spite of her large build. She was five months pregnant.

"Might we ask wheer you've been to?" inquired Mrs Marriott, very erect, very dangerous. She was only polite when she was very angry.

"I'n bin ter th' match."

"Oh indeed!" said the mother-in-law. "And why couldn't we be told as you thought of jaunting off?"

"I didna know mysen," he answered, sticking to his broad Derbyshire.

"I suppose it popped into your mind, an' so you darted off," said the mother-in-law dangerously.

"It didna. It wor Chris Smitheringale who exed me."

"An' did you take much invitin'?"

"I didna want ter goo."

"But wasn't there enough man inside your jacket to say no."

He did not answer. Down at the bottom he hated her. But he was, to use his own words, all messed up with having lost his strike-pay, and with knowing the man was dead. So he was more helpless before his mother-in-law, whom he feared. His wife neither looked at him nor spoke, but kept her head bowed. He knew she was with her mother.

"Our Maud's been waitin' for some money, to get a few things in," said the mother-in-law.

In silence, he put five and sixpence on the table.

"Take that up, Maud," said the mother.

Maud did so.

"You'll want it for us board,* shan't you?" she asked, furtively, of her mother.

"Might I ask if there's nothing you want to buy yourself first?"

"No, there's nothink I want," answered the daughter.

Mrs Marriott took the silver and counted it.

"And do you," said the mother-in-law, towering upon her shrinking son, but speaking slowly and statelily, "do you think I'm going to keep you an' your wife, for five and sixpence a week?"

"It's a' I've got," he answered, sulkily.

"You've had a good jaunt, my sirs, if it's cost four and sixpence. You've started your game early haven't you?"

He did not answer.

"It's a nice thing! Here's our Maud an' me been sitting, since eleven o'clock this morning! Dinner waiting and cleared away, tea waiting and washed up, then in he comes crawling with five and sixpence. Five and sixpence, for a man-an-wife's board for a week, if you please!"

Still he did not say anything.

"You must think somethink of yourself, Ephraim Wharmby!" said his mother-in-law. "You must think somethink of yourself. You suppose, do you, *I'm* going to keep you an' your wife, while you make a holiday, off on the nines to* Nottingham, drink an' women."

"I've neither had drink nor women, as you know right well," he said.

"I'm glad we know summat about you. For you're that close, anybody 'd think we was foreigners to you. You're a pretty little jockey,* aren't you. Oh it's a gala time for you, the strike is. That's all men strike for, indeed. They enjoy themselves, they do that. Ripping* and racing and drinking, from morn till night, my Sirs!"

"Is there ony tea for me?" he asked, in a temper.

"Hark at him, hark-ye! Should I ask you whose house you think you're in. Kindly order me about, do. Oh it makes him big, the strike does. See him land home after being out on the spree for hours, and give his orders, My Sirs! Oh Strike sets the men up, it does. Nothing have they to do but guzzle and gallivant to Nottingham. Their wives'll keep them, oh yes. So long as they get something to eat at home, what more do they want! What more *should* they want, prithee? Nothing! Let the women an' children starve and scrape, but fill the man's belly, and let him have his fling. My Sirs, indeed, I think so! Let tradesmen go—what do they matter! Let rent go—let children get what they can catch—only the man will see *he's* all right. But not here though!"

"Are you goin' ter gi'e me ony bloody* tea?"

His mother-in-law started up.

"If tha dare's ter swear at me, I'll lay thee flat."

"Are yer—goìn' ter—gì'e me—any blasted, ròtten, còssed,* blòody tèa," he bawled, in a fury, accenting every other word deliberately.

"Maud!" said the mother-in-law, cold and stately, "if you gi'e him any tea after that, you're a trollops."*

Whereupon she sailed out to her other daughter's.

Maud quietly got the tea ready.

"Shall y'ave your dinner warmed up?" she asked.

"Ay."

She attended to him. Not that she was really meek. But—he was *her* man—not her mother's.*

# Delilah and Mr. Bircumshaw*

"He looked," said Mrs. Bircumshaw to Mrs. Gillatt. "He looked like a positive saint—one of the noble sort, you know, that will suffer with head up and with dreamy eyes. I nearly died of laughing."

She spoke of Mr. Bircumshaw, who darted a look at his wife's friend. Mrs. Gillatt broke into an almost derisive laugh. Bircumshaw shut tight his mouth and set his large, square jaw. Frowning, he lowered his face out of sight.

Mrs. Bircumshaw seemed to glitter in the twilight. She was like a little uncanny machine, working unheard and unknown, but occasionally snapping a spark. A small woman, very quiet in her manner, it was surprising that people should so often say of her, 'she's *very* vivacious.' It was her eyes. They were brown, very wide-open, very swift and ironic. As a rule she said little. This evening her words and her looks were quick* and brilliant. She had been married four years.

"I was thankful, I can tell you, that you didn't go," she continued to Mrs. Gillatt. "For a church pageant, it was the most astonishing show. People blossomed out so differently. *I* never knew what a fine apostle was lost in Harry. When I saw him, I thought I should scream—."

"You looked sober enough every time I noticed you," blurted Harry in deep bass.

"You were much too rapt to notice *me*," his wife laughed gaily. Nevertheless, her small head was lifted and alert, like a fighting bird's. Mrs. Gillatt fell instinctively into rank with her, unconscious of the thrill of battle that moved her.

Mr. Bircumshaw, bowing forward, rested his arms on his knees, and whistled silently as he contemplated his feet. Also, he listened acutely to the women. He was a large-limbed, clean, powerful man—and a bank clerk. Son of a country clergyman, he had a good deal of vague, sensuous religious feeling, but he lacked a Faith. He would have been a fine man to support a cause, but he had no cause. Even had he been forced to work hard and unremittingly he would have remained healthy in spirit. As it was, he was a bank clerk, with a quantity of unspent energy turning sour in his veins, and a fair amount of barren leisure torturing his soul. He was degenerating—and now his wife turned upon him.

She had been a school-teacher. He had had the money and the position. He was inclined to bully her, when he was not suited—which was fairly often.

"Harry was one of the 'Three Wise Men'. You should have seen him, Mrs. Gillatt. With his face coming out of that white forehead band, and the cloth that hung over his ears—he looked a picture. Imagine him!"

Mrs. Gillatt looked at Bircumshaw, imagining him. Then she threw up her hands and laughed aloud. It *was* ludicrous to think of Bircumshaw, a hulking, frequently churlish man, as one of the Magi. Mrs. Gillatt was a rather beautiful woman of forty, almost too full in blossom. Better off than the Bircumshaws, she assumed the manner of patron and protectress.

"Oh," she cried, "I *can* see him—I can see him looking great and grand—Abraham!* Oh, he's got that grand cut of face, and plenty of size."

She laughed rather derisively. She was a man's woman, by instinct serving flattery with mockery.

"That's it!" cried the little wife deferentially. "Abraham, setting out to sacrifice. He marched—his march was splendid—" the two women laughed together. Mrs. Gillatt drew herself up superbly, laughing, then coming to rest.

"And usually, you know," the wife broke off, "there's a good deal of the whipped schoolboy about his walk."

"There is, Harry," laughed Mrs. Gillatt, shaking her white and jewelled hand at him. "You just remember that for the next time, my lad." She was his senior by some eight years. He grinned sicklily.

"But now," Mrs. Bircumshaw continued, "he marched like a young Magi. You could see a look of the Star in his eyes."

"Oh," cried Mrs. Gillatt. "Oh! the look of the Star—!"

"Oftener the look of the Great Bear,* isn't it?" queried Mrs. Bircumshaw.

"That is quite true, Harry," said the elder woman, laughing.

Bircumshaw* cracked his strong fingers brutally.

"Well, he came on," continued the wife, "with the light of the Star in his eyes and his mouth fairly sweet with Christian resignation—"

"Oh," cried Mrs. Gillatt. "Oh—and he spanks the baby! Christian resignation—" She laughed aloud. "Let me hear of you spanking that child again, Harry Bircumshaw, and I'll Christian-resignation you—"

Suddenly she remembered that this might implicate her friend.

"I came in yesterday," she explained, "at dinner. 'What's the matter, baby?' I said, 'what are you crying for?'...'Dadda beat baby—naughty baby'. It was a good thing you had gone back to business, my lad, I can tell you."

Mrs. Bircumshaw glanced swiftly at her husband. He had ducked his head and was breaking his knuckles tensely. She turned her head with a quick, thrilled movement, more than ever like a fighting bird.

"And you know his nose," she said, blithely resuming her narrative, as if it were some bit of gossip. "You know it usually looks a sort of 'Mind-your-own-business-or-you'll-get-a-hit-in-the-jaw' nose?"

"Yes," cried Mrs. Gillatt, "it does—" and she seemed unable to contain her laughter. Then she dropped her fine head, pretending to be an angry Buffalo glaring under bent brows, seeking whom he shall devour,* in imitation of Harry's nose. Mrs. Bircumshaw bubbled with laughter.

"Ah!" said Mrs. Gillatt, and she winked at her friend as she sweetened Harry's pill—"I know him—I know him." Then: "And what *did* his nose look like?" she asked of the wife.

"Like Sir Galahad* on Horseback," said Ethel Bircumshaw, spending her last shot.

Mrs. Gillatt drew her hand down her own nose, which was straight with thin, flexible nostrils.

"How does it feel, Harry," she asked, "to stroke Galahad on Horseback?"

"I don't know, I'm sure," he said icily.

"Then stroke it, man, and tell me," cried the elder woman, with which *her* last shot was sped. There was a moment of painful silence ...

"And the way the others acted—it was screamingly funny," the wife started. Then the two women, with one accord, began to make mock of the other actors in the pageant, people they knew, ridiculing them, however, only for blemishes that Harry had not, pulling the others to pieces in places where Harry was solid, thus leaving their man erect like a hero among the litter of his acquaintances.

This did not mollify him, it only persuaded him he *was* a fine figure, not to be carped at.

Suddenly, before the women had gone far, Bircumshaw jumped up. Mrs. Gillatt started. She got a glimpse of his thick* form, in its blue serge, passing before her. Then the door banged behind him.

Mrs. Gillatt was really astonished. She had helped in clipping this ignoble Samson, all unawares, from instinct. She had no idea of what she had been doing. She sat erect and superb, the picture of astonishment that is merging towards contempt.

"Is it someone at the door?" she asked, listening.

Mrs. Bircumshaw, with alert, attentive* eyes, shook her head quickly with a meaning look of contempt.

"Is he mad?" whispered the elder woman. Her friend nodded. Then Mrs. Gillatt's eyes dilated and her face hardened with scorn. Mrs. Bircumshaw had not ceased to listen. She bent forward.

"Praise him," she whispered, making a quick gesture that they should play a bit of fiction. They rose with zest to the game. "Praise him" whispered the wife. Then she herself began.

Every woman is a first-rate actress in private. She leaned forward, and in a slightly lowered yet very distinct voice, screened as if for privacy, yet penetrating clearly to the ears of her husband—he had lingered in the hall she could hear—

"You know, Harry really acted splendidly," she said.

"I know," said Mrs. Gillatt eagerly. "I know. I know he's a really good actor."

"He is. The others did look paltry beside him, I have to confess."

Harry's pride was soothed but his wrath was not appeased.

"Yes," he heard the screened voice of his wife. "But for all that, I don't care to see him on the stage. It's not manly, somehow. It seems unworthy of a man with any character, somehow. Of course, it's all right for strangers—but for anyone you care for—anyone *very* near to you——"

Mrs. Gillatt chuckled to herself. This was a thing well done. The two women, however, had not praised very long—and the wife's praise was sincere by the time she had finished her first sentence—before they were startled by a loud 'thud!' on the floor above their heads. Both started. It was dark, nearly nine o'clock. They listened in silence. There came another 'thud!'.

Mrs. Bircumshaw gave a little spurt of bitter-contemptuous laughter.

"He's not—?" began Mrs. Gillatt.

"He's gone to bed, and announces the fact by dropping his boots as he takes them off," said the young wife bitterly. Mrs. Gillatt was wide-eyed with amazement.

"You don't mean it!" she exclaimed.

Childless, married to an uxorious man whom she loved, this state of affairs was monstrous to her. Neither of the women spoke for a while. It was dark in the room. Then Mrs. Gillatt began in a sotto voce:

"Well, I could never have believed it. No, not if you'd told me forever. He's always been so very considerate—"

So she went on. Mrs. Bircumshaw let her continue. A restrained woman herself, the other's outburst relieved her own tension. When she had sufficiently overcome her own emotion, and when she knew her husband to be in bed, she rose.

"Come into the kitchen, we can talk there," she said. There was a new hardness in her voice. She had not 'talked' before to anyone, had never mentioned her husband in blame.

The kitchen was bare, with drab walls glistening to the naked gas-jet. The tiled floor was uncovered, cold and damp. Everything was clean, stark and cheerless. The large stove, littered with old paper, was black—black-cold. There was a baby's high chair in one corner, and a teddy-bear and a tin pigeon. Mrs. Bircumshaw threw a cloth on the table that was pushed up under the drab-blinded window, against the great, black stove which radiated coldness—since it could not radiate warmth.

"Will you stay to supper?" asked Mrs. Bircumshaw.

"What have you got?" was the frank reply.

"I'm afraid there's only bread and cheese."

"No thanks, then," declined the older woman, "I don't eat bread and cheese for supper, Ethel, and you ought not."

They talked—or rather Mrs. Gillatt held forth for a few minutes on 'Suppers'. Then there was a silence.

"I never knew such a thing in my life," began Mrs. Gillatt, rather awkwardly, as a tentative—she wanted her friend to unbosom. "Is he often like this?" she persisted.

"Oh yes."

"Well, I can see now," Mrs Gillatt declared. "I can understand now. Often have I come in and seen you with your eyes all red. But you've not said anything—so I haven't liked to. But I know now. Just fancy, the brute! And will he be all right when you go to bed?"

"Oh no."

"Will he keep it up tomorrow?" Mrs. Gillatt's tone expressed nothing short of amazed horror.

"Oh yes, and very likely for two or three days."

"Oh the brute!—the brute! Well, this *has* opened my eyes. I've been watching a few of these men, lately and I tell you——. You'll not sleep with him tonight, shall you?"

"It would only make it worse."

"Worse or not worse, I wouldn't. There's the other bed. Take the baby and sleep there."*

"It would only make it worse," said Mrs. Bircumshaw weariedly. Mrs. Gillatt was silent a moment.

"Well, you're better to him than I should be, I can tell you," she said. "Oh, the brute, to think he should always be so good and gracious to my face and I think him so nice. But let him touch that child again—! Haven't I seen her with her little arms red. 'Gentlemanly'—so fond of quoting his 'gentlemanly'! Eh, but this has opened my eyes, Ethel—. Only let him touch that child again, to my knowledge. I only wish he would."

Mrs. Bircumshaw listened to this threat in silence. Yet she did wish she could see the mean bully in her husband matched by this spoiled, arrogant, generous woman.

"But tell him, Ethel," said Mrs. Gillatt, bending from her handsome height and speaking in considerate tones. "Tell him that I saw nothing—nothing. Tell him I thought he had suddenly been called to the door. Tell him that—and that I thought he'd gone down the Drive with a caller. Say that—you can do it, it's perfectly true—I did think so. So tell him, the brute!"

Mrs. Bircumshaw listened patiently, occasionally smiling to herself. She would tell her husband nothing, would never mention the affair to him. Moreover, she intended her husband to think he had made a fool of himself before this handsome woman whom he admired so much.

Bircumshaw heard his wife's friend take her leave. He had been in torment while the two women were together in the far-off kitchen. Now the brute in him felt more sure, more triumphant. He was afraid of *two* women—he could cow one. He felt he had something to punish, that he had his own dignity and authority to assert. And he was going to punish, going to assert.

"I should think," said Mrs. Gillatt in departing, "that you won't take him any supper."

Mrs. Bircumshaw felt a sudden blaze of anger against him. But she laughed deprecatingly.

"You *are* a silly thing if you do," cried the other. "My word, I'd starve him if I had him."

"But you see you haven't got him," said the wife quietly.

"No, I'm thankful to say. But if I had—the brute!"

He heard her go and was relieved. Now he could lie in bed and sulk to his heart's content, and inflict penalties of ill-humour on his insolent wife. He was such a lusty, emotional man—and he had nothing to do. What was his work to him? Scarcely more than nothing. And what was to fill the rest of his life—nothing! He wanted something to do—and he thought he wanted more done for him. So he got into this irritable, sore state of moral debility. A man cannot respect himself unless he does something. But he can do without his own positive self-respect so long as his wife respects him. But when a man who has no foothold for self-esteem sees his wife and his wife's friends despise him, it is Hell—he fights for very life. So Bircumshaw lay in bed in this state of ignoble misery. His wife had striven for a long time to pretend he was still her hero but he had tried her patience too far. Now he was confounding heroism, mastery with brute tyranny. He would be a tyrant if not a hero.

She, downstairs, occasionally smiled to herself. This time she had given him his due. Her mind was triumphant, but her heart was pained and anxious. She could still smile. She had clipped a large lock from her Samson and her smile rose from the depth* of her woman's nature.

After having eaten a very little supper, she worked about the house till ten o'clock. Her face had regained that close impassivity which many women wear when alone. Still impassive, at the end of her little tasks she fetched the dinner-joint and made him four sandwiches carefully seasoned and trimmed. Pouring him a glass of milk, she went upstairs with the tray, which looked fresh and tempting.

He had been listening acutely to her last movements. As she entered, however, he lay well under the bed-clothes, breathing steadily, pretending to sleep. She came in quite calmly.

"Here is your supper," she said in a quiet, indifferent tone, ignoring the fact that he was supposed to be asleep. Another lock fell from his strength. He felt virtue depart from him,* felt weak and watery in spirit, and he hated her. He made no reply, but kept up his pretence of sleep.

She bent over the cot of the sleeping baby, a bonny child of three. The little one was flushed in her sleep. Her fist was clenched in a tangle of hair over her small, round ears, while even in sleep she pouted in her wilful, imperious way. With very gentle fingers, the mother loosened the bright hair and put it back from the full, small brow.* The father felt that he was left out, ignored. He would have wished to whisper a word to his wife, and so bring himself into the trinity, had he not been so wrath.* He retired further into his manly bulk, felt weaker and more miserably insignificant—and at the same time more enraged.

Mrs. Bircumshaw slipped into bed quietly, settling to rest at once, as far as possible from the broad form of her husband. Both lay quite still, although, as each knew, neither slept. The man felt he wanted to move, but his will was so weak and shrinking he could not rouse his muscles. He lay tense, paralysed with self-conscious shrinking, yet bursting to move. She nestled herself down, quite at ease. She did not care, this evening, how he felt or thought. For once she let herself rest in indifference.

Towards one o'clock in the morning, just as she was drifting into sleep, her eyes flew open. She did not start or stir, merely she was wide awake. A match had been struck.

Her husband was sitting up in bed, leaning forward to the plate on the chair. Very carefully, she turned her head just enough to see him. His big back bulked above her. He was leaning forward to the chair. The candle, which he had set on the floor, so that its light should not penetrate the sleep of his wife, threw strange shadows on the ceiling, and lighted his throat and underneath his strong chin. Through the arch of his arm she could see his jaw and his throat working. For some strange reason, he felt that he could not eat in the dark. Occasionally she could see his cheek bulged with food. He ate rapidly, almost voraciously, leaning over the edge of the bed and taking care of the crumbs. She noticed the weight of his shoulder muscles at rest upon the arm on which he leaned.

"The strange animal!" she said to herself, and she laughed, laughed heartily within herself.

"Are they nice?" she longed to say, slyly.

"Are they *nice*?"—she must say it—"*Are* they nice?"

The temptation was almost too great. But she was afraid of this lusty animal startled at his feeding. She dared not twit him.

He took the milk, leaned back, almost arching back over her as he drank. She shrank with a little fear, a little repulsion, which was nevertheless half pleasurable. Cowering under his shadow, she shrugged with contempt, yet her eyes widened with a small excited smile. This vanished and a real scorn hardened her lips...when he was sulky his blood was cold as water, nothing could rouse it to passion...he resisted caresses as if he had thin acid in his veins. "Mean in the blood," she thought.

He finished the food and milk, licked his lips, nipped out the candle, then stealthily lay down. He seemed to sink right into a grateful sleep.

"Nothing on earth is so vital to him as a meal," she said to herself. She lay a long time thinking before she fell asleep.

# Once—!

The morning was very beautiful. White packets of mist hung over the river, as if a great train had gone by leaving its steam idle, in a trail down the valley.* The mountains were just faint grey-blue, with the slightest glitter of snow high up in the sunshine. They seemed to be standing a long way off, watching me, and wondering. As I bathed in the shaft of sunshine that came through the wide-opened window, letting the water slip swiftly down my sides, my mind went wandering through the hazy morning, very sweet and far-off and still, so that I had hardly wit enough to dry myself. And as soon as I had got on my dressing gown, I lay down again idly on the bed, looking out at the morning that still was greenish from the dawn, and thinking of Anita.*

I had loved her when I was a boy. She was an aristocrat's daughter, but she was not rich. I was simply middle-class. Then, I was much too green and humble-minded to think of making love to her. No sooner had she come home from school than she married an officer. He was rather handsome, something in the Kaiser's fashion,* but stupid as an ass. And Anita was only eighteen. When at last she accepted me as a lover, she told me about it.

"The night I was married," she said, "I lay counting the flowers on the wall-paper, how many on a string; he bored me so."

He was of good family, and of great repute in the army, being a worker. He had the tenacity of a bull-dog, and rode like a centaur. These things look well from a distance, but to live with they weary one beyond endurance, so Anita says.

She had her first child just before she was twenty: two years afterwards, another. Then no more. Her husband was something of a brute. He neglected her, though not outrageously, treated her as if she were a fine animal. To complete matters, he more than ruined himself owing to debts, gambling and otherwise, then utterly disgraced himself by using government money and being caught.

"You have found a hair in your soup," I wrote to Anita.

"Not a hair, a whole plait," she replied.

After that, she began to have lovers. She was a splendid young creature, and was not going to sit down in her rather elegant flat in Berlin, to run to seed. Her husband was officer in a crack regiment. Anita was superb to look at. He was proud to introduce her to his friends. Then moreover she had her own relatives in Berlin,* aristocratic but also rich, and moving in the first society. So she began to take lovers.

Anita shows her breeding: erect, rather haughty, with a good-humoured kind of scorn. She is tall and strong, her brown eyes are full of scorn, and she has a downy, warm-coloured skin, brownish to match her black hair.

At last she came to love me a little. Her soul is unspoiled. I think she has almost the soul of a virgin. I think, perhaps, it frets her that she has never really loved. She has never had the real respect—Ehrfurcht*—for a man. And she has been here with me in the Tyrol these last ten days. I love her, and I am not satisfied with myself. Perhaps I too shall fall short.

"You have never *loved* your men?" I asked her.

"I loved them—but I have put them all in my pocket," she said, with just the faintest disappointment in her good-humour. She shrugged her shoulders at my serious gaze.

I lay wondering if I too were going into Anita's pocket, along with her purse and her perfume and the little sweets she loved. It would almost have been delicious to do so. A kind of voluptuousness urged me to let her have me, to let her put me in her pocket. It would be so nice. But I loved her: it would not be fair to her: I wanted to do more than give her pleasure.

Suddenly the door opened on my musing, and Anita came into my bedroom. Startled, I laughed in my very soul, and I adored her, she was so natural! She was dressed in a transparent lacy chemise, that was slipping over her shoulder, high boots, upon one of which her string-coloured stocking had fallen, and she wore an enormous hat, black, lined with white, and covered with a tremendous creamy-brown feather, that streamed like a flood of brownish foam, swaying lightly.* It was an immense hat on top of her shamelessness, and the great, soft feather seemed to spill over, fall with a sudden gush, as she put back her head.

She looked at me, then went straight to the mirror.

"How do you like my hat?" she said.

She stood before the panel of looking glass, conscious only of her hat, whose great feather-strands swung in a tide. Her bare shoulder glistened, and through the fine web of her chemise, I could see all her body in warm silhouette, with golden reflections under the breasts and arms.* The light ran in silver up her lifted arms, and the gold shadow stirred as she arranged her hat.

"How do you like my hat?" she repeated.

Then, as I did not answer, she turned to look at me. I was still lying on the bed. She must have seen that I had looked at her, instead of at her hat, for a quick darkness and a frown came into her eyes, cleared instantly, as she asked, in a slightly hard tone:

"Don't you like it?"

"It's rather splendid," I answered. "Where did it come from?"

"From Berlin this morning—or last evening," she replied.

"It's a bit huge," I ventured.

She drew herself up.

"Indeed not!" she said, turning to the mirror.

I got up, dropped off my dressing gown, put a silk hat quite correctly on my head, and then, naked save for a hat and a pair of gloves, I went forward to her.

"How do you like my hat?" I asked her.

She looked at me and went off into a fit of laughter. She dropped her hat onto a chair, and sank onto the bed, shaking with laughter. Every now and then she lifted her head, gave one look from her dark eyes, then buried her face in the pillows. I stood before her clad in my hat, feeling a good bit of a fool. She peeped up again.

"You are lovely, you are lovely!" she cried.

With a grave and dignified movement I prepared to remove the hat, saying:

"And even then, I lack high-laced boots and one stocking."

But she flew at me, kept the hat on my head, and kissed me.

"Don't take it off," she implored. "I love you for it."

So I sat down gravely and unembarrassed on the bed.

"But don't you like my hat?" I said in injured tones. "I bought it in London last month."

She looked up at me comically, and went into peals of laughter.

"Think," she cried, "if all those Englishmen in Piccadilly went like that!"

That amused even me.

At last I assured her her hat was adorable, and, much to my relief, I got rid of my silk and into a dressing gown.

"You *will* cover yourself up," she said reproachfully. "And you look so nice with nothing on—but a hat."

"It's that old Apple I can't digest,"* I said.

She was quite happy in her shift and her high boots. I lay looking at her beautiful legs.

"How many more men have you done that to?" I asked.

"What?" she answered.

"Gone into their bedrooms clad in a wisp of mist, trying a new hat on?"

She leaned over to me and kissed me.

"Not many," she said. "I've not been *quite* so familiar before, I don't think."

"I suppose you've forgotten," said I. "However, it doesn't matter." Perhaps the slight bitterness in my voice touched her. She said almost indignantly:

"Do you think I want to flatter you and make you believe you are the first that ever I really—*really*—"

"I don't," I replied. "Neither you nor I is so easily deluded."

She looked at me peculiarly and steadily.

"I know all the time," said I, "that I am 'pro tem.', and that I shan't even last as long as most."

"You are sorry for yourself?" she mocked.

I shrugged my shoulders, looking into her eyes. She caused me a good deal of agony, but I didn't give in to her.

"I shan't commit suicide," I replied.

"'On est mort pour si longtemps',"* she said, suddenly dancing on the bed. I loved her. She had the courage to live, almost joyously.

"When you think back over your affairs—they are numerous, though you are only thirty-one—"

"Not numerous—only several—and you *do* underline the thirty-one—," she laughed.

"But how do you feel, when you think of them?" I asked.

She knitted her eyebrows quaintly, and there was a shadow, more puzzled than anything, on her face.

"There is something nice in all of them," she said. "Men are really fearfully good," she sighed.

"If only they weren't all pocket-editions," I mocked.

She laughed, then began drawing the silk cord through the lace of her chemise, pensively. The round cap of her shoulder gleamed like old ivory: there was a faint brown stain towards the arm-pit.

"No," she said, suddenly lifting her head and looking me calmly into the eyes, "I have nothing to be ashamed of—that is,—no, I have nothing to be ashamed of!"

"I believe you," I said. "And I don't suppose you've done anything that even *I* shouldn't be able to swallow—have you—?"

I felt rather plaintive with my question. She looked at me and shrugged her shoulders.

"I know you haven't," I preached. "All your affairs have been rather decent. They've meant more to the men than they have to you."

The shadows of her breasts, fine globes, shone warm through the linen veil. She was thinking.

"Shall I tell you," she asked, "one thing I did?"

"If you like," I answered. "But let me get you a wrap." I kissed her shoulder. It had the same fine, delicious coldness of ivory.

"No—yes you may," she replied.

I brought her a Chinese thing of black silk with gorgeous embroidered dragons, green as flame, writhing upon it.

"How white against that black silk you are," I said, kissing the half globe of her breast, through the linen.

"Lie there," she commanded me. She sat in the middle of the bed, whilst I lay looking at her. She picked up the black silk tassel of my dressing gown, and began flattening it out like a daisy.

"Gretchen!" I said.

"'Marguerite with one petal'," * she answered in French, laughing. "I am ashamed of it, so you must be nice with me—"

"Have a cigarette!" I said.

She puffed wistfully for a few moments.

"You've got to hear it," she said.

"Go on!"

"I was staying in Dresden* in quite a grand hôtel;—which I rather enjoy: ringing bells, dressing three times a day, feeling half a great lady, half a cocotte. Don't be cross with me for saying it: look at me! The man was at a garrison a little way off. I'd have married him if I could—"

She shrugged her brown, handsome shoulders, and puffed out a plume of smoke.

"It began to bore me after three days. I was always alone, looking at shops alone, going to the opera alone—where the beastly men got behind their wives' backs to look at me. In the end I got cross with my poor man, though of course it wasn't his fault, that he couldn't come."

She gave a little laugh as she took a draw at her cigarette.

"The fourth morning I came downstairs—I was feeling fearfully good-looking and proud of myself. I know I had a sort of café au lait coat and skirt, very pale—and its fit was a *joy*!"

After a pause, she continued: "—And a big black hat with a cloud of white ospreys. I nearly jumped when a man almost ran into me. O jeh!,* it was a young officer, just bursting with life, a splendid creature: the German aristocrat at his best. He wasn't over tall, in his dark blue uniform, but simply firm with life. An electric shock went through me, it slipped down me like fire, when I looked into his eyes. O jeh!, they just flamed with consciousness of me—And they were just the same colour as the soft-blue revers* of his uniform. He looked at me—ha!—and then, he bowed, the sort of bow a woman enjoys, like a caress.

"'Verzeihung, gnädiges Fräulein!'*

"I just inclined my head, and we went our ways. It felt as if something mechanical shifted us, not our wills.

"I was restless that day, I could stay nowhere. Something stirred inside my veins. I was drinking tea on the Brühler Terrasse, watching the people go by like a sort of mechanical procession, and the broad Elbe* as a stiller background, when he stood before me, saluting, and taking a seat, half apologetically, half devil-may-care. I was not nearly so much surprised at him, as at the mechanical parading people. And I could see he thought me a Cocotte—"

She looked thoughtfully across the room, the past roused dangerously in her dark eyes.

"But the game amused and excited me. He told me he had to go to a Court ball tonight—and then he said, in his nonchalant yet pleadingly passionate way:

"'And afterwards—?'

"'And afterwards—!' I repeated.

"'May I—?' he asked.

"Then I told him the number of my room.

"I dawdled to the hôtel, and dressed for dinner, and talked to somebody sitting next to me, but I was an hour or two ahead, when he would come. I arranged my silver and brushes and things, and I had ordered a great bunch of lilies of the valley; they were in a black bowl. There were delicate pink silk curtains, and the carpet was a cold colour, nearly white, with a tawny pink and turquoise ravelled border, a Persian thing, I should imagine. I know I liked it.—And didn't that room feel fresh, full of expectation, like myself!

"That last half hour of waiting—so funny—I seemed to have no feeling, no consciousness. I lay in the dark, holding my nice pale blue gown of crêpe de chine against my body for comfort. There was a fumble at the door, and I caught my breath. Quickly he came in, locked the door, and switched on all the lights. There he stood, the centre of everything, the light shining on his bright brown hair. He was holding something under his cloak. Now he came to me, and threw on me from out of his cloak a whole armful of red and pink roses. It was delicious! Some of them were cold, when they fell on me. He took off his cloak: I loved his figure in its blue uniform; and then, oh jeh!, he picked me off the bed, the roses and all, and kissed me—*how* he kissed me!"

She paused at the recollection.

"I could feel his mouth through my thin gown. Then, he went still and intense. He pulled off my saut-de-lit,* and looked at me. He held me away from him, his mouth parted with wonder, and yet, as if the Gods would envy him—wonder and adoration and pride! I liked his worship. Then he laid me on the bed again, and covered me up gently, and put my roses on the other side of me, a heap just near my hair, on the pillow.

"Quite unashamed and not the least conscious of himself, he got out of his clothes. And he *was* adorable—so young, and rather spare, but with a *rich* body, that simply glowed with love of me. He stood looking at me, quite humbly; and I held out my hands to him.

"All that night we loved each other. There were crushed, crumpled little rose-leaves on him when he sat up, almost like crimson blood! Oh and he was fierce, and at the same time, tender—!"

Anita's lips trembled slightly, and she paused. Then, very slowly, she went on:

"When I woke in the morning he was gone, and just a few passionate words on his dancing-card with a gold crown, on the little table beside me, imploring me to see him again in the Brühler Terrasse in the afternoon. But I took the morning express to Berlin—"

We both were still. The river rustled far off in the morning.

"And—?" I said.

"And I never saw him again—"

We were both still. She put her arms round her bright knee, and caressed it, lovingly, rather plaintively, with her mouth. The brilliant green dragons on her wrap seemed to be snarling at me.

"And you regret him?" I said at length.

"No," she answered, scarcely heeding me.—"I remember the way he unfastened his sword-belt and trappings from his loins, flung the whole with a jingle on the other bed—"

I was burning now with rage against Anita. Why should she love a man for the way he unbuckled his belt!

"With him," she mused, "everything felt so inevitable."

"Even your never seeing him again," I retorted.

"Yes!" she said, quietly.

Still musing, dreaming, she continued to caress her own knees.

"He said to me, 'We are like the two halves of a walnut'."

And she laughed slightly.

"He said some lovely things to me.—'Tonight, you're an Answer.'* And then 'Whichever bit of you I touch, seems to startle me afresh with joy.' And he said, he should never forget the velvety feel of my skin.—Lots of beautiful things he told me."

Anita cast them over pathetically in her mind. I sat biting my finger with rage.

"—And I made him have roses in his hair. He sat so still and good while I trimmed him up, and was quite shy. He had a figure nearly like yours—."

Which compliment was a last insult to me.

"—And he had a long gold chain, threaded with little emeralds, that he wound round and round my knees, binding me like a prisoner, never thinking."

"And you wish he had kept you prisoner," I said.

"No," she answered. "He couldn't!"

"I see! You just preserve him as the standard by which you measure the amount of satisfaction you get from the rest of us."

"Yes," she said, quietly.

Then I knew she was liking to make me furious.

"But I thought you were rather ashamed of the adventure?" I said.

"No," she answered, perversely.

She made me tired. One could never be on firm ground with her. Always, one was slipping and plunging on uncertainty.* I lay still, watching the sunshine streaming white outside.

"What are you thinking?" she asked.

"The waiter will smile when we go down for coffee."

"No—tell me!"

"It is half past nine."

She fingered the string of her shift.

"What were you thinking?" she asked, very low.

"I was thinking, all you want, you get."

"In what way?"

"In love."

"And what do I want?"

"Sensation."

"Do I?"

"Yes."

She sat with her head drooped down.

"Have a cigarette," I said. "And are you going to that place for sleighing today?"

"Why do you say I only want sensation?" she asked quietly.

"Because it's all you'll take from a man.—You *won't* have a cigarette?"

"No thanks—and what else could I take—?"

I shrugged my shoulders.

"Nothing, I suppose—" I replied.

Still she picked pensively at her chemise string.

"Up to now, you've missed nothing—you haven't felt the lack of anything—in love," I said.

She waited awhile.

"Oh yes I have," she said gravely.

Hearing her say it, my heart stood still.*

# New Eve and Old Adam*

## 1

"After all," she said, with a little laugh, "I can't see it was so wonderful of you, to hurry home to me, if you are so cross* when you do come."

"You would rather I stayed away?" he asked.

"I wouldn't mind."

"You would rather I had stayed a day or two in Paris—or a night or two?"

She burst into a jeering "pouf!" of laughter.

"You!" she cried. "You and Parisian Nights' Entertainments!* What a fool you would look."

"Still," he said, "I could try."

"You *would*!" she mocked. "You would go dribbling up to a woman—'Please take me—my wife is so unkind to me'."

He drank his tea in silence. They had been married a year.* They had married quickly, for love. And during the last three months there had gone on almost continuously that battle between them which so many married people fight, without knowing why. Now it had begun again. He felt the physical sickness rising in him. Somewhere down in his belly the big, feverish pulse began to beat, where was the inflamed place caused by the conflict between them.

She was a beautiful woman of about thirty, fair, luxuriant, with proud shoulders and a face borne up by a fierce, native vitality. Her green eyes had a curious puzzled* contraction just now. She sat leaning on the table against the tea-tray, absorbed. It was as if she battled with herself in him. Her green dress reflected in the silver, against the red of the firelight. Leaning abstractedly forward, she pulled some primroses from the bowl, and threaded them at intervals in the plait which bound round her head in the peasant fashion. So, with her little starred fillet of flowers, there was something of the Gretchen about her.* But her eyes retained the curious half-smile.

Suddenly her face lowered gloomily. She sank her beautiful arms, laying them on the table. Then she sat almost sullenly, as if she would not give in. She was looking away out of the window. With a quick movement she glanced down at her hands. She took off her wedding ring, reached to the bowl for a long flower-stalk, and shook the ring glittering round and round upon it, regarding the spinning gold, and spinning it as if she would spurn it.* Yet there was something about her of a fretful, naughty child, as she did so.

The man sat by the fire, tired, but tense. His body seemed so utterly still because of the tension in which it was held. His limbs, thin and vigorous, lay braced like a listening thing, always vivid for action, yet held perfectly still. His face was set and expressionless. The wife was all the time, in spite of herself, conscious of him: as if the cheek that was turned towards him had a sense which perceived him. They were both rendered elemental, like impersonal forces, by the battle and the suffering.

She rose and went to the window. Their flat was the fourth, the top storey of a large house. Above the high-ridged, handsome red roof opposite was an assembly of telegraph wires, a square, squat framework, towards which hosts of wires sped from four directions, arriving in darkly stretched lines out of the white sky. High up, at a great height, a seagull sailed. There was a noise of traffic from the town beyond.

Then, from behind the ridge of the house-roof opposite a man climbed up into the tower of wires, belted himself amid the netted sky, and began to work, absorbedly. Another man, half hidden by the roof-ridge, stretched up to him with a wire. The man in the sky reached down to receive it. The other, having delivered, sank out of sight. The solitary man worked absorbedly. Then he seemed drawn away from his task. He looked round, almost furtively, from his lonely height, the space pressing on him. His eyes met those of the beautiful woman who stood in her afternoon gown, with flowers in her hair, at the window.

"I like you," she said, in her normal voice.

The husband in the darkening room with her looked round slowly and asked:

"Whom do you like?"

Receiving no answer, he resumed his tense stillness.

She remained watching at the window, above the small, quiet street of large houses. The man, suspended there in the sky, looked across at her and she at him. The city was far below. Her eyes and his met across the lofty space. Then, crouching together again into his forgetfulness, he hid himself in his work. He would not look again. Presently he climbed down, and the tower of wires was empty against the sky.

The woman glanced at the little park at the end of the clean, grey street. The diminished, dark-blue form of a soldier was seen passing between the green stretches of grass, his spurs giving the faintest glitter to his walk.

Then she turned hesitating from the window, as if drawn by her husband. He was sitting still motionless, and detached from her, hard: held absolutely away from her by his will. She wavered, then went and crouched on the hearthrug at his feet, laying her head on his knee.

"Don't be horrid with me!" she pleaded, in a caressing, languid, impersonal voice.

He shut his teeth hard, and his lips parted slightly with pain.

"You know you love me," she continued, in the same heavy, sing-song way.

He breathed hard, but kept still.

"Don't you?" she said, slowly, and she put her arms round his waist, under his coat, drawing him to her. It was as if flames of fire were running under his skin.

"I have never denied it," he said, woodenly.

"Yes," she pleaded, in the same heavy, toneless voice. "Yes. You are always trying to deny it." She was rubbing her cheek against his knee softly. Then she gave a little laugh, and shook her head. "But it's no good." She looked up at him. There was a curious light in her eyes, of subtle victory. "It's no good, my love, is it?"

His heart ran hot. He knew it was no good his trying to deny he loved her. But he saw her eyes, and his will remained set and hard. She looked away into the fire.

"You hate it that you have to love me," she said, in a pensive voice through which the triumph flickered faintly. "You hate it that you love me—and it is petty and mean of you. You hate it that you can't stay away from me. You hate it that you had to hurry back to me from Paris."

Her voice had become again quite impersonal, as if she were talking to herself.

"At any rate," he said, "it is your triumph."

She gave a sudden, bitter-contemptuous laugh.

"Ha!" she said. "What is triumph to me, you fool. You can have your triumph. I should be only too glad to give it you."

"And I to take it."

"Then take it," she cried, in hostility. "I offer it you often enough."

"But you never mean to part with it."

"It is a lie. It is you, you, who are too paltry to take a woman. How often do I fling myself at you—!"

"Then don't—don't—"

"Ha—and if I don't—I get nothing out of you. Self!—self!—that is all you are."

His face remained set and expressionless. She looked up at him. Suddenly she drew him to her again, and hid her face against him.

"Don't kick me off, Pietro,* when I come to you," she pleaded.

"You *don't* come to me," he answered stubbornly.

She lifted her head a few inches away from him and seemed to listen, or to think.

"What do I do then?" she asked, for the first time quietly.

"You treat me as if I were a piece of cake, for you to eat when you wanted."

She rose from him with a mocking cry of scorn, that yet had something hollow in its sound.

"Treat you like a piece of cake, do I!" she cried. "I, who have done all I have for you—!"

There was a knock, and the maid entered with a telegram. He tore it open.

"No answer," he said, and the maid softly closed the door.

"I suppose it is for you," he said, bitingly, rising and handing her the slip of paper.

She read it, laughed, then read it again, aloud:

"'Meet me Marble Arch* 7.30—theatre—Richard.' Who is Richard?" she asked, looking at her husband rather interested. He shook his head.

"Nobody of mine," he said. "Who is he?"

"I haven't the faintest notion," she said, flippantly.

"But," and his eyes went bullying, "you *must* know."

She suddenly became quiet, and jeering, took up his challenge.

"Why must I know?" she asked.

"Because it isn't for me, therefore it must be for you."

"And couldn't it be for anybody else?" she sneered.

"'Moest, 14 Merrilies Street'," he read, decisively.

For a second she was puzzled into earnestness.

"Pah, you fool," she said, turning aside. "Think of your own friends," and she flung the telegram away.

"It is not for me," he said, stiffly and finally.

"Then it is for the man in the moon—I should think *his* name is Moest,"* she added, with a pouf of laughter against him.

"Do you mean to say you know nothing about it?" he asked.

"'Do you mean to say'," she mocked, mouthing the words, and sneering. "Yes I do mean to say, poor little man."

He suddenly went hard with disgust.

"Then I simply don't believe you," he said coldly.

"Oh—don't you believe me," she jeered, mocking the touch of sententiousness in his voice. "What a calamity—the poor man* doesn't believe!"

"It couldn't possibly be any acquaintance of mine—" he said slowly.

"Then hold your tongue," she cried harshly. "I've heard enough of it."

He was silent, and soon she went out of the room. In a few minutes he heard her in the drawing-room, improvising furiously. It was a sound that maddened him; something yearning, yearning, striving, and something perverse, that counteracted the yearning. Her music was always working up towards a certain culmination, but never reaching it, falling away in a jangle. How he hated it. He lit a cigarette, and went across to the side board for whisky and soda. Then she began to sing. She had a good voice, but she could not keep time. As a rule it made his heart warm with tenderness for her, hearing her ramble through the songs in her own fashion, making Brahms sound so different by altering all his time. But today he hated her for it. Why the devil couldn't she submit to the natural laws of the stuff!

In about fifteen minutes she entered laughing. She laughed as she closed the door, and as she came to him where he sat.

"Oh," she said, "you silly thing, you silly thing! Aren't you a stupid clown?"

She crouched between his knees and put her arms round him. She was smiling into his face, her green eyes, looking into his, were bright and wide. But somewhere in them, as he looked back, was a little twist that could not come loose to him, a little cast, that was like an aversion from him, a strain of hate for him. The hot waves of blood flushed over his body, and his heart seemed to dissolve under her caresses. But at last, after many months, he knew her well enough. He knew that curious little strain in her eyes, which was waiting for him to submit to her, and then would spurn him again. He resisted her while ever it was there.

"Why don't you let yourself love me?" she asked, pleading, but a touch of mockery in her voice. His jaw set hard.

"Is it because you are afraid?"

He heard the slight sneer.

"Of what?" he asked.

"Afraid to trust yourself?"

There was silence. It made him furious that she could sit there caressing him and yet sneer at him.

"What *have* I done with myself?" he asked.

"Carefully saved yourself from giving all to me, for fear you might lose something."

"Why should I lose anything?" he asked.

And they were both silent. She rose at last and went away from him to get a cigarette. The silver box flashed red with firelight in her hands. She struck a match, bungled, threw the stick aside, lit another.

"What did you come running back for?" she asked, insolently, talking with half-shut lips because of the cigarette. "I told you I wanted peace—I've had none for a year. And for the last three months you've done nothing but try to destroy me."

"You have not gone frail on it," he answered sarcastically.

"Nevertheless," she said, "I am ill inside me. I am sick of you—sick. You make an eternal demand, and you give nothing back. You leave one empty." She puffed the cigarette in feminine fashion, then suddenly she struck her forehead with a wild gesture. "I have a ghastly, empty feeling in my head," she said. "I feel I simply *must* have rest—I must."

The rage went through his veins like flame.

"From your labours?" he asked, sarcastically, suppressing himself.

"From you—from *you*!" she cried, thrusting forward her head at him. "You, who use a woman's soul up, with your rotten life.—I suppose it is partly your health, and you can't help it," she added, more mildly. "But I simply can't stand it—I simply can't, and that is all."

She shook her cigarette carelessly in the direction of the fire. The ash fell on the beautiful asiatic rug. She glanced at it, but did not trouble. He sat, hard with rage.

"May I ask how I use you up, as you say?" he asked.

She was silent a moment, trying to get her feeling into words. Then she shook her hand at him passionately, and took the cigarette from her mouth.

"By—by following me about—by not leaving me *alone*. You give me no peace.—*I* don't know what you do, but it is something ghastly."

Again the hard stroke of rage went down his veins.*

"It is very vague," he said.

"I know," she cried. "I can't put it into words—but there it is.—You—you don't love. I pour myself out to you, and then—there's nothing there—you simply aren't there."

He was silent for some time. His jaw had set hard with fury and hate.

"We have come to the incomprehensible," he said.—"And now, what about Richard?"

It had grown nearly dark in the room. She sat silent for a moment. Then she took the cigarette from her mouth and looked at it.

"I'm going to meet him," her voice, mocking, answered out of the twilight.

His heart went molten, and he could scarcely breathe.

"Who is he?" he asked, though he did not believe the affair to be anything at all, even if there were a Richard.

"I'll introduce him to you when I know him a little better," she said. He waited.

"But who is he?"

"I tell you, I'll introduce him to you later."

There was a pause.

"Shall I come with you?"

"It would be like you," she answered, with a sneer.

The maid came in, softly, to draw the curtains and turn on the light. The husband and wife sat silent.

"I suppose," he said, when the door was closed again, "you are wanting a Richard for a rest?"

She took his sarcasm simply as a statement.

"I am," she said. "A simple, warm man who would love me without all these reservations and difficulties. That is just what I do want."

"Well, you have your own independence," he said.

"Ha," she laughed. "You needn't tell me that. It would take more than you to rob me of my independence."

"I meant your own income," he answered quietly, while his heart was plunging with bitterness and rage.

"Well," she said, "I will go and dress."

He remained without moving, in his chair. The pain of this was almost too much. For some moments the great, inflamed pulse struck through his body. It died gradually down, and he went dull. He had not wanted to separate from her at this point of their union: they would probably, if they parted in such a crisis, never come together again. But if she insisted, well then, it would have to be. He would go away for a month. He could easily make business in Italy. And when he came back, they could patch up some sort of domestic arrangement, as most other folk had to do.

He felt dull and heavy inside, and without the energy for anything. The thought of having to pack and take a train to Milan appalled him, it would mean such an effort of will. But it would have to be done, and so he must do it. It was no use his waiting at home. He might stay in town a night, at his brother-in-law's,* and go away the next day. It were better to give her a little time to come to herself. She was really impulsive. And he did not really want to go away from her.

He was still sitting thinking, when she came downstairs. She was in costume and furs and toque. There was a radiant, half wistful, half perverse look about her. She was a beautiful woman, her bright, fair face set among the black furs.

"Will you give me some money?" she said. "There isn't any."

He took two sovereigns, which she put in her little black purse. She would go without a word of reconciliation. It made his heart set hard again.

"You would like me to go away for a month?" he said, calmly.

"Yes," she answered, stubbornly.

"All right then, I will. I must stop in town for tomorrow, but I will sleep at Edmund's."

"You could do that, couldn't you?" she said, accepting his suggestion, a little bit hesitating.

"If you want me to."

She knitted her brow, and put up her face pathetically.

"I'm so *tired*!" she lamented.

But there was exasperation and hate in the last word, too.

"Very well," he answered.

She finished buttoning her glove.

"You'll go, then?" she said, suddenly brightly, turning to depart. "Goodbye."

He hated her for the flippant insult of her leavetaking.

"I shall be at Edmund's tomorrow," he said.

"You will write to me from Italy, won't you?"

He would not answer the unnecessary question.

"Have you taken the dead primroses out of your hair?" he asked.

"I haven't," she said.

And she unpinned her hat.

"Richard *would* think me cracked," she said, picking out the crumpled, creamy fragments.

"Lovable and pathetic," he answered, sarcastic and bitter.*

She strewed the withered flowers carelessly on the table, set her hat straight.

"Do you *want* me to go?" he asked, again, rather yearning.

She knitted her brows. It irked her to resist the appeal. Yet she had in her breast a hard, repellant* feeling for him. She had loved him, too. She had loved him dearly. And—he had not seemed to realise her. So that now she *did* want to be free of him for a while. Yet the love, the passion she had had for him clung about her. But she did want, first and primarily, to be free of him again.

"Yes," she said, half pleading.

"Very well," he answered.

She came across to him, and put her arms round his neck. Her hatpin caught his head, but he moved, and she did not notice.

"You don't mind very much, do you, my love?" she said caressingly.

"I mind all the world, and all I am," he said.

She rose from him, fretted, miserable, and yet determined.

"I *must* have some rest," she repeated.

He knew that cry. She had had it, on occasions, for two months now. He had cursed her, and refused either to go away or to let her go. Now he knew it was no use.

"All right," he said. "Go and get it from Richard."

"Yes."—She hesitated. "Goodbye," she called, and was gone.

He heard her cab whirr away. He had no idea whither she was gone—but probably to Madge, her friend.*

He went upstairs to pack. Their bedroom made him suffer. She used to say, at first, that she would give up anything rather than her sleeping with him. And still they were always together. A kind of blind helplessness drove them to one another, even when, after he had taken her, they only felt more apart than ever. It had seemed to her that he had been mechanical and barren with her. She felt a horrible feeling of aversion from him, inside her, even while physically she still desired him. His body had always a kind of fascination for her. But had hers for him? He seemed, often, just to have served her, or to have obeyed some impersonal instinct for which she was the only outlet, in his loving her. So at last she rose against him, to cast him off. He seemed to follow her so, to draw her life into his. It made her feel she would go mad. For he seemed to do it just blindly, without having any notion of her herself. It was as if she were sucked out of herself by some non-human force. As for him, he seemed only like an instrument for his work,* his business, not like a person at all. Sometimes she thought he was a big fountain pen which was always sucking at her blood for ink.

He could not understand anything of this. He loved her—he could not bear to be away from her. He tried to realise her and to give her what she wanted. But he could not understand. He could not understand her accusations against him. Physically, he knew, she loved him, or had loved him, and was satisfied, or had been satisfied* by him. He also knew that she would have loved another man nearly as well. And for the rest, he was only himself. He could not understand what she said about his using her and giving her nothing in return. Perhaps he did not think of her, as a separate person from himself, sufficiently. But then he did not see, he could not see that she had any real personal life, separate from himself. He tried to think of her in every possible way, and to give her what she wanted. But it was no good, she was never at peace. And lately there had been growing a breach between them. They had never come together without his realising it, afterwards. Now he must submit, and go away.

And her quilted dressing gown—it was a little bit torn, like most of her things—and her pearl-backed mirror, with one of the pieces of pearl missing—all her untidy, flimsy, lovable things, hurt him as he went about the bedroom, and made his heart go hard with hate, in the midst of his love.

## 2

Instead of going to his brother-in-law's, he went to an hôtel for the night. It was not till he stood in the lift with the attendant at his side that he began to realise that he was only a mile or so away from his own house, and yet further away than any miles could make him. It was about nine o'clock. He hated his bedroom. It was comfortable, and not ostentatious: its only fault was the neutrality necessary to an hôtel apartment. He looked round. There was one semi-erotic Florentine picture of a lady with cats' eyes, over the bed. It was not bad. The only other ornament on the walls was the notice of hours and prices of meals and rooms. The couch sat correctly before the correct little table, on which the writing sachet* and inkstand stood mechanically. Down below, the quiet street was half illuminated, the people passed sparsely, like stunted shadows. And of all times of the night, it was a quarter past nine. He thought he would go to bed. Then he looked at the white-and-glazed doors which shut him off from the bath. He would bath to pass the time away—in the bath-closet everything was so comfortable and white and warm—too warm: the level, unvarying heat of the atmosphere, from which there was no escape anywhere, seemed so hideously hôtel-like; this central-heating forced a unity into the great building, making it more than ever like an enormous box with incubating cells. He loathed it. But at any rate the bath-closet was human, white and business-like and luxurious.

He was trying, with the voluptuous warm water, and the exciting thrill of the shower-bath, to bring back the life into his dazed body. Since she had begun to hate him, he had gradually lost that physical pride and pleasure in his own physique which the first months of married life had given him. His body had gone meaningless to him again, almost as if it were not there. It had wakened up, there had been the physical glow and satisfaction about his movements, of a creature which rejoices in itself; a glow which comes on a man who loves and is loved passionately and successfully. Now this was going again. All the life was accumulating in his mental consciousness, and his body felt like a piece of waste. He was not aware of this. It was instinct which made him want to bathe. But that, too, was a failure. He went under the shower-spray with his mind occupied by business, or some care of affairs, taking the tingling water almost without knowing it, stepping out mechanically, as a man going through a barren routine. He was dry again, and looking out of the window, without having experienced anything during the last hour.

Then he remembered that she did not know his address. He scribbled a note and rang to have it posted.

As soon as he had turned out the light, and there was nothing left for his mental consciousness to flourish amongst, it dropped, and it was dark inside him as without. It was his blood, and the elemental male in it, that now rose from him: unknown instincts and unperceived movements out of the depths of his physical being rose and heaved blindly. The darkness almost suffocated him, and he could not bear it, that he was shut in this great, warm building. He wanted to be outside, with space springing from him. But again, the reasonable being in him knew it was ridiculous, and he remained staring at the dark, having the horrible sensation of a roof low down over him; whilst that dark, unknown being, which lived below all his consciousness in the eternal gloom of his blood, heaved and raged blindly against him.

It was not his thoughts that represented him. They spun like straws or the iridescence of oil on a dark stream. He thought of her, sketchily, spending an evening of light amusement with the symbolical Richard. That did not mean much to him. He did not really speculate about Richard. He had the dark, powerful sense of her, how she wanted to get away from him and from the deep, underneath intimacy which had gradually come between them, back to the easy, everyday life, where one knows nothing of the underneath, so that it takes its way apart from the consciousness. She did not want to have the deeper part of herself in direct contact with or under the influence of any other intrinsic being. She wanted, in the deepest sense, to be free of him. She could not bear the close, basic intimacy into which she had been drawn. She wanted her life for herself. It was true, her strongest desire had been previously to know the contact through the whole of her being, down to the very bottom. Now it troubled her. She wanted to disengage her roots. Above, in the open, she would give. But she must live perfectly free of herself, and not, at her source, be connected with anybody.— —She was using this symbolical Richard as a spade to dig him away from her. And he felt like a thing whose roots are all straining on their hold, and whose elemental life, that blind source, surges backwards and forwards darkly in a chaos,* like something which is threatened with spilling out of its own vessel.

This tremendous swaying of the most elemental part of him continued through the hours, accomplishing his being, whilst superficially he thought at random of the journey, of the Italian he would speak, how he had left his coat in the train, and the rascally official interpreter had tried to give him twenty lire for a sovereign—how the man in the hat-shop in the Strand* had given him the wrong change—of the new shape in hats, and the new felt—and so on. Underneath it all, like the sea under a pleasure-pier, his elemental, physical soul was heaving in great waves through his blood and his tissue, the sob, the silent lift, the slightly-washing fall away again. So his blood, out of whose darkness everything rose, being moved to its depths by her revulsion, heaved and swung towards its own rest, surging blindly to its own re-settling.

Without knowing it, he suffered that night almost more than he had ever suffered during his life. But it was all below his consciousness. It was his life itself at storm, not his mind and his will engaged at all.

In the morning he got up, thin and quiet, without much movement anywhere, only with some of the clearness of after-storm. His body felt like a clean, empty shell. His mind was limpidly clear. He went through the business of the toilet with a certain accuracy, and at breakfast, in the restaurant, there was about him that air of neutral correctness which makes men seem so unreal.

At lunch there was a telegram for him. It was like her to telegraph. "Come to tea, my dear love."

As he read it, there was a great heave of resistance in him. But then he faltered. With his consciousness, he remembered how impulsive and eager she was when she dashed off her telegrams, and he relaxed. It went without saying that he would go.

## 3

When he stood in the lift going up to his own flat, he was almost blind with the hurt of it all. They had loved each other so much, in this his first home. The parlour-maid opened to him, and he smiled at her, affectionately. In the golden-brown and cream-coloured hall—Paula would have nothing heavy or sombre about her—a bush of rose-coloured azaleas shone, and a little tub of lilies twinkled naïvely.

She did not come out to meet him.

"Tea is in the drawing-room," the maid said, and he went in while she was hanging up his coat. It was a big room, with a sense of space, and a spread of whitey carpet—almost the colour of unpolished marble—and grey and pink border; of pink roses on big white cushions, pretty Dresden China, and deep, chintz-covered chairs and sofas which looked as if they were used freely. It was a room where one could roll in soft, fresh comfort, a room which had not much breakable in it, and which seemed, in the dusky spring evening, fuller of light than the streets outside.

Paula rose, looking queenly and rather radiant, as she held out her hand. A young man, whom Peter scarcely noticed, rose on the other side the hearth.

"I expected you an hour ago," she said, looking into her husband's eyes. But though she looked at him, she did not see him. And he sank his head.

"This is another Moest," she said, presenting the stranger. "He knows Richard, too."

The young man, a German of about thirty, with a clean-shaven aesthetic face, long black hair brushed back a little wearily or bewildered from his brow, and inclined to fall in an odd loose strand again, so that he nervously put it back with his fine hand, looked at Moest and bowed. He had a finely cut face, but his dark blue eyes were strained, as if he did not quite know where he was. He sat down again, and his pleasant figure took a self-conscious attitude, of a man whose business it was to say things that should be listened to. He was not conceited or affected—naturally sensitive and rather naïve; but he could only move in an atmosphere of literature and literary ideas; yet he seemed to know there was something else, vaguely, and he felt rather at a loss. He waited for the conversation to move his way, as inert an insect waits, for the sun to set it flying.

"Another Moest," Paula was pronouncing emphatically. "Actually another Moest, of whom we have never heard, and under the same roof with us."

The stranger laughed, his lips moving nervously over his teeth.

"You are in this house?" Peter asked surprised.

The young man shifted in his chair, dropped his head, looked up again.

"Yes," he said, meeting Moest's eyes as if he were somewhat dazzled. "I am staying with the Lauriers, on the second flat."*

He spoke English slowly, with a quaint, musical quality in his voice, and a certain rhythmic enunciation.

"I see, and the telegram was for you?" said the host.

"Yes," replied the stranger, with a nervous little laugh.

"My husband," broke in Paula, evidently repeating to the German what she had said before, for Peter's benefit this time, "was quite convinced I had an *affaire*"—she pronounced it in the French fashion—"with this terrible Richard."

The German give his little laugh, and moved, painfully self-conscious, in his chair.

"Yes," he said, glancing at Moest.

"Did you spend a night of virtuous indignation," Paula laughed to her husband, "imagining my perfidy?"

"I did not," said her husband. "Were you at Madge's?"

"No," she said. Then, turning to her guest: "Who is Richard, Mr Moest?"

"Richard," began the German, word by word, "is my cousin." He glanced quickly at Paula, to see if he were understood. She rustled her skirts, and arranged herself comfortably, lying, or almost squatting, on the sofa by the fire. "He lives in Hampstead."*

"And what is he like?" she asked, with eager interest.

The German gave his little laugh. Then he moved his fingers across his brow, in his dazed fashion. Then he looked, with his beautiful blue eyes, at his beautiful hostess.

"I—" he laughed again nervously—"He is a man whose parts—are not very much—very well known to me. You see," he broke forth, and it was evident he was now conversing to an imaginary audience;—he grasped at the air with his hand, and his eyes had the blind look of one thinking hard—"I cannot easily express myself in English.—I—I never have talked it. I shall speak, because I know nothing of modern England, a kind of Renaissance English."

"How lovely!" cried Paula. "But if you would rather, speak German. We shall understand sufficiently."

"I would rather hear some Renaissance English," said Moest.

Paula was quite happy with the new stranger. She listened to descriptions of Richard, shifting animatedly on her sofa. She wore a new dress, of a rich red tile colour, glossy and long and soft, and she had threaded daisies, like buttons, in the braided plait of her hair.

Her husband hated her for these familiarities. But she was beautiful too, and warm-hearted. Only, through all her warmth and kindliness, lay, he said, at the bottom, an almost feline selfishness, a coldness.

She was playing to the stranger—nay, she was not playing, she was really occupied by him. The young man was the favorite disciple of the most famous present-day German poet and 'Meister'.* He himself was occupied in translating Shakspere. Having been always a poetic disciple, he had never come into touch with life save through literature, and for him, since he was a rather fine-hearted young man with a human need to live, this was a tragedy. Paula was not long in discovering what ailed him, and she was eager to come to his rescue.

It pleased her, nevertheless, to have her husband sitting by, watching her. She forgot to give tea to anyone. Moest, and the German, both helped themselves, and the former attended also to his wife's cup. He sat rather in the background, listening, and waiting. She had made a fool of him with her talk to this stranger of "Richard"; lightly and flippantly she had made a fool of him. He minded, but was used to it. Now she had absorbed herself in this dazed, starved, literature-bewildered young German, who was, moreover, really lovable, evidently a gentleman. And she was seeing in him her mission—"Just as," said Moest bitterly to himself, "she saw her mission in me, a year ago. She is no woman. She's got a big heart for everybody, but it must be like a common room: she's got no private, sacred heart, except perhaps for herself, where there's no room for a man in it."

At length the stranger rose to go, promising to come again.

"Isn't he adorable!" cried Paula, as her husband returned to the drawing-room. "I think he is simply adorable."

"Yes!" said Moest.

"He called this morning to ask about the telegram.—But poor devil, isn't it a shame, what they've done to him!"

"What who have done to him?" her husband asked, coldly, jealous.

"Those literary creatures.—They take a young fellow like that, and stick him up among the literary gods, like a mantel-piece ornament, and there he has to sit, being a minor ornament, while all his youth is gone.—It is criminal."

"He should get off the mantel-piece then," said Moest.

But inside him his heart was black with rage against her. What had she, after all, to do with this young man, when he himself was being smashed up by her. He loathed her pity and her kindliness, which was like a charitable institution. There was no core to the woman. She was full of generosity and bigness and kindness, but there was no heart in her, no security, no place for one single man. He began to understand now syrens and sphinxes and the other Greek fabulous, female things. They had not been created by fancy, but out of bitter necessity of the man's human heart to express itself.

"Ha!" she laughed, half contemptuous. "Did *you* get off your miserable starved isolation by yourself?—you didn't. You had to be fetched down, and I had to do it."

"Out of your usual charity," he said.

"But you can sneer at another man's difficulties," she said.

"Your name ought to be Panacea, not Paula,"* he replied.

He felt furious and dead against her. He could even look at her without the tenderness coming. And he was glad. He hated her. She seemed unaware. Very well, let her be so.

"Oh, but he makes me so miserable, to see him!" she cried. "Self-conscious, can't get into contact with anybody, living a false literary life like a man who takes poetry as a drug.—One *ought* to help him."

She was really earnest and distressed.

"Out of the frying-pan into the fire," he said.

"I'd rather be in the fire any day, than in a frying-pan," she said, abstractedly, with a little shudder. She never troubled to see the meaning of her husband's sarcasms.

They remained silent. The maid came in for the tray, and to ask him if he would be in to dinner. He waited for his wife to answer. She sat with her chin in her hands, brooding over the young German, and did not hear. The rage flashed up in his heart. He would have liked to smash her out of this false absorption.

"No," he said to the maid. "I think not. Are you at home for dinner, Paula?"

"Yes," she said.

And he knew by her tone, easy and abstracted, that she intended him to stay too. But she did not trouble to say anything.

At last, after some time, she asked:

"What did you do?"

"Nothing—went to bed early," he replied.

"Did you sleep well?"

"Yes thank you."

And he recognised the ludicrous civilities of married people, and he wanted to go. She was silent for a time. Then she asked, and her voice had gone still and grave:

"Why don't you ask me what I did?"

"Because I don't care—you just went to somebody's for dinner."

"Why don't you care what I do? Isn't it your place to care?"

"About the things you do to spite me?—no!"

"Ha!" she mocked. "I did nothing to spite you. I was in deadly earnest."

"Even with your Richard."

"Yes," she cried. "There *might* have been a Richard. What did you care?"

"In that case you'd have been a liar and worse, so why should I care about you then?"

"You *don't* care about me," she said, sullenly.

"You say what you please," he answered.

She was silent for some time.

"And did you do absolutely nothing last night?" she asked.

"I had a bath and went to bed."

Then she pondered.

"No," she said, "you don't care for me—"

He did not trouble to answer. Softly, a little china clock sang six.

"I shall go to Italy in the morning," he said.

"Yes."

"And," he said, slowly, forcing the words out, "I shall stay at the Aquila Nera at Milan*—you know my address."

"Yes," she answered.

"I shall be away about a month. Meanwhile you can rest."

"Yes," she said, in her throat, with a little contempt of him and his stiffness.

He, in spite of himself, was breathing heavily. He knew that this parting was the real separation of their souls, marked the point beyond which they could go no further, but accepted the marriage as a comparative failure. And he had built all his life on his marriage. She accused him of not loving her. He gripped the arms of his chair. Was there something in it? Did he only want the attributes which went along with her, the peace of heart which a man has in living to one woman, even if the love between them be not complete; the singleness and unity in his life that made it easy; the fixed establishment of himself as a married man with a home; the feeling that he belonged to somewhere, that one woman existed—not was paid, but *existed*,—really to take care of him; was it these things he wanted, and not her? But he wanted her for these purposes—her, and nobody else. But was that not enough for her. Perhaps he wronged her—it was possible. What she said against him was in earnest. And what she said in earnest he had to believe, in the long run, since it was the utterance of her being. He felt miserable and tired.

When he looked at her, across the gathering twilight of the room, she was staring into the fire and biting her finger nail, restlessly, restlessly, without knowing. And all his limbs went suddenly weak, as he realised that she suffered too, that something was gnawing at her. Something in the look of her, the crouching, dogged, wondering look, made him faint with tenderness for her.

"Don't bite your finger nails," he said quietly, and obediently, she took her hand from her mouth. His heart was beating quickly. He could feel the atmosphere of the room changing. It had stood aloof, the room, like something placed round him, like a great box. Now everything got softer, as if it partook of the atmosphere, of which he partook himself, and they were all one.

His mind reverted to her accusations, and his heart beat like a caged thing against what he could not understand. She said he did not love her. But he knew that, in his way he did. In his way—but was his way wrong? His way was himself, he thought, struggling. Was there something wrong, something missing in his nature, that he could not love? He struggled madly, as if he were in a mesh, and could not get out. He did not want to believe that he was deficient in his nature. Wherein was he deficient? It was nothing physical. She said he could not come out of himself, that he was no good to her, because he could not get outside himself. What did she mean? Get outside himself! It seemed like some acrobatic feat, some slippery contortionist trick. No, he could not understand. His heart flashed hot with resentment. She did nothing but find fault with him. What did she care about him, really, when she could taunt him with not being able to take a light woman when he was in Paris.—Though his heart, forced to do her justice, knew that for this she loved him, really.

But it was too complicated and difficult, and already, as they sat thinking, it had gone wrong between them, and things felt twisted, horribly twisted, so that he could not breathe. He must go. He could dine at the hôtel and go to the theatre.

"Well," he said, casually, "I must go. I think I shall go and see 'The Black Sheep'."*

She did not answer. Then she turned and looked at him with a queer, half bewildered, half perverse smile that seemed conscious of pain. Her eyes, shining rather dilated and triumphant, and yet with something heavily yearning behind them, looked into his. He could not understand, and, between her appeal and her defiant triumph, he felt as if his chest were crushed so he could not breathe.

"My love," she said, in a little singing, abstract fashion, her lips somehow sipping towards him, her eyes shining dilated: and yet he felt as if he were not in it, himself.

His heart was a flame that prevented his breathing. He gripped the chair like a man who is going to be put under torture.

"What?" he said, staring back at her.

"Oh my love!" she said softly with a little, intense laugh on her face, that made him pant. And she slipped from her sofa and came across to him, quickly, and put her hand hesitating on his hair. The blood struck like flame across his consciousness, and the hurt was keen like joy, like the releasing of something that hurts as the pressure is relaxed and the movement comes, before the peace. Afraid, his fingers touched her hand, and she sank swiftly between his knees, and put her face on his breast. He held her head hard against his chest, and again and again the flame went down his blood, as he felt her round, small, nut of a head between his hands pressing into his chest where the hurt had been bruised in so deep. His wrists quivered as he pressed her head to him, as he felt the deadness going out of him; the real life, released, flowing into his body again. How hard he had shut it off, against her, when she hated him. He was breathing heavily with relief, blindly pressing her head against him. He believed in her again.

She looked up, laughing, childish, inviting him with her lips. He bent to kiss her, and as his eyes closed, he saw hers were shut. The feeling of restoration was almost unbearable.

"Do you love me?" she whispered, in a little ecstasy.

He did not answer, except with the quick tightening of his arms, clutching her a little closer against him. And he loved the silkiness of her hair, and its natural scent. And it hurt him that the daisies she had threaded in should begin to wither. He resented their hurting her by their dying.

He had not understood. But the trouble had gone off. He was quiet, and he watched her from out of his sensitive stillness, a little bit dimly, unable to recover. She was loving to him, protective, and bright, laughing like a glad child too.

"We must tell Maud I shall be in to dinner," he said.

That was like him—always aware of the practical side of the case, and the appearances. She laughed a little little bit ironically—why should she have to take her arms from round him, just to tell Maud he would be in to dinner?

"I'll go," she said.

He drew the curtains and turned on the light in the big lamp that stood in a corner. The room was dim, and palely warm. He loved it dearly.

His wife, when she came back, as soon as she had closed the door, lifted her arms to him in a little ecstasy, coming to him. They clasped each other close, body to body. And the intensity of his feeling was so fierce, he felt* himself going dim, fusing into something soft and plastic between her hands. And this connection with her was bigger than life or death. And at the bottom of his heart was a sob.

She was gay and winsome, at the dinner. Like lovers, they were just deliciously waiting for the night to come up. But there remained in him always the slightly broken feeling which the night before had left.

"And you won't go to Italy," she said, as if it were an understood thing.

She gave him the best things to eat, and was solicitous for his welfare—which was not usual with her. It gave him deep, shy pleasure. He remembered a verse she was often quoting as one she loved. He did not know it for himself:

"On my breasts I warm thy foot-soles
Wine I pour, and dress thy meats;
Humbly, when my lord disposes
Lie with him on perfumed sheets—"*

She said it to him sometimes, looking up at him from the pillow. But it never seemed real to him. She might, in her sudden passion, put his feet between her breasts. But he never felt like a lord, never more pained and insignificant than at those times. As a little girl, she must have subjected herself before her dolls. And he was something like her lordliest plaything. He liked that too. If only——.

Then, seeing some frightened little way of looking at him, which she had, the pure pain came back. He loved her, and it would never be peace between them, she would never belong to him, as a wife. She would take him and reject him, like a mistress. And perhaps for that reason he would love her all the more: it might be so.

But then, he forgot. Whatever was or was not, now she loved him. And whatever came after, this evening he was the lord. What matter if he were deposed tomorrow, and she hated him!

Her eyes, wide and candid, were staring at him a little bit wondering, a little bit forlorn. She knew he had not quite come back. He held her close to him.

"My love," she murmured consolingly. "My love."

And she put her fingers through his hair, arranging it in little, loose curves, playing with it and forgetting everything else. He loved that dearly, to feel the light lift and touch-touch of her finger-tips making his hair, as she said, like an Apollo's.* She lifted his face to see how he looked, and, with a little laugh of love, kissed him. And he loved to be made much of by her. But he had the dim, hurting sense, that she would not love him tomorrow, that it was only her great need to love that exalted him tonight. He *knew* he was no king: he did not feel a king, even when she was crowning and kissing him.

"Do you love me?" she asked, playfully whispering.

He held her fast and kissed her, while the blood hurt in his heart-chambers.

"You know," he answered, with a struggle.

Later, when he lay holding her with a passion intense like pain, the words blurted from him:

"Flesh of my flesh—Paula!—Will you— —?"*

"Yes my love," she answered, consolingly.

He bit his mouth with pain. For him it was almost an agony of appeal.

"But Paula—I mean it—flesh of my flesh—a wife—?"

She tightened her arms round him without answering. And he knew, and she knew that she put him off like that.

## 4

Two months later, she was writing to him in Italy: "Your idea of your woman is that she is an expansion, no, a *rib* of yourself, without any existence of her own. That I am a being by myself is more than you can grasp.—I wish I could absolutely submerge myself in a man—and *so I do*, I *always* loved you.— — — —

"You will say 'I was patient.' Do you call that patient, hanging on for your needs, as you have done? The innerest* life you have *always* had of me, and you held yourself aloof because you were afraid.

"The unpardonable thing was you told me you loved me.—Your *feelings* have hated me these three months, which did not prevent you from taking my love and every breath from me.—Underneath you undermined me, in some subtle, corrupt way that I did not see because I believed you, when you told me you loved me.— —

"The insult of the way you took me these last three months I shall never forgive you. I honestly *did* give myself, and always in vain and rebuffed. The strain of it all has driven me quite mad.

"You say I am a tragédienne, but I don't do any of your perverse undermining tricks. You are always luring one into the open like a clever enemy, but you keep safely under cover all the time.— — —

"This practically means, for me, that life is over, my belief in life.—I hope it will recover, but it never could do so with you— — —"

To which he answered: "If I kept under cover it is funny, for there isn't any cover now.—And you can hope, pretty easily, for your own recovery apart from me. For my side, without you, I am done.—But you lie to yourself. You *wouldn't* love *me*, and you won't be able to love anybody else—except generally."*

# APPENDIX I

## *'TWO SCHOOLS' FRAGMENT*

## Note on the text

This manuscript fragment (Roberts E396), located at UCB, is written in pencil on seven sides of a single folding of twelve leaves, with the remaining five sides blank; the paper is watermarked 'Boots/Cash Stationers', measuring 16.5 × 20.4 cm. (6½ × 8 inches), and is identical to that of a number of manuscripts known to date from DHL's period in Croydon (see Introduction p. xxviii). Deletions in the manuscript are here marked ⟨ ⟩: insertions are marked ⌜ ⌝.

Editorial emendations to the text consist of the addition of full stops at the end of sentences (187:14, 29), a comma after 'Sturgess' (189:10) and the replacement of Lawrence's ampersand by 'and'.

## 'Two Schools' fragment

There were, three years back, two schools in the mining village of High Park; a National and a British—The head of the national school was a well known figure in the village, having been in office for twenty five years. ⟨Everyone⟩ ⌜No one⌝ looked out as Gaffer Sturgess* strode off down the main street every morning at about five minutes to nine. He was not popular, save with a few of his cronies. He was a ⟨middle-sized man,⟩ ⌜man of middle height,⌝ broad, and, now he was forty eight, getting stout. He was of the sturdy British Bull-dog type; with a big walrus moustache, a round heavy jowl that gave him the look of a sulk. That was in the street. At home he was very handsome, with his fair forehead, short black hair, neat nose, and swift, proud brown eyes, whose look could be very kind, whose smile winning and delightful.

Mr Sturgess was conservative. He stuck to the old ideas, the old methods, and cared not a jot for anybody, unless he were angered or thwarted, then he ran into extraordinary passionate vehemence of rancour. Frankly, the shop-keepers and the tradesmen, who formed the aristocracy of the mining village,* bored him. He preferred the miners. But these he patronised. Therefore he was quite friendless in a place where he had lived for nigh thirty years.

Mr Culverwell,* master of the British School, was a very different specimen of the same type as Gaffer Sturgess. The younger man was tall, but would grow heavy. He had the same appearance of sulk about the jaw, ⟨it⟩ indication of the same vigor, and scorn for his compatriots. For the rest, he suggested the sea, where Sturgess suggested the land, the best of the ⟨...⟩ ⌜yeomanry⌝. Culverwell was tall, straight, ⟨creat,⟩ a commanding man in presence. He had stiff brown hair cut short on a round, bullet ⟨head⟩, but not small head. He had a thick reddish moustache cut level over a full red mouth. Lastly, he had fine, forget-me-not coloured blue eyes that, very slightly protuberant, could blaze blue lightening the moment his passion was roused.

The master of the British school was a native of High Park, who had spent six or seven years away teaching in Lancashire. When he was twenty seven years old he won the appointment of headmaster in his own old school. He was unmarried, unengaged. By nature an orator and a boon companion, moreover a commander, he held after two years in position, a fairly high place in the estimation of the miners, and those aristocrats, the shop-keepers.

When he came to the British school he found, somewhat to his embarrassment, that Miss Fanny Sturgess was there before him as one of his assistants: he only had three. She taught the Standards One and Two, the little children. He was not prejudiced against her, but he found it awkward. She had nothing against him, so long as he did not eclipse her father. Conditions such, they met.

Truth to tell, she was a bad teacher. The unruly little boys of the miners were too much for her. She was a brilliant girl, ⟨with⟩ slender, vivid. Her colouring was high, her movements swift and impulsive. Strange to say, she had, in one brown pupil, a grey segment. One ⟨hal⟩ fifth of her left eye was grey, the rest brown. When Culverwell saw that, he was dumbfounded.

"Well, strike me lucky!" he exclaimed in his heart.

She knew what amazed him so, but, instead of hiding her eyes, stared him full and challengingly.

"Very well," said her brilliant eyes, "look, look as long as you like. I am here to be seen."

Under her wide-flung gaze, he was the first to quaver. He put his head forward, still in bull-dog style, like a strange and antagonistic dog, searching her, as it were. She flared back at him. He grew red, looked aside, and stumbled for words.

⟨It⟩At the end of the first day, she declared at teatime to her father—rash and impulsive she was to ⟨a⟩ the last degree:

"He's common, Dadda."

"I've only seen him once," said Mr Sturgess, in his musical baritone, "but *that* was evident."

At the end of the first week:

"He's a great bully, Dadda. The boys hate him, and everybody will when they know him. He's a common bully."

"Well," said her father, "let him try it long enough, his bullying, and these miners will settle him. You've only to ⟨see⟩ look ⟨h⟩ at his head to see he's a bully." Mr Sturgess glanced suddenly, with affectionate ⟨brown⟩ quick brown eyes, under his fine eyebrows at his daughter. She smiled. Then both engaged in the most winning and winsome of smiles, father and daughter. She, Fanny, was his great friend.

At the end of the first month:

"Father, he's a beast, and I'm not going to stop there," said Fanny.

"You needn't stop a day,⟨"⟩ my girl, not a day longer than you want," said that aristocrat, her father. "You've only to let me apply to have you transferred."

"He bawls out to your class, when you're in the middle of a lesson, and frightens the poor little things out of their lives."

"It won't take him long," said Mr Sturgess, "to run to the end of his rope at that rate. Wait till he sets these people⟨'⟩s' backs up."

Mr Culverwell did set the people's backs up, but it was no good. He bullied the complainers roundly, looking at them with scorn. Mr Sturgess was by nature a rather courteous man. He was, like many reserved people, very pleasant when actually faced. Culverwell, on the other hand, always found himself in company, and always found himself bullying his companions into subordination. Once he had established himself, once he was unquestioned and unchallenged, he was perfect, easy, intimate, jovial, strong, clever, nay, an admirable man. So High Park concluded.

So at last Fanny Sturgess concluded. He bullied her class into order, made things smooth for her, took away all her difficulties, and then, because she still was antagonistic, determined to show her the nice side of him.

[end of manuscript]

# APPENDIX II

# *'DELILAH AND MR BIRCUMSHAW' FRAGMENT*

## Note on the text

This manuscript fragment (Roberts E90.5a), located at UCB, is written in ink on eleven leaves torn from notebooks; the unwatermarked paper measures (leaf 1) 14.3 × 21.25 cm. (5⅝ × 8⅜ inches) and (leaves 2–11) 15.75 × 20.2 cm. (6³⁄₁₆ × 7¹⁵⁄₁₆ inches). The pages were originally numbered 9–19: a later hand renumbered them 1–11. Deletions in the manuscript are here marked ⟨ ⟩: insertions are marked ⌜ ⌝.

Editorial emendations to the text are the addition of full stops at the ends of two sentences (194:16 and 195:5).

# 'Delilah and Mr Bircumshaw' fragment

Then "Come into the kitchen," said Mrs Bircumshaw, and they went down the long, dark passage to the back room. This was ⟨dark⟩ cold, rather bare. Mrs Bircumshaw kept no maid. The ⟨immense⟩ ⌜large⌝ black stove, littered with paper, looked exceedingly chilly, black-chilly when the gas was lighted. The scarlet bricks of the floor seemed slightly moist. For the rest, the room was drab in colour, very small. There was a baby's high chair in ⌜one corner, and⌝ ⟨On the st⟩ the litter of a child on the floor, a ⟨little⟩ tin pigeon, and a teddy-bear. Mrs Bircumshaw swiftly straightened the house, then threw a cloth on the table, that was pushed to the wall under the drab-blinded window, and near to the great black cold stove.

"Will you stay to supper?," she asked.

"What have you got?," frankly inquired the elder woman.

"I'm afraid there's nothing but bread and cheese."

"No thanks, then. No, Nance—I oughtn't to leave Mr Cullen* alone. You ought to come to supper with me."

They talked a few moments,—then there was silence.

"Well!," Mrs Cullen exclaimed, "I never knew such a thing in my life. Is he often like it."

"Oh yes," replied the other reservedly.

"Well, I know now," Mrs Cullen declared. "I know now. Often have I come in ⟨and⟩ ⌜in⌝ the morning and seen you with your eyes red, but you've not said anything, so I haven't. I thought perhaps you'd been feeling poorly, as you often do. But I know now—the brute!—the great disagreeable brute!! And will he be all right when you go to bed."

"Oh no," said Mrs Bircumshaw.

"Will he keep it up tomorrow?."

"Oh yes—and very likely for two or three days."

"The brute—oh, this *has* opened my eyes. You'll not sleep with him tonight, shall you?"

"It would only make it worse," said the wife.

"Worse or not worse, I wouldn't. You've got another bed aired—

you had your cousin till yesterday—it's aired. Take the baby and sleep there."

"It would only make it worse," said Mrs Bircumshaw.

"Well—you're better than I should be to him, I can tell you. The great brute! But let him touch that child again when I'm in. Haven't I seen her with her little arms red! And he's always been so fair to my face: you'd think he was one of the most gentlemanly—! I tell you, I've been watching a few men lately, and it's opened my eyes to them. They're a wretched lot, these men—brutes, nothing else. But I wish he'd beat that little child when I'm in, I only wish he would—!"

Mrs Bircumshaw listened to this threat in silence. Yet she too, wished for the occasion. Mrs Cullen, in her full vigour, ⟨spoiled⟩ ⌜always spoiled by men⌝ and fearless, would match the bully which occasionally, too often, broke out in her husband.

"But tell him, Nance," said the elder, bending from her handsome height, "tell him, with perfect truth, that I saw nothing. Tell him I thought he'd suddenly gone to door to somebody who had called. Tell him that. And say that I thought he'd gone out with them—with whoever called—tell him—the brute!—or else he'll never get over it."

Mrs Bircumshaw listened patiently. Occasionally she laughed. She would tell her husband nothing—she would never ⟨le⟩ mention the affair. But she would let it sink into him that he had made a fool and a brute of himself before this handsome, spoiled woman.

Bircumshaw heard his wife's friend go. He had lain in torment while the two women talked in the far-off kitchen. To tell the truth, he was miserable. A big-limbed, fairly 'clever' man, he was intolerably stupid in private relations, blind as a bat to the real feelings of his wife. She merely reserved her inner self proudly, and was wife to him, ⟨but not⟩ ⌜never⌝ comrade.

Such a frame for ⟨physi⟩ work he had, and nothing to do but ⟨bank⟩ clerking and occasional tennis. Often, as he put on the jacket of his pyjamas, she thought, 'If only he went with Lieutenant Shackleton discovering the South Pole,* or had to break a farm in Canada, he'd be splendid.' For she really loved him.

But, with his humours, his brutality, his nothingness, he became rather ignoble. He did nothing with zest except eat, or play tennis, act, and occasionally discuss politics.

"I should think," said Mrs Cullen in departing, "that you won't be so silly as to take him any supper."

Mrs Bircumshaw felt a sudden lift of anger against him. But she laughed deprecatingly.

"You *are* a silly thing. My word—I'd starve him if I had him," said the other.

"But you haven't got him, you see," replied the wife.

"Indeed I haven't, the brute."

So long as he was unmarried, there was still something to conquer. So long as he had no children, there was ⟨a⟩ something to await. But with a two-year old baby, and an income fixed at £200 a year, with little hope of rising, nothing remained.

He lay in bed, sullen and angry. He didn't know what ailed him, why he was angry, why he hated his wife although part of him loved her. He merely lay awake in a wretched state of torment, hating everything, but as if paralysed, unable to act in any direction.

Truth to tell, his ⟨wi⟩ life had no purpose. His clerking represented five or six hours a day not unpleasantly neutral. He had nothing else to do: he had no real value. A man, never convinced of his own personal worth, must be looked-up-to if he is to keep his own, inner self-esteem: if he is to be healthy, he must have something to accomplish. But for his soul even to live, he must be somebody's hero. A woman can live ⟨without⟩ by herself, unpropped by esteem, so long as she has some weak thing to cherish. A man cannot.

Bircumshaw began to feel that he was not his wife's hero: if not her's, no one's. She, unconsciously perhaps, strove to maintain him in his heroic capacity, but was occasionally impatient. Life turned black and bitter in the mouth. He lay in bed, full of stupid anger of despair, hating his wife because he was not her hero.

She, downstairs, occasionally smiled to herself. This time she had triumphed. Usually, after a bout of his ill-temper, she was left hurt, weeping bitterly. This time she smiled, though her heart was anxious and pained. Nevertheless, she could not restrain a slight exultation. ⟨She sl sm⟩ ⌜Her smile⌝ rose from the deep of her subtle nature. She ate a very little supper, worked about the house until almost ten o'clock. Her face had regained that close impassivity which so many woman wear when alone. Still impassive, she fetched the dinner-joint and made him four sandwiches, seasoned exactly as he liked them. Pouring him a glass of milk and went up to bed with the tray.

Hearing her coming, he lay well under the bed-clothes, as if asleep. She entered calmly.

"Here is your supper," she said quietly, setting the tray on the chair at his side, and ignoring the fact that he was asleep. This made him feel the reverse of heroic. Down went the subconscious mercury of his self esteem: he felt he should almost dwindle to nothing, and he hated her. He made no reply. ⟨S⟩ She bent over the cot of the sleeping baby, a winsome, bonny girl. The child had pouted wilfully down among the bedclothes, and lay asleep, still proudly pouting in her childish way; but strands and rings of shiny hair stuck to her hot cheeks, and her brows had a little impatient, debonnair lilt, very pretty. The mother's eyes moistened. With very gentle fingers, she loosened the hair, put it back from the girlish brow, and disclosed the little ⟨white⟩ ⌜round⌝ flower of an ear. The father felt the silence of love: but he would not look. He shrank deeper into his manly bulk.

Mrs Bircumshaw slipped into bed quietly, and settled to rest immediately, as far as possible from the broad form of the man. Both lay quite still, yet, as each knew, neither slept. The man felt he wanted to move, but imposed a strict immobility upon himself. He lay stiffly. She nestled ⟨up,⟩ ⌜herself,⌝ nor did she want to stir. This evening she neither knew nor cared how he felt towards her. She let herself rest for once in victory.

Towards one oclock in the morning, just as she was drifting into sleep, she started awake. Her spirit started, not her body. She merely opened her eyes.

A match had been struck. Her husband was sitting up in bed, leaning forward to the plate on the chair. She could not resist the temptation: she must look at him. Very quietly she turned her head.

His big⟨, hulking back was towards her.⟩ ⌜back hulked above her. He was⌝ leaning forward, stretching for the sandwiches. He got one. He had lighted the candle and set it on the floor, so that it should not illuminate the bed. Somehow, he did not care to eat in the dark, feeling as if he would be chewing darkness with sandwich. The candle-light lit up his face and black hair. Occasionally she could see his cheek bulged out with food. He ate rapidly, with gusto, leaning over the edge of the bed because of the falling crumbs. As he rested on his right elbow, she saw the heavy shoulder-muscles piled under his sleeping jacket, and occasionally saw the working of his thick bare throat as he swallowed with gusto.

"The animal," she said to herself, and she laughed, laughed within herself heartily.

"Are they nice?," she longed to say, slyly. "Are they nice?"—she must say it—"are they nice?" The temptation was almost too great. But she was afraid of this lusty young man startled at his feeding. She dared not twit him.

He took the milk, leaned back, almost arching backwards over her as he drank. She quickened with a little pleasurable fear lest he should slip back from his elbow and crush her. She cowered under his shadow, small, smiling daringly at her fear. It was some sort of pride to own a man so physically big: she almost forgot how idiotic he was, how disagreeable, and she felt inclined to kiss him. Then her lip curled with scorn at the thought of how he would behave. His sulky, gloomy temper could not even be cajoled. When he was sulky, she could not even kindle his passion for her. He was mean in the blood, she said, petty.

He devoured the rest of the sandwich, swallowed the rest of the milk in noisy gulps, nipped out the candle, and lay down, sighing with relief. He seemed to sink gratefully right into sleep.

"Pah!," she said to herself. "He likes a meal better than anything else on earth—a meal gives him more pleasure than even me when we're at our best."

She shrugged her shoulders and went to sleep.

[end of manuscript]

# APPENDIX III

## *'BURNS NOVEL' FRAGMENTS*

# Note on the text

The manuscript fragments (Roberts E59.3), located at UT, are written in black ink on thirteen leaves of cream-coloured, unlined, unwatermarked wove paper measuring 20.5 × 34.5 cm. (8⅜ × 13½ inches). The major section covers eleven sheets and five lines of the twelfth sheet, numbered 1–12. The other fragment is written on a separate sheet, numbered 1. Several blank sheets of identical paper today separate the two fragments, having been bound up with them, probably in the late 1950s. Although he made no reference to them at the time, Edward Nehls probably acquired the blank pages together with the fragments, the first of which was sent to him by Else Jaffe on 1 April 1954; the second, on 3 April with the note 'Belongs to the Burns Novel I sent yesterday' (Nehls, i. 561–2, n. 38). There is now no way of telling which of the fragments Lawrence wrote first; the coincidence of the paper, and the historical setting of the second fragment, probably confirm Else Jaffe's assertion that it belonged to the major section.

Deletions in the manuscript, alterations in the first printing (A1) and editorial emendations are recorded in the Textual apparatus.

# 'Burns Novel' fragments

## Chapter I.

There was the clear sound of a man's whistling, but no one was to be seen on the common. The afternoon of the beautiful November day was drawing to a close. Overhead the sky was of fine, high blue, but in the west it grew mild as turquoise, then glistened green near the dark rim of the hill. Under the blue sky the fawn-coloured leaves standing dry and chavelled* upon the young oaks shone sharply as the levelling light caught them. Then two women were seen, with reddish kerchieves over their heads, bending among the oak-scrub. They were piling into a little heap the brushwood they had been cutting.

The whistling ceased, there was heard the sharp quick strokes of an axe. The women disappeared among the tangle of sere young oaks. A bird fluttered in distinct little leaps of flight over the brush wood to the open spaces. Everything, twigs, leaves, gorse-bushes, rags of heather shone sharply defined. One young holly tree stood alone in a little space cleared of the ravel-leaved* brown oaks. It was a perfectly healthy young tree, erect, with all its berries burning among the dark and glittering leaves. Quite alone it stood, and radiant.

One of the women came rustling through the withered oaks. Her arms were full of brushwood, she wore a crimson and fawn kerchief tied round her cheeks. Her hair was red as a squirrel about her pink and white face. She walked valiantly with her great armful of twigs. She glanced at the radiant young holly tree. A donkey that had been feeding lifted its head as she passed. It was almost invisible on the common, in its greyness. Moreover it was belted round with sackcloth fawn like the oak-leaves.

The girl plunged in her heavy clogs, rustling with a hiss through the trees. The little brilliant holly tree stood alone in its charmed circle. The donkey was invisible again. As the light grew richer, the leaves and shrubs became solid with their sharply defined edges. But away across the valley the wooded slope was hazy blue, the water below lay vague as smoke. Then behind towards the west the sky was brilliantly green, the rim of the hill was dark.

Quickly the light was withdrawn. Down where the water was, all grew shadow. The girl came tramping back into the open space, and stood before the holly tree. She was a slim, light thing of about eighteen. Her dress was of weathered blue, her kerchief crimson. She went up to the little tree, reached up, fingering the twigs. The shadow was creeping uphill. It went over her unnoticed. She was still pulling down the twigs to see which had the thickest bunch of berries. All the clearing died and went cold. Suddenly the whistling stopped. She stood to listen. Then she snapped off the twig she had chosen and stood a moment admiring it.

A man's voice, strong and cheerful, shouted:

"Bill—Bill—Bi—ill!"

The donkey lifted its head, listened, then went on eating.

"Go on!" said the girl, waving her twig of holly at it. The donkey walked stolidly two paces from her, then took no notice.

All the hillside was dark. There was a tender flush in the east. Away among the darkening blue and green over the west, a faint star appeared. There came from far off a small jangling of bells—one two three—one two three four five! The valley was all twilight, yet near at hand things seemed to stand in day.

"Bill—Bill!" came the man's voice from a distance.

"He's here!" shrilled the girl.

"Wheer?" came the man's shout, nearer, after a moment.

"Here!" shrilled the girl.

She looked at the donkey that was bundled in its cloth.

"Why don't ye go, dummy!" she said.

"Wheer is 'e?" said the man's voice, near at hand.

"Here!"

In a moment a youth strode through the bushes.

"Bill, tha chump!"* he said.

The donkey walked serenely towards him. He was a big boned, limber youth of twenty. His trousers were belted very low, so that his loins remained flexible under the shirt. He wore a black felt hat, from under which his brown eyes gazed at the girl.

"Was it you as shouted?" he said.

"I knowed it was you," she replied, tapping her skirt with the richly berried holly sprig.

"Been getting holly?" he said.

He had advanced towards her, leading the donkey by the head.

"It's a rare red bush," he said, looking at the tree.

There was a moment of silence.

"But it's bad luck to get it afore Christmas,"* he added.

"Who says?" she replied.

"They say," he answered.

In the little clearing that had now gone cold with evening, he stood lounging against his donkey, a dark-eyed, limber youth, just near to her who stood with her averted face.

"Wheer are ye from?" he asked her.

"Jacksdale," she replied.

He looked at her more closely. Her small face was closed and averted.

"Which house?" he asked.

"The cottages by the brook."

"Colliers?"

"My father's come fra Alfreton to th' gin-pit,"* she said.

"An' what's your name?"

"Renshaw."*

"An' what else?"

"Mary."

"*Mary Renshaw*!—do yer like it?"

The girl looked at him suddenly. Her blue eyes, startled, seemed to ask him for something.

"Why?" she said.

"It's pretty-sounding.—I'm from the Haggs."

She looked at him questioning.

"From th' farm over there." He pointed down the valley to a wood that was dark-purple among the grey land. Then, having roused himself, he leaned once more on the donkey, half lying, in a loose, limber fashion, just in front of the girl.

"How did you know it was our donkey?" he said.

"'Cause I've 'eered you singin', an' I could tell your voice."

"An' 'ad you seed* me?"

"No."

He got up suddenly, with a quick motion that startled her.

"'Appen you'll be goin' top road," he said. "Been sticking?"*

"Yes."

"By yourself?"

"With the woman next door."

"Are yer *goin'* th' top road?"

"No, I mun go by myself—wi' th' woman—"

"Why?"

"Because I mun.—I on'y 'eered yer singin'."

She began to move away from him.

"There'll be a dance a Sat'day night ower th' Robin Hood at Sels'on. Should I take yer?"

"I dunna go to th' dances," she replied.

He began to hum a tune, and went spinning a dozen paces in a dance round his donkey. She walked away without bidding any farewell, and presently he heard her voice talking quietly, reserved, to the other woman.

He led his donkey away to where stood a good pile of faggots and twigs, beside a long wagon. The common was quite still.

"Stand there!" he said to the donkey.

Then he began to load his cart. It consisted, the wagon, of a long beam which carried the cross-bars of the axle trees, and rode upon low, rude wheels. The side-rails were slung with chains, making a sort of loose cradle. Into this he put his big bundles of twigs, arranging them neatly. Then he packed the faggots above them.

He worked quickly and easily, as if he were not at all tired. His hands and wrists were big, raw-boned as he grasped the purple and grey twigs, but they moved with an intimate intelligence. The common was silent. It was growing quickly dusk. His supple young body alone seemed active. The donkey might have been a great stone that allowed itself a little life.

At last he was finished. The donkey was harnessed in a moment. The youth pulled on his coat, and set off with his wagon, whose small wheels swung freely, so that the long load seemed sinuous as it wound its way over the rough common down the hill.

Above the dark, shaggy common, the sky was bright green and purple, but it gave off no light. The earth was a great shadow. One big white star hung between the purple and the darkening green of the west. The youth watched it as he walked trailing behind his load. The donkey took its own way. They came out on a sandy lane between gorse bushes, and began to climb a hill, slowly.

The youth gripped the long switch he carried, and went in silence. Suddenly he lifted his head and began to sing. He had a fine tenor voice that rang out in the frosty, clear evening. The girl, climbing the hill in the other direction, bowed beneath her load of wood, heard the wild singing as she tramped.

"That's Jack Haseldine," said the woman accompanying her. "He knows more songs* than any lad i' th' country."

"And a good singer," said the girl.

"It wins him his 'lowance, I'm tellin' yer," said the woman. "When Jock sings in a public,* the men flock in."

The youth trudged along beside his load. On his left was the west with the big naked star; on his right, where the hill sloped down, the great curve of the darkening heavens began to glitter faintly. The wooded hill opposite across the valley was blacker than the sky.

He turned down a track beside a hedge, and descended the rough hill. Soon he was skirting the wood's edge, and the thick darkness was on his right hand. At last he came to a gate across the path, against the looming of buildings. In a moment he was in the farm-yard, that made a square with the wood on one side. There was a light in one window. He went along with his load to a big shed, and, without taking the donkey out of the shafts, he heaved over his wagon, and tipped the contents with a hiss into the dark wooden buildings. Fowls chawked and remonstrated. He lightly righted his wagon, led it away.

The farm kitchen was a poor little place, with none of the appearance of plenty that bigger houses have. It was a pokey room, all corners and angles. Two men sat by the fire that burned on the hearth. A candle stood in a bracket on the wall, its tin reflector casting a ruddy light over the room where a small woman was taking plates from the rack.

"Tha'rt late enow," said the father,* turning from the fire as he entered.

"Nowt ter fret about,"* replied the youth.

"No, there's nowt ter fret about," repeated the father, turning again to the fire. There was silence.

The father was a stern-looking, hard-featured man who had evidently wrung a living from the land by will and work. He sat half dreaming over the fire, his big, gnarled hands folded and asleep, his white hair glistening rose against the glow. His elder son, seated opposite him, a smaller, stiff, resolute-looking young man, was nodding and waking, thrusting forward a stick into the fire, watching the pot, dozing, waking, thrusting forward the black sticks into the red glow.

Presently the four sat down to supper. The father asked a blessing, in his stern fashion. The men noisily supped the broth thickened with barley from their wooden spoons. Alfred, the elder son, dropped brown bread into his pot of red earthenware and ponched* it with his spoon till his broth was a solid mess. It irritated John, the younger son. His dark brown eyes flashed proudly.

"Tha mun well be a thick-set stodge-belly,"* he said to his brother. The other took no notice.

Soon the supper was cleared away. The father and Alfred returned to the fire to half-sleep. John took two books off a shelf that hung by cords against the wall, and began to work on a slate. He had a young, eager, peasant face. His black hair fell in thick straight locks over his forehead. His clumsy-looking fingers marked laboriously on a slate. He was doing arithmetic. For some time he concentrated on his work. Then suddenly he put down the slate and the marker with a clatter, got up, washed himself, and tied a scarf like a stock round his neck.

"Art goin' out again?" asked his father.

"I want to look at my snares," he said.

The night was brilliant with stars, the wood was black. He walked down the high, bald fields, along the hedgerow. Orion was just heaving up above the wooded hill opposite. Everywhere the ground was dark, everywhere the heavens glittered. He clenched his hands, wanting to grasp something. So he slunk along the hedge in the dark. He stood and listened. There was scarce a sound anywhere. And yet the night seemed to breathe. He felt his breast burning. Again he went forward down the hedge. Suddenly he started. There was a rush and a flurry down in the hedge. It was a rabbit in one of his snares.* He bent down over it. The creature spurted away, to be choked back. The wire ring that throttled it was tightly pegged. He put out his hand to get hold of it. Like a bullet it bounded the other way. But it could not escape. He pulled up the pegs and took the rabbit up in his hands. Suddenly, in its black eye, he saw a point of light glitter with fear and agony. The thing was afraid of him. It gave his heart a shock. There alone in the darkness with the rabbit, that crouched now still, too terrified to move, feeling its little heart quivering, his wrists went weak and his heart melted like fire in him. He looked close at its black eye. It was watching him. It was a little live thing with his wire round its neck.

He had snared and killed hundreds, but this one frightened him. It was a living little rabbit-person with dark eyes, and it was afraid of him. He held it in his big hands against his chest, murmuring:

"Are ter frit, my little missie. Are ter frit, Tiss, Tissie?"*

But he was more frightened himself. He dared not kill it. Feeling the palpitating thing crouch and warm his breast, he was stifled. The stars glittered, staring like thousands of eyes. Slowly, very carefully, fumbling, he felt for the twine round the rabbit's neck. It gave a convulsed movement. His heart leaped like a ball of fire. Half trembling, he loosed the noose. When it was free of the rabbit, he began to breathe again. He cuddled the thing against his breast.

"Say nowt!" he said. "Say nowt."

Then glancing round, he lowered the little beast and set it on the grass. It sat there in a bunch, not moving. He stood quite still. Suddenly, like a shot, it was gone into the darkness. He felt a load off his breathing. The night seemed to expand big and clear again. He stood and looked round. It seemed another world than that he knew by daylight. He was half frightened.

There was something he wanted, out of the glittering night. He stood quite still, fronting it all. He ought to be going back to the house, but he did not want to. He wanted to get away from something—he wanted something. Turning swiftly, he set off across the fields up-hill. After walking about a mile he saw the lights of the quarry cottages, the farms, the inn at Underwood. He did not want to go to the 'Brick and Tile.' Keeping along the rutty road, he descended the hill on the other side, into Jacksdale that lay in the dark hollow. But he went past the inn and the houses. On the stone bridge he halted. Set back there was the row of cottages where the girl lived. He guessed she lived in the end house. There was a dim light in the window. He half lay across the stone parapet of the bridge, watching. Suddenly her door opened, and she appeared, sheltering her candle with one hand. He saw her small, serious face ruddy as a moon crouching by the door. Softly, he began to whistle a tune.* She looked round into the darkness. She was getting some of the coal from the little heap near the door. Crouching by the coal, her candle lighting up her figure, she looked round. He went quickly to the gate.

"It's a fine night," he called softly.

"Yes," she answered, clear and distinct.

She lingered by the coals. The door stood open, showing a chair or so in the fire-light.

"Come an' ha'e a word wi' me," he pleaded, leaning against the gate in the dark. She left the candle burning among the coal, and came down the path.

"All alone?" he asked, as she drew near.

"The children's in bed—father will be coming directly."

"Aren't you frightened by yourself?"

"No."

He asked her questions. She said she had two brothers and a sister. The youngest was eight. Her mother had been dead five years. Her father wouldn't be later than nine.

As she talked, she stood just out of reach of him. He leaned on the gate in the dark, his face turned up to her. He could see her neat, delicate features and bunches of hair.

"Shan't you come a bit of a walk?" he asked.

"The children are in bed," she replied quietly.

He raised himself, pushed open the gate.

"I s'll have to be goin' in," she said.

"Stop with me just a minute," he said, caressively.

"The candle's swalin' away,"* she said.

"Then take it in the house and come back," he said.

She did not move.

"I must be goin' in," she said.

"Are you frightened of your father?" he asked.

"Yes," she said.

He put his arms round her, and folded her to him suddenly.

"'He's here!'", he suddenly said, curiously and lovingly imitating the voice in which she had called to him on the common. "'He's here'!—I thought it was a witch o' the woods callin'."

He had got her tightly clasped to his bosom, and was trembling.

"What made thee ca' to me?" he asked.

"I niver thought," she replied.

"'He's here!' " he repeated softly, "that's what I heard. An' Bill vanished clean out o' my mind, as if he'd gone off in a wisp.—I wonder if you could shout again like that—?"

"Like what?" she asked.

"Like that. You called straight to me."

"I'd heered you singin' an' whistlin'," she said.

"What did I sing?" he asked.

"You sung 'Gentle Annie'."*

He held her fast in his arms, very warm.

"I catched a rabbit tonight an' I let it go again," he said.

"What for?"

"I dunno!"

She mused over this.

"Art warm?" he murmured.

She made a little sound, nestling closer in to him.

"Hasn't ter nobody ter hold thee besides me?"

She put her face on his bosom, and he felt her small hands clinging to his shoulders. His heart going fast, he bent his head and kissed her. He shook his head quickly, tickled by her hair. She put up her mouth to him. He found her lips. The end of her small nose, quite cold, brushed his cheek. He was breathless and astonished in all his being. Holding her fast, he moved his lips over her face, her cheeks, her shut eyes, her brows. The discovery was amazing. The whole secret of the night and the stars was in these soft, smooth grooves and mounds and hollows. It was her face! Yet it seemed to include big distances and wonderful things. The flashing lights overhead were no further off than the strange roughness of her eyebrows under his lips, the arched, dark sky didn't frighten him more than the firm domes of her eyes under the softly closed eyelids. And she was breathing against him, live and warm like the rabbit. And it was the darkness he was kissing, discovering. It was the night he had his mouth upon.

Suddenly she sighed, and raised her face from him.

"Dost love me?" he murmured, not knowing. "Dost love me?"

"I mun go," she moaned.

"Then dost love me?" he repeated.

"I dunno!" She had drawn away. "Does thee me?"

He took her close in his arms again. She let her self melt against him quite naturally, as he pressed her to his breast.

"I do," he whispered. "I do! I do!"

She sighed again as he kissed her.

Suddenly a door of one of the cottages opened, with a sharp clack of the latch. The girl put her fingers upon his face in the dark, almost mournfully, and withdrew from him. The ruddy light from the open door fell across the garden, the plants showed up raggedly, then vanished. The door banged.

Mary was back at her coal heap, crouching. Haseldine stood at the gate, watching. She went indoors, her candle perched upon the dust-pan with its coals. He saw the dark ruddiness vanish from the interior as she mended the fire. Then she closed the door. He still stood watching. She wanted him to go, then!

Feeling warm, with a warm, rich sensation in his chest and arms, he turned away, accepting her dismissal because his heart was glad and grateful to her. The bare cottages straggled along the sides of the road. When he came to the inn, he hesitated. Then he mounted the two steps and went into the passage.

The inn was only the kitchen of a house. At the two small tables, and by the fire, sat half a dozen men, drinking from mugs. A fat man jumped up from his seat by the fire, crying:

"Jock, ma beauty, come thy ways! Sit thee down lad—sit thee theer."

"I'll sit by th' table," said the youth.

The fat man put his hand on his shoulder affectionately.

"Nay," he said, "if I sit theer ony longer I s'll be sizzlin' in my fat—climb up, lad."

The fire place was curious.* It was a brick hearth raised about two feet from the ground, on which the fire burned merrily in the wide, black chimney. The chimney seats were also raised, so that one climbed onto the hearth, and perched aloft in the high brown seat, with one's shoes near the red fire, one's pots on the brick hearth. And this was the throne. There was room for two persons on either side of the fire. These, the elect, sat hot and red, looking down upon their meaner comrades who were seated at ground-level at the tables. Jack took his seat, putting his hat on the high mantel-piece.

He was a raw-boned, big youth, with a high domed head on which the black hair hung straight. He was swarthy and ruddy, his dark eyes were full of fire and laughter. It being Thursday, all the men had five-days' growth of beard, otherwise they were mostly clean-shaven, if grimy. Jack arranged the skirts of his blue coat, and sat comfortably. He was something of a king among the men, because he was clever, and a great singer, and something of a fiddler. The landlady gave him a mug of beer. He turned his flashing dark eyes on the company in the little room, laughing.

"What brings thee this far?" asked the fat man deferentially.

"Oh," he said, "I wanted a bit o' cump'ny."

"An' tha's come 'n ter th' right place, boy," said his protector. Jock was proud at being flattered by these grown men. The landlady took her seat again by her table, and continued knitting. All the men talked together for a while, waving the red points of their clay pipes excitedly.

[end of fragment]

He had wakened before it was time to get up. But there was a stealthy look about the room that seemed like dawn. He was relieved, watching the small window, when he saw it was so distinctly lighter outside than in.

The night had gone then, and he was glad. He had slept, but a sleep that was almost like an ache, and which wearied him more than work would. He lay quite still, watching the window, seeing nothing, neither conscious nor unconscious, but like the dawn, indefinite, only silting towards realisation.

When he looked again, the furniture of the room stood out black against the pale suffusion of light. There were only two stools—or chairs without backs—a rough table, and the bed. He could hear birds rustling in the thatch overhead. His brother was still asleep. The clothes of the two youths lay in a dark jumble on the bed. James was breathing regularly.

Soon, into the ashy, colourless dawn, crept the warmth of day. The gold came up behind the hill, and with it, joy for everything. He had wakened up too soon, but with the sky full of glow, he forgot the night immediately. In the next room he heard his father coughing as he got up, then the staircase creaked. He would have to rise himself.

[end of manuscript]

# APPENDIX IV

## *NOTTINGHAMSHIRE AND CROYDON*

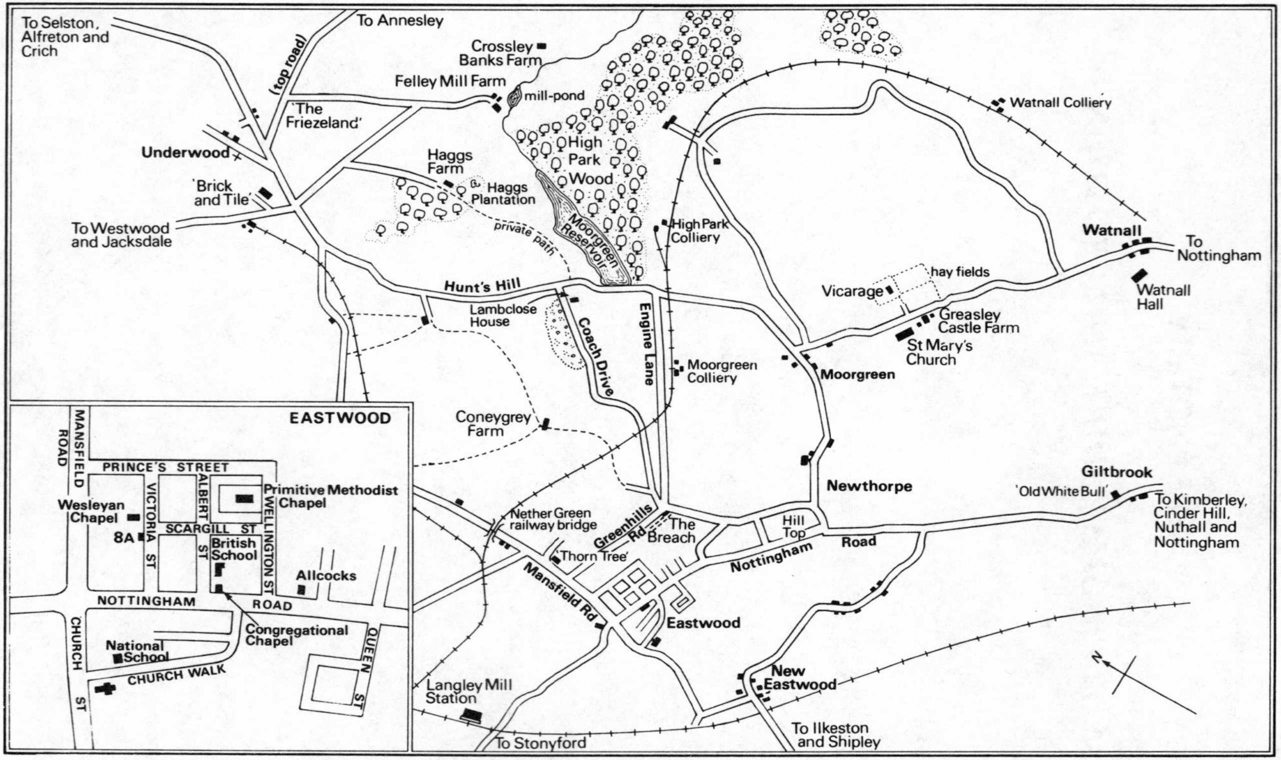
To Selston, Alfreton and Crich
To Annesley
(top road)
Crossley Banks Farm
Felley Mill Farm
mill-pond
'The Friezeland'
Underwood
'Brick and Tile'
To Westwood and Jacksdale
Haggs Farm
Haggs Plantation
High Park Wood
Moorgreen Reservoir
private path
High Park Colliery
Watnall Colliery
Watnall
To Nottingham
Watnall Hall
hay fields
Vicarage
Greasley Castle Farm
St Mary's Church
Hunt's Hill
Lambclose House
Coach Drive
Engine Lane
Moorgreen Colliery
Moorgreen
Coneygrey Farm
Newthorpe
Giltbrook
'Old White Bull'
To Kimberley, Cinder Hill, Nuthall and Nottingham
Nether Green railway bridge
Greenhills Rd
The Breach
Hill Top
Road
'Thorn Tree'
Nottingham
Mansfield Rd
Eastwood
New Eastwood
Langley Mill Station
To Stonyford
To Ilkeston and Shipley
N
EASTWOOD
MANSFIELD ROAD
PRINCE'S STREET
VICTORIA ST
ALBERT ST
SCARGILL ST
WELLINGTON ST
Primitive Methodist Chapel
Wesleyan Chapel
8A
British School
Allcocks
NOTTINGHAM ROAD
Congregational Chapel
QUEEN ST
National School
CHURCH WALK
CHURCH ST

Map 1 Eastwood and region *c.* 1910

## (i) Nottinghamshire

In a number of pieces in this volume ('A Prelude', 'A Modern Lover', 'Love Among the Haystacks', 'The Miner at Home', 'Her Turn', 'Strike-Pay', 'Delilah and Mr. Bircumshaw', the fragment 'Two Schools' and the 'Burns Novel' fragments), Lawrence recreated his own home township of Eastwood, in Nottinghamshire, and the industry, country and communities around it. Eastwood itself appears as 'High Park' in 'Two Schools'—actually the name of a local colliery; as 'Bestwood' in 'Strike-Pay' (the name he gave it in *Sons and Lovers*), and as 'Eastwood' in 'The Miner at Home'. Victoria Street, where he was born in 1885 (at no. 8a) is the setting of the Wesleyan Chapel mentioned in 'Strike-Pay'; running into Victoria Street is Scargill Street (also in 'Strike-Pay'), and parallel to it is Albert Street, where the 'British School' of 'Two Schools' was situated. All three streets were built around the blocks of colliery company houses in the 1860s, known locally as 'the Squares' (the name given in 'Strike-Pay'). Also in the Squares was the Primitive Methodist Chapel, where 'Strike-money is paid' (134:2). Off the Nottingham Road on the other side is Queen Street (again in 'Strike-Pay'); at no. 39 Nottingham Road was Wm. Allcock's furniture shop (in 'Her Turn'), and in the other direction Church Walk led to the 'National School' of 'Two Schools'. Going out of the township on the Mansfield Road, the 'Thorn Tree' public house used to stand on the right shortly before the Nether Green railway arch; this appears as the 'Golden Horn' in 'Her Turn'. Shortly before the site of the 'Thorn Tree', Greenhills Road turns off to the right; this leads to the Coach Drive towards Lambclose House, the 'Drive' mentioned in 'Delilah and Mr. Bircumshaw'. Stonyford, in 'Her Turn', is a hamlet 2 miles n.w. of Eastwood; in the other direction, Shipley and its colliery (mentioned in 'The Miner at Home') are 2½ miles s.w.

Lawrence himself went frequently to the Chambers family at Haggs Farm, Underwood, between 1901 and 1908; but instead of taking the Mansfield Road towards Underwood, he would (like Cyril Mersham in 'A Modern Lover') leave Eastwood by the track to 'Coney Grey Farm'; from the brow of the hill just beyond the farm, Mersham is aware of the 'large ponds ... farms, the fields, the far-off coal mine' (29:6). These must be

Moorgreen Reservoir, the Haggs Farm, Felley Mill Farm, and High Park Colliery. The first is referred to as 'Nethermere' at the end of 'A Modern Lover' (the name Lawrence gave it in *The White Peacock*); it is also the 'large natural reservoir' (137:23) of 'Strike-Pay' and the 'water ... vague as smoke' (202:1) of the 'Burns Novel'. The Haggs Farm itself appears as 'Crossleigh Bank' (taken from the name of a farmhouse a mile to the east) in 'A Modern Lover', as the unnamed home farm of 'A Prelude' and under its own name in the 'Burns Novel'. Felley Mill Farm, half a mile east of the Haggs, appears as 'Ramsley Mill' in 'A Prelude'. 'Strelley Mill', in 'The Fly in the Ointment', is (as in *The White Peacock*) a combination of both Haggs Farm and Felley Mill Farm.

Edmund Chambers, of the Haggs Farm, rented two large hay-fields in Greasley, which Lawrence recreated in 'Love Among the Haystacks'; he told Blanche Jennings in 1908 about 'two great fields at Greasley, running to the top of a sharp, irregular hillside, with ... the Vicar's garden on one side' (*Letters*, i. 67). They bordered Greasley Vicarage, and looked out to the east towards Nottingham; to the south were the 'old church and the castle farm' of 'Love Among the Haystacks' (88:30)—the Church of St Mary, Greasley, and just to its east Greasley Castle Farm, which retains traces of the castle on whose site it was built. The 'far-off hooting of a pit' (98:2) comes either from High Park Colliery or Moorgreen Colliery, as does the colliery smoke. At night, from the crest of the hill, Maurice and Paula see the red glare of an iron foundry; perhaps the foundry at Ilkeston, with its town lights (Lawrence saw its 'purple gloom' by day in 1908; *Letters*, i.67). At the bottom of the field runs the main road between Alfreton (mentioned in the 'Burns Novel', 6 miles n.w. of Eastwood) and Nottingham; this goes past Moorgreen Reservoir and up Hunt's Hill (118:15). Just outside Underwood, a turning off to the right takes one to the 'lane-end' of Haggs Farm (118:15). Gertrude in 'Love Among the Haystacks' is planning to go to Crich, a village nine miles n.w. of Eastwood, only 'ten mile to walk' from Greasley (118:14); or she could go by train from Langley Mill to Ambergate, the nearest station to Crich.

In 'Strike-Pay', a party of colliers walk from Eastwood to Nottingham. They stop at the 'White Bull' at Giltbrook (once the 'Old White Bull', now the 'Hayloft'), and again at Kimberley Top, either at the 'Queen's Head', or the 'Gate', or the 'Lord Clyde'. They do not stop at 'Nuttall' (local spelling of Nuthall), but pass St Patrick's Church; they turn off the main road and thus miss Cinder Hill, but cross the fields to Bulwell, to an unidentifiable small public house. In Nottingham, they go to the Meadow Lane Ground (home of Notts. County Football Club from 1910), to see the match; afterwards, John Wharmby will be playing at the 'Punch Bowl Vaults' at 1, Peck Lane, Nottingham.

The start of the 'Burns Novel' is set on the common Lawrence celebrated as 'The Wild Common' (*Complete Poems*, ed. Pinto and Roberts, ii. 897-8), locally known as 'The Friezeland', above the valley and the 'wooded slope' (201:33) of Moorgreen Reservoir and High Park wood. The 'top road' (203:37), which also appears in 'A Prelude' (7:37), is probably that to Underwood along the top of the ridge from Annesley. Jack Haseldine returns to the Haggs Farm (see above), and then—avoiding the 'Brick and Tile' public house in Underwood—walks to Jacksdale, 2 miles n.w. of Underwood, to the 'cottages by the brook' (203:15) in the centre of the village. On his way home he stops at a pub: probably Lawrence's recreation of 'The Gate' in Westwood, on the road from Jacksdale to Underwood (see Explanatory note on 210:15). The 'Robin Hood at Sels'on' (204:7) is also mentioned; there was no such public house in Selston (1 mile n. of Underwood) but the name was popular locally: Lawrence referred to the 'Robin Hood' in Brinsley in 'Two Marriages' (see *The Prussian Officer*, ed. Worthen, note on 210:12).

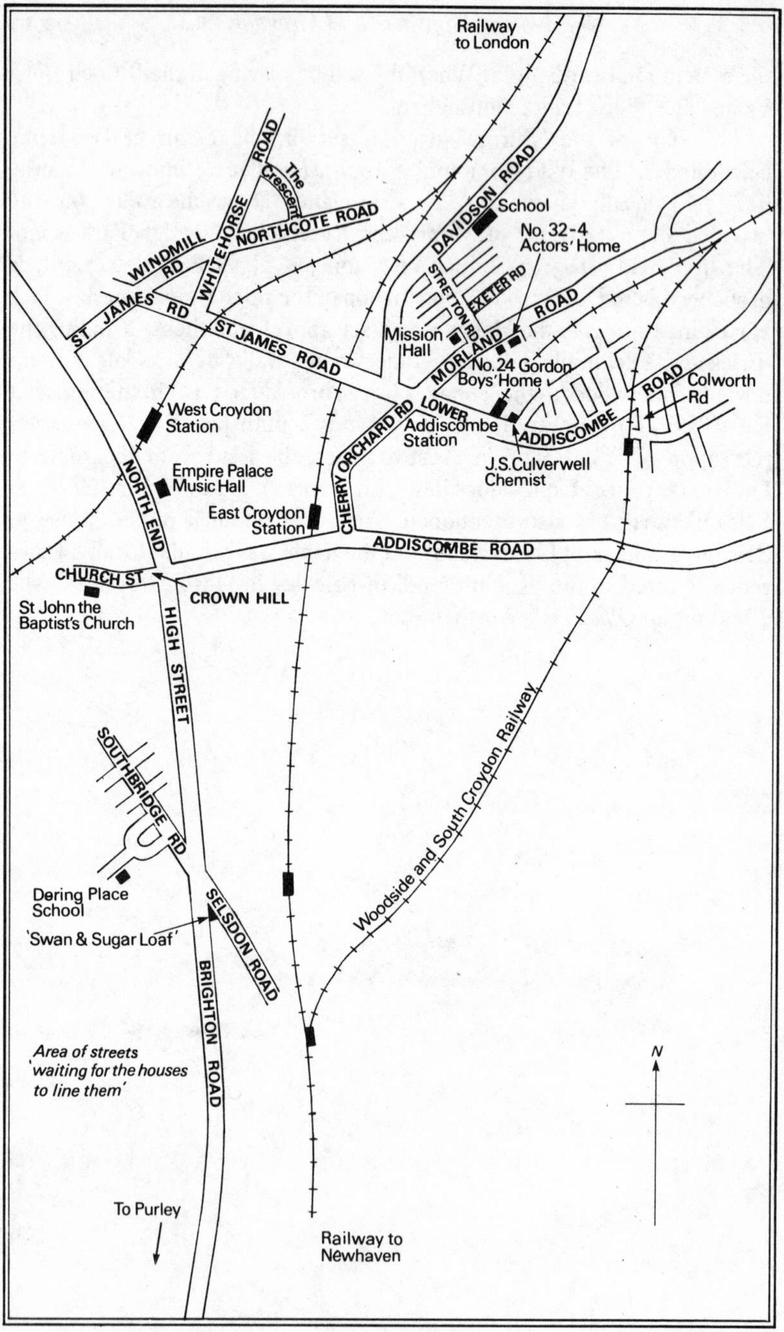


Map 2 Croydon *c.* 1911

## (ii) Croydon

Lawrence lived in Croydon during term-time between October 1908 and December 1911; a number of stories in this volume recreate it ('A Lesson on a Tortoise', 'Lessford's Rabbits', 'The Fly in the Ointment', 'The Witch à la Mode' and 'The Old Adam'). In 'The Fly in the Ointment' and 'The Old Adam' he uses numerous details of the family, house and garden at his first lodging, no. 12 on the w. side of Colworth Road; the glass door leading to the garden (see *Letters*, i. 115), the high embankment at the end of the garden where the trains of the Woodside and South Croydon Railway passed, 'as if suspended in the air ... bright and yellow' (*Letters*, i. 118), the garden where he played with the children; but what was in real-life 'our little garden' (*Letters*, i. 115) is here 'large for a London suburb' (73:1). The house itself, of two storeys, appears as a three storey house in 'The Old Adam' (though houses on the opposite side of the road had three storeys); but in 'The Fly in the Ointment' he describes the kitchen, the yard outside, and the 'hand's-breadth of garden backed up by the railway embankment' (50:20).

In 1908–9, Colworth Road ('the still little street' of *Letters*, i. 118) was the most recently completed and built-up street on the east side of Croydon, 'on the very edge of town' (*Letters*, i. 115). On his half-mile walk to school, Lawrence would have walked through the 'sordid streets' of 'A Lesson on a Tortoise', the 'mean streets' of 'The Fly in the Ointment', like Exeter Road (mentioned as the home of the poor and thieving youth). Also on Lawrence's way to school was the St Martin's Church of England Mission Hall, at the corner of Morland Road and Stretton Road, probably where the children have free dinners in 'Lessford's Rabbits'. In Morland Road itself, at no. 24, was the Croydon Gordon Boys' Home, where the six Gordon Home boys in 'A Lesson on a Tortoise' come from. A few doors further on, at nos. 32–4, were the 'two great houses' (*Letters*, i. 314) of the Home for the children of actors mentioned in 'A Lesson on a Tortoise'.

The school itself, Davidson Road School, had only been opened earlier in 1908, in a road also only built that year: it was a 'great big new red-brick imposing handsome place' (*Letters*, i. 83). Lawrence describes in 'Lessford's Rabbits' the 'six short flights of stone stairs' he had to climb, up to the art room at the top of the building, with its 'strip of blackboard' (21:12); the latter was recalled by Frank W. Turner, one of Lawrence's Croydon pupils: 'In a room below the roof, a continuous blackboard runs around the upper part of the room, and even now, I can picture "D.H." standing some feet away, with an arm outstretched to draw on the board' (Nehls, i. 91). In 'A Lesson on a Tortoise', he refers to the playground in front of the school; the west facing room looking out across the town is one of the class rooms opening off the great hall (*Letters*, i. 96).

Travelling to and from Croydon, Lawrence used East Croydon station, with its direct line to Charing Cross station in London (*Letters*, i. 307). Bernard Coutts, travelling up from Newhaven on the south coast, comes into the same station in 'The Witch à la Mode'; like Lawrence in 1911, he goes down to Purley by the tram which left from Crown Hill, in the town centre. Laura MacCartney's house and garden at 8 Purley Park Road are recreated in the same story, as is the return journey to Croydon, either by the tram which goes to West Croydon station (taken by Miss Syfurt, who leaves 'not later than ten o'clock' (59:14); the last tram from Purley to Croydon on weekday evenings in 1911 started at 10.55 p.m., but she has to change at West Croydon terminus to catch a train to Sutton and Ewell) or by walking (like Coutts and Winifred Varley) over the hill, along the roads built 'waiting for the houses to line them' (60:18). They can see below them the Brighton Road, running s. from Croydon; they descend to the 'Swan and Sugar Loaf' public house, at the junction of Selsdon Road with the Brighton Road. This was a tram and bus stop; the couple take the tram up to West Croydon terminus, and then walk to Winifred Varley's home. This is Lawrence's recreation of the house of Helen Corke and her parents, at no. 75, The Crescent. Winifred walks 'from West Croydon every day' (59:31), just as Helen Corke would have done on her way to and from the Dering Place School.

Other features of Croydon mentioned by Lawrence include the fifteenth-century church of St John the Baptist in Church Street (running on and down from Crown Hill), and the Empire Palace Music Hall at 84, North End, where Lessford spends his money in 'Lessford's Rabbits'. The Chemist's shop owned by John Sayer Culverwell, just beside Addiscombe Station, which Lawrence must have walked past many times between 1908 and 1911, may have contributed the name 'Culverwell' to 'Two Schools' (see note on 187:22).

# EXPLANATORY NOTES

# EXPLANATORY NOTES

## A Prelude

5:1 **A Prelude** Jessie Chambers (1887–1944), the intimate friend of DHL in his early years, considered it a 'sentimental little story' with 'a rather charming picture of my parents and my elder brother' (*D. H. Lawrence Review*, xii, Spring–Summer 1979, 113): see note on 5:3. She herself is recreated as 'Muriel' at 31:31 below, one of the names DHL adopted for her; actually the first name of her sister May (see note on 5:3).

5:2 **"Sweet is pleasure after pain……"** *Alexander's Feast* (1697), by John Dryden (1631–1700), l. 60: 'Rich the treasure; / Sweet the pleasure; / Sweet is pleasure after pain.'

5:3 **a little woman** Recreation of Sarah Ann Chambers (1859–1937), wife of Edmund Chambers (1863–1946; here 'Henry', 7:27), and mother of Alan (1882–1946; here 'Fred', 6:2), Muriel May (1883–1955), Jessie, Hubert and Bernard (b. 1888 and 1890; here 'the two at the pit' and 'The younger, Arthur', 6:20 and 7:15), Mary ('Mollie', b. 1896), and Jonathan David (1898–1970).

Several family particulars are also recreated; married twenty-six years ('twenty-seven' in the story — 6:18), at 25 Edmund Chambers already had three (not two) children (6:25); like 'Fred', Alan Chambers was 25 in 1907. The family's white bull terrier Trip appears at 10:3 (DHL still recalled 'Trip floundering round' when he wrote to J. D. Chambers on 14 November 1928); a horse called 'Chris' appears at 13:25; their farm, the Haggs at Underwood, appears *passim*.

The family is also recreated in 'A Modern Lover' (Bernard as 'Benjamin'), in 'Love Among the Haystacks' (Alan as 'Henry', Hubert as 'Geoffrey' and Bernard as 'Maurice') and in the 'Burns novel' (Alan as 'Alfred', Bernard as 'Jack', perhaps Hubert as 'James'). Jessie appears as 'Muriel' in 'A Modern Lover' and in 'The Fly in the Ointment'. See also notes on 9:21, 32:40, 33:12, 33:22, 33:31, 33:37, 48:5, 49:2, 87:1, 87:17, 98:15, 117:32 and 205:28.

6:8 **oven.** At this point in Per appeared the first of the cross headings which must have been inserted into DHL's MS by the *Nottinghamshire Guardian*: 'THE DEPRESSED INDUSTRY'. All are listed in the Textual apparatus.

6:22 **two beast—"** 'Beast' is still commonly used as a collective noun.

7:34 **Nellie Wycherley,** Cf. 'Nell Wycherley' in *The White Peacock*, ed. Andrew Robertson (Cambridge, 1983), 9:20.

8:22 **the guysers** Or 'Guisers': mummers or masqueraders performing a St George play at Christmas-time, in disguise, with grotesque masks or blackened faces. Guisers (normally extemporising their lines) enter without knocking; King Christmas gives a prologue; the valiant knight enters, followed by his rival; they fight, and one of them is killed. The doctor enters, and restores him to life. A grotesque figure (often Betty, or Betty Beelzebub: see 8:36), normally carrying a dripping pan (see 10:35) appeals to the generosity of the onlookers, and collects money; glasses of wine or ale are also provided. The longer the troupe of boys or young men remains unrecognised, the better. DHL described guisers again in *The Rainbow*, chap. v.

8:25 **a gathered face,** Affected with a 'gathering': a pus-filled sore or swelling.

9:21 **as the Bedouins do,** J. D. Chambers remembered DHL's fondness for dressing up Alan Chambers 'in some oriental costume, as an Arab chief or a Jewish prophet' ('Memories of D. H. Lawrence', *Renaissance & Modern Studies*, xvi, 1972, 12).

9:34 **burnouse** 'Mantle or cloak with a hood ... extensively worn by Arabs and Moors' (*OED*).

11:8 **a lady's; thanks** E1 (p. 40) emended to 'a lady's thanks', which may well be correct.

14:23 **song of Giordani's ... is sore.** One of the numerous English versions of 'Caro mio ben', the only well-known song by Guiseppe Giordani (1744–98); cf. *Letters*, i. 67. See too 'Laetitia: Fragment I' in *The White Peacock*, ed. Robertson, 341:24.

## A Lesson on a Tortoise

16:8 **November** See Introduction for discussion of the story's date of composition.

16:27 **six Gordon Home boys,** DHL first wrote 'Gordon', altered it to 'Gregory' (and 'Gordons' to 'Gregories'), then back again on each appearance in MS (p. 2 etc.). From 1903 the Church of England Society for Providing Homes for Waifs and Strays ran the Croydon Gordon Boys' Home at 24 Morland Road; in December 1908 DHL had in his class 'eight lads from the Gordon Home; waifs and strays living by charity. They are of insolent, resentful disposition ... they make me jolly mad, but I am sorry for them' (*Letters*, i. 97). Cf. Helen Corke, *In Our Infancy* (Cambridge, 1975), p. 153.

16:28 **five boys ... Home for the children of actors,** DHL altered 'actors' to 'authors' and then back again on each appearance in MS (p. 2 etc.). '1908–14 the Actors' Orphanage Fund (now the Actors' Charitable Trust) rented 32–4 Morland Road, Croydon, to accommodate orphans and illegitimate children of actors and actresses' (*Letters*, i. 97 n. 1). In December 1908 DHL had six in his class: 'They are delightful boys, refined, manly, and aimiable' (*Letters*, i. 97).

16:30 **broken enormous boots,** Cf. DHL to Louisa ('Louie') Burrows (1888–1962, DHL's fiancée from December 1910 to February 1912) in March 1909: 'Louisa, do any of your youngsters limp to school; through the snow or the fine weather, limp to school because they are crippled with broken boots. Have you seen wounds on the feet of your boys, from great mens boots they wear which are split across' (*Letters*, i. 124).

17:16 **the grains** Small, hardish, rounded particles; figuratively 'the smallest possible'.

## Lessford's Rabbits

21:5 **free breakfasts. Dinners ... in a Church Mission room** DHL wrote to Louie Burrows about the school's free breakfasts on 28 March 1909: 'half a pint of milk and a lump of bread – eighty boys and girls sitting down the bare boards' (*Letters*, i. 124); he had also told May Holbrook about the canteen dinners and free breakfasts on 2 December 1908 (*Letters*, i. 97). St Martin's Church of England Mission Hall, run by the Rev. W. E. Jones in 1908, was at the corner of Stretton Road and Morland Road.

21:6 **the feeding of the five thousand.** The feeding of the four thousand is described by Mark viii. 1–9, that of the five thousand by Matthew xiv. 15–21. DHL told May Holbrook that the canteen 'is a mission room, with pictures of the feeding of the ten thousand and Peter smiting the rock' (*Letters*, i. 97).

21:10 **to be late.** Followed in MS by the deleted: 'I inherited it from my mother's side' (p. 1).

21:23 **vises ... a fish kettle,** I.e. vices ... a long oval vessel for boiling fish.

21:30 **the Infant mistress** Named as 'Miss Culloch' below; probably a recreation of Miss A. Rollston, teacher at the Davidson Road school, 1908–11; see *Letters*, i. 194 n. 7.

22:14 **said confidentially to me, thrusting** In MS DHL first wrote 'said, thrusting', then inserted the other three words (p. 2); his insertion mark, however, appeared the wrong side of the comma. E1's emendation (p. 1) has been adopted.

22:35 **rat-tailed hair,** Replacing DHL's first MS reading: 'hair like rows of butcher's hooks in their necks' (p. 3).

23:2 **'Let us ... we die'."** A conflation of Luke xii. 19, 'eat, drink, and be merry' (echoing Ecclesiastes viii. 15: 'A man hath no better thing under the sun, than to eat, and to drink, and to be merry'), with St Paul's reaction to the idea of there being no resurrection in 1 Corinthians xv. 32: 'let us eat and drink; for tomorrow we die'.

23:29 **Halket** A name also used in *The White Peacock*, ed. Robertson, 58:18.

23:36 **unrelievedly poor people.** Substituted in MS for 'poor low slum dwellers' (p. 5).

25:24 **when the register was closed.** When it was too late in the day to be included in the register of the pupils' attendance.

## A Modern Lover

28:1 **A Modern Lover** Cf. the novel of the same name (1883) by George Moore (1852–1933). DHL knew at least three other novels by him (see *Letters*, i. 154 and note on 40:5), and it is likely that he knew *A Modern Lover* (with its artist hero) as well. The story's title also suggests the poem-cycle 'Modern Love' (1862) by

George Meredith (1828–1909) which DHL recommended to Louie Burrows as 'very fine indeed' in March 1911 (*Letters*, i. 242). The original title, deleted on MS p. 1, was 'The Virtuous'.

See Introduction for some of the circumstances surrounding the writing of the story. In 1933, Jessie Chambers recalled 'Lawrence's complete change of attitude towards our relationship' in December 1909: 'He came up to our house [the Haggs Farm] on Christmas Eve and from his first glance I was aware of a difference. When I went with him over the fields he told me he had found out – he had really loved me all along and not realised it... He said that all our long association was in reality a preparation for this "une intimité d'amour". It came as a shock to me, very disturbing, yet at the same time inevitable...' (Delavenay, ii. 702). DHL himself commented on the change in the relationship in *Letters*, i. 154.

28:30 **glamourous,** DHL's spelling in MS (p. [3]), accepted as alternative to 'glamorous' by *OED*.

29:4 **on the brink** In MS, DHL deleted 'the' (p. [3]), but the 1933 typist must have restored it (it appeared in both Per and E1, pp. 258 and 12); it has been adopted here.

30:1 **folded** Otherwise unrecorded, and perhaps DHL's coinage: presumably, 'in a fold'.

30:2 **Orion ... the Twins** The Twins: Gemini, with Castor and Pollux. Orion plays a particular role in DHL's private symbolism: see ll. 21–24 in 'Hymn to Priapus': 'He's the star of my first beloved / Love-making. / The witness of all that bitter-sweet / Heart-aching' (*Complete Poems*, ed. V. de S. Pinto and W. Roberts, 1964, i, 198). See references below at 45:30, 60:23 and in *Sons and Lovers*, chap. VIII and *The Rainbow*, chap. V.

31:1 **Cyril!** Cf. the name 'Cecil' used by DHL for the autobiographical character in *The White Peacock*.

31:37 **torses,** Alternative (from the French) to the Italian 'torsos'.

32:15 **clambered** Otherwise unrecorded in this sense; but cf. 'to clam' (Nottinghamshire dialect), 'to clutch, seize, grope at'.

32:40 **"Daily News."** Popular daily newspaper; DHL and Jessie Chambers read G. K. Chesterton's regular Saturday column in it (see *Letters*, i. 43 and n. 1). Jessie Chambers also remembered 'father in his corner engrossed in the *Daily News*' (E. T. 115).

33:12 **water-colours ... the Countess'** Helen Corke saw at least one picture by DHL when she visited the Chambers family late in 1910 (*The Croydon Years*, Austin, 1965, p. 26) ... the chair is mentioned again in 'The Shades of Spring'; see *The Prussian Officer*, ed. John Worthen, Cambridge 1983, 104:5 and n.

33:22 **"Jane Eyre"** [33:16] **... William James.** In the period up to the end of 1909, DHL knew the following books and authors out of the list:

*Jane Eyre* (1847), by Charlotte Brontë; in November 1908 one of his 'favourite English books' (*Letters*, i. 88); for Jessie Chambers, a book 'that exercised a real fascination over him' (E.T. 98).

George Eliot; DHL 'adored' *The Mill on the Floss* (1860), and knew *Adam Bede* (1859) and *Romola* (1863) (E.T. 97–8); 'I am very fond of her' (*Letters*, i. 101).

Thomas Carlyle; DHL declared himself suffering 'acutely from Carlyliophobia' (*Letters*, i. 49) in 1906, when he read *Sartor Resartus* (1834), *The French Revolution* (1837) and *Heroes and Hero-Worship* (1841) (E.T. 101–2).

John Ruskin; DHL read *Sesame and Lilies* (1865), probably in 1908 (E.T. 107).

Arthur Schopenhauer (1788–1860); DHL read essays by him in 1907–8 (E.T. 111–12), in the selection edited by Mrs Rudolf Dircks (Walter Scott Publishing Co. Ltd, 1903) (Nehls, i. 66).

Charles Darwin (1809–82); DHL had read some Darwin, probably *On the Origin of the Species* (1859) (E.T. 112) by October 1907 (*Letters*, i. 36).

Thomas Henry Huxley (1823–95); DHL read *Man's Place in Nature* (originally *Evidence as to Man's Place in Nature*, 1863) *c.*1907 (E.T. 112).

'The Rubáiyát of Omar Khayyám', translated (1839) by Edward Fitzgerald (1809–83); DHL gave Jessie Chambers a copy one Christmas between 1902 and 1909 (E.T. 101).

DHL had read *Anna Karenina* (tr. 1884) by Leo Tolstoy and thought it 'the greatest novel in the world' (E.T. 114) by 1905 (Nehls, iii. 593); he read *War and Peace* (tr. 1886) by 1909 (*Letters*, i. 127). He liked the work of Ivan Turgenev (1818–83) 'immensely' (E.T. 121), reading *Fathers and Sons* (tr. 1867) and *Rudin* (probably as *Dmitri Rudine*, tr. 1873). By 1908, he had read Maxim Gorky (1868–1936), 'but didn't care much for him' (E.T. 121); 'I'm very much an English equivalent of his' (*Letters*, i. 209). He read *Crime and Punishment* (tr. 1886), by Feodor Dostoievsky, in 1909 (*Letters*, i. 126–7); 'It's very great, but I don't like it' (E.T. 123).

Henrik Ibsen; by 1909 he knew *Lady Inger*, *The Vikings*, *The Pretenders*, *The Lady from the Sea*, *Hedda Gabler* and *Rosmersholme* (*Letters*, i. 112–13 and nn. 3 and 2), in *Ibsen's Prose Dramas*, ed. Archer (tr. 1890–1).

Honoré de Balzac (1799–1850); from 1907, DHL had 'a great admiration' for him, in particular for 'La Peau de Chagrin' (E.T. 105–7) and *Eugénie Grandet* (1833), 'one of the finest works out of the heart of a man' (*Letters*, i. 89, 91–2).

Guy de Maupassant (1850–93); DHL gave Jessie Chambers 'Tales' in January 1906 (E.T. 107).

DHL probably read *Madame Bovary* (1857), by Gustave Flaubert, in the spring of 1906 (E.T. 107).

Friedrich Nietzsche; DHL found books by him (e.g. *Thus Spake Zarathustra*, tr. 1899) in the public library at Croydon after 1908 (E.T. 120).

*Pragmatism* (1907) by William James (1842–1910) 'especially appealed' to DHL; he probably read it 1908–09.

33:29 **sweating down.** Unlike feathers, down can be extruded ('sweated') through the fabric of a cushion.

33:31 **The two photographs of himself** At twenty-one (see 34:36–7). Two photographs of DHL taken on his twenty-first birthday survive; he gave a copy of at least one of them to the Chambers family in 1906 (E.T. 135). See Corke, *The Croydon Years*, p. 26.

33:37 **leaving the farm come Lady-day.** 25 March, Annunciation of the Virgin Mary, one of the four quarter days on which tenancy of houses and farms usually began and ended (25 March, 24 June, 29 September, 25 December). (The Chambers family left the Haggs farm on 25 March 1910.)

34:23 **creatures** DHL originally wrote 'a pack of boors' (MS, p. [20]), but failed to delete the 'a' when revising; the 1933 typist must have ignored it, and it has been omitted here.

34:36 **"Ah, the pity!** Substituted in MS for 'Which is regrettable!' (p. [21]). Cf. *Othello* IV. i. 191: 'but yet the pity of it, Iago, the pity...'

35:22 **'Men at ... fates etcetera.'"** Cf. W. E. Henley (1849–1903), *Echoes* (1888), 'Invictus': 'I am the master of my fate: / I am the captain of my soul' (ll. 15–16).

36:20 **carding ... carded** To prepare wool, etc., for spinning by combing out impurities and straightening the fibres with a card.

38:20 **"iron-men" ... electric haulage ... a working electrician** Coal-cutting machines (*OED* first reference 1897) ... electric winding machinery replacing steam driven haulage (also underground, replacing pit ponies 'on the main roads'), introduced into the Eastwood collieries 1906–7 ... named as 'Tom Vickers' below; cf. 'Palmer' in *Women in Love*, ed. David Farmer, Lindeth Vasey and John Worthen (Cambridge, 1987), 117:26.

39:18 **Miel?** I.e. 'Muriel'; also 'honey' (French).

40:1 **xy and yx.** 2xy.

40:5 **one of the men ... across the floor.** In *Evelyn Innes* (1898), by George Moore, Sir Owen Asher (about to elope with Evelyn) considers the future: 'keep women you couldn't; he had long ago found out that. Marry them, and they came to hate the way you walked across the room...' (chap. VI). DHL asked Blanche Jennings for the novel on 1 November 1909 (*Letters*, i. 142), and loaned it to Helen Corke on 8 December 1909 (see *The Trespasser*, ed. Elizabeth Mansfield, Cambridge, 1982, p. 289). According to Jessie Chambers, he was 'extremely enthusiastic' about it (Delavenay, ii. 686–7). In *The Rainbow*, chap. VI, Anna, thinking of her husband Will, 'loved and rejoiced in the way he crossed the floor...'.

41:3 **You only ... for you."** Replacing the deletion in MS: 'You want to understand—sympathise, that's the same—with you landlady's troubles, and she'll love you; you must also understand her weaknesses, and overlook them—then she'll respect you; lastly you must have no faults of your own but the faults of generosity and quick temper; then she'll always forgive you. In the end, you can turn her round your little finger' (p. [36]).

41:39 **twitched** The 1933 typist probably typed 'twinkled' (the reading of Per, p. 276). E1 (p. 33) adjusted this to 'wrinkled'.

42:16 **"Honour and Arms."** Used by DHL as the title of a story he wrote in 1913 (see *The Prussian Officer*, ed. Worthen, note on 1:2); an aria in the oratorio *Samson* (1743), music by George Frideric Handel (1685–1759), words (after Milton) by Newburgh Hamilton.

42:18 **'sois triste et sois belle'"** Charles Baudelaire (1821–67), *Fleurs du Mal*, 3rd edn (1868), 'Madrigal Triste': 'Que m'importe que tu sois sage! / Sois belle! et sois triste!...' (ll. 1–2): 'What does it matter to me whether you're well-behaved! / Be beautiful! and be melancholy!...' (French). See note on 75:19.

42:19 **'Du bist wie eine Blume' ... 'Pur dicesti.'"** Poem by Heinrich Heine (1797–1856), 'Du bist wie eine Blume, / So hold und schön und rein': 'You are like a flower, / so sweet and lovely and pure' (German); there are musical settings by Liszt, Rubinstein and Schumann ... Song by Antonio Lotti (1667–1740), 'Pur dicesti, o bocca bocca bella': 'But you have said, oh beautiful, beautiful mouth'. Deleted in MS: 'Caro mi' ben' (p. [40]); see note on 14:23.

42:32 **"The Octopus."** *The Octopus: a story of California* (London, 1901), by Benjamin Franklin [Frank] Norris (1870–1902); there was a 1907 Nelson's Library cheap reprint. First novel of an unfinished trilogy entitled *The Epic of the Wheat*, the book deals with the war between the wheat grower and the railroad trust. See *Letters*, i. 172.

44:5 **Owbridge's?** A 'Lung Tonic'; 'The most up-to-date, best known and most successful Remedy in the World for COUGHS AND COLDS' (1912 advertisement).

44:20 **luminous, and wonderful.** DHL rewrote this part of the sentence several times in MS, and left it reading 'a luminous, and wonderful', after deleting the final noun 'transfiguration' (p. [45]).

45:6 **"Sic transit,"** 'Sic transit gloria mundi' ('Thus passes the glory of the world') in *De Imitatione Christi*, chap. III, by Thomas à Kempis (1380–1471).

45:6 **a blossom.** DHL rewrote the end of this sentence several times in MS; the earliest version read: 'a blossom at the mercy of the gardener who has patiently watched in the garden to see Life moving unseen about the buds' (p. [47]).

46:17 **how they pollinate ... over them.** A debate continued in *Women in Love*: '"isn't it better that [the children] should see as a whole, without all this pulling to pieces, all this knowledge?" "Would you rather, for yourself, know or not know that the little red flowers are there, putting out for the pollen?"' (ed. Farmer, Vasey and Worthen, 40:5–8).

46:19 **"you won't** [46:14] **... dazing fairies."** Replacing the deletion in MS: 'No! I'm sure I shan't! I examine things too much! It's like Christian baptism-with-spirit—if you're decently well-behaved, and look at things honestly, you don't get it. You have to shut your eyes. Same with love. My eyes won't be shut' (p. [50]).

47:26 **"one need not blunder into calamities."** Cf. Paul to Miriam in *Sons and Lovers*, chap. XI: 'there's not much risk for you really—not in the Gretchen way. You can trust me there?' (see note on 156:25).

48:5 **creeping together in the dark—"** Replacing 'underhand—even—' (deleted in MS, p. [54]). Jessie Chambers recalled of her new relationship with DHL, starting at Christmas 1909, that 'The feature that presented most difficulty was the necessity to be clandestine, and the holiday actually ended on a note of disagreement because I said it seemed "not honourable" to take advantage of Mrs Jones's [see note on 49:6] hospitality' (Delavenay, ii. 702).

48:36 **goodbye.** In MS, DHL started a new paragraph, but deleted the single line he wrote: 'He stumbled a little as he hurried down' (p. [56]).

## The Fly in the Ointment

49:2 **Muriel ... some mauve primroses,** See note on 5:3. Cf. *The White Peacock*, ed. Robertson, p. 262, where 'Emily' (a recreation of Jessie Chambers) sends 'Cecil' (see note on 31:1) some winter aconites. In February–March 1909, Louie Burrows sent DHL snowdrops, primroses, winter aconites and violets (*Letters*, i. 117·21); in March 1910 he asked her (*Letters*, i. 156) for a box of 'hazel catkins' (49:4).

49:3 **rosettes,** Cf. DHL to Louie Burrows, 27 March 1911: 'The hedges are in rosettes. Hawthorn leaves, opened no further than half blown rosettes, on a wet evening, are the vividest green things I know' (*Letters*, i. 241).

49:6 **Mrs Williams,** DHL's landlord and landlady in Croydon 1908–11 were John William (1868–1956) and Marie (1869–1950) Jones, first at 12 and later at 16 Colworth Road; see *Letters*, i. 82 n.2 and i. 83. J. W. Jones was Superintendent of Attendance Officers on Croydon Education Committee.

49:25 **her looking** Per's reading 'her, while she looked' (p. 595) might just possibly be an authorial proof correction; it is more likely to be a compositor or magazine editor assisting a difficult sentence. If DHL had corrected proof himself, he would almost certainly have made more changes than this (the only major change between TS and Per).

50:22 **the oilcloth** Canvas enamelled with oil to make it waterproof, and used to cover chairs, floors etc.

51:8 **'im,** I.e. the poker; the preceding sentence (rewritten by DHL in MS, p. 4) originally ran: 'Stop that idiotic commotion, and put down that poker.' Per (p. 596) and O1 (p. 222) both altered ''im' to 'me'.

51:26 **a low breed.** MS (p. 5) originally read 'the lowest class', altered to 'the lowest breed'; the current reading was inserted in TS (p. 5).

52:5 **chelp."** Impertinent talk or chatter.

52:26 **in his chair.** In a passage DHL rewrote in MS, the narrator had originally 'handed him a wooden chair' (p. 5) before himself sitting down.

53:8 **"if a man ... his hire,** Cf. Luke x. 7: 'for the labourer is worthy of his hire'.

53:17 **a knock-out ... sleering** Overwhelming (first usage 1892 in *A Supplement to the OED*, ed. R. W. Burchfield, vol. II, Oxford, 1976) ... see note on 130:12.

53:28 **unpassable** Dialect form of 'impassable'.

53:30 **a blot,** The story's original title, deleted on MS (p. 1).

## The Witch à la Mode

54:1 **The Witch à la Mode** Helen Corke recalled, of 1911:

> Sometimes I spend an evening with Laura M. and her father [see notes on 55:18 and 55:36 below] in their little villa at Purley. Laura will arrange a

muscial evening to which David is also invited ... (A collection of D. H. Lawrence's short stories published after his death includes one entitled 'The Witch à la Mode', which recalls this evening. Reading it, I could understand much in his attitude and behaviour of the time then incomprehensible. The story itself is a skilful blend of fact and fiction, with an entirely imaginary *dénouement.*) (*In Our Infancy*, p. 210)

See also Nehls, i. 143.

54:2 **Coutts** A common name in the Eastwood region; cf. Bertha Coutts in *Lady Chatterley's Lover*, chap. XIV, and Sam Coutts in 'Strike-Pay' below, at 135:22.

54:6 **Connie's forlorn spot** A vicarage in Yorkshire, according to details given below; in the early draft, Roberts E438a, at Ingleton, on the North Yorkshire moors (p. 1). DHL's fiancée in 1911, Louie Burrows, lived at Gaddesby in Leicestershire during term-time: a small village $8\frac{1}{2}$ miles n.e. of Leicester.

54:13 **an evening of March.** Cf. DHL's letter to Helen Corke of 14 March 1911 (*Letters*, i. 238–40) for its suggestions of a relationship similar to that in the story. The sentence concluded 'an evening of April' before being revised in Roberts E438a (p. 1).

54:23 **smiled a little, roused.** DHL first corrected MS, p. 2, to read 'smiled with pleasure' in MS, p. 2, then deleted 'with pleasure' and inserted 'a little exultation': he may not have meant to delete 'with'. Clayton typed 'smiled a little in exultation' in TS (p. 2), which DHL revised to 'smiled a little, roused'. Although his final revision was prompted by Clayton's unauthorised alteration, it is a sufficiently new development to count as an authentic authorial revision, and has been adopted.

55:3 **"It is like a knife ... he said,** DHL records such a conjunction in a letter to Louie Burrows of 1 May 1911: '"Bless you, you little devil of a weapon", I said' (*Letters*, i. 264).

55:14 **alyssome** The spelling of MS (p. 3); E1 revised to 'alyssam' (p. 104); *OED* has 'alyssum'. Sweet alyssum (*Koniga maritima*) has white flowers. May Chambers described DHL's account of his home garden, *c.*1905: '"the white flower all over the grotto here is *alyssum.* I like it, don't you?" And he spelled the word out' (Nehls, iii. 605).

55:18 **Mrs Braithwaite** DHL's recreation (with first name 'Laura') of Miss Laura MacCartney, sister to H. B. MacCartney, Helen Corke's "Siegmund" (see Introduction to *The Trespasser*, ed. Elizabeth Mansfield, Cambridge, 1982, pp. 4–5). She lived in Purley; Helen Corke introduced DHL to her. See *Letters*, i. 253, 265, 279 and 300–1. 'Mrs Braithwaite' is a widow of two years; H. B. MacCartney had died in August 1909.

55:27 **skin and black hair,** DHL first wrote 'skin and hair' (MS, p. 3), then deleted 'hair' and inserted 'black hair'. In a subsequent revision, he inserted 'in' between 'and' and 'hair'. Clayton, realising that 'skin and in black hair' must be wrong, added 'her' after 'in' (TS, p. 3). It seems likely that DHL's addition of 'in' was done carelessly; rather than adopt Clayton's emendation, this edition has reverted to DHL's original revision.

55:36 **A rosy old gentleman,** Named as 'Mr Cleveland' below. See *Letters*, i. 279 for DHL's description of Laura MacCartney's father, and cf. Helen Corke, *In Our Infancy*, p. 173.

56:34 **Free Will** Reflecting the mid-nineteenth-century debate between an increasingly scientific determinism (fostered by theories like evolution), and the idea that man's freedom lies in obeying the moral law, not in admitting himself subject wholly to scientific law. To revive *that* debate would be 'passé' (56:36): 'out of date, behind the times'.

57:12 **Miss Bunbury,"** 'Bunbury' was an invalid, offering a continuing excuse for visiting the country, used by Algernon Moncrieff in *The Importance of Being Earnest* (1895) by Oscar Wilde.

57:18 **Winifred** Deleted in MS (p. 6): 'Enid'. DHL's recreation of his Croydon friend Helen Corke (1882–1978); see *Letters*, i. 129 n. 2. She was 'Margaret Varley' in the story's first draft (Roberts E438a, p. 9).

57:31 **When are . . . well off."** Cf. DHL's letter to his fiancée Louie Burrows, 27 January 1911: 'Look, Louie: I – we both have agreed that we cannot marry unless I have £100 in cash and £120 a year income' (*Letters*, i. 223); by 24 July the sum had risen to 'an assured income of £150, and a hundred quid to marry on . . .' (*Letters*, i. 293).

58:1 **a German lady** Named below as 'Miss Syfurt', 'a little woman of forty', living in Ewell; cf. DHL's acquaintance with Miss Emma Herbert, 'German lady, 45 (circa)', who lived in Peckham (*Letters*, i. 308 and n. 1).

58:31 **deep grey water.** DHL first wrote 'the deep grey water in a canal' (MS, p. 9), but then deleted the last three words. Clayton did not type 'the' (TS, p. 8); his emendation has been adopted.

59:2 **Laura played . . . a Grieg Sonata,** Laura MacCartney 'plays Chopin's nocturnes very well indeed' (*Letters*, i. 253); Helen Corke recorded an evening when she and Laura MacCartney performed a Grieg violin sonata (*In Our Infancy*, p. 210).

60:5 **set the man on edge. It** In MS, DHL first wrote 'affected Coutts: it' (p. 11); he then deleted the first two words and inserted 'set the man on edge.'. This edition respects the full stop of his revision and adjusts accordingly.

63:6 **an almond tree . . .theatrical effect.** Cf. DHL's 1910 poem 'Letter from Town: The Almond Tree' (*Complete Poems*, ed. Pinto and Roberts, i. 58). Croydon's almond blossom was fully out in 1911 by 27 March (*Letters*, i. 241).

63:36 **voiceless."** The reading of MS (p. 17) and TS (p. 16); altered to 'scentless' in TS by a hand unlike DHL's in his corrections of words on pp. 1, 2, 9 and 26 of TS.

64:36 **the score of 'Walküre.'** *Die Walküre* (written 1852–6, performed 1870), music drama by Richard Wagner (1813–83); Helen Corke quoted from its musical score in her autobiographical novel *Neutral Ground* (1933), pp. 216–17.

65:22 **you tilt—"** Coutts originally replied: '"Windmills," he laughed' (deleted in MS, p. 21). The reference is to *Don Quixote*, Book I, chap. VIII.

65:27 **"Meredith—very healthy,"** DHL referred to poetry by George Meredith ('Love in a Valley', 'Woods of Westermain' and 'Modern Love') in a letter of 27 March 1911 (*Letters*, i. 242); he was reading the novel *The Tragic Comedians* (1880) on 2 April 1911 (*Letters*, i. 250). See note on 28:1.

66:10 **Q.E.F."** Quod erat faciendum: 'Which was to be done' (Latin).

66:22 **we should . . . become abnormal."** Cf. DHL to Helen Corke, 14 March 1911 (*Letters*, i. 239), and Helen Corke, *In Our Infancy*, p. 204.

66:29 **Euripides' 'Bacchae':** DHL referred to the play on 26 April 1911: '*Bacchae* I like exceedingly for its flashing poetry' (*Letters*, i. 261). He had read it in May 1910 (*Letters*, i. 160).

67:4 **the Kobolds** In German folklore, either gnomes which haunt dark and solitary places, or domestic spirits. DHL probably means the former; cf. Coutts' reply in the original reading of Roberts E438a: '"Do you know," he said, "that's a woman exactly. All knowledge rolls along down the deep stream of her subconscious twilight soul and she loves a man because he, a mere naked bird born of her, can dive and fish her out the wonders, flourish them in the face of her, her own undiscoverables."' (p. 29).

67:9 **Lady-of-Shalott-looking-glass** The mirror which was the Lady of Shalott's only way of viewing the real world, in Tennyson's poem (1832) of that title. DHL read it 'time after time' to Jessie Chambers, *c.*1902, and 'somehow hinted' that it 'applied to me' (E.T. 95).

67:17 **the Gods the suet and intestines:** Blood sacrifice by the Greeks and Romans normally involved the burning of some part of the animal, wrapped in fat or suet. See William Smith, *Dictionary of Greek and Roman Antiquities* (1853): 'it was the almost general practice to burn only the legs . . . enclosed in fat, and certain parts of the intestines' (p. 999).

67:26 **all the Addios in 'Traviata'** Cf. the 'farewell' in DHL's letter to Louie Burrows of 6 April 1911: 'Addio – I can hear Sammarco in *Traviata* 'Addi-i-i-i-o' (*Letters*, i. 253 and n. 4). DHL must have seen Verdi's *La Traviata* at Covent Garden between 1908 and 1911; he here alludes to the final duet between Violetta and Alfredo. Cf. *The Trespasser*, ed. Mansfield, 150:31–5.

## The Old Adam

71:1 **The Old Adam** See Romans vi. 6, and the Service of Publick Baptism of Infants (*Book of Common Prayer*): 'O Merciful God, grant that the old Adam in this child may be so buried . . .' A favourite phrase of DHL's for the unregenerate man (see first note on 'New Eve and Old Adam'): also a slang phrase for the penis (see *Slang and its Analogues*, ed. John S. Farmer, 1890).

A letter DHL wrote from his lodgings in Croydon in April 1911 suggests some of the story's background: 'Pa [J. W. Jones] is out tonight . . . so Mrs Jones and I are "en famille". I believe she enjoys the house best, and I'm sure I do, when we are thus on our own. Pa is really a bit gênant ['troublesome']. There are rather rotten rows occasionally. But there, it's not my business to talk.' The same letter continues: 'I meant to write a story – but I'm a bit out of the humour' (*Letters*, i. 253–4). The story was first written in June; see Introduction.

71:27 **oaks kindle green like a low fire** Cf. DHL's poem 'The Enkindled Spring' as first written in 1911, ll. 17–18: 'bonfires green, / Of wild, of puffing emerald trees and bushes' (Roberts E320.1); and his reference on 7 May 1911 to beech-trees 'as if afire with the vividest green' (*Letters*, i. 266).

72:13 **flower-border was . . . girl of three,** The sentence in MS (p. 3) originally ran 'There, running . . . flower-border, was'. When DHL deleted 'There,' he failed to remove the second comma: this edition has done so . . . The second child of the Jones family (see note on 49:6), Hilda Mary, was three on 13 March 1911.

72:32 **Menad.** A frenzied woman; from the female participants in the orgiastic rites of Dionysus.

73:6 **Mrs Thomas** 'Gertie' ('Mabel' twice deleted in MS, pp. 14–15); see note on 49:6.

73:9 **a bacchanal.** A priest, priestess or devotee of Bacchus, drunken and inspired; the American edition of *A Modern Lover*, New York, 1934, emended unnecessarily here and elsewhere to 'a bacchante' (p. 42).

73:40 **come to lodge . . . a month old.** When DHL came to lodge with the Jones family in October 1908, Hilda Mary Jones was almost seven months old.

74:19 **thirty-four years old,** In MS, DHL first made Mrs Thomas 'five years older' than Severn (p. 12), then altered it to 'eight'; Severn is 'twenty-seven' (78:15).

75:19 **a volume of French verse.** Jessie Chambers recalled that, while DHL was in Croydon, 'the two great poetic lights in his firmament were Verlaine and Baudelaire' (E.T. 121); DHL owned a copy of Baudelaire's *Fleurs du Mal* from September 1910 (*Letters*, i. 179).

76:21 **Mr Thomas** 'Joe' (81:26); see note on 49:6, and cf. the description of his mouth ('small and nervously pinched' — 79:7) with *Letters*, i. 263.

79:35 **Councillor Jarndyce,** DHL had known since 1902 (E.T. 96) Dickens's *Bleak House* (1852), with its connection between 'Jarndyce' and the practice of the law.

80:29 **the Woman's Bill,** Seven Suffrage Bills were defeated from 1906; the Second 'Conciliation' Bill was passed by a majority of 167 on its second reading on 5 May 1911; the Government, however, announced on 29 May that it did not intend to provide time for it to continue further that session. A Suffragist demonstration on 17 June had 40,000 people in a five-mile procession; DHL told Louie Burrows about it in the same letter in which he told her about the first draft of 'The Old Adam' (*Letters*, i. 276–7).

82:33 **'Beware the fearful avalanche.'"** Cf. 'Excelsior' (1838), by H. W. Longfellow (1807–82), ll. 26–7: 'Beware the pine-tree's withered branch! / Beware the awful avalanche!'

83:8 **struggling** MS originally read 'struggling, still laughing, to his feet' (p. 21); when DHL deleted 'still laughing,' he failed to delete its preceding comma; TCC (p. 21) removed it.

83:12 **sod,** E1 (p. 66) failed to print the word; from *c.*1880, a term of abuse.

83:34 **his met** DHL originally wrote 'his eyes met' MS (p. 22), but deleted 'eyes'. TCC's emendation to 'he met' (p. 22) is unnecessary.

## Love Among the Haystacks

87:1 **Love Among the Haystacks** DHL and Alan Chambers 'spent some days together thatching haystacks in the fields at Greasley' (E.T. 107), probably in 1908; he would also 'spend whole days working with my father and brothers in the fields at Greasley. These fields lay four miles away [from the Haggs farm], and we used to pack a big basket of provisions to last all day, so that hay harvest had a picnic flavour' (E.T. 31). Cf. the description in *Letters*, i. 60. DHL camped out with Alan Chambers and another friend the night of 27 August 1908, when a tramp joined them; see *Letters*, i. 64–5, 67–8. Jessie Chambers commented in 1934: 'Of course, there is not a shred of factual foundation for the story. Lawrence and my eldest brother [Alan] once slept out a night in those fields, and felt starved to death in the morning' (Delavenay, ii. 684).

87:14 **winrows,** The lines into which hay is raked for drying.

87:17 **The two brothers** See note on 5:3. They are named below as 'Geoffrey' and 'Maurice'; cf. the brothers Geoffrey and Maurice Leivers in *Sons and Lovers*, chap. VI. The family name 'Wookey' was DHL's revision of 'Field' (MS, p. [51]). Jessie Chambers felt that DHL 'caught the essential characteristics of my two brothers, and their attitude to one another with great sureness' (Delavenay, ii. 683).

87:32 **"tha thowt … didna ter?"** 'You thought you'd put one over me, didn't you?'

88:9 **'ud ha'e ter stop** 'Would have to stop'.

88:13 **Didna my feyther** 'Didn't my father'.

88:40 **'*er* 'd be theer** '*She* would be there'.

89:7 **"Ich bin … Christ allein."** Traditional German children's prayer: 'I am small, my heart is pure / There is no-one in it [d'rin = darin] except Christ alone.'

89:10 **Can thee thy prayers … German,"** DHL originally wrote '*Tha* canna say thy prayers', but decisively crossed out the first three words and inserted 'Can thee' (MS, p. 4). TCC (p. 4) followed his text; E1 reintroduced the word 'say'. DHL's 'Can' is probably a local version of 'Ken' (to know), though the dialect form is otherwise unrecorded. An error in deleting 'say' is possible … MS shows the addition in pencil of the upper part of a question-mark over the comma (p. 4). Not all the pencil emendations of MS appear to be by DHL; the original comma has therefore been retained.

89:19 **"An' there's . . . her bosom,"** MS before revision read 'Her bosom's just two good handfuls', and described Maurice's tone as 'common' (p. 5).

89:23 **mother, in** DHL originally wrote 'mother. In' (MS, p. 5), but then altered the capital 'I' to lower-case and the full-stop into a large comma, which Clayton interpreted (TCC, p. 5) as an ampersand.

89:27 **the two** DHL first wrote 'these two', and then overwrote 'these' with 'the' (MS, p. 5). TCC read 'these' (p. 5).

89:31 **morbid** Unhealthy, sickly.

89:32 **The foreign governess at the Vicarage,** A position at Greasley Vicarage had a certain local reputation; cf. DHL's play 'The Merry-Go-Round':

HARRY: I can never make out why she [Rachel] went in service at the vicarage.

BAKER: Can't you? I've had many a nice evening up there. Baron an' Baroness go to bed at nine o'clock and then—— Oh, all the girls know the advantage of being at the vicarage.

HARRY: Oh—an' does she ha'e thee up in the kitchen?

BAKER: Does she not half. (*Complete Plays*, 1965, p. 411)

90:7 **nettled** I.e. stung by nettles.

91:6 **sheered with . . . the scotches.** To sheer is to swerve or lurch . . . a scotch is a block placed under a wheel, cask or load to prevent it slipping.

91:13 **to teem** 'To empty out'.

91:19 **the blue . . . fork glittering** DHL first wrote 'and the blue . . . fork glittered'; he then altered 'glittered' to 'glittering', but failed to delete 'and' (MS, p. 8). TCC followed him (p. 8); this edition accepts the emendation of E1 (p. 8).

92:3 **moiled . . . hollin' it,** 'Hot, sweaty and weary . . . throwing it'.

92:17 **drawing in** I.e. narrowing and tapering.

92:40 **An' tha non ca's** 'And you don't call'.

93:7 **going to** In MS, DHL first wrote 'going ta', then altered 'ta' to 'to' (p. 11).

93:12 **"Thaïgh,"** 'Thee'.

93:36 **his oldest brother** Named as 'Henry' below; see note on 5:3 and 87:1.

94:23 **Bill,"** Presumably 'the laborer' of 94:15.

94:37 **the vicar.** Named below as 'Mr Inwood'. Perhaps DHL's recreation of the Rev. Cyprian Thornton (1878–1939), vicar of Greasley 1907–12, and recreated as 'Mr Colbran' in 'A Fragment of Stained Glass': see *The Prussian Officer*, ed. Worthen, note on 88:13.

96:12 **"Nowt as I know on,"** 'Nothing I know about'.

96:21 **'wanting'.** 'Weak-minded'.

96:24 **a Pole, named Paula Jablonowsky:** The Polish origin (and name) suggest a parallel with Lydia Lensky, in the first part of *The Rainbow* (finished initially in May 1914), who also goes to work for an English clergyman in the Midlands (chaps. I and II). 'Paula'—here pronounced in the German way, 'Powla'

(109:12)—was the name Frieda Lawrence adopted for herself in many of her written memoirs (see *The Memoirs and Correspondence*, ed. E. W. Tedlock, 1961, pp. 3–123).

98:3 **loose 'a,"** Loose-all; the afternoon colliery shift would end with a whistle or hooter blown at 4.00 p.m.

98:10 **horses ... pick** DHL first wrote ''osses', then altered it to 'horses' (MS, p. [20]); TCC's 'hosses' (p. 20) arose from a misreading of the alteration ... pitch or throw; a 'picking-fork' is a hay fork.

98:15 **the float** A low-bodied crank-axled cart. Edmund Chambers ran a milk-round with a 'milk-float' (E.T. 27), and it may have also been employed in the Greasley hay-harvest.

99:6 **the *Nation*,** For DHL in 1911, 'a sixpenny weekly, of very good standing' (*Letters*, i. 324); it printed his poems in November 1911 and 'The Miner at Home'.

100:10 **a winder!"** Something that takes one's breath away; a blow that 'knocks the wind' out of one.

101:31 **bacca** 'Tobacco'.

102:5 **a mean crawl** Not recorded in this sense elsewhere; *OED* defines 'crawler' as 'one who acts in a mean or servile way', and this variant undoubtedly means the same.

103:1 **A good grind,** 'A good fuck'; the earliest recorded example in *A Supplement to the OED*, ed. Burchfield, vol. I (Oxford 1972).

103:16 **horse-raking.** The raking of the cut hay into the winrows (see note on 87:14). DHL describes working at the horse-rake in his letter of 30 July 1908 (*Letters*, i. 67).

104:20 **a large lime tree teemed with scent** Cf. DHL's letter of 30 July 1908 about the Greasley hay-harvest: 'big lime trees, murmuring, and full of the scent of nectar' (*Letters*, i. 67).

106:13 **"Coop lass!"** 'Come up lass!'

108:11 **sheered** 'Swerved': cf. 'sheering down' at 108:15.

108:25 **fast** Unable to escape; natural for a German speaker, as the German 'fest' has an identical meaning.

109:8 **should we sit** DHL first wrote 'come here 'an we'll sit', then deleted the first three words and inserted 'should we' (MS, p. [38]). TCC (p. 38) inserted a dash between 'we' and 'we'll'; this edition has assumed that DHL meant to delete 'we'll' but failed to do so.

111:1 **snipe** Either a contemptuous term for someone, suggesting insignificance; or a cheat, a fraud.

111:31 **he asked.** In MS, the following sentence is roughly deleted in pencil: 'He was perfectly honorable, and sorry for her.' (p. [42]). Most of the pencil adjustments in MS do not appear to be authorial; this, however, resembles the pencil deletions DHL made in the MS Roberts E438b ('The White Woman') in July 1913, and has therefore been accepted.

112:10 **'Gormin''** Staring vacantly, gaping; thus, stupid and awkward.

112:26 **glossy.** 'Glossy skin' was taken as a sign of 'morbid symptoms' (*OED*) or illness.

114:31 **It was eerie. Silence again.** In MS, after 'eerie.', DHL first wrote 'The' (probably the start of 'There was silence', or its equivalent): deleted it, and wrote 'Silence again': deleted that and wrote 'Silence fell again': then deleted 'fell' (p. [47]). TCC (p. 48) took the 'S' of 'Silence' as lower case, and produced 'It was eerie silence again.'

115:2 **clinched** 'Interlocked, fastened'.

115:12 **his own road."** 'His own way'.

115:32 **blue-green blotches of light** In a sentence deleted in MS (p. [49]), Geoffrey rubs his hands with the match head so that they glow, and Lydia can see them; the matches are probably of the old style phospherous type, prohibited in Britain after 1908.

116:26 **'câline'.** Soft, sweet, caressable (French).

117:1 **bruise the lips of the scornful . . . unabateable.** Not a quotation, but cf. Psalms i. 1 ('the seat of the scornful') and references to bruising at Genesis iii. 15 . . . DHL's coinage (cf. 'unabated' and 'unabatingly'): that which cannot be abated, cannot be brought down.

117:13 **"Lydia,"** The name DHL gave to the Polish woman in the first part of *The Rainbow* (see note on 96:24); also his own mother's name.

117:32 **to Canada** There is a deep fascination with North America in DHL's fiction, first experienced by the Saxton family in *The White Peacock* (part II, chap. IV), felt in 'Daughters of the Vicar', 'The Thorn in the Flesh', 'The Fox', 'You Touched Me' and *The Lost Girl* (chap. XVI). At least four members of the Chambers family emigrated there, as well as DHL's cousin Alvina; Helen Corke's landlord and landlady also emigrated (see *Letters*, i. 553); and while the Lawrences were in Italy in 1914, DHL found that 'Here almost every man has spent his time in America' (*Letters*, ii. 148).

119:25 **make me stay here** Replacing 'you want to have me all night', deleted in MS (p. [55]).

120:25 **a bit sin."** Just now: 'a bit since'.

121:20 **Bits of hay . . . to advantage.** Reminiscent of the appearance of Anita (a recreation of Frieda) in 'A Hay-Hut Among the Mountains', written August–September 1912: '"Do I look horrid?" she asked. She was huddled in her coat: her tousled hair was full of hay'.

121:28 **take the stack-cloth up."** Lift it up and carry it down to the ground.

## The Miner at Home

123:2 **Bower** 'John Bower' is a butty at 'Bretty' [Brinsley] pit in *Sons and Lovers*, chap. IV, and DHL also used the name in 'Odour of Chrysanthemums'; see *The Prussian Officer*, ed. Worthen, note on 190:9.

123:18 **panchion,** More often 'pancheon' or 'panshen'.

123:28 **"Gi'e ower,"** 'Give over', i.e. stop it.

124:10 **the strap,** The belt.

124:28 **screets . . . iver.** 'Cries . . . ever'.

125:8 **February 14, 1912.** The Miners' Federation had threatened national strike action from early February 1912; on 2 February it proposed a new schedule of wages, and 'strike tickets' (126:20) went out for signatures 12–14 February. The strike began 26 February 1912, at Alfreton in Derbyshire; the Eastwood pits closed on 28 February. The strike ended in most places 9–11 April 1912.

125:22 **arena you?"** 'Aren't you?'

125:30 **th' last two strikes** The Eastwood collieries of Barber Walker & Co. were closed January–March 1908 and June–November 1910; see note on 128:18.

125:35 **Yorkshire an' Welsh colliers . . . that bug** The Yorkshire and Welsh miners had voted for the National Strike of 1912 with majorities of 6–1 and 5–1 respectively . . . 'that conceited, vain'.

126:7 **th' Minimum Wage? Butties** The Miners' Federation of Great Britain had decided in 1911 on the principle of the individual minimum wage as an immediate demand. In Nottinghamshire the minimum day wage demand for coal-getters (piece workers at the face) was 7s. 6d. . . . Cf. a deleted passage in the manuscript of *Sons and Lovers*: 'A butty is a contractor. Two or three butties are given a certain length along a seam of coal, which they are to mine forward to a certain distance. They were paid something like 3/4 [i.e. 3s. 4d.] for every ton of coal they turned out. Out of this, they had to pay the men, holers and loaders, whom they hired by the day, and also for tools, powder, and so on' (*Sons and Lovers: A Facsimile of the Manuscript*, ed. Mark Schorer, Berkeley, 1977, p. 26).

126:13 **'am-pat.** Dialect expression not recorded elsewhere. 'Pat' means 'perfectly', 'fluently', 'appropriately', and so the expression may be ironical. Alternatively, as 'ham-sam' means 'confused, in confusion' in North Country dialect, ''am-pat' may mean 'fluently, but muddled up'.

126:25 **chunterin' . . . scroddy** 'Muttering, grumbling, complaining . . . rotten'.

126:36 **to addle,** 'To earn'.

126:39 **day man . . . ostler . . . mester?** One who works and is paid by the day . . . one in charge of pit ponies . . . master.

127:2 **hang my rags,** Damn it; cf. 'Dash my rags', *The Lost Girl*, ed. John Worthen (Cambridge, 1981), 205:3. There is perhaps some connection with the slang phrases 'smash a rag' (lose one's—paper—money) and 'flash one's rags' (display one's money): see *Slang and Its Analogues*, ed. Farmer.

127:7 **sided wi'** 'Agreed with'.

127:17 **flig** 'Pleased'.

## Her Turn

128:14 **Radford** Very common local name, used in the March–October 1911 draft of 'Paul Morel' for the characters named Clara and Baxter Dawes in *Sons and Lovers*.

128:18 **Eighteen months ... eleven weeks ... eleven shillings strike-pay** The Eastwood collieries of the real-life Barber Walker & Co. were closed twenty-two weeks, 13 June–25 November 1910; cf. DHL's reference to a 'fifteen weeks' closure in 'A Sick Collier', *The Prussian Officer*, ed. Worthen, 167:16 ... Full members of the Union were entitled to ten shillings (half a sovereign) a week strike-pay, with one shilling extra for each child (see 'Strike-Pay' 135:4). TCC reads 'ten' (p. 1): DHL must have made the alteration in proof for Per.

128:19 **the second strike** See note on 125:8.

128:22 **the publican's wife at the "Golden Horn."** Cf. the publican's wife Mrs Houseley in *Aaron's Rod*, chap. IX; both appear to be recreations of Ellen Wharton in the 'Thorn Tree' public house, Nether Green (see Appendix IV).

129:8 **weigh,** The reading of TCC (p. 2); 'way' in Per is judged to be a normalisation either by Douglas Clayton in his 1913 TS, or by the editor of Per.

129:38 **have no ... his ailment.** The reading of Per; TCC reads 'never see when he wasn't well,' (p. 4).

130:12 **sleering** Covertly sneering; talking with sly offensiveness. Cf. *The White Peacock*, ed. Robertson, note on 22:32.

130:21 **rib ... ha'e a smite** The reading of TCC (p. 5); Per's 'rise' has been judged a normalisation provided either by Douglas Clayton in his 1913 TS, or by the editor of Per ... 'Have a bit'.

130:29 **tan-tafflins** Nottinghamshire form of 'tantadlin': a small tart, a light delicacy.

130:36 **paid th' Union** Paid the strike-pay for members of the Nottinghamshire Miners' Association.

131:13 **Mr. Allcock,** William Allcock, in 1912 Boot Manufacturer and House Furnisher at 39, Nottingham Road, Eastwood.

131:17 **"strap."** 'Goods on credit'.

131:29 **wakkened up betimes,"** 'Woken early'.

132:18 **a corker!"** Something stunning.

132:33 **a winder!"** See note on 100:10.

133:13 **a shilling.** Contrast Mr Morel in *Sons and Lovers*, who 'from eighteen [shillings wage] ... kept a shilling; from sixteen he kept sixpence' (chap. I). Mrs Radford is generous in giving her husband one eleventh of their joint income.

## Strike Pay

134:10 **Forty years ago ... opened their pits,** The 'Squares' (see Appendix IV) were built *c.*1866, at the height of the expansion and development of the Eastwood collieries; between 1852 and 1872, Underwood, High Park, Willey Lane, Moorgreen and Watnall New collieries were all remodelled or reopened.

134:17 **ponches,** Local spelling and pronunciation of 'poaches' (confirmed by deletion in MS, p. 1, where 'pestle' replaces 'ponche'), wooden instruments resembling 'dollies' used in washing; in South Nottinghamshire, shaped like a cross, with a long handle. Cf. Explanatory note on 206:4.

134:31 **Sorry … shovin' up."** 'The word is a form of address, corruption probably of "Sirrah"' ('A Sick Collier', *The Prussian Officer*, ed. Worthen, 169:8) … pushing forward.

135:18 **'Diddle-diddle … suit on'"** See the *Oxford Dictionary of Nursery Rhymes*, ed. J. and P. Opie (1951), No. 275 ['… with his trousers on …'].

135:22 **Sam Coutts!"** See note on 54:2.

135:28 **tha's addled it,** You've earned it.

136:2 **"Does your collar** [135:15] **… pay on delivery—."** An earlier draft of this passage is deleted in MS (perhaps as self-censorship: see too notes on 136:14 and 141:38):

"Eight children!" shouted the crowd.

"Howiver did yer do it!" exclaimed Ben, handing over the cash. "Haight children under thirteen!—Sam Coutts!"

"Wife's got a white leg!" roared the crowd.

Sam came up for his money, amid coarse jokes.

"Fred Sagar."

"Two children!" shouted the men in ecstasy. "Twins ter him, mester."

Fred came up cursing.

"Yi," said Ben suavely. "But not in wedlock, not in wedlock I'm sorry to say."

"Keep thy sorrer to thy sen," said Fred.

"It's *thy* sorrow, my friend, tha canna lay it onto me," said the pay master smoothly.

"Thy button, thy button, look if thy button's undone!" jeered the crowd.

Sagar glanced downwards, then pushed his way out, cursing. (p. 3)

136:6 **the half-sovereigns clicked.** See note on 128:18.

136:9 **a gleamy day** Rain-clouds and sunshine blended are called 'gleamy' weather.

136:14 **"He hasna** [136:10] **… some time.** An earlier draft of this passage is deleted in MS:

"He's tired," said somebody, and a laugh went up.

"What's 'e tired wi'?" asked another pertinent voice.

"Stoppin' i' bed," said Chris Smitheringale …

"'E wor up as soon as any on yer," protested the young man.

"I'll bet 'e wor—an' stopped up longest," said Chris.

There was a roar of laughter.

"Bed's the ruin of a young married feller," said Chris. "Keep out on it, Ephraim. Dunn ta'e thy boots off, that's the idea." (p. 4)

136:19 **the match between Notts and Aston Villa.** See note on 139:21.

136:40 **clipt up** Climbed up; to clip up a tree is to climb it by clasping it with the arms and knees.

137:4 **the Colonel. Luthee** A recreation of Lancelot Rolleston (1847–1941) of Watnall Hall, in 1912 Hon. Lieut. Colonel (from 1914, Hon. Colonel) of the South Notts. Hussars ... 'Look thee'; Per's reading 'Lu' thee' is probably an unauthorised clarification; TCC reverted to the safer 'Sithee' (p. 6).

137:7 **heered,** The reading of Per (p. 2). Six substantive variants from Per have been accepted, as almost certainly the result of DHL's revision of the (missing) typescript which Douglas Clayton made from MS in July 1913 (see Introduction), or of DHL's proof correction of Per: see Textual apparatus at 137:7(1), 137:9(2), 137:21, 137:31, 137:38 and 138:9. Substantive variants in Per (not including cuts or adjustments resulting from cuts) which have not been accepted appear in the Textual apparatus at 136:10(2), 136:15, 138:39, and 139:1: all four are characteristic of the 'improvements' to DHL's text which Clayton sometimes made. For occasions where Per's emendation of the text (whether or not authorial) has been judged necessary and also accepted, see Textual apparatus at 134:34(1), 135:37(1), 137:7(2), 138:20 and 138:30.

137:9 **they'n com'n out i' Germany ... i' France simbilar,"** The British strike leaders did not ask for sympathetic strikes from the Continental Unions, only for production to be curtailed. The Unions on the International Miners' Federation agreed to try to prevent coal exports to Britain from Germany, France, Belgium and Austria.

137:12 **a twenty perzent rise."** Food prices 1896–1910 had risen 25% in Britain.

137:19 **gaffer."** The one in charge: employer, head of household, foreman, etc.

137:23 **rassivoy** Local pronunciation of 'reservoir' (see Appendix IV for the reservoir in question).

137:33 **no trains were running ... a troop of pit ponies.** Many passenger services were cancelled by the Great Northern and the Great Central Railway companies during the 1912 coal strike ... See the report in the *Nottinghamshire Guardian* of Saturday 16 March 1912: 'Messrs Barber, Walker & Co. have brought the ponies out of all five pits, but they have made no other changes...' (p. 13).

137:37 **skewbawd** Skewbald; normally brown and white.

138:6 **Taffy** Common name for pit ponies; one 'Taff' was working in Brinsley pit in Eastwood in 1907, and another was killed there in an accident on 30 December 1914 (R. W. Storer, *Some Aspects of Brinsley Colliery*, Selston 1985, pp. 89, 91). Mr Morel in *Sons and Lovers* refers to 'one little 'oss—we call 'im Taffy' (chap. IV).

138:26 **I'n foraged** 'I've searched'.

139:13 **Ephraim the Unhappy** Cf. Ethelred the Unready, King of England 978–1016.

139:21 **It was [139·17] ... two goals through.** In the match between Notts. County and Aston Villa at the Meadow Lane ground on Wednesday 13 March 1912, William Arthur ('Billy') Flint (1890–1955), born in Underwood and playing for Notts as an inside-forward 1909–26, scored one of the two goals (the other being scored by Billy Matthews (1883–1916), born in Derby).

139:29 **an accident near the football ground.** Cf. the report in the *Nottinghamshire Guardian*, Saturday 16 March:

> SUFFOCATED IN SLUDGE
> Remarkable Fatality in Nottingham
>
> Just as the crowd of football enthusiasts was assembling at the Meadow Lane Ground for the Notts. and Aston Villa match on Wednesday afternoon a remarkable fatality occurred.
>
> Abutting on to the sixpenny side is some waste land on which there is a depression, and for some time past the Health Department have been levelling up by means of clinkers from the Eastcroft destructor.
>
> On Wednesday afternoon a carter, named Chas. Shaw, was engaged in the work, when the horse attached to his cart bolted. It is supposed that the animation and unaccustomed sounds of people proceeding to the match caused the animal to take fright. To the horror of the many witnesses, the man was dragged for some distance towards a big pool of sludge, emptied by the men of the Works and Ways Department, between the Cattle Market entrance and the entrance to the football field.
>
> The horse continued its mad career till it plunged into the filth, carrying man and cart with it.
>
> With all speed the man was extricated, but efforts to resuscitate him were unavailing, death having taken place from suffocation.
>
> The body was removed to the Leen-side Mortuary, to await an inquest.
>
> Shaw, who lived in Shaftesbury-street, and was a widower, was between 60 and 70 years of age. He was an old servant of the Corporation, and bore the character of an industrious workman. (p. 9)

The discrepancies between the newspaper account and the story suggest that DHL had heard a first-hand, but not entirely accurate, account.

139:40 **dark.** The addition (see Textual apparatus) in Per (p. 2) is not a proof revision by DHL, but the re-introduction—presumably by the magazine editor—of a phrase cut from the previous paragraph (see Textual apparatus for 139:37).

140:36 **for us board,** For our food.

141:17 **off on the nines to** Otherwise unrecorded; phrases such as 'dressed up to the nines' or 'one over the eight' throw no light on it. It is, however, a manuscript substitution for 'and have your fling in' (MS p. 13), and probably means the same.

141:22 **jockey,** Half-affectionate, half-contemptuous term for someone not quite as they should be.

141:24 **Ripping** 'Swearing'.

141:38 **bloody** Cut by Per in 1913; three lines later DHL first wrote 'sòddin' but himself altered it to 'blasted' (MS, p. 14).

142:1 **còssed,** 'Cursed'.

142:5 **a trollops."** A dirty, idle, slovenly woman.

142:11 **not her mother's.** Replacing the original ending in MS: 'and a man she must have. He might leave her if she gave him no tea.' (p. 15).

## Delilah and Mr. Bircumshaw

143:1 **Delilah and Mr. Bircumshaw** Delilah: the woman loved by Samson (Judges xvi. 4–20). He told her that 'if I be shaven, then my strength will go from me': she betrayed him to the Philistines. Bircumshaw was a common name in Eastwood.

143:15 **quick** The reading of Per (p. 257). TS's 'quiet' (p. 1) appears to be a typist's misreading of DHL's writing.

144:18 **Abraham!** Setting out to sacrifice (144:23): Genesis xxii. 3.

144:34 **the Great Bear,** I.e. bad temper; cf. the star constellation Ursa Major.

144:37 **Bircumshaw** At this point TS (p. 2) began a new unindented line, although there was room for 'Bircumshaw' at the end of the previous line. It is probable that TS simply followed the frequently confusing paragraphing of DHL's early manuscripts; the reading of Per, which inserted a paragraph (p. 259), has been adopted.

145:20 **seeking whom he shall devour,** 1 Peter v. 8: 'your adversary the devil, as a roaring lion, walketh about, seeking whom he may devour'.

145:25 **Sir Galahad** In Arthurian legend, the most virtuous knight of the Round Table, destined to recover the Holy Grail. TS's spelling 'Gallahad' (p. 4) may be a typist's error (though made twice): it is also a common German spelling of the name.

146:4 **thick** Per's reading 'strict' (p. 260) is probably a typist's or type-setter's misreading of 'thick'; it is unlikely to be DHL's meaning.

146:11 **attentive** Probably DHL's revision of 'listening' (Per, p. 260), but possibly an unauthorised alteration of the oxymoron 'listening eyes'.

148:9 **There's the ... sleep there."** The similarity between the reading of Per (see Textual apparatus) and the early MS Roberts E90.5a (see Appendix II, 193:34–194:3) is one of the few pieces of evidence that Per may predate TS (see Introduction).

149:25 **due. Her mind ... from the depth** Per reads: 'dues. Though her heart was pained and anxious, still she smiled: she had clipped a large lock from her Samson. Her smile rose from the deep' (p. 264).

149:38 **virtue depart from him,** Cf. Mark v. 30: 'knowing in himself that virtue had gone out of him'.

150:6 **small brow.** Per reads: 'small brow, that reminded one of the brow of a little Virgin by Memling.' (p. 265). Hans Memling (*c.*1430–94), painter from the Netherlands, produced many paintings of the Virgin; DHL may have known the Donne Altarpiece, with Virgin and Child, in the National Gallery in London.

150:8 **wrath.** E1 (p. 90) emended to 'wroth', but 'wrath', though 'somewhat rare' (*OED*) as an adjective, was used both by Thackeray (1860) and Bulwer Lytton (1862).

## Once—!

152:4 **the valley.** The landscape described here is that of the Isartal near Icking, s. of München, where DHL and Frieda lived June–August 1912. Later in the story the setting is 'here ... in the Tyrol' (153:15), which for DHL was 'beyond Innsbrück' (*Letters*, i. 431); he and Frieda lived in Mayrhofen in the Austrian Tyrol 10–26 August. See next note, and footnote 54 to the Introduction.

152:13 **Anita.** In 'Once—!', 'A Chapel Among the Mountains' and 'A Hay-Hut Among the Mountains' (the latter two both probably drafted at Mayrhofen in August 1912), DHL uses the name Anita for a character with many of the characteristics of Freida Weekley; here, however, the details of her marriage and children are taken directly from those of Frieda's sister Johanna von Richthofen (1882–1971), who married Max G. V. von Schreibershofen (1864–1944), an officer stationed in the von Richthofens' home town of Metz, in August 1900. In 1903 he was transferred to the General Staff Headquarters in Berlin (see 153:3). Johanna's first child, Anita, was born in 1901; her son Hadubrand four years later. Her husband left the army in 1908 after what appears to have been a scandal (cf. 152:32). DHL described her in May 1912 as 'very beautiful, married to a brute [cf. 152:29] of a swanky officer in Berlin – and, in a large, splendid way – cocotte [cf. 156:33]' (*Letters*, i. 395).

152:18 **in the Kaiser's fashion,** The fashion of Kaiser Wilhelm II (1859–1941), King of Prussia 1888–1918.

153:5 **her own relatives in Berlin,** Johanna and Frieda's Berlin relatives included Oswald von Richthofen (1847–1906), Secretary of State under Chancellor Bernhard von Bülow (1902–06), and their aunts Anna von Elbe and Elisabeth von Plessen: see *Frieda Lawrence: The Memoirs and Correspondence*, ed. Tedlock, pp. 65–8.

153:15 **Ehrfurcht** Deep, even solemn, respect (German).

153:35 **an enormous hat ... swaying lightly.** Frieda wrote to Edward Garnett on 7 September 1912: 'My sister [Johanna], who is elegant has just sent me 4 baldachino hats – L. is trying them on in an undescribable get-up and the most beautiful Asphodel pose! [Lawrence interjects: – by "get-up", she means "sans anything". She always was a brazen bitch.]' (*Letters*, i. 449).

154:4 **and through ... breasts and arms.** This part of the sentence appears between square brackets pencilled into MS by 'an editor', according to DHL. Clayton queried whether he should type such sentences in July 1913 (see Introduction), and inserted ink brackets around them when he made the surviving typed carbon copy E296b in 1930. Similar 'editorial' brackets occur around 'and the gold shadow stirred' (154:4–5), 'The round cap ... the arm-pit' (155:39–40), 'The shadows ... the linen veil' (156:11–12) and '"All that night ... same time, tender—!"' (158:28–31).

155:3 **"It's that old Apple I can't digest,"** I.e. shame at nakedness, resulting from the Fall (Genesis iii. 6–7).

155:26 **"'On est mort pour si longtemps',"** 'One is dead for such a long time' (French). A recollection either of 'Le délire bachique' by Marc-Antoine Désaugiers (1772–1827): 'Quand on est mort, c'est pour longtemps, / Dit un adage / Fort sage' (*Chansons et Poésies diverses*, 1808–16), or of the probable source of his 'adage': Mascarille, in *Dépit amoureux* (1656), v. iii. 1576, by Molière (1622–73), remarks 'On ne meurt qu'une fois, et c'est pour si longtemps!' ('One only dies once, and it is for such a long time!').

156:25 **"Gretchen ... Marguerite with one petal',"** Diminutive form of Margarete, the innocent, virtuous, devotedly loving and seduced heroine of Goethe's *Faust* (1808: 1832); she bears Faust's child. For Frieda's comments on Gretchen, see *The Memoirs and Correspondence*, ed. Tedlock, pp. 52–3 ... 'Marguerite' is the French form of 'Margarete', who decides whether Faust loves her by picking off the petals of a flower. She finds one petal left: he loves her. The reference is probably to the version of the scene in Act II of the opera *Faust* (1859) by Charles Gounod (1818–93).

156:31 **Dresden** City, now in the German Democratic Republic, where Max von Schreibershofen was born.

157:9 **O jeh!,** DHL's spelling of the more common German 'oje', the short form of 'ojemine' (abbreviation of 'O Jesus Domine'). The interjection normally suggests sympathy—'oh dear' would be the English equivalent; but here it clearly suggests surprise—'my word!'

157:14 **revers** I.e. part of a coat of which the edge is turned back to exhibit the under surface. DHL erroneously wrote 'reveres' in MS (p. 8), and has been followed by all subsequent texts.

157:17 **"'Verzeihung, gnädiges Fräulein!'** 'I beg your pardon, young lady!' (German): 'gnädiges Fräulein' is the form of address to an unmarried woman of superior social class.

157:23 **the Brühler Terrasse ... the broad Elbe** The Brühlsche Terrasse (spelled 'Terasse' by DHL in MS, pp. 8, 10) in Dresden was built by Heinrich, Graf Brühl (1700–63), Chief Minister to Friedrich Augustus II, King of Saxony 1733–63; it was the garden to his palace beside the river Elbe (130 metres wide at Dresden).

158:18 **saut-de-lit,** A loose dressing-gown (French).

159:17 **you're an Answer.'** Cf. DHL's poem 'Bei Hennef' (first drafted May 1912), l. 14: 'You are the call and I am the answer' (*Complete Poems*, ed. Pinto and Roberts, i. 203).

159:38 **uncertainty**. The probable reading of MS (p. 12); neither 't' is crossed. Clayton first typed 'uncertainly', but in TCC he deleted the 'l' and inserted a 't' (p. 13). He probably did not make this alteration to the ribbon copy: E1 printed 'uncertainly' (p. 95) from a typescript he supplied. Secker's 1933 reprint (p. 146) restored 'uncertainty', but the alteration was probably made without reference to MS or TCC.

160:27 **She awaited awhile ... heart stood still.** These lines must have appeared on the final page of the ribbon copy typescript used as setting-copy for E1, but TCC lacks the page [15] on which they would have appeared. Clayton's name, address and telephone number, however, are typed on the verso of page 14; he normally inserted these on the verso of the last page, or on a new and separate page, so he must either have failed to make a carbon of page [15] or not have added it to TCC.

## New Eve and Old Adam

161:1 **New Eve and Old Adam** DHL's first title was 'Eve and the Old Adam'; this was revised to 'Renegade Eve and the Old Adam', then to 'The New Eve and the Old Adam', finally to the present title on MS (p. 1). By 1910 (when he gave a copy of the English translation to Alan Chambers), DHL knew the novel *Der alte Adam und die neue Eva* (1895), tr. as *The Old Adam and the New Eve* (1898), by Rudolf Golm (pseud. of Rudolf Goldscheid, 1870–1931), which concentrates on the dilemma of 'the new Eve, who finds it hard to bear the fetters of her dependence on man, but is lost when she attempts to shake them off' (p. xviii). Both 'old Adam' and 'new Eve' were favourite images for DHL; see note on 71:1, and *Letters*, ii. 662.

161:4 **cross** Inserted in Frieda's hand, replacing DHL's 'tame' (MS, p. 1). As we have no record of the stage at which the alteration was made, or under what conditions, it has been accepted.

161:11 **Parisian Nights' Entertainments!** Cf. *The Arabian Nights' Entertainment*, a collection of oriental folk tales dating from the tenth century.

161:16 **married a year.** DHL and Frieda eloped on 3 May 1912; although they were not married until 13 July 1914, DHL remarked in late May 1913 (the date this story was written) 'I have been married for this last year' (*Letters*, i. 553).

161:25 **puzzled** Inserted in Frieda's hand in MS, replacing DHL's 'inhuman' (p. 1); see note on 161:4. After 'just now.' (161:25), a sentence in MS is deleted: 'There was a faint smile of cruelty about her.' (p. 1). The sentence may have been deleted by Frieda, but has not been restored here; it helps explain 'her eyes retained the curious half-smile' at 161:32.

161:32 **fillet ... Gretchen about her.** Head-band ... see note on 156:25.

162:6 **spinning it as if she would spurn it.** Cf. Clara Dawes in *Sons and Lovers* (chap. x) spinning her wedding ring on a table.

164:14 **Pietro,** DHL's nickname 'Lorenzo' apparently dates from before April 1913: 'L. stands for Lorenzo. Mrs. Anthony's kid calls me Lorenzo ...' (*Letters*, i. 538). Signore Pietro di Paoli was the Lawrences' 'Padrone' in Gargnano, 1912–13 (*Letters*, i. 458). 'Giovanni' is deleted in MS (p. 2).

164:31 **Marble Arch** Monument and latterly underground railway station, at the w. end of London's Oxford Street.

165:7 **Moest,"** From here to the end of MS, the name appears uncorrected as 'Cyriack', but a note in DHL's hand on MS p. 1 reads: 'note: for "Cyriack" write "Moest"'. The name 'Cyriack' (for the couple, 'Cyriacks') probably derives from

Antonia Almgren, née Cyriax (1881–1927), who came to Gargnano to stay with the Lawrences *c.* 1 March 1913; see *Letters*, i. 520 and n. 2, 521–3, and note on 164:14 above.

165:14 **the poor man** DHL's revision in MS of 'Thomas Thomas' (p. 3).

167:11 **veins.** Typed as 'mind' in TCC (p. 11); perhaps an attempt to improve the text. Cf. 'stick' typed for 'stand' at 166:40.

168:20 **his brother-in-law's,** Named as 'Edmund' below; perhaps a recreation of DHL's brother-in-law to be, Edgar Jaffe, married to Frieda's sister Else (1874–1973), and recreated as 'Alfred' in *Mr Noon*, ed. Lindeth Vasey (Cambridge, 1984); see chap. XIII and note on 100:10.

169:15 **"Lovable and ... and bitter.** Omitted in TCC (p. 14); the typist's eye skipped a line of MS (p. 6). Also omitted in TCC (pp. 19, 24) where lines of MS (pp. 8, 10) were skipped: 'and unperceived ... darkness almost' (172:9–11): 'he grasped ... thinking hard—' (175:30–1).

169:20 **repellant** DHL uses a normal nineteenth-century spelling; TCC at first typed it, then altered it to 'repellent' (p. 14).

169:40 **Madge, her friend.** Cf. Madge Bradley, a close Nottingham friend of Frieda and Ernest Weekley (*Letters*, i. 388 n.2).

170:16 **like an instrument for his work,** Cf. Frieda to Edward Garnett, 17 May 1913: DHL 'goes on working and it's simply ghastly, he becomes a writing machine, that works itself out...' (*Letters*, i. 549).

170:23 **satisfied, or had been satisfied** TCC (p. 16) omitted the comma and the last four words (an interlinear insertion in MS, p. 7); they were probably overlooked rather than bowdlerised.

171:12 **the writing sachet** Perhaps from the French 'un sachet de papier'—a packet of paper.

173:1 **forwards darkly in a chaos,** DHL first wrote 'forwards, in a chaos'; he then deleted the comma and inserted 'darkly' after 'in' to create the obscure 'forwards in darkly a chaos' (p. 8). TCC read 'forwards darkly, in a chaos' (p. 20); its repositioning of 'darkly' (though not its restoration of the comma) has here been adopted.

173:8 **twenty lire for a sovereign ... the Strand** In 1912–13, the exchange rate was 24–6 lire to a pound sterling ... Street in London running between Charing Cross and Fleet Street.

175:2 **on the second flat."** The German uses 'flat' in its original (and old-fashioned) sense of 'storey' or 'floor'; E1 adjusted to 'floor'.

175:22 **Hampstead."** Fashionable and mostly middle and upper class suburb of n. London; DHL's relations Ethel and Max Hunger lived there (*Letters*, i. 183–4), and DHL had met Ernest Rhys and H. G. Wells there in 1909 (*Letters*, i. 144).

176:7 **the most famous ... poet and 'Meister'.** DHL listed what were to him the most famous present-day German poets in a letter to Else Jaffe, 10 February 1913 (*Letters*, i. 513). Included is Stefan George (1868–1933), the most appropriate choice as 'Meister' (Master) here; he was an acquaintance of the Webers in Heidelberg, and known to Else Jaffe (see Martin Green, *The von Richthofen Sisters*, New York, 1974, p. 189).

177:14 **Panacea, not Paula,"** For 'Paula', see note on 96:24; and cf. DHL to Edward Garnett, 21 May 1912: 'Frieda – "The Peaceful"' (*Letters*, i. 409). The joke about 'Panacea' is repeated in *Mr Noon*, ed. Vasey, 165:4 and n.

178:28 **the Aquila Nera at Milan** The Black Eagle; no hotel of that name appears to have existed in Milan, but DHL and Frieda stayed at the Hôtel Europa E Aquila Nera in Verona *c.*11–14 April 1913 (*Letters*, i. 539–40).

180:4 **'The Black Sheep'."** At least four plays of that title are known: a comedy by Joseph Stirling Coyne (1803–68), produced in 1861; a drama (1868) written jointly by E. D. Yates (1831–94) and John Palgrave Simpson (1807–87); a 'panto pastoral' by Mark André Raffalovitch (*fl.* 1884–96), produced in 1894; and a sketch performed at the Brixton Empress in 1909. However, it seems likely that DHL had none of these in mind, but was instead joking with the title of the play *The Blue Bird* by Maurice Maeterlinck (1862–1949), produced in London for the first time at the Haymarket theatre in 1909.

181:17 **he felt** DHL failed to delete part of his original reading when he made an interlinear revision in MS (p. 13); TCC's decision to omit 'he would' (below 'he felt') is clearly correct (p. 34).

181:33 **"On my breasts ... perfumed sheets—"** George Meredith, 'A Preaching from a Spanish Ballad', ll. 33–6 ['At my ... cool thy footsoles; ... I dress ... lord it pleases, ...']. Cf. *Women in Love*: 'She made great professions, to herself, of her willingness to warm his foot-soles between her breasts, after the fashion of the nauseous Meredith poem' (ed. Farmer, Vasey and Worthen, 264:35–8).

182:14 **like an Apollo's.** Cf. the wavy hair (with stylised bunch on top) of the Apollo Belvedere in the Vatican Museum, Rome.

182:26 **"Flesh of my flesh ... Will you——?"** Genesis ii. 23 ... Originally in MS 'Will you be it?' (p. 14).

183:2 **innerest** Obsolete (since 1483) in *OED*; E1 printed 'innermost' (p. 165).

183:22 **else—except generally."** In MS DHL first wrote 'else—"', then added the last two words (p. 14); TCC misread the last as 'yourself' (p. 38).

## 'Two Schools' fragment

187:6 **a National and a British ... Gaffer Sturgess** In DHL's recreation of nineteenth-century Eastwood (see Appendix IV), he ignores the local school he himself attended (the Board School at Beauvale) and refers to the 'National School' in Church Walk (founded 1863 by the Anglican National Society for the Education of the Poor in the Principles of the Established Church) and the 'British School' (founded 1874 by the Non Conformist Voluntary Society, in Albert Street from 1876). In 1899 an Undenominational School was opened in New Eastwood. DHL taught at the British School between October 1902 and September 1906 ...

'Gaffer': dialect for 'Master'. John Sheldon was Master of the National School from 1866 to December 1905.

187:19 **the aristocracy of the mining village,** Cf. DHL's ironical analysis of the social system of 'Woodhouse' in *The Lost Girl*, ed. Worthen, p. 1.

187:22 **Mr Culverwell,** George Holderness (b. 1857) was Master of the British School from June 1881 to July 1909. DHL used the name 'Culverwell' again in the fragment Roberts E209b (printed, as 'Elsa Culverwell', as an Appendix to *The Lost Girl*, ed. Worthen, pp. 343–58). See Appendix IV for a suggestion of the name's origin.

## 'Delilah and Mr Bircumshaw' fragment

193:16 **Mr Cullen** A name taken from the Cullen family of Eastwood, friends of DHL's family (see *Letters*, i. 234 n. 1), and used as models for the central characters in *The Lost Girl*, ed. Worthen, p. xxi; see too *The White Peacock*, ed. Robertson, 340:12. DHL changed the name to 'Gillatt' in the final version.

194:34 **Lieutenant Shackleton ... South Pole,** Sir Ernest Henry Shackleton (1874–1922) led an expedition to Antarctica 1907–9, during which the south magnetic pole was located.

## 'Burns Novel' fragments

201:8 **chavelled** Torn or chewed-up (in Derbyshire, 'to chavel' is to tear with the teeth); cf. *The White Peacock*, ed. Robertson, note on 306:8.

201:18 **ravel-leaved** With leaves entangled.

202:32 **tha chump!"** You fool; 'gormey' (deleted in MS p. 3) is 'a foolish, staring person'.

203:4 **bad luck ... afore Christmas,"** Not gathering, but taking holly into the house before Christmas Eve was widely believed unlucky.

203:17 **th' gin-pit,"** A shallow pit-shaft worked by a crane with a winch. Cf. *Sons and Lovers*: 'these small mines, whose coal was drawn to the surface by donkeys that plodded wearily in a circle, round a gin' (chap. 1).

203:19 **"Renshaw."** Renshaw was a common name in the Moorgreen district, and was also the name of some of DHL's relations (*Letters*, i. 199); it is DHL's manuscript revision for 'Burns' (MS p. 3). 'Mary' (203:21) suggests the 'Highland Mary' of his enquiry to A. W. McLeod (see Introduction, p. xxxvii), i.e. possibly Mary Campbell (d. 1786), described by W. E. Henley in an essay with which DHL became acquainted in January 1913 as either 'a paragon ... or ... a national delusion' (*Poetry of Robert Burns*, ed. Henley and Henderson, Edinburgh, 1896, iv. 292). For Lockhart, whose biography DHL read in December 1912, she was 'the object of by far the deepest passion that ever Burns knew' (J. G. Lockhart, *Life of Burns*, Dent's Everyman's Library, 1907, p. 55).

203:34 **An' 'ad you seed** 'And had you seen'.

203:37 **sticking?"** Gathering sticks for firewood.

205:4 **Haseldine ... more songs** A common name in the Eastwood region: here and at 210:22 and 28 'Jack', later 'John' (206:5 and 10) and—suggesting some hesitation over the character's Scottishness—'Jock' (205:7, 210:9 and 35). The character would apparently have been DHL's recreation of Robert Burns (1759–96) ... Burns noted that *A Select Collection of English Songs* 'was my *vade mecum.* I pored over them, driving my cart, or walking to labour, song by song, verse by verse' (Lockhart, *Life of Burns*, p. 10).

205:7 **his 'lowance ... a public,** His allowance of free drink ('drink' is deleted in MS, p. 6) ... a public bar or house.

205:28 **Two men ... a small woman ... the father,** Cf. the Chambers family discussed in Explanatory note on 5:3. The focus of the 'Burns Novel' on the 'younger son' Jack suggests, too, DHL's April 1910 project to write 'a "bright" story with Bernard Chambers (b. 1890) 'as hero' (E. T. 181).

205:30 **"Tha'rt late enow ... Nowt ter fret about,"** 'You're late enough' ... 'nothing to worry about'.

206:4 **ponched** Pressed down as with a 'ponche' (see Explanatory note on 134:17).

206:7 **"Tha mun well ... stodge-belly,"** 'You certainly are a podgy belly-stuffer'.

206:29 **a rabbit in one of his snares.** Cf. the poem 'Rabbit Snared in the Night' in the *Look! We Have Come Through!* (1917) sequence; its placing there suggests a composition date in the winter 1912–13. The 'spark glittering at me' of the rabbit's eye starts 'a strange fire ... mounting, mounting up in me' (*Complete Poems*, ed. Pinto and Roberts, i. 241, ll. 19–21).

207:3 **"Are ter frit ... Tiss, Tissie?"** 'Are you frightened'; cf. Burns' poem 'To a Mouse': '... tim'rous *beastie*, / O what a panic's in thy breastie!' (*Poems and Songs*, ed. J. Kinsley, Oxford 1971, pp. 101–2) ... 'Tiss, Tissie' appears to be neither Scots nor dialect, though it is suggestive of a number of names in Burns' poems (e.g. 'Maggie', 'Mallie', 'Tibby').

207:32 **to whistle a tune.** Cf. Lockhart's description of the 'rural lover' of Burns' time: 'After the labours of the day are over, nay, very often after he is supposed by the inmates of his own fireside to be in his bed, the happy youth thinks little of walking many long Scotch miles to the residence of his mistress, who, upon the signal of a tap at her window, comes forth to spend a soft hour or two beneath the harvest moon' (*Life of Burns*, p. 19). See, too, Burns' song 'O whistle, and I'll come to ye, my lad' (*Poems and Songs*, ed. Kinsley, p. 556):

> O whistle, and I'll come to ye, my lad ...
> But warily tent, when ye come to court me,
> And come nae unless the back-yett be a-jee;
> Syne up the back-style and let naebody see,
> And come as ye were na comin' to me— (ll. 1, 5–8)

208:18 **swalin' away,"** 'Melting or guttering away'.

208:38 **'Gentle Annie'."** Reminiscent of many songs by Burns, e.g. 'Fair Jenny', 'My Nanie' and 'It was upon a Lammas night' when 'I held awa to Annie' (*Poems and Songs*, ed. Kinsley, pp. 9–10); but actually a popular nineteenth-century song by Stephen Foster (1826–64), 'Thou wilt come no more' (see *The Merry-Go-Round*, *Collected Plays*, p. 440).

210:15 **The fire place was curious.** DHL found similar inns and fire-places in a number of places on Lake Garda. There, 'the inn is always the family living room' (*Letters*, i. 483); here, 'only the kitchen of a house' (210:6); for DHL, the kitchen *was* the working-class family living room. In an inn at Bogliaco, there was 'a great open fireplace, about level with your knees, for the guest of honor' (*Letters*, i. 508, emended from Nehls, iii. 627); he described another such inn and fireplace on 2 December 1912 (*Letters*, i. 483), which may well have been the one he saw in Muslone or Piovere and wrote about in 'John', *Twilight in Italy* (1916); 'The chimneys are like the wide, open chimney-places of old English cottages, but the hearth is raised about a foot and a half or two feet from the floor, so that the fire is almost level with the hands; and those who sit in the chimney-seats are raised above the audience in the room, something like two gods flanking the fire . . .'

# TEXTUAL APPARATUS

# TEXTUAL APPARATUS

In the Apparatus, whenever the reading of the base-text is adopted (see the Note on the texts), it appears within the square bracket with no symbol. Corrupt or superseded readings follow the square bracket, in chronological sequence, with their first source denoted. When a reading from a source later than the base-text has been preferred, it appears within the square bracket with its source symbol. This is always followed by the reading of base-text. Further variants from later states follow in chronological order.

In the absence of information to the contrary, the reader should assume that a variant recurs in all subsequent states.

The following symbols are used editorially:

*Ed.* = Editor
~ = Repeated word in recording a punctuation variant
*Om.* = Omitted
/ = Line or page break resulting in a punctuation, hyphenation or spelling error
*P* = Paragraph division
# = Internal division
*R* = Autograph corrections, by DHL unless otherwise stated, to a state of the text (e.g. *TSR* in 'The Fly in the Ointment')

## A Prelude

*Per* = *Nottinghamshire Guardian*, 7 December 1907, p. 17
*E1* = *A Prelude* (Merle Press, Thames Ditton, 1949), pp. 29–47

5:1 **A Prelude** *Ed.*] **AN ENJOYABLE CHRISTMAS, A PRELUDE** *Per* **A PRELUDE** *E1*
5:2 "*Sweet* ... *pain* ......" *E1*] "*Sweet* ... *pain* ......"/BY JESSIE CHAMBERS / HAGGS FARM / UNDERWOOD / JACKSDALE, NOTTS. *Per*
5:12 and setting] ~, ~ *E1*
5:22 clocks in many] many clocks in *E1*
5:22 kitchens,] ~ *E1*
5:23 half an hour] half-an-hour *E1*
5:26 approach. *P* There] ~. There *E1*
5:28 and,] ~ *E1*
5:30 iron shod] iron-shod *E1*
5:33 heavily] *Om. E1*
6:5 it's ... it's *E1*] its ... its *Per*
6:8 oven. *E1*] oven. *P* THE DEPRESSED INDUSTRY. *Per see notes*
6:9 Well] ~, *E1*
6:9 pleasant] ~, *E1*
6:17 Christmas,] ~— *E1*

6:23 If—!] ~... *E1*
6:23 Besides] ~, *E1*
6:23 in] ~, *E1*
6:28 He'd only ... got married.] *Om. E1*
6:37 pit!] ~. *E1*
638 and"——] ~..." *E1*
6:38 they] he *E1*
7:3 fire. *P* Looking] ~. Looking *E1*
7:5 said: *P* "You] ~: "You *E1*
7:13 heavy,] ~ *E1*
7:17 whiteness *E1*] whitness *Per*
7:21 There] ~, *E1*
7:25 shy,] ~ *E1*
7:26 doubtful. *E1*] doubtful. *P* HOLLY BERRIES. *Per*
7:34 Wycherley,] ~ *E1*
7:36 father.] ~, *E1*
8:12 'cause] because *E1*
8:12 th' town] the town *E1*
8:20 father;] ~, *E1*
8:21 a laughing] a-laughing *E1*
8:25 an' Wardy's] and Ward's *E1*
8:28 Arthur. *E1*] Arthur. *P* THE GUYSERS. *Per*
8:29 ye what!] you what, *E1*
8:32 fun. Hey] fun." *P* "Hey *E1*
8:36 You,] ~ *E1*
9:3 don't] don' *E1*
9:12 richly berried] richly-berried *E1*
9:16 it is] it's *E1*
9:17 that!" *Ed.*] that!" *P* A BEDOUIN. *Per* that." *E1*
9:22 moustache] moustaches *E1*
9:23 naked,] ~ *E1*
9:26 exclaimed] said *E1*
9:34 burnouse] burnous *E1*
9:35 face] face in *E1*
9:36 to the] from the *E1*
9:39 mill] Mill *E1*
10:3 and] ~, *E1*
10:4 quieted. *E1*] quieted. *P* CHRISTMAS PLAY. *Per*
10:5 tones, *P* "Dun] ~, "Dun *E1*
10:18 away,] ~ *E1*
10:18 laughing,] ~ *E1*
10:22 as near to them] to them as near *E1*
10:26 Devil feels] Devils feel *E1*
10:33 his] the *E1*
10:35 dripping-pans] ~, *E1*
10:36 end. *Ed.*] end. *P* AFTER THE PLAY. *Per*
10:38 next,] ~? *E1*
11:8 lady's;] ~ *E1 see notes*
11:9 blushed,] ~ *E1*
11:12 to] *Om. E1*
11:14 arm-chair] armchair *E1*
11:17 St.] Saint *E1*
11:18 this] the *E1*
11:20 burnouse] burnous *E1*
11:24 frown] ~, *E1*
11:30 sleeves. *E1*] sleeves. *P* A MAIDEN'S HEART. *Per*
12:11 pretty!] ~, *E1*
12:16 miserable," faltered Nellie, "and] miserable and *E1*
12:22 see——] ~ ... *E1*
12:26 him!] ~? *E1*
12:30 Blanche, *E1*] ~," *Per*
12:32 then." *E1*] then." *P* THE DISCONSOLATE LOVER. *Per*
12:35 to] *Om. E1*
13:5 had she invited him] if she had invited himself *E1*
13:6 how could he have asked her;] *Om. E1*
13:9 likes.] ~, *E1*
13:12 think] say *E1*
13:13 sometimes." *P* Then] ~." Then *E1*
13:19 care!" *E1*] care!" *P* THE SERENADE. *Per*
13:36 though,] *Om. E1*
13:38 Blanche.] ~, *E1*
14:1 Nellie *E1*] Blanche *Per*
14:5 her] ~, *E1*
14:14 'Good] ~ *E1*
14:14 Wenceslaus?'] ~? *E1*
14:17 he said,] *Om. E1*
14:18 shining. "Let] ~, "let *E1*
14:23 thee,] ~ *E1*
14:28 finished,] ~; *E1*

14:30 but—"Nell] ~— *P* "Nell *E1*
14:32 kitchen,] ~ *E1*
14:34 rocking-chair] ~, *E1*
14:38 old,] ~ *E1*

## A Lesson on a Tortoise

*MS* = Autograph MS (Roberts E196.5a, Lazarus)
*E1* = *Phoenix II* 24–8.

16:3 half past ... half past] half-past ... half-past *E1*
16:19 flat,] ~ *E1*
16:22 walk"] ~," *E1*
16:22 myself. "And *Ed.*] ~ "And *MS* ~, "and *E1*
16:27 Gordon] London *E1*
17:7 Sir *E1*] sir *MS*
17:19 enough] ~. *E1*
17:32 interrupted. *Ed.*] ~ *MS* ~— *E1*
18:17 Gordons, *Ed.*] "~," *MS* "~" *E1*
18:17 noticeable.] ~: *E1*
18:18 them, *E1*] ~ *MS*
18:19 are:—] ~— *E1*
18:32 Gordons *Ed.*] '~' *MS* "~" *E1*
18:37 said] ~. *E1*
18:39 Well"] ~." *E1*
18:39 me] ~, *E1*
18:40 us—!" *P* This] ~—!" This *E1*
19:3 what *E1*] What *MS*
19:7 Well"] ~," *E1*
19:7 myself. *Ed.*] ~ *MS* ~, *E1*
19:7 Isn't] isn't *E1*
19:8 your] you *E1*
19:20 see"] ~," *E1*
19:21 up"] ~," *E1*
19:36 'I] "~ *E1*
19:36 nobody';] ~" *E1*
19:38 assistant-monitor, assistant monitor *E1*
20:5 convicted] convinced *E1*
20:28 class room,] classroom *E1*
20:30 Sir" *E1*] ~." *MS*

## Lessford's Rabbits

*MS* = Autograph MS (Roberts E196.4a, Lazarus)
*E1* = *Phoenix II* 18–23

21:9 morning *E1*] ~, *MS*
21:11 'art'] "~" *E1*
21:12 black-board] blackboard *E1*
21:18 roof,] ~ *E1*
21:30 Infant *Ed.*] infant *MS*
22:2 a walrus] walrus *E1*
22:4 good-morning] good morning *E1*
22:13 said ... me, *E1*] said, ... me *MS see notes*
22:24 and *E1*] ~, *MS*
22:30 three quarters] three-quarters *E1*
22:33 "and ... Amen." *E1*] '~ ... ~.' *MS*
23:2 die'.] ~.' *E1*
23:6 squatting] squalling *E1*
23:23 Sir,"] ~" *E1*
23:23 very *E1*] ~, *MS*
23:26 inquiries,] inquirer *E1*
23:30 work] ~, *E1*
23:39 furtively] ~, *E1*
24:32 Eat, *E1*] ~. *MS*
24:35 true"] ~," *E1*
24:35 said] ~. *E1*
25:4 No"] ~," *E1*
25:4 time—.] ~ — *E1*
25:5 believe"] ~," *E1*
25:11 Well"] ~," *E1*
25:11 said] ~, *E1*
25:23 half past *E1*] half-past *MS*
25:25 heaving; he *Ed.*] ~; He *MS* ~. He *E1*
25:27 exclaimed] ~, *E1*
25:30 on"] ~," *E1*
25:34 half out] half-out *E1*

25:37 open?" *P* Lessford] ~?" Lessford *E1*
26:6 Halket: *P* "Please] ~: "Please *E1*
26:25 bread.] ~, *E1*
26:32 them." —He *Ed.*] ~."—he *MS* ~,"—he *E1*
26:34 green-grocer] greengrocer *E1*
26:36 Eight-pence] Eightpence *E1*
26:38 He *E1*] he *MS*
27:2 Halket *E1*] ~; *MS*
27:2 wisely] widely *E1*
27:8 field——.] ~—— *E1*

## A Modern Lover

*MS* = Autograph MS (Roberts E240.7, NYPL)
*Per* = *Life and Letters*, ix (Sept.–Nov. 1933), 257–86.
*E1* = *A Modern Lover* 11–44.

28:2 **1.**] I *Per*
28:10 grass lands] grassland *Per*
28:12 The *Per*] ~, *MS*
28:14 land,] ~ *Per*
28:20 statues] ~, *Per*
28:30 glamourous,] glamorous *Per*
29:4 on the *Per*] on *MS see notes*
29:4 South-Country] south country *Per* South Country *E1*
29:11 only the] the only *E1*
29:12 him:] ~; *E1*
29:18 slowly lapsing] slowly-lapsing *Per*
29:18 days.] ~? *Per*
29:41 rose,] ~ *Per*
30:1 sheep:] ~; *E1*
30:2 west] West *E1*
30:5 **2.**] II *Per*
30:16 porch,] ~; *Per*
30:18 started;] ~, *Per*
30:25 table] ~, *Per*
30:25 bread and butter] bread-and-butter *Per*
30:26 dark] ~, *E1*
30:29 nights] night *Per*
30:29 submission, *MS*, *E1*] ~ *Per*
31:12 a long *MS*, *E1*] his *Per*
31:13 window] ~, *Per*
31:16 South *MS*, *E1*] south *Per*
31:18 outside," *E1*] ~", *MS* ~', *Per*
31:21 tree,] ~: *Per*
31:21 bitterly] ~, *Per*
31:23 records":] ~': *Per* ~;" *E1*
31:26 news",] ~', *Per* ~," *E1*
31:31 time] ~, *Per*
31:37 torses] torsos *Per*
31:38 a] *Om. Per*
32:5 cow-sheds *Per.*] cowsheds *MS*
32:6 haltingly:] ~; *E1*
32:11 Southern *MS*, *E1*] southern *Per*
32:11 heavily sounded] heavily-sounded *Per*
32:16 bread and butter] bread-and-butter *Per*
32:18 him. Without] ~; without *Per*
32:28 power,] ~ *Per*
32:32 well!",] ~!' *Per* ~!" *E1*
32:32 farm work] farm-work *E1*
32:34 knees, *Per*] ~ *MS*
32:35 shirt-sleeves,] ~ *Per*
32:40 "Daily News." *MS*, *E1*] *Daily News. Per*
33:1 parlour Cyril!] ~, ~. *Per*
33:1 you!] ~? *Per*
33:6 **3.**] III *Per*
33:9 little,] ~ *Per*
33:12 chair—] ~ *Per*
33:12 Countess'—] ~, *Per*
33:16 "Jane Eyre" *MS*, *E1*] *Jane Eyre Per*
33:19 Khayyam *MS*, *E1*] Khayyám *Per*
33:20 Balzac,] ~; *Per*
33:20 Madame Bovary.] *Madame Bovary. Per* "Madame Bovary." *E1*
33:21 "Madame Bovary". *Ed.*] 'Madame Bovary'. *MS*

*Madame Bovary*. *Per* "Madame Bovary." *E1*
33:26 side] side of *Per*
33:32 honor] honour *Per*
33:32 mantel-piece,] mantelpiece; *Per*
33:33 be; *MS*, *E1*] ~: *Per*
33:33 good-looking,] ~ *Per*
33:37 Lady-day *MS*, *E1*] Lady Day *Per*
33:38 boisterously, *MS*, *E1*] ~: *Per*
34:1 unconscious] ~, *Per*
34:14 tea-times, *MS*, *E1*] ~ *Per*
34:15 Ay!"—] ~! *Per* ~!" *E1*
34:18 kindly.] ~: *E1*
34:19 Ah] ~, *Per*
34:21 Nay"] ~," *Per*
34:21 bitterly, *Ed.*] ~ *MS* ~; *Per*
34:23 creatures *Per*] a creatures *MS* *see notes*
34:24 mind"] ~," *Per*
34:24 easily] ~. *Per*
34:24 —if] If *Per*
34:25 is!—] ~! *Per*
34:25 handsome; *MS*, *E1*] ~: *Per*
34:26 back *MS*, *E1*] ~, *Per*
34:27 eyes:] ~. *Per*
34:28 Oh] ~, *Per*
34:28 well"] ~," *Per*
34:31 think—?" she] ~?' She *Per* ~?" She *E1*
34:32 head.—] ~. *Per*
34:34 Ah *MS*, *E1*] ~! *Per*
34:35 —No]—no, *Per* —No, *E1*
34:37 mantel-piece] mantelpiece *Per*
34:39 nice—] ~, *Per*
34:40 really!] ~. *Per*
35:1 She too *MS*, *E1*] ~, ~, *Per*
35:4 voluptuously] ~, *Per*
35:4 chair:] ~. *Per*
35:5 all—*MS*, *E1*] ~—— *Per*
35:6 him] ~, *Per*
35:7 mean"] ~," *Per*
35:11 laughed:] ~. *Per* ~. *E1*
35:14 word"] ~," *Per*
35:16 listened:] ~. *Per*
35:17 true"] ~," *Per*
35:17 said] ~. *Per*
35:18 yourself] ~, *Per*
35:18 treat—] ~! *Per*
35:19 life!'—you] ~." You *Per* ~.' You *E1*
35:22 fates etcetera.'"] ~", etcetera.' *Per* ~,' etcetera." *E1*
35:25 Well—!] ~, *Per*
35:25 lying] ~, *E1*
35:25 smiling,— *P* "Isn't it] smiling, 'isn't that *Per* smiling, "isn't that *E1*
35:27 am,—] ~— *E1*
35:28 voice: *P* "Then *MS*, *E1*] ~: 'Then *Per*
35:30 Yes"] ~," *Per*
35:30 I?"—she] ~?' She *Per* ~?" She *E1*
35:32 Nay"] ~," *Per*
35:32 said] ~, *Per*
35:33 meekly,] ~ *E1*
35:33 excuse: *P* "It's *MS*, *E1*] ~: 'It's *Per*
35:36 asked—?] ~? *Per*
35:38 course—!] ~! *Per*
35:38 said] ~, *Per*
36:2 serious, "supposing] ~. 'Supposing *Per* ~. "Supposing *E1*
36:3 myself. *Ed.*] ~ *MS* ~? *Per*
36:8 rate"] ~," *Per*
36:8 said] ~, *Per*
36:11 pupil] pupils *Per*
36:12 see"] ~," *Per*
36:12 said] ~, *Per*
36:13 steel] a steel *Per*
36:14 sparks] spark *Per*
36:15 me. *Ed.*] ~ *MS* ~? *Per*
36:17 see"] ~," *Per*
36:17 usual] ~; *Per* ~: *E1*
36:17 "—thought] "~ *Per*
36:21 together—see?—] ~, ~? *Per*
36:24 Yes—?] ~? *Per*
36:25 you—." *P* He] ~——' He *Per* ~—" He *E1*
36:27 But"] ~," *Per*
36:27 huskily] ~, *Per*
36:30 Fibber!"—] ~!' *Per* ~!" *E1*
36:31 him] ~— *Per*
36:31 clearly!] ~. *Per*

36:36 cried] ~, *Per*
36:36 herself,] ~; *Per*
36:37 couldn't.—Quite *E1*] ~.—quite *MS* ~. Quite *Per*
36:40 Ah] ~, *Per*
37:2 he] He *Per*
37:3 voice] ~, *Per* ~. *E1*
37:3 don't] ~, *E1*
37:5 Not"] ~," *Per*
37:5 Not] not *Per*
37:8 else—] ~, *Per*
37:12 bicycle bell] bicycle-bell *Per*
37:17 Him?"—he] him?' He *Per* Him?" He *E1*
37:17 mantel-piece *Ed.*] mantel piece *MS* mantelpiece *Per*
37:22 not!—besides] not. Beside *Per* not. Besides *E1*
37:23 place—.] ~. *Per*
37:24 No—] ~, *Per*
37:24 deeply, *Ed.*] ~ *MS* ~. *Per*
37:25 altogether—"—then] ~.' Then *Per* ~." Then *E1*
37:25 whimsically "but] ~, 'But *Per* ~, "But *E1*
37:28 bitterness] ~, *Per*
37:32 bitterness:] ~. *Per*
37:33 me!] ~. *Per*
37:34 ironical—"and] ~. 'And *Per* ~. "And *E1*
37:36 **4.**] IV *Per*
37:38 now,] ~ *Per*
37:38 looked] ~, *Per*
38:6 Muriel *MS, E1*] ~, *Per*
38:13 house—.] ~. *Per*
38:19 technicalities;] ~, *Per*
38:23 check, *Per*] ~ *MS*
38:23 taunting,] ~: *Per*
38:25 Oh is she!] ~, ~ ~? *Per*
38:25 in,] ~: *Per* ~; *E1*
38:25 be"—he] ~.' He *Per* ~." He *E1*
38:34 rose, *MS, E1*] ~ *Per*
38:37 sweethearts] sweetheart *Per*
38:38 visitor] ~, *Per*
38:39 Yes!] ~. *Per*
39:1 set up] set-up *E1*
39:5 steady] ~, *Per*
39:6 head] ~, *Per*
39:29 arm-chair *MS, E1*] armchair *Per*
39:13 intruding"] ~," *Per*
39:14 not"] ~!" *Per*
39:18 we] ~, *Per*
39:25 'badly'] ~ *Per*
39:27 that"] ~," *Per*
39:31 see"] ~," *Per*
39:31 yet] and yet *Per*
39:33 eyelids *MS, E1*] eyebrows *Per*
39:35 that"] ~," *Per*
39:36 a chair *MS, E1*] the chair *Per*
39:38 solid, *MS, E1*] ~ *Per*
40:1 xy and yx *MS, E1*] *xy* and *yx* *Per*
40:4 wife— *MS, E1*] ~.... *Per*
40:12 late"] ~," *Per*
40:17 dead white] dead-white *Per*
40:20 second hand] second-hand *Per*
40:25 Well—] ~, *Per*
40:28 alike,] ~: *Per* ~; *E1*
40:37 he?—] ~? *Per*
40:39 think—!] ~! *Per*
40:40 true"] ~," *Per*
41:4 Mersham— *Ed.*] ~—" *MS* ~. *Per*
41:6 emphatically—"it's] ~,—'~ *Per* ~, "—~ *E1*
41:7 husband"] ~," *Per*
41:9 end—] ~ *Per*
41:10 you!—] ~. *Per*
41:10 poor women!—] Poor women! *Per* Poor woman! *E1*
41:12 it—isn't] ~. Isn't *Per*
41:13 Oh quite!] ~, ~. *Per*
41:13 home brewed] home-brewed *Per*
41:14 'ad infinitum'.] *ad infinitum. Per ad infinitum? E1*
41:15 better"] ~," *Per*
41:16 change"] ~," *Per*
41:16 Mersham—"Now] ~. 'Now, *Per* ~. "Now, *E1*
41:24 husband] ~, *Per*
41:28 Why"] ~," *Per*
41:28 intervening] ~, *Per*
41:29 quietly] ~, *Per*

41:31 tried] had *Per*
41:32 said] ~: *Per*
41:33 purple:—] ~—*E1*
41:33 is in] ~, ~ *E1*
41:35 added] ~: *Per*
41:39 twitched] twinkled *Per* wrinkled *E1 see notes*
42:1 5.] V *Per*
42:4 away] ~, *Per*
42:12 well"] ~," *Per*
42:13 But"] ~—" *Per*
42:13 Mersham "—but] ~—'~ *Per* ~—"~ *E1*
42:13 you really—?] ~ ~——? *Per* ~, ~? *E1*
42:14 Yes] ~, *Per*
42:14 course—play] ~. Play *Per*
42:18 sois] Sois *Per*
42:18 belle'"—he *Ed.*] ~'."—he *MS* ~!' He *Per* ~.'" He *E1*
42:18 suggestively "—try] ~. 'Try *Per* ~. "Try *E1*
42:19 Blume'] ~", *Per* ~,' *E1*
42:23 song, *MS*, *E1*] ~ *Per*
42:25 Daffodils!] ~, *Per*
42:28 by line] ~ ~, *Per*
42:29 Blume". *Ed.*] ~" *MS* ~'. *Per* ~." *E1*
42:31 whole] *Om. Per*
42:32 "The Octopus." *MS*, *E1*] *The Octopus. Per*
42:36 philosophy,—] ~— *Per*
43:3 Life"] ~," *Per*
43:4 Life] life *Per*
43:6 white hot] white-hot *Per*
43:9 merry"] ~," *Per*
43:13 age,] ~ *Per*
43:14 do"] ~," *Per*
43:15 Oh] ~, *Per*
43:20 But then] ~, ~, *E1*
43:22 And"] ~," *Per*
43:22 Mersham] ~, *Per*
43:23 understand—.] ~— *Per* ~. *E1*
43:30 Oh] ~, *Per*
43:31 but] ~, *E1*
43:31 all—!" For] ~...!' *P* For *Per* ~...!" *P* For *E1*
43:32 lover,] ~; *Per*
43:35 goodbye] good-bye *E1*
43:37 'showing-off'] 'showing off' *Per* "showing off" *E1*
44:3 whooping cough] whooping-cough *Per*
44:4 row"] ~," *Per*
44:5 she,] ~— *Per* ~?— *E1*
44:5 her—.] ~.*Per*
44:6 rate—do] ~. Do *Per*
44:7 devils—?] ~? *Per*
44:8 laughed,] ~ *E1*
44:9 Mind"] ~," *Per*
44:11 Thanks!] ~, *Per*
44:18 bicycle lamp] bicycle-lamp *E1*
44:19 luminous, *Ed.*] a luminous, *MS* luminous *Per see notes*
44:21 razor line] razor-line *Per*
44:23 all"] ~," *Per*
44:23 Mersham] ~, *Per*
44:23 beautiful,] ~; *Per*
44:27 dimness] ~, *Per*
44:29 movements,] ~ *Per*
44:31 have"] ~," *Per*
44:31 himself] ~, *Per*
44:34 man,] ~ *Per*
44:35 know] ~, *Per*
44:35 twin soul] twin-soul *Per*
45:2 nothing. They] ~. *P* They *Per*
45:4 goodnight] Good-night *Per* good-night *E1*
45:5 Sic transit *MS*, *E1*] *Sic transit Per*
45:7 in *MS*, *E1*] into *Per*
45:16 hearth-rug *Ed.*] hearthrug *MS*
45:21 ankle deep] ankle-deep *Per*
45:24 hand"] ~," *Per*
45:24 hand in hand] hand-in-hand *Per*
45:30 front. There] ~. *P* There *Per*
45:32 fairy tales] fairy-tales *Per*
45:34 unknown] *Om. Per*
45:35 onto] on to *Per*
45:36 wood-fence *MS*, *E1*] wood fence *Per*
45:37 meadow] meadows *Per*
46:1 Yes!] ~. *Per*
46:8 *him*] him *Per*
46:9 But"] ~," *Per*

46:9 certainty] ~, *Per*
46:11 don't!] ~. *Per*
46:11 love;—] ~: *Per* ~; *E1*
46:13 will"] ~," *Per*
46:13 sadly: "you] ~. 'You *Per* ~. "You *E1*
46:15 then] ~, *Per*
46:17 them.—] them. *Per* to them. *E1*
46:18 you:] ~; *E1*
46:18 intimate, *MS, E1*] ~ *Per*
46:19 wonderful] ~, *Per*
46:21 "—And] '~ Per "~ *E1*
46:22 words] ~, *Per*
46:23 Well"] ~," *Per*
46:23 said] ~, *Per*
46:23 wonderful] ~, *Per*
46:25 *you*] you *Per*
46:25 wonderful] ~, *Per*
46:25 person." She] ~.' *P* She *Per* ~." *P* She *E1*
46:26 gently.] ~: *Per*
46:29 ass——] ~. . . . *Per* ~. . . *E1*
46:33 myself—" he] ~. . .' He *Per* ~. . ." He *E1*
46:34 am—?"—] ~?' *Per* ~?" *E1*
46:35 her,] ~ *E1*
46:36 No!] ~, *Per*
46:36 beautiful] ~, *Per*
46:37 is!] ~. *Per*
46:38 ever—"—she] ~——' She *Per* ~—" She *E1*
47:1 But] ~, *Per*
47:5 directly"—there *Ed.*] ~—" there *MS* ~.' There *Per* ~." There *E1*
47:6 resumed] ~: *Per*
47:7 debt—.] ~— *Per*
47:10 youth—? *MS, E1*] ~? *Per*
47:11 No—, *Ed.*] ~—. *MS* ~, *Per*
47:12 you?—and—] ~? And *Per*
47:13 naturally;] ~, *Per*
47:15 reluctant?—will] ~? Will *Per*
47:21 silence] ~, *Per*
47:23 but] ~, *Per*
47:25 wise"] ~," *Per*
47:25 answered, *MS, E1*] ~ *Per*
47:25 gently, "one *Ed.*] ~ "one *MS* ~. 'One *Per* ~. "One *E1*
47:28 Yes] ~, *Per*
47:33 fear, "there *Ed.*] ~ "there *MS* ~. 'There *Per* ~. "There *E1*
47:35 know"] ~," *Per*
47:35 replied, *MS, E1*] ~ *Per*
47:36 so— *MS, E1*] ~—— *Per*
47:38 books—.] ~. *Per* ~— *E1*
47:39 but—.] ~—— *Per* ~— *E1*
47:40 he] He *Per*
48:5 dark— *MS, E1*] ~. . . . *Per*
48:6 him;—] ~; *Per*
48:6 once, *MS, E1*] ~ *Per*
48:7 frail] fine *Per*
48:16 No"] ~," *Per*
48:16 drearily] ~; *Per*
48:18 thorn tree] thorn-tree *Per*
48:24 wild fowl] wild-fowl *Per*
48:25 North *MS, E1*] north *Per*
48:29 Beyond *MS, E1*] ~, *Per*
48:32 Goodbye!] ~, *Per*
48:33 me—goodbye] ~. Goodbye *Per*

## The Fly in the Ointment

*MS* = Autograph MS (Roberts E135.5a, Clarke)
*TS* = Ribbon copy TS (Roberts E135.5b, UT)
*TSR* = Autograph corrections to TS
*Per* = *New Statesman*, i (16 August 1913), 595–7
*O1* = Ada Lawrence and G. Stuart Gelder, *Young Lorenzo* (Florence, 1932), pp. 215–30

49:2 weather beaten] weather-beaten *Per*
49:3 honeysuckle-twine] honeysuckle, twine *O1*

49:5 box, *MS*, *O1*] ~ *Per*
49:6 Williams, *MS*, *O1*] ~; *Per*
49:7 tone] tune *O1*
49:7 day: *MS*, *O1*] ~. *Per*
49:8 reluctant *TSR*] tender *MS*, *O1*
49:9 these,] ~ *Per*
49:9 winter-trodden] winter—trodden *O1*
49:10 primroses, *MS*, *O1*] ~ *Per*
49:11 Altogether,] ~ *O1*
49:14 purple, *MS*, *O1*] ~ *TS*
49:17 purple *TSR*] purple pall *MS*, *O1*
49:22 thought *TS*] though *MS*
49:23 midlands] Midlands *Per*
49:25 her looking *MS*, *O1*] her, while she looked *Per see notes*
49:26 eyes] ~, *O1*
49:27 Meanwhile *MS*, *O1*] ~, *Per*
49:30 myself: *P* "This *MS*, *O1*] ~: "This *TS*
49:31 do—"] ~"— *TS* ~," *Per*
49:32 Muriel:] ~. *O1*
49:34 'robins', *MS*, *O1*] "~," *Per*
50:2 about *MS*, *O1*] ~, *Per*
50:4 had a grass-hopper ... read their *TSR*] got mixed up with you. 'If the interest on a certain Muriel be——' That {be—' that *O1*} was arithmetic. And I've read the *MS*, *O1* had a grasshopper ... read their *Per*
50:7 Pancakes *MS*, *O1*] pancakes *Per*
50:7 saw *TSR*] seen *MS*
50:7 thinking—] ~ *Per*
50:8 primrose flowers *MS*, *O1*] primrose flower *TS* primroses flower *TSR*
50:8 now *TSR*] *Om. MS*, *O1*
50:8 plum-trees ... with *TSR*] plum-trees. They are black plums, with very *MS*, *O1*
50:9 bark—' *TSR*] ~. *MS*, *O1* ~.' *Per*
50:9 You like *TSR*] She is fond of *MS*, *O1*
50:10 hard *MS*, *O1*] ~, *Per*
50:10 gum—if ... get so *TSR*] gum. Then her lips get *MS*, *O1* gum. If ... get so *Per*
50:10 sticky——" *Ed.*] ~——' *MS* ~—'—. *TS* ~——." *TSR* ~..." *Per* ~'". *O1*
50:12 dim *TSR*] blind, dim *MS*, *O1*
50:13 of putting] putting *O1*
50:15 Strelley *MS*, *O1*] Stretley *TS*
50:19 hand's-breadth *TSR*] hand-breadth *MS*, *O1* hand's breadth *Per*
50:19 garden backed up *MS*, *O1*] garden, backed *TS*
50:24 pushed *TSR*] pushed the door *MS*, *O1*
50:24 harder] ~. *Per* ~, *O1*
50:25 space *TSR*] space of the door *MS*, *O1*
50:27 wonder *TSR*] curiosity *MS*, *O1*
50:28 The shock ... me to *TSR*] Perhaps I ought to say I {that I *O1*} opened my eyes a little *MS*, *O1*
50:30 wondered, and ... disturbed: ... of me *TSR*] did not feel alarmed: I *MS*, *O1* wondered ... disturbed; ... of me *Per*
50:31 midlands *MS*, *O1*] Midlands *Per*
50:31 and blinking *TSR*] in dull curiosity *MS*, *O1*
50:32 said,] ~ *Per*
50:32 helplessly *TSR*] quite mildly *MS*, *O1*
50:33 shrunk *MS*, *O1*] shrank *Per*
50:34 and the] and *O1*
50:36 me—don't *MS*, *O1*] ~! Don't *Per*
50:36 me—I'll *MS*, *O1*] ~! I'll *Per*
50:37 poker—I *MS*, *O1*] ~. I *Per*
50:37 you—don't *MS*, *O1*] ~. Don't *Per*
50:38 coward. *MS*, *O1*] ~! *Per*
50:40 dazed *TSR*] amazed *MS*, *O1*

51:1 I came awake, sick *TSR*] It went cool *MS*, *O1*
51:2 pain. It ... seen before, *TSR*] disgust. I was not unaccustomed {was accustomed *O1*} to displays of the kind *MS*, *O1* pain. It ... seen before *Per*
51:3 helplessness *TSR*] contempt *MS*, *O1*
51:5 slum-rat] slum rat *O1*
51:6 still *MS*, *O1*] ~, *Per*
51:7 row. *MS*, *O1*] ~! *Per*
51:7 children.] ~? *TS*
51:8 Ah] ~, *Per*
51:8 you touch 'im,] you touch me; *Per* yer touch me, *O1* *see notes*
51:8 you come] yer come *O1*
51:10 frenzy,] ~ *O1*
51:11 fool,—" I] ~,—." I *TS* ~"—I *Per* ~!" *P* I *O1*
51:12 stove, *MS*, *O1*] ~ *Per*
51:13 and, *MS*, *O1*] ~ *Per*
51:13 crazy *MS*, *O1*] ~, *Per*
51:13 state, *MS*, *O1*] ~ *Per*
51:15 second hand] secondhand *TS* second-hand *O1*
51:16 clatter. I *MS*, *O1*] ~. *P* I *TS*
51:17 him like ... heart began *TSR*] further contempt for the nerveless knave. Yet {knave, yet *TS*} my own heart had begun *MS*, *O1*
51:19 and then ... collapse, *TSR*] *Om. MS*, *O1*
51:22 mantel piece] mantel-piece *TS* mantelpiece *Per*
51:26 a low *TSR*] the lowest *MS*, *O1* *see notes*
51:28 topping", *MS*, *O1*] ~," *Per*
51:30 doin'] doing *O1*
51:30 harm"] ~," *TS*
51:30 whined, *MS*, *O1*] ~ *Per*
51:31 you, *MS*, *O1*] ~; *Per*
51:33 Be quiet" *Ed.*] Shut up" *MS* Shut up," *TS*, *O1* Be quiet," *TSR*
51:33 You'll wake ... the people. *TSR*] Do you want to wake the baby and fetch everybody down? Keep your mouth shut! *MS*, *O1*
51:34 door, *MS*, *O1*] ~ *Per*
51:37 ugly and shapeless *TSR*] chill and dreary *MS*, *O1*
51:40 ricketty] rickety *Per*
51:40 rocking chair *MS*, *Per*] rocking-chair *TS*
52:1 almost pleading *TSR*] curious *MS*, *O1*
52:2 Well"] ~," *TS*
52:2 insolently "an' *MS*, *O1*] ~. "An' *TS*
52:2 go somewhere, *TSR*] be, *MS*, *O1* go somewhere *Per*
52:3 you 'edn't] you'ed n't *TS* you edn't *Per* you 'adn't *O1*
52:3 this. *MS*, *O1*] ~? *TS*
52:4 here"] ~," *Per*
52:4 coldly, a ... blood, "none *TSR*] coldly "None *MS* coldly, "none *TS* coldly, a ... blood; "none *Per* coldly. "None *O1*
52:5 chelp *TSR*] sauce *MS*, *O1*
52:6 Well] ~, *Per*
52:6 warm" *MS*, *O1*] ~," *Per*
52:6 afraid ... defiant *TSR*] meekly *MS*, *O1*
52:8 No you didn't, *TSR*] Nor blarney either *MS* Nor blarney either, *TS*, *O1*
52:8 take *TSR*] pinch *MS*, *O1*
52:8 something. *Per*] ~, *MS*
52:8 What did ... unhappily *TSR*] it's no use saying you didn't.—{didn't. *O1*} What should you have taken?", {taken?" *O1*} I asked, curiously *MS*, *O1*
52:13 said, with ... 'food'. And ... it is." *TSR*] said simply. For the moment, {moment *O1*} he could not help speaking the truth. *P* "And what right have you to pinch boots from people who can't afford to buy any

more?" I said. *MS*, *O1* said, with ... "food." And ... it is." *Per*

52:18 time——] ~—— *TS* ~. *O1*

52:19 swine *TSR*] creep *MS*, *O1*

52:23 you don't] do you *O1*

52:24 except—] ~ *O1*

52:24 laundry—] ~.... *TS* ~—— *Per* ~ — *O1*

52:25 thieving *TSR*] stealing *MS*, *O1*

52:27 uncomfortable,] ~ *O1*

52:31 stubborn, *MS*, *O1*] ~ *TS*

52:32 corners] corner *O1*

52:34 girls, *MS*, *O1*] ~ *Per*

52:34 passers-by] the passers-by *O1*

52:35 But"] ~," *Per* ~", *O1*

52:35 said] ~, *Per*

52:35 what are ... to do *TSR*] what's going to become of you *MS*, *O1*

52:36 fidgetted] fidgeted *O1*

52:39 asked, *MS*, *O1*] ~ *Per*

53:2 him. *MS*, *O1*] ~? *TS*

53:3 And *TSR*] You'll *MS*, *O1*

53:3 corners] corner *O1*

53:3 rotten?] ~, *O1*

53:4 sullenly:] ~. *TS*

53:5 Well] ~, *Per*

53:5 job" *MS*, *O1*] ~," *Per*

53:3 replied, *MS*, *O1*] ~ *Per*

53:5 insolence. He *MS*, *O1*] ~: *P* He *TS*

53:6 but *MS*, *O1*] ~, *Per*

53:8 No" *TSR*] But" *MS* No," *Per* But," *O1*

53:8 said] ~; *TS* ~, *O1*

53:9 you *are* a man *TSR*] you're one *MS*, *O1*

53:11 And would ... Then *TSR*] It beats me that any woman 'ud let you touch her," I said. *P* And then *MS*, *O1*

53:13 primroses, *MS*, *O1*] ~ *Per*

53:15 Then, that ... a father. *TSR*] *Om. MS*, *O1* Then that, ... a father. *Per*

53:16 it's a knock-out *TSR*] you're beyond me *MS* You're beyond me *O1*

53:17 look *TSR*] look from his sore eyes *MS*, *O1*

53:18 everyfing] everything *O1*

53:19 wondered. *P* And *MS*, *O1*] ~. And *TS*

53:22 said, *MS*, *O1*] ~ *Per*

53:22 go. *TSR*] go. But for God's sake, {sake *O1*} steal in different streets. *MS*, *O1*

53:23 me, *MS*, *O1*] ~: *Per*

53:24 path. *TS*] ~,. *MS*

53:25 lamp posts] lamp-posts *TS*

53:28 unpassable *MS*] impassable *TS* *see notes*

53:28 fact *TSR*] rock *MS*, *O1*

53:29 I could ... him; I ... hated him. *TSR*] *Om. MS*, *O1* I could ... him. I ... hated him. *Per*

53:30 stairs. *TS*] ~,. *MS*

53:31 mind *TSR*] soul *MS*, *O1*

53:31 heavy out of *TSR*] heavy, *MS* heavy *TS*, *O1*

53:32 extricate myself *TSR*] decipher *MS*, *O1*

53:34 sick. *P* "No, *MS*, *O1*] ~. "No! *TS*

53:35 perfect *MS*, *O1*] ~, *Per*

53:36 her." *P* And *MS*, *O1*] ~." And *TS*

## The Witch à la Mode

*MS* = Autograph MS, 'The White Woman' (Roberts E438b, BucU)
*TS* = Ribbon copy TS (Roberts E438c, BucU)
*TSR* = Autograph corrections to *TS*
*TCC* = Carbon copy TSS (Roberts E438d, UCB, and E438e, Viking Press)
*Per* = *Lovat Dickson's Magazine*, ii (June 1934), 697–718
*E1* = *A Modern Lover* 103–28

54:1 The Witch à la Mode *TSR*] The White Woman *MS*
54:7 easiest!" He] ~." *P* He *TS* ~?" *P* He *TSR*
54:8 tram-car: *P* "I] ~: "I *TS*
54:9 Purley,] ~. *TCC*
54:11 desires,] ~ *TCC*
54:14 Church *MS*, *E1*] church *Per*
54:16 thought—] ~. *TS*
54:16 confessed, secretly,] ~ ~ *TS*
54:20 sparks, *Ed.*] sparks *MS* spark *TS* spark, *TSR*
54:23 smiled a little, roused *TSR*] smiled, a little exultation *MS* smiled a little in exultation *TS* *see notes*
54:31 star,] ~ *TCC*
55:3 said,] ~ *TS*
55:4 Then] ~, *TCC*
55:8 full tilt] full-tilt *TS*
55:12 up-hill] uphill *TS*
55:12 a] the *TS*
55:14 alyssome] alyssam *E1*
55:16 daffodils,] ~ *TCC*
55:19 cried] exclaimed *TS*
55:22 things:] ~; *E1*
55:26 rich,] ~ *E1*
55:27 and *Ed.*] and in *MS* and in her *TS* *see notes*
55:30 course], *TCC*
55:31 meeting] seeing *TCC*
55:33 led] let *TS*
55:33 room,] ~ *TCC*
55:33 dark] ~, *TCC*
55:34 hangings,] ~ *TS*
55:39 puzzled] ~, *TCC*
56:3 why yes] ~, ~ *TCC*
56:3 Coutts!—hm?—Ay] ~!—Hm—ay *TS* ~! H'm—ay *TCC*
56:4 hm] h'm *TCC*
56:5 Ay!—] ~! *TS*
56:6 you?—] ~?... *TCC*
56:6 Come] come *TS*
56:6 along,] ~; *TCC*
56:7 I'll] I will *TS*
56:9 bell-push] bell-pull *TS*
56:10 done] ~, *TS*
56:10 in in] in *E1*
56:11 high] ~, *TCC*
56:15 man,] ~ *TS*
56:16 presence:] ~; *E1*
56:19 away—why] ~. Why *TCC*
56:21 fidgetted] fidgeted *TS*
56:25 suppose;] ~, *TCC*
56:27 Pater,] ~? *TS*
56:29 Eh?—Why] Ay?—why *TS* Ay—why *TCC*
56:32 Eh?—Oh.] ~?—oh *TS* ~? Oh! *TCC*
56:32 Well] ~, *TCC*
56:34 it—" he] ~—" He *TS* ~..." He *TCC*
56:35 laughed—] ~, *TS*
56:36 Oh,] ~! *TCC*
56:36 'passé'] *passe*, *TCC* *passé*, *Per*
56:40 things?—now] ~?—Now *TS* ~? Now, *TCC*
56:40 things." *P* "I] ~?" *P* "I *TCC*, *E1* ~? I *Per*
57:2 it.—Eh?—what] ~—eh?—What *TS* ~—eh? What *TCC*
57:3 laughed,] ~. *TCC*
57:4 said] ~, *TS*
57:11 know] ~, *TCC*
58:18 used] used to *TCC*
57:24 have] have had *TCC*
57:31 know—when] ~.—When *TCC* ~—When *E1*
58:2 half past] half-past *TCC*
58:6 suffered] ~, *TCC*
58:9 white,] ~ *TCC*
58:10 twenty eight] twenty-eight *TS*
58:17 timbre] *timbre* *TCC*
58:18 half closed) half-closed *TCC*
58:19 you—at least—.] ~. At least... *TCC*
58:19 indefinitely—] ~. *TS*
58:21 rectory] Rectory *TS*
58:22 lived:] ~; *E1*
58:26 play] ~, *TS*
58:27 drawing room] drawing-room *TCC*
58:28 chimney-piece *MS*, *Per*] chimneypiece *TCC*, *E1*

58:29 new] ~, *TCC*
58:31 deep *TS*] the deep *MS see notes*
59:7 figure:] ~; *E1*
59:7 corsets:] ~; *E1*
59:8 resolute,] ~ *E1*
59:10 an isolated woman *TSR*] and shut off from contact *MS*
59:11 All] All the *TS*
59:12 continually] ~, *TS*
59:13 ah] ~! *TS*
59:22 tram terminus] tram-terminus *TCC*
59:25 along] ~, *TS*
59:29 frail] fail, *TCC* frail, *Per*
59:29 lady] ~, *TS*
59:31 day:] ~; *E1*
59:33 Aren't] aren't *TS*
59:34 back in supplication] ~, ~ ~, *TCC*
60:2 child-like] childlike *TCC*
60:4 the 'Swan'.] 'The Swan'. *TS* 'The Swan.' *Per*
60:4 intense,] ~ *TS*
60:5 edge. It *Ed.*] ~.: it *MS* ~: it *TS*, *Per* ~; it *TCC*, *E1 see notes*
60:5 or more often] ~ ~ ~, *TS* ~, ~ ~, *TCC*
60:7 violin:] ~; *E1*
60:12 half a mile] half-a-mile *TCC*
60:18 night,] ~ *TCC*
60:23 west] West *TS*
60:24 long] ~, *E1*
60:24 arc-lamps] arc lamps *TS*
60:26 faint] ~, *TCC*
60:31 low] ~, *TCC*
60:33 answered. "Both] ~, "both *TS* ~; "both *TCC*
60:38 half stubborn] half-stubborn *TCC*
60:38 half pleading] half-pleading *TCC*
60:39 one] ~, *TCC*
61:1 dovetailed] dove-tailed *TS*
61:4 hair's breadth] hair's-breadth *TCC*
61:5 privacy:] ~; *E1*
61:11 throat] threat *E1*
61:11 gold and black] gold-and-black *TCC*
61:12 full] ~, *TCC*
61:18 know:] ~; *E1*
61:18 there . . . *TCC*] ~. . *MS* ~. . . . . *TS*
61:21 *life*] life *TS*
61:22 was] were *TS*
61:28 her:] ~; *TS* ~, *TCC*
61:28 dinner is] dinner's *TS*
61:29 on— —but—] ~. . ~. . . . *TS* ~; ~. . . *TCC*
61:29 things—] ~. . . . *TS* ~. . . *TCC*
61:31 speak:] ~; *TCC*
61:35 Trouble.—] ~— *TS* ~. . . *TCC*
61:36 Vexations] Vexation *TCC*
61:36 trouble—:] ~: *TS* ~; *TCC*
61:37 soul,] ~— *TCC*
61:37 had—.] ~. *TS*
61:38 again,] ~ *TS*
61:38 sharply:] ~; *TCC*
62:3 myself 'Wish',] ~, '~,' *TCC*
62:3 back] ~, *TCC*
62:4 again] ~, *TCC*
62:4 fool',] ~,' *TCC*
63:5 hurry] ~, *TCC*
62:11 hand in hand] hand-in-hand *TCC*
62:14 know— —,] ~. . . . . ., *TS* ~. . . *TCC*
62:15 don't—,] ~. . . . , *TS* ~. . . *TCC*
62:17 Yes,] ~; *TCC*
62:22 symbolism] ~, *TCC*
62:24 fog— —.] ~. . . . . . *TS* ~. *TCC*
62:26 candles,] candle, *TS*
62:27 forth] ~, *TS*
62:27 wronger] more wrong *TS*
62:30 ignis fatuus] *ignis fatuus TS*
62:30 rate,] ~? *TCC*
62:31 May be] Maybe *TCC*
62:31 in a] in the *TS*
62:39 'Swan *MS*, *TSR*] ~ *TS* "~ *Per*
62:39 Sugar Loaf'] Sugar Loaf, *TS* Sugar Loaf,' *TSR* Sugar-Loaf', *TCC* Sugar-Loaf," *Per*
63:2 lamps,] ~ *TS*
63:3 dark,] ~ *TS*
63:4 almond tree] almond-tree *TCC*

63:5 glittered] glistered *TS* glistened *E1*

63:5 street-lamp] street lamp *TS*

63:7 said,] ~: *TCC* ~; *E1*

63:8 midnight] mid-night *TS*

63:8 lamplight] lamp-light *TS*

63:12 him] ~, *TCC*

63:12 usual] ~, *TCC*

63:13 her drawing room] the drawing-room *TS*

63:13 same,] ~: *TCC* ~; *E1*

63:14 appointment:] ~; *TCC*

63:14 ivory-coloured *TS*] ivory coloured *MS*

63:14 blond *TSR*] blonde *MS*

63:15 rugs:] ~; *TCC*

63:15 armchairs] arm-chairs *TS*

63:16 cushions:] ~; *TCC*

63:16 it:] ~; *TCC*

63:18 piano candles] piano-candles *TS*

63:20 said. "This] ~, "this *TS* ~; "this *TCC*

63:21 anemones,] ~ *TCC*

63:23 Why? *TS*] ~?, *MS*

63:32 purple:] ~, *TCC*

63:33 cannot] can't *TS*

63:36 voiceless] scentless *TSR see notes*

63:40 know—] ~… *TCC*

64:7 said, quietly] ~ ~, *TS*

64:9 see—to] ~.—To *TCC* ~—To *E1*

64:9 conclusions,] ~? *TS*

64:12 I will] I'll *TS*

64:16 house,] ~ *TCC*

64:16 formal:] ~; *E1*

64:17 superiority,] ~; *TCC*

64:18 she] she was *TS*

64:23 her too] ~, ~ *TCC*

64:25 rectory] Rectory *TS*

64:26 Vaguely,] ~ *TS*

64:28 was not] ~ ~, *TCC*

64:28 be] ~, *TCC*

64:29 not frank] ~ ~, *TCC*

64:31 each,] ~ *TS*

64:33 Winifred—she] ~. She *TCC*

64:33 and unnatural,] ~ ~— *TS*

64:36 'Walküre.'] '*Walküre*'. *TS* 'Walkure'. *TCC* "Walkure." *Per* "Walküre." *E1*

65:3 times:] ~; *E1*

65:3 blue,] ~; *TCC*

65:4 tenderness,] ~; *TCC*

65:5 animal's. He] ~. *P* He *TS*

65:7 uncorseted] uncorsetted *TS*

65:10 loose:] ~; *TCC*

65:10 elbows] elbow *E1*

65:11 acknowledgement,] ~ *TS*

65:15 life:] ~; *E1*

65:16 result:] ~; *E1*

65:19 said] ~, *TS*

65:22 tilt—" she] ~…." she *TS* ~…" She *TCC*

65:22 ending.—] ~. *TS*

65:26 she] She *TS*

65:27 Meredith—very] ~. Very *TCC*

65:28 quickly,] quickly at *TS*

65:29 Now] ~, *E1*

65:30 Oh] ~, *TCC*

65:31 finish] ~, *TCC*

65:32 But—but—] ~ … ~ … *TCC*

65:36 on—] ~. *TCC*

65:37 battle field] battlefield *TS*

65:38 her:] ~; *TCC*

65:39 witch-like] ~, *TCC*

66:1 every-day] everyday *TS*

66:7 But—] ~ … *TCC*

66:10 business,] ~ ;*TCC*

66:10 amiable *TS*] aimiable *MS*

66:14 his] His *TCC*

66:14 self mistrust] self-mistrust *TS*

66:17 began, *TSR*] began heavily, *MS* began; *TCC*

66:17 *all*] all *TCC*

66:19 not?—] ~? *TCC*

66:19 because] Because *TCC*

66:22 abnormal. *TSR*] abnormal. And it would destroy us. *MS*

66:27 head] ~, *TS*

66:29 'Bacchae'] "~" *Per*

66:33 the] a *TS*

66:35 Ah yes] Oh yes, *TS* Oh, yes, *TCC*

66:35 deadlock,] ~ *TS*

66:38 bad,] ~? *TS*

66:40 But," —] ~ ," *TS* ~" — *TCC*
66:40 irritably. "Is] ~ .—"Is *TS* ~ — "is *TCC*
67:1 answered—] ~; *TCC*
67:1 smiling "you] ~, "You *TS* ~: "You *TCC*
67:6 'genius'. *TS*] "~". *MS* '~.' *Per*
67:7 Ah] ~, *TCC*
67:9 Shalott-looking] Shalott looking *TCC*
67:11 symbols.] ~! *TCC*
67:12 Ah] ~, *TCC*
67:13 He] She *TS*
67:16 Gods] gods *TCC*
67:17 least] ~, *TCC*
67:18 Goddess] goddess *TCC*
67:20 answered,] ~ *TS*
67:22 sadly. All *MS*, *E1*] ~. *P* All *Per*
67:23 said, "I] ~: I *TCC* ~: "I *Per*
67:24 Winifred:] ~; *TCC*
67:24 eleven"—then *Ed.*] ~—" then *MS* ~—" Then *TS* ~ . . ." Then *TCC*
67:25 laughter—"though] ~. "Though *TCC*
67:26 Addios] *Addios* *TCC*
67:27 vague] ~, *TCC*
67:29 at her,] ~ ~ *TS*
67:30 throat,] ~ *TS*
67:31 sense,] ~ *TCC*
67:32 fire glow] fireglow *TS* fire-glow *TCC*
67:34 length,] ~; *TCC*
67:39 harness,] ~ *TS*
67:40 bridled,] ~ *TS*
68:2 be.] ~? *TS*
68:3 I am] I'm *TS*
68:5 Ah] ~! *TCC*
68:6 steady] steadily *TCC*
68:7 sunset:] ~; *E1*
68:8 asked, at last.] asked. *TS*
68:13 the] a *TS*
68:14 Oh dear,] ~, ~, *TCC* ~, ~ *E1*
68:17 up-tilted *MS*, *Per*] uptilted *TS*, *E1* up-/tilted *TCC*
68:18 his throat] himself *TS*
68:21 rapidly chasing] rapidly-chasing *TCC*
68:23 gravely,] ~; *TCC*
68:28 Goodbye *MS*, *TCC*] Good-bye *TS*, *Per*
68:28 small] ~, *TS*
68:29 sound] noise *TS*
68:29 face,] ~ *TCC*
68:34 onto] on to *Per*
68:40 and the] and a *TS*
69:4 full] ~, *TS*
69:14 startled:] ~; *E1*
69:15 stark; *MS*, *E1*] ~: *TS*
69:16 half sunk] half-sunk *TS*
69:17 knew] knew that *TS*
69:18 him,] ~; *TCC*
69:19 kiss:] ~; *TCC*
69:19 and] ~, *TCC*
69:23 death:] ~; *E1*
69:28 quavered *MS*, *Per*] quivered *TCC*, *E1*
69:29 tightened] had lightened *TS*
69:38 coming,] ~; *TCC*
69:39 drawing room] drawing-room *TS*
69:40 onto *TSR*] on *MS* on to *Per*
69:40 flame *TSR*] fire *MS*
70:4 burning red] burning-red *TCC*
70:5 blindly] ~, *TS*

## The Old Adam

*MS* = Autograph MS (Roberts E286a, Lazarus)
*TCC* = Carbon copy TS (Roberts E286b, Viking Press)
*E1* = *A Modern Lover* 47–71

71:15 sea bird] sea-bird *TCC*
71:15 wings] wing *TCC*
71:29 evening: must be] ~; must be, *TCC*
71:32 pause,] ~; *TCC*
72:1 laughed] ~, *TCC*
72:5 dining room] dining-room *TCC*

72:6 evening:] ~; *E1*
72:6 dusk blue] dusk-blue *TCC*
72:10 grape vine] grape-vine *TCC*
72:12 flower-border *Ed.*] ~, *MS see notes*
72:22 Com'] Come *TCC*
72:37 in her] in hers *TCC*
73:39 him,] ~; *TCC*
73:4 caterpillars,] ~ *TCC*
73:8 Severn *TCC*] Thomas *MS*
73:10 wild cat] wild-cat *TCC*
73:11 said—] ~. *TCC*
73:12 *swing*] swing *TCC*
73:14 said] ~, *TCC*
73:14 half smothered] half-smothered *TCC*
73:19 pendant *TCC*] pendent *MS*
73:24 Oh no,] ~, ~! *TCC*
72:29 Oh] ~, *TCC*
73:35 laughter,] ~; *TCC*
74:12 high waisted] high-waisted *TCC*
74:13 bread and butter] bread-and-butter *TCC*
74:16 pleasure:] ~; *E1*
74:21 dark blue] dark-blue *TCC*
74:24 rocking chair] rocking-chair *TCC*
74:25 close] *Om. TCC*
74:29 close cut] close-cut *TCC*
75:1 No no] ~, ~ *TCC*
75:1 low,] ~ *E1*
75:1 dog-licks ] dog-lick, *TCC*
75:8 me] ~, *TCC*
75:12 aside:] ~; *E1*
75:14 nicely——." *Ed.*] ~——". *MS* ~—" *TCC*
75:17 dark:] ~; *E1*
75:18 arm chair] arm-chair *TCC*
75:22 white flannelled] white-flannelled *TCC*
75:25 evening,] ~? *TCC*
75:27 reading. She] ~. *P* She *TCC*
75:29 peculiar] ~, *TCC*
76:5 Oh no,] ~, ~; *TCC*
76:5 It's *TCC*] Its *MS*, *E1*
76:5 do." *P* Mrs] ~." Mrs. *TCC*
76:12 sunk his head] sank his head, *TCC*
76:13 north east] north-east *TCC*
76:17 way] ~, *TCC*
76:18 Well] ~, *TCC*
76:25 other] ~, *TCC*
76:32 away,] ~? *TCC*
76:33 superb] ~, *TCC*
76:37 little,] ~ *TCC*
76:38 bowed,] ~ *TCC*
76:39 curiously:] ~; *E1*
76:39 her: and] ~. And *TCC*
77:10 lamp shade] lamp-shade *TCC*
77:20 There] ~, *TCC*
77:25 overlapped,] ~; *TCC*
77:30 said] ~, *TCC*
77:34 No] ~, *TCC*
77:36 feel] ~. *E1*
77:38 bewildered:] ~; *E1*
77:40 jeopardy. *P* She] ~. She *TCC*
78:5 greeting:] ~; *E1*
78:32 half past] half-past *TCC*
79:4 thickly built] thickly-built *TCC*
79:4 good looking] good-looking *TCC*
79:6 jaw:] ~; *TCC*
79:13 movement,] ~ *TCC*
79:19 book. Severn] ~. *P* Severn *TCC*
79:24 said] ~, *TCC*
79:25 then.] ~? *TCC*
79:35 are] Are *TCC*
79:36 Gertie—?] ~? *TCC*
79:40 Courteous] courteous *TCC*
79:40 Gentleman— —] ~— *TCC*
80:2 to——] ~... *TCC*
80:3 heeded ...] ~. *TCC*
80:4 chairman.] Chairman. *TCC* Chairman *E1*
80:5 congratulation:] ~; *E1*
80:6 staff:] ~; *E1*
80:6 is *one*] is one *TCC*
80:7 sure:—] ~— *E1*
80:7 *law:*] *law; E1*
80:9 chairman] Chairman *TCC*
80:11 table;] ~, *TCC*
80:12 Hear!'. *Ed.*] ~!.' *MS* ~!' *TCC*
80:14 indifferent. Mr] ~. *P* Mr. *TCC*

80:15 bread and butter] bread-and-butter *TCC*
80:27 mantel-piece] mantelpiece *TCC*
80:37 nimble witted] nimble-witted *TCC*
81:3 meanwhile] meantime *TCC*
81:3 the] *Om. E1*
81:4 angry:] ~; *E1*
81:11 over heated] overheated *TCC*
81:12 half frenzied] half-frenzied *TCC*
81:13 opponent's] opponent to *TCC*
81:17 aside] ~, *TCC*
81:20 purpose:] ~; *E1*
81:23 box.] ~? *TCC*
81:32 situation:] ~; *E1*
82:7 little,] ~ *TCC*
82:8 hands,] ~ *TCC*
82:11 impedimenta] impediments *E1*
82:16 pleasure Sir] ~, sir *TCC*
82:20 behind. *TCC*] ~, *MS*
82:21 Gertie,] ~? *TCC*
82:28 anxious] ~, *TCC*
82:32 slip, *TCC*] ~ *MS*
82:32 bottommost] bottom-most *E1*
82:33 avalanche. *Ed.*] ~ *MS* ~! *TCC*
82:37 turn] ~, *TCC*
83:7 banister] bannister *E1*
83:8 struggling *TS*] ~, *MS see notes*
83:12 You sod] You—— *E1 see notes*
83:21 blows] blow *TCC*
83:22 Thomas'] Thomas's *TCC*
83:27 scattered:] ~; *E1*
83:29 self possession:] self-possession; *TCC*
83:31 face,] ~; *E1*
83:34 his] he *TCC see notes*
83:40 banisters *Ed.*] bannisters *MS*
84:2 shame. *P* He] ~. He *TCC*
84:9 stand up,] ~ ~; *TCC*
84:13 Kate,—] ~— *E1*
84:18 its] *Om. TCC*
84:18 little,] ~ *TCC*
84:21 little] ~, *TCC*
84:21 grief-stricken: he] ~. He *TCC*
84:26 stairs] ~, *TCC*
84:26 watching. For] ~: For *TCC* ~: for *E1*
84:27 time,] ~ *TCC*
84:31 self abnegation] self-abnegation *TCC*
85:1 pity] ~, *TCC*
85:16 fomentation] fomentations *TCC*
85:18 sat, *TCC*] ~ *MS*
85:21 sea-side] seaside *E1*
85:34 you—it is] ~; it's *TCC*
85:34 Goodnight] Good-night *TCC*
85:37 dressing gown] dressing-gown *TCC*
85:37 Thomas'] Thomas's *TCC*
85:38 bed] ~, *TCC*
86:1 looked,] ~ *TCC*
86:1 tenderness,] ~ *TCC*
86:1 friend:] ~. *TCC*
86:6 own,] ~ *TCC*
86:11 Oh] ~, *TCC*
86:16 bearing] ~, *E1*
86:19 'betters',] "~," *E1*

## Love Among the Haystacks

*MS* = Autograph MS (Roberts E211a, Private)
*TCC* = Carbon copy TS (Roberts E211b, UCB)
*E1* = *Love Among the Haystacks* (The Nonesuch Press, 1930), pp. 1–56

87:2 1.] I *E1*
87:5 half way] half-way *E1*
87:10 further] farther *E1*
87:20 hedge tops] hedge-tops *E1*
87:21 slightly hollowed] slightly-hollowed *E1*
87:21 hot] ~, *E1*
87:23 half submerged] half-submerged *E1*
87:26 twenty one] twenty-one *TCC*
87:26 debonnair] debonair *E1*
87:32 tha 'd] tha'd *TCC*

88:8 off—"] ~"— *E1*
88:9 us 'ud] us'ud *TCC*
88:10 turn——] ~— *TCC* ~—— *E1*
88:12 off,] ~ *TCC*
88:14 coal—] ~—— *E1*
88:29 deep-hedged *MS*, *E1*] deep hedged *TCC*
88:29 high-road] high road *E1*
88:36 think—] ~—— *TCC* ~—— *E1*
88:40 '*er* 'd … theer] 'er'd … thur *TCC*
89:6 rein] ~, *E1*
89:10 thee] thee say *E1* *see notes*
89:10 German, *Ed.*] ~? *MS* ~? *TCC* *see notes*
89:14 Sorry] Sonny *E1*
89:23 mother,] mother and *TCC* *see notes*
89:27 broad tongued,] broad-tongued *TCC*
89:27 the two] these two *TCC* *see notes*
90:3 onto] into *TCC*
90:9 said. *P* She] ~. She *TCC*
90:11 do-ock] dock *TCC*
90:11 repeated. *P* He] ~. He *TCC*
90:17 golden brown] golden-brown *E1*
90:18 small] ~, *E1*
90:19 remained arrested] ~, ~, *TCC*
90:35 re-appeared] reappeared *E1*
90:35 holding] holding up *TCC*
91:6 back] back again *TCC*
91:11 Oh] ~, *E1*
91:19 the blue *E1*] and the blue *MS* *see notes*
91:25 dully;] ~: *TCC*
91:31 judgment] judgement *E1*
92:2 forkful *TCC*] fork-ful *MS*
92:3 fool?] ~! *TCC*
92:5 I'n] I'v' *TCC* I've *E1*
92:5 cart-bottom] cart bottom *TCC*
92:16 out,] ~? *E1*
92:18 you.] ~? *E1*
92:20 corner—] ~—— *E1*
92:24 What—here … ? *Ed.*] ~ —.~..?.*MS* ~—~? *TCC*
92:30 tha 'rt] tha'rt *TCC*
92:31 elbowed] and elbowed *E1*
92:32 foot hold] foothold *TCC*
92:35 father—] ~; *E1*
92:39 Tha 'll … tha 'rt] Tha'll … tha'rt *TCC*
92:40 work, "An *Ed.*] ~. "An *MS* ~, "an *TCC*
93:7 to] ta *TCC* *see notes*
93:11 shovin' *E1*] ~ *MS*
93:12 sneer. *P* And] ~, and *TCC*
93:16 resistance *E1*] resistence *MS*
93:25 voice: *P* "Feyther] ~: "Feyther *TCC*
93:29 nearer,] ~ *E1*
93:32 Then] ~: *E1*
93:33 Ah-h!—] ~! *TCC*
93:36 oldest] eldest *E1*
93:38 What *ever*] What ever *TCC* Whatever *E1*
93:41 Ehe] Eh *TCC*
94:15 to,] ~; *E1*
94:20 —Fetch—?.] —~—? *TCC* ~? *E1*
94:27 on—.] ~. *TCC*
94:27 *always*] always *TCC*
94:35 brother,] ~ *E1*
94:38 moaning] ~, *E1*
94:40 muted] united *TCC*
95:4 father, *TCC*] Father, *MS* father *E1*
95:10 eh?,] ~? *TCC*
95:19 headforemost] head foremost *TCC*
95:21 not-to-be] not to be *TCC*
95:23 out.—] ~. *TCC*
95:25 stack.] ~? *E1*
95:34 that *TCC*] his that *MS*
96:7 said, "Eh?,] ~, "~? *TCC* ~. "~? *E1*
96:13 in] in a *E1*
96:18 Oh] ~, *E1*
96:21 wanting'.] ~.' *E1*
96:23 Nay] ~, *E1*
96:28 languorously] ~, *TCC*
96:40 Marjery?,] Margery? *E1*
97:5 bit, *TCC*] ~ *MS*
97:12 the] his *TCC*

97:16 she— —] ~ – – – – *TCC* ~—— *E1*
97:21 looked] and looked *E1*
97:31 raïght?,] ~? *TCC*
98:1 **2.**] II *E1*
98:6 Now] ~, *E1*
98:9 Jim?—] ~? *TCC*
98:10 horses] hosses *TCC see notes*
98:10 and you] ~ ~, *E1*
98:24 highroad] high road *E1*
98:25 some one] someone *E1*
98:34 spread,] ~: *E1*
98:36 Eh] eh *E1*
99:6 *Nation E1*] 'Nation' *MS* "Nation" *TCC*
99:7 Er's]'Er's *E1*
99:10 mid-way] midway *E1*
99:16 Gi'e] Give *TCC*
99:19 hm] him *TCC*
99:33 name—] ~—— *E1*
99:35 name—,] ~— *TCC* ~—— *E1*
99:36 son—] ~. *TCC*
100:16 Paris!!] ~! *E1*
100:25 "—I] "~ *TCC*
100:26 "you] "You *TCC*
100:26 you.] ~? *E1*
100:32 thought,] ~ *TCC*
100:35 braggadocio *TCC*] braggadacio *MS*
100:38 Han] Have *TCC*
100:39 yer] you *TCC*
101:11 '*E TCC*] *E MS*
101:11 '*E TCC*] *E MS*
101:13 he] ~, *E1*
101:21 parasitic] ~, *TCC*
101:24 'n] '~' *E1*
101:26 embarrassed *E1*] embarassed *MS*
101:29 help?,] ~? *TCC*
101:37 small, and] ~ ~ *TCC*
102:7 nedn't] nedn&t *TCC* needn't *E1*
102:8 contemptuously. *P* He] ~. He *TCC*
102:9 ricketty] rickety *E1*
102:10 nedn't] needn't *E1*
102:20 *you*] you *TCC*
102:22 flashed,] ~ *TCC*
102:30 here] ~, *E1*
102:36 rising . . . off] rising, . . . of *E1*
103:2 half understood] half-understood *E1*
103:3 off?,] ~? *TCC*
103:6 hypersensitive;] hyper-sensitive, *TCC* hyper-sensitive: *E1*
103:8 her?—it's] ~? It's *TCC*
103:12 me——] ~, *TCC*
103:14 **3.**] III *E1*
103:15 all] all the *E1*
103:36 Somebody 'll] Somebody'll *TCC*
104:1 Nay] ~, *E1*
104:8 know——] ~ . . . *E1*
104:20 lime tree] lime-tree *E1*
104:32 sickly smelling] sickly-smelling *E1*
105:4 velvetty] velvety *E1*
105:18 particularly] ~, *E1*
105:25 elder bush] elder-bush *E1*
105:27 quarter past] quarter-past *E1*
105:29 No] ~, *E1*
105:35 want—"] ~"— *TCC*
105:36 laïke] laike *TCC*
105:37 run] ~, *E1*
106:8 We *TCC*] we *MS*
106:8 horse?,] ~? *TCC*
106:9 What, *TCC*] ~ *MS*
106:9 bareback?,] ~? *TCC*
106:10 say?"—] ~?" *E1*
106:13 Coop] ~, *E1*
106:17 up-hill *Ed.*] uphill *MS*
106:25 off] ~, *E1*
106:25 iron foundry] iron-foundry *E1*
106:26 town-lights] town lights *TCC*
106:40 her] ~, *TCC*
107:6 excitement,] ~; *E1*
107:6 behind,] ~ *TCC*
107:30 cried. "Up] ~, "up *TCC*
107:30 burden. *P* "Yes] ~. "Yes *TCC*
107:32 Fumblingly,] ~ *TCC*
107:33 top. "I] ~. *P* "I *TCC*
107:40 you?,] ~? *TCC*
108:4 **4.**] IV *E1*
108:6 highroad] high road *E1*
108:12 rain-drops] raindrops *E1*
108:25 here?,] ~? *TCC*

108:30 rain-drops *Ed.*] rain drops *MS* raindrops *E1*

108:33 tone,] ~ *TCC* ~— *E1*

108:34 rate] ~, *E1*

108:38 You … Mind!'.] you … ~!' *TCC*

104:1 do!] ~? *TCC*

104:2 but *TCC*] But *MS*

104:5 plaintive] plaintively *TCC*

104:6 excitement,] ~ *E1*

104:7 we *Ed.*] we we'll *MS* we—we'll *TCC see notes*

109:11 right] raïght *TCC*

109:13 Minnie?" It] ~?" *P* It *TCC*

109:14 Minne!] Minnie? *TCC*

109:20 sure?,] ~? *TCC*

109:32 rain-drops] raindrops *E1*

110:4 round: what] ~. What *TCC*

110:5 waist;] ~, *TCC*

110:6 him;] ~, *TCC*

110:11 soon:] ~; *E1*

110:20 heavily,] ~ *E1*

110:23 panting *P* "Now] ~ "Now *TCC* ~ 'Now, *E1*

111:9 off,] ~ *TCC*

111:13 think?—] ~? *TCC*

111:14 though] through *TCC*

111:15 teemin' *TCC*] ~ *MS*

111:15 rain.—] ~. *TCC*

111:27 beaten—] ~, *TCC*

111:29 Why … through,] ~, … ~! *E1*

111:34 horse rug] horse-rug *E1*

112:10 Gormin'"] ~', *TCC*

112:11 eat!] ~? *E1*

112:16 but she] but *TCC*

112:26 his,] ~ *E1*

113:9 *all*] all *TCC*

113:33 pitch dark] pitch-dark *E1*

114:1 don't. And] ~, and *TCC*

114:18 dead"—] ~," *TCC*

114:19 doggedly] ~, *TCC* ~: *E1*

114:22 while: *P* "Have *Ed.*] ~. *P* "Have *MS* ~, "Have *TCC* ~: 'Have *E1*

114:26 Twenty three] Twenty-three *TCC*

114:27 twenty three] twenty-three *TCC*

114:30 eerie. Silence] ~, silence *TCC see notes*

114:34 stable man] stableman *TCC*

114:35 horse dealers] horse-/dealers *E1*

114:38 moss— —] ~. . . . *TCC*

114:39 baby.] ~? *TCC*

115:3 say,] ~ *TCC*

115:3 sympathetically, *P* "You *Ed.*] ~ *P* "You *MS* ~, "You *TCC* ~: "You *E1*

115:7 dying." He … silent. *P* "But] dying.' *P* He … silent. 'But *E1*

115:8 whatever] what ever *TCC*

115:8 do?,] ~? *TCC*

115:19 feet—!] ~! *TCC*

115:22 No] ~, *E1*

115:29 Well] ~, *E1*

115:30 match box] match-box *E1*

116:26 'câline'.] '~.' *TCC câline. E1*

116:29 down,] ~ *TCC*

116:33 5.] V *E1*

117:8 open eyed] open-eyed *E1*

117:8 him:] ~; *E1*

117:9 golden brown *Ed.*] golden-brown *MS*

117:37 fortunes,] ~; *E1*

117:40 Crich?] Crick. *TCC*

118:2 farm-labourer] farm laborer *TCC* farm labourer *E1*

118:8 service,—] ~— *TCC*

118:10 me] ~, *E1*

118:13 Crich] Crick, *TCC*

118:16 money—] ~, *E1*

118:33 Bredon'! *TCC*] ~!' *MS*

119:6 loomed] looked *TCC*

119:12 wondered] ~, *TCC*

119:17 exclaimed. *P* Then] ~. Then *TCC*

119:24 here—] ~—— *E1*

119:25 lies— —.] ~— *TCC* ~—— *E1*

119:27 here—,] ~— *TCC* ~—— *E1*

119:29 *mean*!!] ~! *E1*

119:32 Maurice] ~, *E1*

119:34 commin] ~' *TCC*

119:36 raïght] ~, *E1*

120:1 slightly,—] ~, *TCC*

120:3 descend *TCC*] descent *MS*

120:4 comin] commin *TCC*
120:5 No;] ~! *TCC*
120:7 comin] commin' *TCC*
120:16 length. *P* Still] ~. Still *TCC*
120:30 Oh] ~— *TCC*
121:8 Hello,] ~. *TCC*
121:12 sticks,] ~? *E1*
121:18 hat-less] hatless *TCC*

## The Miner at Home

*Per* = *The Nation*, x (16 March 1912), 981–2
*E1* = *Phoenix* 775–9

123:6 squeal,] ~; *E1*
123:7 ascertained,] ~ *E1*
123:16 ready] ~, *E1*
123:17 in] *Om. E1*
123:18 red] *Om. E1*
123:22 this] the *E1*
124:1 steel] *Om. E1*
124:3 that] the *E1*
124:4 in——] ~... *E1*
124:5 doesn't,] ~ *E1*
124:11 spluttering] sputtering *E1*
124:25 hands,] ~? *E1*
125:3 said: *P* "Bill] ~: "Bill *E1*
125:6 whitey-blue] whity-blue *E1*
125:8 "February] ~ *E1*
125:8 14th] 14 *E1*
125:9 "To] ~ *E1*
125:10 "I] ~ *E1*
125:12 "Signed——."] ~—— *E1*
126:1 *he's*] he's *E1*
126:2 *want*] want *E1*
126:7 butties 'll] butties'll *E1*
126:9 shillin',] ~' *E1*
126:11 the] th' *E1*
126:11 on...] ~. *E1*
126:15 an' what] what *E1*
126:24 chunterin'] chaunterin' *E1*
126:26 then] *Om. E1*
126:29 doesna] ~' *E1*
126:30 to it] it *E1*
126:32 minimum wage] Minimum Wage *E1*
126:35 much] *Om. E1*
126:39 day man] day-man *E1*
127:13 the] th' *E1*
127:15 do——] ~... *E1*
127:18 strike] ~, *E1*
127:21 ears.] ~? *E1*

## Her Turn

*Per* = *Westminster Gazette*, 6 September 1913, p. 2
*TCC* = Carbon copy TS (Roberts E159.5b, Viking Press)
*E1* = *A Modern Lover* 75–83

128:1 **Her Turn** *TCC*] STRIKE PAY.—I.: HER TURN. *Per*
128:3 wife] woman *TCC*
128:4 such] ~, *E1*
128:6 them, as... with] them; he was so, even to *TCC*
128:10 enemies] ~, *TCC*
128:10 good humour] fresh interest in life *TCC*
128:10 him] his presence *TCC*
128:10 welcome] agreeable *TCC*
128:11 plenty] always plenty *TCC*
128:11 a] always a *TCC*
128:18 eleven] ten *TCC*
128:25 sipping a] sipping a very *TCC*
128:27 scans] surveys *TCC*
128:30 warm and] warm, *TCC*
128:32 most important to her.] who interests her most. *TCC*
129:7 highly-coloured *TCC*] highly coloured *Per*
129:7 wheer——.] ~... *TCC, E1*
129:8 weigh *TCC*] way *Per see notes*
129:22 peculiar] ~, *TCC*
129:24 Always] ~, *TCC*
129:25 of him] *Om. TCC*

129:29 time] ~, *TCC*
129:31 life,] ~. *TCC*
129:35 ahead....] ~. *TCC*
129:38 have ... ailment.] never see when he wasn't well, *TCC*
129:39 wanted——."] ~—" *Per* ~——" *E1*
129:40 So] ~, *TCC*
130:1 and] and therefore *TCC*
130:6 while] ~, *TCC*
130:7 good-night] goodnight *TCC*
130:8 quarter-past *Per, E1*] quarter past *TCC*
130:10 fat,] ~ *E1*
130:11 satirical;] ~, *TCC*
130:19 rib *TCC*] rise *Per see note on* 130:21
130:21 missis] Missis *TCC*
130:25 think] ~, *TCC*
130:25 night] ~, *TCC*
130:27 jam tarts] jam-tarts *TCC*
130:29 tan-tafflins 'll] tan tafflins'll *TCC*
130:30 they! *TCC*] ~? *Per*
130:31 suavely] amiably, but determined *TCC*
130:34 this hour,] *Om. TCC*
130:35 th'] the *TCC*
130:39 ha'ep'ny] ha'p'ny *TCC*
131:1 so!] ~. *TCC*
131:5 cried,] said. *TCC*
131:8 day] ~, *TCC*
131:9 up-town] up town *TCC*
131:18 breakfast service] breakfast-service *TCC*
131:25 half-way] halfway *TCC*
131:26 woman] ~, *TCC*
131:27 big] ~, *TCC*
131:27 hand] ~, *TCC*
131:31 scaley] scaly *TCC*
131:38 breakfast cups] breakfast-cups *TCC*
131:39 up-town] up town *TCC*
132:1 seemly!] ~. *TCC*
132:6 sang] said *TCC*
132:6 insidious] ~, *TCC*
132:7 right;] ~, *TCC*
132:7 Radford. The] ~. *P* The *TCC*
132:8 carrying] with *TCC*
132:10 An'] '~ *TCC*
132:10 asked Radford] he asked *TCC*
132:11 yer] *Om. TCC*
132:12 gi'e *TCC*] gie' *Per*
132:15 well-being,] ~ *TCC*
132:16 herself. The] ~. *P* The *TCC*
132:19 They ... entry.] *Om. TCC*
132:20 There's th'] Now the *TCC*
132:24 street] ~, *TCC*
132:27 Give] Gi'e *TCC*
132:28 thy-sen] thysen *TCC*
132:30 carter] ~, *TCC*
132:34 enough."] ~," she replied. *TCC*
132:38 half-crowns;] ~, *TCC*
132:38 ivery] every *TCC*
133:5 out] ~, *TCC*

## Strike-Pay

*MS* = Autograph MS (Roberts E381a, Lazarus)
*Per* = *Westminster Gazette*, 13 September 1913, p. 2
*TCC* = Carbon copy TS (Roberts E381b, Viking Press)
*E1* = *A Modern Lover* 87–100

134:1 Strike-Pay] STRIKE-PAY.— II. / EPHRAIM'S HALF-SOVEREIGN. *Per*
134:5 The Primitive ... 'Squares' ... miner's ... square, unpaved ... drying ground ... women's washing.] *Om. Per* The Primitive ... "squares" ... miners' ... square ... drying-ground ... women's washing. *TCC*
134:16 Chapel, *MS, TCC*] chapel *Per*
134:16 thud-thud-thud!] thud-thud-thud *TCC*
134:17 ponches] pouches *TCC*

134:19 clothes lines] clothes-lines *Per*
134:24 man *MS, TCC*] ~, *Per*
134:25 schoolroom *MS, TCC*] Methodist Schoolroom *Per*
134:25 name after name *MS, TCC*] *Om. Per*
134:27 Ben dodged … list … the fore.] *Om. Per* Ben dodged … list, … the fore. *TCC*
134:30 Now] ~, *Per*
134:33 Queen Street *MS, TCC*] Queen-street *Per*
134:33 Queen Street *MS, TCC*] Queen-street *Per*
134:34 Joe, *Per*] ~. *MS*
135:2 That is] That's *TCC*
135:5 Sedgwick— *MS, TCC*] ~. *Per*
135:7 was a] was *E1*
135:9 Yes,] ~. *TCC*
135:9 money—] ~—— *Per* ~. *TCC*
135:10 thysen *MS, TCC*] thy-sen *Per*
135:11 No.— *MS, TCC*] ~— *Per, E1*
135:11 John … Nine. 'Diddle-diddle … on' "—came … half-sovereign … [135:21] loftily. *Ed.*] John … Nine. 'Diddle-diddle … on"—came … half sovereign … loftily, *MS Om. Per* John … Nine. *P* 'Diddle-diddle … on,'" *P* came … half-sovereign … loftily. *TCC*
135:22 pay-master] paymaster *Per*
135:23 Now] ~, *Per*
135:25 neer-do-well] ne'er-do-well *Per*
135:27 a-Monday *MS, TCC*] a' Monday *Per*
135:28 it, Sam,] ~, ~; *TCC*
135:28 be-out *MS, TCC*] bi-out *Per*
135:29 'im ha'e] him ha' the *TCC*
135:29 bob *MS, TCC*] bobs *Per*
135:29 mister," … awkwardly. *MS, TCC*] mister." *Per*
135:32 pay-master] paymaster *Per*
135:33 week——] ~—— *Per* ~— *TCC*
135:34 Nay nay] ~, ~, *Per*
135:34 voice, "pay] ~; "pay *Per* ~. "Pay *TCC*
135:35 theer] there *TCC*
135:36 money] ~, *Per*
135:37 Union *Per*] union *MS*
135:37 florin, *MS, TCC*] ~ *Per*
135:39 "Good … acclaimed … slim lad … Gi'e … Nay … Townsend, … delivery—… [136:3] laughter.] *Om. Per* "Good … exclaimed … lad … Gi' … Nay, … Townsend; … delivery … laughter. *TCC*
136:3 spirits. In] ~. *P* In *TCC*
136:5 market place] market-place *Per*
136:5 public-houses *Per*] public houses *MS*
136:7 Coutts] Couuts, *TCC* Coutts, *E1*
136:8 twenty two] twenty-two *Per*
136:10 hasna] has na *TCC*
136:10 the *MS, TCC*] th' *Per*
136:14 The … time. *MS, TCC*] *Om. Per*
136:15 wi's,] wi' us, *Per* wi's; *TCC*
136:17 nine miles] nine-miles *Per*
136:22 black haired] black-haired *Per*
136:23 declared. *P* "I … niver … [136:27] minutes." *P* He *MS, TCC*] declared. He *Per* declared. *P* … nivir … *P* He *E1*
136:28 It … 'instrument' … [136:33] entirely. *MS, TCC*] *Om. Per* It … "instrument" … entirely. *E1*
136:34 Brook,] ~; *Per* ~. *TCC*
136:35 Kimberley top *MS, TCC*] Kimberley-top *Per*
136:39 churchyard *TCC*] church-yard *MS* Churchyard *Per*
137:3 pit. "Sithee] ~, "sithee *TCC*
137:4 Luthee] Lu' thee *Per* Sithee *TCC see notes*
137:7 heered *Per*] heard *MS, TCC see notes*
137:7 Sorry—, *Ed.*] ~—. *MS* ~, *Per*
137:7 they'n] they'm *TCC* they're *E1*

137:8 riotin'. *Ed.*] ~' *MS* ~'? *Per*
137:9 commin'] comin' *E1*
137:9 simbilar *Per*] simbitar *MS*, *TCC*
137:11 much ... perzent ... easy! They] "they *Per* much ... per zent ... They *TCC*, *E1*
137:16 willin'!] ~', *TCC*
137:16 laugh. The *MS*, *TCC*] ~. *P* The *Per*
137:21 ower *Per*] over *MS*, *TCC*
137:22 Nowt! *MS*, *TCC*] ~, *Per*
137:22 Th' *MS*, *TCC*] The *Per*
137:23 rassivoy] cassivoy *E1*
137:23 There ... simile. *MS*, *TCC*] *Om. Per*
137:28 working men] working-men *Per*
137:29 It ... that way. *MS*, *TCC*] *Om. Per*
137:31 then *Per*] *Om. MS*, *TCC*
137:32 pit ponies *MS*, *TCC*] pit-ponies *Per*
137:33 Of all ... red ... the field. *MS*, *TCC*] *Om. Per*
137:36 th'] the *TCC*
137:36 pit 'osses *MS*, *TCC*] pit-'osses *Per*
137:36 Sam. "Let's *MS*, *TCC*] ~, "let's *Per*
137:37 uns *MS*, *TCC*] 'uns *Per*
137:38 warmly *Per*] *Om. MS*, *TCC*
138:1 pie-bald *MS*, *TCC*] piebald *Per*
138:1 white, *MS*, *TCC*] ~ *Per*
138:2 'growing-day,'] "growing day," *Per*, *E1* 'growing day', *TCC*
138:5 The younger ... But having *MS*, *TCC*] Having *Per*
138:8 above-ground *MS*, *TCC*] above ground *Per*
138:9 movement *Per*] life *MS*, *TCC*
138:9 They looked ... them. *MS*, *TCC*] *Om. Per*
138:13 The horses ... element. *P* Performing *MS*, *TCC*] Performing *Per*
138:15 feat, *MS*, *TCC*] ~ *Per*
138:20 strike-pay *Per*] strike pay *MS*
138:27 a *MS*, *TCC*] a' *Per*
138:29 An't *MS*, *TCC*] An' *Per*
138:29 Ephraim. *P* He] ~. He *TCC*
138:30 half-sovereign *Per*] half sovereign *MS*
138:31 He ... possession. *MS*, *TCC*] *Om. Per*
138:33 went, four ... and *MS*, *TCC*] went and *Per*
138:35 wes'll] we s'll *Per*
138:39 shamefully *MS*, *TCC*] shamefacedly *Per*
139:1 in *MS*, *TCC*] at *Per*
139:2 benches *MS*, *TCC*] ~, *Per*
139:2 The central ... amount drunk. *MS*, *TCC*] *Om. Per*
139:6 skittle board] skittle-board *Per*
139:8 'backers.'] "~." *Per*, *E1* '~'. *TCC*
139:9 Chris,] ~ *TCC*
139:9 the man ... favour *MS*, *TCC*] *Om. Per*
139:15 bread and cheese] bread-and-cheese *TCC*
139:15 half past] half-past *Per*
139:17 between ... well known ... putting ... [139:21] through] *Om. Per* between ... well known ... pulling ... through *TCC* between ... well-known ... putting ... through *E1*
139:22 the match *MS*, *TCC*] it *Per*
139:23 He ... 'Punch Bowl,' ... [139:27] go.] *Om. Per* He ... 'Punch Bowl', ... go. *TCC* He ... "Punch Bowl," ... go. *E1*
139:29 football ground *MS*, *TCC*] football-ground *Per*
139:29 navvy] ~, *E1*
139:30 onto *MS*, *TCC*] on to *Per*, *E1*
139:31 ooze,] ~ *TCC*
139:37 went ... [139:40] He *MS*, *TCC*] *Om. Per*
139:40 dark *MS*, *TCC*] dark (vaguely impressed with a sense of death, and loss, and strife) *Per* *see notes*

140:1 Queen Street *MS*, *TCC*] Queen-street *Per*
140:2 sixty four] sixty-four *Per*
140:7 His wife ... months pregnant. *MS*, *TCC*] *Om. Per*
140:12 She ... angry. *MS*, *TCC*] *Om. Per*
140:15 Oh *MS*, *TCC*] ~, *Per*
140:21 It] I *TCC*
140:22 "An' ... ter goo." *MS*, *TCC*] *Om. Per*
140:24 inside] beside *TCC*
140:24 no.] 'No' *Per* no? *TCC*
140:26 strike-pay,] ~ *Per*
140:31 in] *Om. TCC*
140:33 silence, *MS*, *TCC*] ~ *Per*
140:38 yourself] ~, *TCC*
141:1 her] the *TCC*
141:2 statelily *MS*, *TCC*] stately *Per*
141:3 an'] and *TCC*
141:3 wife,] ~ *Per*
141:4 answered, *MS*, *TCC*] ~ *Per*
141:5 four and sixpence] four-and-sixpence *TCC*
141:8 sitting,] ~ *Per*
141:10 up,] ~; *TCC*
141:11 Five and sixpence,] Five-and-sixpence *TCC*
141:11 man-an-wife's] man-an'-wife's *Per* man an' wife's *TCC*
141:13 Still ... somethink ... mother-in-law ... somethink ... any-body 'd ... you. Oh ... [141:24] Sirs!" *Ed.*] Still ... somethink ... mother in law ... somethink ... anybody 'd ... you. Oh ... Sirs!" *MS Om. Per* Still ... something ... mother-in-law ... something ... anybody'd ... you? Oh, ... sirs!" *TCC*
141:26 him, hark-ye] ~! Hark-ye *TCC*
141:27 in.] ~? *Per*
141:27 Oh] ~, *Per*
141:29 My Sirs] my sirs *TCC*
141:29 Oh Strike] ~, Strike *Per* ~, strike *E1*
141:32 want! *MS*, *TCC*] ~? *Per*
141:33 an'] and *TCC*
141:34 Sirs] sirs *TCC*
141:35 go— *MS*, *TCC*] ~, *Per*
141:35 matter! *MS*, *TCC*] ~? *Per*
141:35 go—let] ~. Let *TCC*
141:36 catch—only] ~. Only *TCC*
141:37 here] ~, *Per*
141:38 ony bloody *MS*, *TCC*] any—— *Per*
141:40 dare's] dares *TCC*
141:40 me, *MS*, *TCC*] ~ *Per*
142:1 goìn'] goin' *Per*
142:1 gì'e] gi'e *Per*
142:1 any blasted, ròtten, còssed, blòody *MS*, *TCC*] any——— *Per*
142:2 tèa,] tea? *Per* tèa? *TCC*
142:5 trollops." *P* Whereupon] ~." Whereupon *Per*
142:9 "Ay ... man,—... mother's.] *Om. Per* "Ay ... man, ... mother's. *TCC*

## Delilah and Mr. Bircumshaw

*MS* = Autograph MS fragment, early version (Roberts E90.5a, UCB)
*TS* = Ribbon copy TS (Roberts E90.5b, UT)
*Per* = *Virginia Quarterly Review*, XVI (Spring 1940), 257–66
*E1* = *Phoenix II* 84–91

143:2 Gillatt. "He] ~, "he *Per*
143:3 saint—] ~: *Per*
143:7 mouth] ~, *Per*
143:10 little] ~, *Per*
143:12 'she's] "She's *Per*
143:13 vivacious.'] ~." *Per*
143:13 eyes. They] ~: they *Per*
143:14 evening] ~, *Per*

143:15 quick *Per*] quiet *TS see notes*
143:20 scream—.] ~. *Per*
143:22 Harry] ~, *Per*
143:30 man—] ~, *Per*
143:31 sensuous] ~, *Per*
143:33 unremittingly] ~, *Per*
144:1 degenerating—] ~: *Per*
144:4 school-teacher] schoolteacher *Per*
144:5 suited—] ~: *Per*
144:7 Men'.] ~.' *Per*
144:9 ears—] ~, *Per*
144:10 him!] ~—! *Per*
144:13 Bircumshaw, *Per*] ~ *TS*
144:16 protectress] protector *Per*
144:17 *can* see] can *see Per*
144:22 wife] ~, *Per*
144:22 Abraham,] ~ *Per*
144:23 splendid—" the] ~." *P* The *Per*
144:30 sicklily] sickly *Per*
144:36 laughing. *P* Bircumshaw *Per*] ~. Bircumshaw *TS see notes*
144:37 fingers] ~, *Per*
144:39 eyes and] eyes, *Per*
144:40 Oh,] ~! *Per*
144:40 Gillatt. "Oh] ~, "oh *Per*
144:40 spanks] beats *Per*
144:40 baby!] ~. *Per*
145:1 resignation—] ~! *Per*
145:1 spanking] beating *Per*
145:4 friend. *P* "I] ~. "I *Per*
145:6 for?' ... *Ed.*] ~?' .. *TS* ~?' *Per*
145:7 baby'.] ~.' *Per*
145:8 you.] ~.... *Per*
145:15 'Mind-your ... the-jaw'] Mind your own business or you'll get a hit in the jaw *Per*
145:19 Buffalo] buffalo *Per*
145:20 nose. Mrs.] ~. *P* Mrs. *Per*
145:23 pill—] ~, *Per*
145:25 Galahad *Per*] Gallahad *TS*
145:25 Horseback] horseback *Per*
145:28 straight] ~, *Per*
145:29 Galahad *Per*] Gallahad *TS*
145:30 Horseback] horseback *Per*
145:32 woman,] ~: *Per*
145:34 silence ... *Ed.*] ~ .. *TS* ~. *Per*
146:1 him,] ~: *Per*
146:1 *was*] was *Per*
146:4 thick] strict *Per see notes*
146:5 her. Then] ~, then *Per*
146:11 attentive] listening *Per see notes*
146:12 quickly] ~, *Per*
146:14 dilated] ~, *Per*
146:18 him"] ~," *Per*
146:18 began. *P* Every] ~. Every *Per*
146:22 hall] ~, *Per*
146:22 hear—] ~—she said: *Per*
146:23 know,] ~ *Per*
146:23 splendidly," she said.] ~." *Per*
146:27 soothed] ~, *Per*
146:28 wife] wife say *Per*
146:30 course,] ~ *Per*
146:31 anyone *very Per*] any one *very TS*
146:32 you——] ~— *Per*
146:33 herself. This] ~: this *Per*
146:36 'thud!'] "Thud!" *Per*
146:38 There] Then *Per*
146:38 'thud!'.] "Thud!" *Per*
146:40 laughter. *P* "He's *Per*] ~. # *P* "He's *TS*
147:2 bitterly. Mrs.] ~. *P* Mrs. *Per*
147:3 amazement. *P* "You] ~. "You *Per*
147:7 began in a] began, *Per*
147:9 it. No] ~, no *Per*
147:10 been so very considerate] so fussy *Per*
147:16 'talked'] "~" *Per*
147:20 stark] ~, *Per*
147:21 black—] ~, *Per*
147:22 teddy-bear *Ed.*] teddy-bear. *MS* teddy bear *TS* teddy-bear, *Per*
147:24 stove] ~, *Per*
147:24 coldness—] ~ *Per*
147:29 thanks, then ... woman, "I] thanks then. I *TS*
147:31 minutes] ~, *Per*
147:32 'Suppers'] suppers *TS*
147:34 tentative—] ~: *Per*
147:35 this] it *Per*
147:36 Oh *MS, Per*] ~, *TS*
147:37 declared.] ~, *Per*

147:38 red. But] ~: but *Per*
147:39 anything—] ~, *Per*
147:40 fancy,] ~— *Per*
147:40 brute! And] ~!—and *Per*
147:41 Oh *MS, Per*] ~, *TS*
148:2 Oh *MS, Per*] ~, *TS*
148:4 Oh *Per*] ~, *TS*
148:4 brute!—] ~! *Per*
148:4 brute!] ~!! *Per*
148:5 men, lately] ~ ~, *Per*
148:5 you——] ~— *Per*
148:8 There's the other bed. Take the] You've got another bed aired—you had visitors till yesterday—there's the bed—take *Per see notes*
148:10 Bircumshaw weariedly *Ed.*] ~ wearily *TS* ~, weariedly *Per*
148:12 Well,] ~— *Per*
148:13 Oh] Ah *Per*
148:13 good and gracious] fair and fussy *Per*
148:14 face] ~, *Per*
148:15 red.] ~? *Per*
148:17 Ethel—.] ~. *Per*
148:23 height] ~, *Per*
148:23 tones. "Tell] ~, "tell *Per*
148:25 door. Tell] ~: tell
148:26 Drive] '~' *Per*
148:26 caller. Say] ~—say *Per*
148:27 him,] ~— *Per*
148:36 women—] ~: *Per*
148:37 punish,] ~: *Per*
148:37 assert. And] ~: and *Per*
148:38 punish,] punish, was *Per*
149:7 go] ~, *Per*
149:11 nothing!] ~. *Per*
149:12 do—] ~, *Per*
149:15 self-respect] ~, *Per*
149:15 a] the *Per*
149:17 friends] friend *Per*
149:17 Hell—] hell: *Per*
149:19 hero] hero: *Per*
149:21 mastery] ~, *Per*
149:21 tyrant] ~, *Per*
149:23 due. Her ... triumphant, but] dues. Though *Per*
149:24 anxious. She ... smile. She] anxious, still she smiled: she *Per*
149:25 Samson and her] Samson. Her *Per*
149:25 depth] deep *Per*
149:30 dinner-joint] dinner joint *Per*
149:30 sandwiches] ~, *Per*
149:34 bed-clothes] bedclothes *Per*
149:36 said] ~, *Per*
150:3 small, round ears] ~ ~ ear *Per*
150:3 while] whilst *Per*
150:4 fingers,] ~ *Per*
150:6 brow.] brow, that reminded one of the brow of a little Virgin by Memling. *Per*
150:8 wrath] wroth *E1 see notes*
150:9 insignificant—] ~, *Per*
150:9 and] *Om. Per*
150:14 shrinking] ~, *Per*
150:15 paralysed] paralyzed *Per*
150:16 down,] ~ *Per*
150:17 thought. For] ~: for *Per*
150:20 stir, merely she was] ~; she was merely *Per*
150:28 arm] ~, *Per*
150:37 *nice*] nice *Per*
150:37 *Are*] are *Per*
150:37 nice?" *P* The] ~?" The *Per*
150:40 back] backwards *Per*
151:3 small] ~, *Per*
151:4 vanished] ~, *Per*
151:4 lips ...] ~: *Per*
151:6 passion ...] ~; *Per*
151:7 thought] said to herself *Per*
151:11 said to herself. She] thought. *P* She *Per*
151:12 thinking] ~, *Per*

## Once—!

*MS* = Autograph MS (Roberts E296a, UT)
*TCC* = Carbon copy TS (Roberts E296b, UCB)
*TCCC* = Corrections to *TCC* [probably by Douglas Clayton]
*E1* = *Love Among the Haystacks* (The Nonesuch Press, 1930), pp. 83–96

152:1 Once—! *MS, TCCC*] ~ *TCC, E1*
152:11 dressing gown] dressing-gown *TCC*
152:15 middle-class. Then,] ~, then. *TCC*
152:23 army] Army *TCC*
152:32 government] Government *TCC*
153:5 Then moreover] ~, ~, *E1*
153:15 Ehrfurcht] *Ehrfurcht TCC*
153:20 good-humour] good humour *E1*
153:26 to her:] ~ ~. *TCC*
153:29 her, she] ~. She *TCC*
153:32 fallen, and] ~. And *TCC*
153:40 looking glass] looking-glass *TCC*
154:2 chemise,] ~ *E1*
154:17 dressing gown] dressing-gown *TCC*
154:22 onto . . . onto] on to . . . on to *E1*
154:36 Piccadilly *TCC*] Picaddilly, *MS*
154:40 dressing gown] dressing-gown *TCC*
155:18 don't] don't know *TCC*
155:18 is] are *TCC*
155:20 'pro tem.'] 'pro tem' *TCC pro tem. E1*
155:26 "'On est . . . longtemps',"] "'*On est mort pour si longtemps*'," *TCC* '*On . . . longtemps*,' *E1*
155:29 thirty-one *TCC*] thirty one *MS*
155:39 cap] caps *TCC*
155:39 shoulder *Ed.*] shoulders *MS*
156:5 you—?] ~? *TCC*
156:16 yes] ~, *E1*
156:23 dressing gown] dressing-gown *TCC*
156:31 hôtel;—] hotel;— *TCC* hotel; *E1*
157:5 café au lait] *café au lait TCC*
157:7 "—And] "~ *TCC*
157:9 jeh!,] ~! *TCC*
157:13 jeh!,] ~! *TCC*
157:13 And] and *E1*
157:14 revers *Ed.*] reveres *MS see notes*
157:6 enjoys,] ~ *TCC*
157:17 Verzeihung . . . Fräulein] *Verzeihung, gnädiges Fräulein TCC*
157:21 Terrasse *Ed.*] Terasse *MS*
157:26 Cocotte—] cocotte—— *TCC*
157:36 hôtel] hotel *TCC*
158:2 it.—] ~. *TCC*
158:4 half hour] half-hour *E1*
158:6 crêpe de chine] crepe de chine *TCC crêpe de Chine E1*
158:7 breath.] ~! *TCC*
158:13 cloak:] ~. *TCC*
158:14 jeh!,] ~! *TCC*
158:18 saut-de-lit] Saut-de-lit *TCC saut-de-lit E1*
158:20 Gods] gods *E1*
158:30 Oh] ~, *E1*
158:30 tender—!] ~! *TCC*
158:36 Terrasse *Ed.*] Terasse *MS*
158:40 again—] ~. *TCC*
159:5 me.—] ~. *TCC*
159:14 me,] ~: *E1*
159:14 walnut'." *P* And *Ed.*] ~'" *P* And *MS* ~.'" And *TCC* ~'." And *E1*
159:15 slightly. *P* "He] ~. "He *TCC*
159:16 me.—] ~— *TCC*
159:17 Answer.'] ~". *E1*
159:17 then] ~, *TCC* ~: *E1*
159:17 touch,] ~ *TCC*
159:18 joy.'] ~". *E1*
159:18 said,] ~ *E1*
159:24 yours—."] ~——" *TCC*
159:26 "—And] "~ *TCC*
159:38 uncertainty *MS, TCCC*] uncertainly *TCC, E1 see notes*

160:3 half past] half-past *TCC*
160:21 suppose—] ~—— *TCC* ~, *E1*
160:25 She waited ... yes I ... stood still.] *Om. TCC* She waited ... yes, I ... stood still. *E1 see notes*

## New Eve and Old Adam

*MS* = Autograph MS (Roberts E268a, UTul)
*TCC* = Carbon copy TS (Roberts E268b, UCB)
*E1* = *A Modern Lover* 131–66

161:2 I] I *E1*
161:4 you,] ~ *TCC*
161:11 Entertainments] Entertainment *TCC*
161:15 woman—] ~. *TCC*
161:15 me'.] ~!' *TCC*
161:25 curious] curiously *TCC*
162:2 She] He *TCC*
162:4 wedding ring] wedding-ring *TCC*
162:7 child,] ~ *TCC*
162:12 him:] ~, *TCC*
162:20 darkly stretched] darkly-stretched *TCC*
162:23 opposite] ~, *TCC*
162:25 half hidden] half-hidden *TCC*
162:29 round,] ~ *TCC*
162:34 The husband] Her husband, *TCC*
162:34 darkening] *Om. TCC*
162:34 her] ~, *TCC*
163:5 clean] clear *TCC*
163:11 hard:] ~; *E1*
163:15 voice. *P* He] ~. He *TCC*
163:18 way. *P* He] ~. He *TCC*
163:26 knee] ~, *TCC*
163:27 her] his *TCC*
163:29 his] *Om. E1*
164:1 fool.] ~? *TCC*
164:8 you—!] ~—? *TCC* ~— *E1*
164:9 don't—"] ~." *TCC*
164:10 Ha—] ~!— *TCC*
164:10 Self!—] ~! *TCC*
164:18 I do] ~ ~, *TCC*
164:24 you—!] ~! *TCC*
164:29 paper. *P* She] ~. She *TCC*
165:1 Street',] ~,' *TCC*
165:7 Moest *TCC*] Cyriack *MS see notes*
165:9 'Do] ~ *TCC*]
165:9 say', *Ed.*] ~' *MS* ~, *TCC*
165:10 sneering. "Yes] ~, "~, *TCC*
165:13 me,] ~! *TCC*
165:14 calamity—the] ~. The *TCC*
165:16 mine—] ~, *TCC*
165:18 tongue,] ~! *TCC*
165:22 him;] ~: *TCC*
165:26 side board] side/ board *TCC* side-/ board *E1*
165:26 whisky and soda] a whisky-and-soda *TCC*
165:30 all] *Om. TCC*
165:33 entered] ~, *TCC*
166:25 peace—] ~. *TCC*
166:37 *you*!] ~P *TCC* ~? *E1*
166:38 life.—] ~. *E1*
166:40 stand] stick *TCC*
167:2 asiatic] Asiatic *E1*
167:9 peace.—] ~— *E1*
167:11 veins] mind *TCC see notes*
167:14 is.—] ~. *TCC*
167:18 said.—] ~. *TCC*
167:24 heart] head *TCC*
168:10 union:] ~; *E1*
168:18 him,] ~; *TCC*
168:24 half wistful] half-wistful *TCC*
168:25 half perverse] half-perverse *TCC*
168:33 right] ~, *TCC*
168:38 She knitted ... face pathetically.] *Om. E1*
169:3 said, suddenly] ~ ~, *TCC*

169:15 "Lovable and ... and bitter.] *Om. TCC see notes*
169:20 repellant] repellent *TCC see notes*
169:38 Yes."—] ~." *E1*
170:17 fountain pen] fountain-pen *TCC*
170:23 satisfied, or had been] *Om. TCC see notes*
170:31 good,] ~; *TCC*
170:35 dressing gown] dressing-gown *TCC*
170:37 things,] ~ *TCC*
171:1 2] II *E1*
171:2 hôtel] hotel *TCC*
171:3 lift] ~, *TCC*
171:3 side] ~, *TCC*
171:7 ostentatious:] ~; *E1*
171:8 hôtel] hotel *TCC*
171:9 cats'] cat's *TCC*
171:12 writing sachet] writing-sachet *TCC*
171:15 quarter past] quarter-past *E1*
171:17 bath] ~, *TCC*
171:17 away—in] ~.—In *TCC* ~. In *E1*
171:18 warm:] ~; *E1*
171:20 hôtel-like] hotel-like *TCC*
171:31 movements,] ~ *TCC*
172:9 him:] ~; *E1*
172:9 and unperceived ... darkness almost] *Om. TCC see note on* 169:15
172:13 But] ~, *TCC*
172:26 life,] ~ *TCC*
172:33 to the *TCC*] the the *MS*
172:34 her roots] his roots *TCC*
172:36 anybody.——] ~.— *TCC* ~. *E1*
173:1 darkly in *Ed.*] in darkly *MS* darkly, in *TCC see notes*
173:5 at random] *Om. TCC*
173:8 given *TCC*] give *MS*
173:10 pleasure-pier] pleasure pier *TCC*
173:21 clearness of] clearing *TCC*
173:26 lunch] ~, *TCC*
173:30 telegrams] telegram *TCC*
173:32 3] III *E1*
173:34 much,] ~ *TCC*
173:35 parlour-maid] parlourmaid *TCC* parlour-/maid *E1*
173:36 her,] ~ *TCC*
174:2 naïvely] naively *TCC*
174:6 carpet—] ~ *TCC*
174:8 China] china *TCC*
174:8 deep,] ~ *TCC*
174:14 man,] ~ *TCC*
174:14 noticed,] ~ *TCC*
174:15 side] side of *E1*
174:25 finely cut] finely-cut *TCC*
174:25 dark blue] dark-blue *TCC*
174:29 naïve] naive *TCC*
174:32 as inert] ~, ~, *TCC*
174:33 waits,] ~ *TCC*
174:38 asked] ~, *TCC*
175:2 flat] floor *E1*
175:5 see,] ~; *E1*
175:9 *affaire*"—*TCC*] ~" *MS*
175:14 indignation,] ~? *TCC*
175:27 he] He *TCC*
175:27 nervously—] ~. *TCC*
175:30 audience;—] ~— *TCC*
175:30 he grasped ... thinking hard—] *Om. TCC see note on* 169:15
175:32 English.—] ~. *TCC*
175:39 red tile] red-tile *TCC*
176:6 favorite] favourite *TCC*
176:7 'Meister'] '*Meister*' *TCC* *Meister E1*
176:8 Shakspere] Shakespeare *TCC*
176:10 man] ~, *TCC*
176:14 Moest, *Ed.*] Cyriack, *MS* Moest *TCC*
176:15 German,] ~ *TCC*
176:18 "Richard";] '~'; *TCC* "~;" *E1*
176:22 Just] just *TCC*
176:22 himself, *TCC*] ~ *MS*
176:24 common room:] common-room: *TCC* common-room; *E1*
176:28 adorable!] ~? *TCC*
176:29 drawing-room *TCC*] drawing room *MS*
176:31 telegram.—] ~. *E1*
176:31 But] ~, *TCC*
176:32 him!] ~? *TCC*

176:35 creatures.—] ~. *TCC*
176:36 mantel-piece] mantel-/piece *TCC* mantelpiece *E1*
176:37 a *TCC*] an *MS*
176:38 gone.—] ~. *E1*
176:39 mantel-piece] mantelpiece, *TCC*
177:2 her.] ~? *TCC*
177:6 syrens] sirens *E1*
177:6 fabulous,] ~ *E1*
177:10 miserable] ~, *TCC*
177:17 well,] ~; *TCC*
177:36 stay] ~, *TCC*
178:1 Yes] ~, *TCC*
178:11 Richard.] ~? *TCC*
178:13 care?] ~! *TCC*
178:22 me—] ~. *TCC*
178:23 sang] rang *E1*
178:32 stiffness. *P* He] ~. He *TCC*
179:3 to] *Om. TCC*
179:3 paid,] ~ *TCC*
179:4 *existed,*—] ~— *TCC*
179:6 her.] ~? *TCC*
179:11 finger nail] finger-nail *TCC*
179:15 look,] ~ *TCC*
179:16 finger nails] finger-nails *TCC*
179:16 and] ~, *TCC*
179:24 way he] ~, ~ *TCC*
179:30 could] would *TCC*
179:31 Get] Het *TCC* Not *E1*
179:32 slippery] ~, *TCC*
179:36 Paris.—] ~?— *TCC* ~? *E1*
180:2 hôtel] hotel *TCC*
180:4 Sheep'.] ~.' *E1*
180:6 half bewildered] half-bewildered *TCC*
180:6 half perverse] half-perverse *TCC*
180:8 into his] at him *TCC*
180:10 were] was *TCC*
180:10 so] so that *TCC*
180:12 dilated:] ~; *TCC*
180:17 Oh] ~, *TCC*
180:17 softly] ~, *TCC*
181:7 little little] little *E1*
181:7 ironically—why] ~. Why *TCC*
181:16 close] closer *TCC*
181:17 he *TCC*] he he would *MS see notes*
181:20 winsome,] ~ *E1*
181:30 foot-soles] ~; *TCC*
181:32 disposes] ~, *TCC*
181:33 sheets—" *P* She] ~." # She *TCC*
181:39 only——.] ~ .... *TCC* ~... *E1*
181:40 him,] ~ *TCC*
182:1 them,] ~; *TCC*
182:3 more:] ~; *E1*
182:13 touch-touch] touch - touch *TCC* touch—touch *E1*
182:16 sense,] ~ *TCC*
182:18 king:] ~; *E1*
182:26 flesh—] ~. *E1*
182:26 you— —] ~ - *TCC* ~— *E1*
182:27 Yes] ~, *TCC*
182:27 answered,] ~ *TCC*
182:30 But] ~, *TCC*
182:30 wife—?] ~? *E1*
182:32 knew] ~, *TCC*
182:33 4 *Ed.*] 3. *MS* 4. *TCC* IV *E1*
182:37 grasp.—] ~. *TCC*
182:38 *do,*] ~. *TCC*
182:38 you.— — — —] ~.... *TCC* ~... *E1*
183:2 innerest] innermost *E1*
183:8 me.— —] ~... *TCC*
183:14 time.— — —] ~.... *TCC* ~. *E1*
183:16 life.—] ~— *E1*
183:17 you— — —] ~.... *TCC* ~... *E1*
183:20 done.—] ~... *TCC*
183:22 generally] yourself *TCC see notes*

## 'Burns Novel' fragments

The following symbols are used to distinguish states of the text:
*MS* = Autograph manuscript (Roberts E59.3, UT)
*A1* = 'Two Fragments of the So-Called "Burns Novel"', Nehls, i. 184–95

The entry to the left of the square bracket usually indicates the final MS reading, with the unidentified entry to the right indicating the reading of the MS before DHL revised it; still earlier readings are indicated by pointed and half brackets. Word fragments and illegible deletions of fewer than three surviving letters have not been recorded. In entries with *Ed.* or *A1*, a reading superseded by DHL's revision appears as *MS draft*.

The following symbols are used editorially:
*MS draft* = Superseded reading
⟨ ⟩ = First deletion in *MS*
⟨⟨ ⟩⟩ = Second deletion in *MS*
⌜ ⌝ = First addition in *MS*
⌜⌜ ⌝⌝ = Second addition in *MS*
*Ed.* = Editor

201:2 I.] ~ *A1*
201:4 The] Tha
201:6 mild] soft
201:8 as] where
201:9 levelling] yellowing
201:11 into a . . . heap the] the
201:12 cutting] cutting into a little heap
201:19 erect,] erect, emblem vigorous,
201:19 burning] burning scarlet and full
201:20 the] the glossy,
201:24 armful] arf
201:32 solid] brilliant
202:6 was of] was of faded,
202:8 creeping] running
202:10 clearing died . . . went cold.] circle went cold.
202:13 shouted: *P* "Bill] ~: "Bill *A1*
202:14 Bi—ill!"] Bi-ill!" *A1*
202:17 paces from her,] paces,
202:20 off a] off a faint
202:22 hand] hands
202:24 here!] ~,
202:25 Wheer] Where
202:29 near at hand.] nearer.
202:31 youth] young man
202:34 chump] gormey
202:34 low, so that] low on his
202:36 his] his ⟨reckless⟩ fine
202:36 gazed] laughed
202:37 Was it . . . as shouted] Not ⟨got⟩ gone yet
202:38 I knowed it was you,"] Just off,"
202:38 tapping her . . . holly sprig.] waving with her hand half explanatorily at the holly bush. "Here's ⟨a tree⟩ ⌜berries⌝ for you⟨,⟩!" she added. He looked.
202:40 Been getting holly?] It's a jewel, that is,
203:1 her, leading . . . the head] her and taken her in his arms
203:2 It's a . . . the tree.] Coming tonight?" he asked tenderly.
203:2 tree. *P* There was . . . silence.] tree. *P* "D'yer want me to?" she replied. *MS draft* tree. There . . . silence. *A1*
203:4 But it's . . . he added.] What art axin' ⌜that⌝ for?" he said, kissing her.
203:5 Who says?" she replied.] The sprig of holly she had gathered pricked his wrist.

203:6 "They say," he answered.] "⟨The⟩ It's bad luck to get it afore Christmas," he said.
203:7 cold] dark
203:17 father's] uncle's
203:19 Renshaw] Burns
203:21 Mary.] ~ ?
203:22 *Renshaw*!] Burns *MS draft Renshaw! A1*
203:32 our] my
204:12 woman.] woman. There was something fine about her, and a certain distinctness, that made her linger in his memory.
204:17 beam which … upon low,] ⟨wicker-work cradle that lay along a beam which carried the axle-trees⟩ beam which … cross-⟨beams⟩ ⌜bars⌝ … low,
204:20 packed] piled
204:28 harnessed *Ed.*] harness *MS* harness[ed] *A1*
204:29 small] whee
204:38 long] youn
205:6 'lowance] drink
205:7 Jock] Jack *A1*
205:12 track] faint track
205:12 beside] between
205:13 hill] road
205:13 darkness] of
205:14 he came … gate across] he came to a place where
205:21 wagon, *Ed.*] ~ *MS* ~[,] *A1*
205:22 kitchen was] was
205:24 Two men … the hearth.] The stairs went up by the door that led to the dairy.
205:26 room] kitchen
205:39 the black] more black
206:2 noisily supped] ate
206:3 from] noisily from
206:4 and] until
206:4 ponched] punched *A1 see notes*
206:5 his broth] it
206:5 mess] stodge
206:9 The] Fat
206:10 two] a few
206:15 slate] ⟨p⟩ ⌜s⌝late
206:23 clenched his hands] put his hands out
206:24 hedge] dark hedge
206:30 tightly] lightly *A1*
206:31 hand] hands
206:37 his heart] h⟨e⟩ ⌜is⌝
206:39 his] a
207:2 murmuring] saying
207:5 was] ⟨wanted⟩ felt
207:14 it] he
207:14 gone into the darkness] gone
207:16 than *A1*] that *MS*
207:22 up-hill] up hill *A1*
207:22 saw] passed
207:24 'Brick and Tile.'] "~ ~ ~." *A1*
207:28 lived.] lived. He wondered what she was really like.
207:32 She] She started and
208:1 the coal] its
208:18 swalin'] gutterin'
208:21 said.] said. "Somebody'll be seein' me."
208:25 here!'",] ~!'" *A1*
208:27 callin'." *P* He] ~'." He *A1*
208:32 in] like
208:33 that—?] ~? *A1*
208:38 sung] ⟨⟨s⟨a⟩⌜u⌝ng⟩⟩ ⌜⌜sung⌝⌝
208:40 rabbit tonight] rabbit *MS draft* rabbit tonight, *A1*
209:2 dunno!"] dunno! 'Cause o' thee, 'appen."
209:5 She made a little sound] ⟨"Um!" she said,⟩ ⌜She murmured⌝ quietly
209:6 thee besides me?"] thee?"
209:10 him.] him simply.
209:11 was] felt
209:11 astonished in all his being.] astonished.
209:13 amazing.] ⟨wonderful.⟩ ⌜almost frightening.⌝
209:15 seemed] seemed comprehensive enough
209:16 lights overhead] stars
209:28 her self] herself *A1*
209:32 clack] clatch
209:35 the plants] then va
210:13 if] If

210:15 fire place] fire
210:15 a brick hearth raised] ⟨raised on a bank⟩ a raised
210:16 on which the fire] and
210:22 ground-level] ground-leval
210:23 high] ~,
210:27 five-days' *A1*] five-day's *MS*
210:29 comfortably] even
210:29 men,] ~.
210:34 cump'ny *A1*] cumpn'y *MS*
210:35 Jock] Jack *A1*
211:11 a] a pale
211:16 day] the day *A1*
211:18 sky] morning

Of the compound words which are hyphenated at the end of a line in this edition, only the following hyphenated forms should be retained in quotation:

37:17 mantel-piece
43:31 old-fashioned
48:2 mole-hills
49:9 winter-trodden
50:8 plum-trees
69:22 cutting-short
79:4 round-shouldered
89:26 loud-mouthed
102:13 callous-looking
111:25 fawn-coloured
128:32 highly-coloured
131:11 furniture-and-upholsterer's
145:2 Christian-resignation
153:8 good-humoured
153:34 creamy-brown
155:30 thirty-one
175:11 self-conscious
195:36 dinner-joint
210:27 clean-shaven

## Pounds, shillings and pence

Before decimalisation in 1971, the pound sterling (£) was the equivalent of 20 shillings (20/- or 20s.). The shilling was the equivalent of 12 pence (12d.).

A price could therefore have three elements: pounds, shillings and pence (£, s., d.). (The apparently anomalous d. is an abbreviation of the Latin *denarius*; but the other two terms were also originally Latin; the pound was *Libra*; the shilling *solidus*.) Such a price might be written as £1. 2s. 6d. or £1/2/6; which was spoken as 'one pound two-and-six', or 'twenty-two and six'.

Prices below a pound were written as (for instance) 19s. 6d. or 19/6, and spoken as 'nineteen and six'. Prices up to £5 were sometimes spoken in terms of shillings: so 'ninety-nine and six' was £4/19/6.

The penny was divided into two half-pence and further into four farthings, but the farthing had minimal value and was mainly a tradesman's device for indicating a price fractionally below a shilling or a pound. So 19/11¾ (nineteen and elevenpence three farthings) produced a farthing's change from a pound, this change often given as a tiny item of trade, such as a packet of pins.

The guinea was £1/1/- (one pound, one shilling) and was a professional man's unit for fees. A doctor would chare in guineas (so £5/5/- = 5 gns). Half a guinea was 10s. 6d. or 10/6 (ten and six).

The coins used were originally of silver (later cupro-nickel) and copper, though gold coins for £1 (sovereign) and 10s. (half-sovereign) were still in use in Lawrence's time. The largest silver coin in common use was the half-crown (two shillings and sixpence, or 2/6). A two-shilling piece was called a florin. Shillings, sixpences and (in Lawrence's time) threepence were the smaller sizes. The copper coins were pennies, half-pence (ha'penny) and farthings.

Common slang terms for money were 'quid' for pound, 'half a crown, 'two bob' for a florin, 'bob' for a shilling, 'tanner' for sixpence, 'threepenny-bit', 'copper' for a penny or half-penny.

The pound since 1971 has had 100 pence, distinguished from the old pennies by being abbreviated to p. instead of d.